CONTINENTAL
PHILOSOPHY
in FEMINIST
PERSPECTIVE

CONTINENTAL PHILOSOPHY *in* FEMINIST PERSPECTIVE

Re-reading the Canon in German

Edited by
HERTA NAGL-DOCEKAL
and
CORNELIA KLINGER

The Pennsylvania State University Press
University Park, Pennsylvania

Library of Congress Cataloging-in-Publication Data

Continental Philosophy in Feminist Perspective : Re-reading the Canon in German / edited by Herta Nagl-Docekal and Cornelia Klinger.

    p.   cm.
Includes bibliographical references and index.
ISBN 0-271-01963-8 (cloth : alk. paper)
ISBN 0-271-01964-6 (pbk. : alk. paper)
    1. Feminist theory.   2. German literature—History and criticism.   3. Sex role in literature.   4. Philosophy, German.   5. Feminist literary criticism.   I. Klinger, Cornelia, 1953– .
II. Nagl-Docekal, Herta.
HQ1190.R47 2000
305.42'01—dc2a   99-21684
                                                                                                                            CIP

Copyright © 2000 The Pennsylvania State University
All rights reserved
Printed in the United States of America
Published by The Pennsylvania State University Press,
University Park, PA 16802–1003

It is the policy of The Pennsylvania State University Press to use acid-free paper for the first printing of all clothbound books. Publications on uncoated stock satisfy the minimum requirements of American National Standard for Information Sciences—Permanence of Paper for Printed Library Materials, ANSI Z39.48–1992.

CONTENTS

Introduction: Feminist Philosophy in German
     Herta Nagl-Docekal and Cornelia Klinger
     (translated by James Dodd)   1

1 Femininity and Critique of Reason in the French Enlightenment
     Lieselotte Steinbrügge
     (translated by Stephanie Morgenstern)   31

2 Julie, or the Feminine Difference: A New Reading of Rousseau's
     Nouvelle Héloïse
     Christine Garbe
     (translated by Melanie Richter-Bernburg)   45

3 Philosophy of History as a Theory of Gender Difference: The
     Case of Rousseau
     Herta Nagl-Docekal
     (translated by Sabrina Völz)   77

4 Schopenhauer or Kant: Gender Difference Between Critique and
     Spirit of the Age
     Ursula Pia Jauch
     (translated by James Dodd)   101

5 The Female as Ethical Resource in the Philosophy of Hegel
   Heidemarie Bennent-Vahle
   (translated by Christine M. Manteghi) 113

6 Woman—Landscape—Artwork: Alternative Realms or
   Patriarchal Reserves?
   Cornelia Klinger
   (translated by James Dodd) 147

7 Is a Feminist Critique of Logic Possible?
   Käthe Trettin
   (translated by George Matthews) 175

8 Georg Simmel: Modernism and the Philosophy of the Sexes
   Ursula Menzer
   (translated by Melanie Richter-Bernburg) 201

9 Explicating the Image of Woman in Psychoanalytic Discourse:
   Sigmund Freud's Theory of Femininity
   Christa Rohde-Dachser
   (translated by Stephanie Morgenstern) 231

10 Fin-de-siècle Vienna: A Movement For or Against Womanhood?
   Some Thoughts on Weininger and Freud
   Ingvild Birkhan
   (translated by Christine Manteghi) 255

11 Woman: The Most Precious Loot in the "Triumph of Allegory":
   Gender Relations in Walter Benjamin's *Passagen-Werk*
   Astrid Deuber-Mankowsky
   (translated by Dana Hollander) 281

12 A Legacy of the Enlightenment: Imagination and the Reality of
   the "Maternal" in Max Horkheimer's Writings
   Mechthild Rumpf
   (translated by Melanie Richter-Bernburg) 303

13 Reason, Gender, and the Paradox of Rationalization
   Elisabeth List 321

Contributors 339

Index 343

INTRODUCTION
Feminist Philosophy in German

Herta Nagl-Docekal and Cornelia Klinger
Translated by James Dodd

"We translate what American women write, they never translate our texts." This complaint, made from the French perspective by Hélène Cixous[1] more than twenty years ago, can be heard today among many women who write in German. To be sure, to say "never" would be an exaggeration today as it was then,[2] yet to point out a lack of attention appears to be justified by all standards. Since a considerable number of interesting studies have been published in Germany, Austria, and Switzerland in the field of feminist the-

---

1. Quoted in Elaine Marks and Isabelle de Courtivron, "Why This Book?" in *New French Feminisms: An Anthology*, ed. Elaine Marks and Isabelle de Courtivron (New York: Schocken Books, 1981), ix.
2. For an overview of translations of French feminist theory since 1973, cf. ibid., note 1.

ory, it is surprising that very little of this material has become known within the English-speaking community.³

A quick look at what is now available in English for someone who wishes to survey research being done in continental Europe clearly reveals an asymmetry among individual regions. Currently, the best represented are without question the works of French authors such as Hélène Cixous, Catherine Clément, Luce Irigaray, Julia Kristeva, or Monique Wittig. With regard to France, the situation has changed decisively: the remark of Hélène Cixous cited above marks the end of the problem she had been addressing. By the beginning of the 1980s, French studies on female subjectivity had elicited broad international interest. The transformation of Lacanian psychoanalysis and the creative appropriation of deconstruction carried out in different ways by individual authors have become a common point of departure for feminist theory in the English-speaking community.⁴ In this context the works of Simone de Beauvoir also have won a new importance that continues to this day.⁵

Recent years have seen intensified translation activities, with the result that feminist studies from a number of other regions in Europe have become available in English. These include, for example, translations of Spanish feminist studies,⁶ as well as collections of essays dedicated to feminist debates in Italy.⁷ In addition, new forms of feminist critique that have been suggested in the former communist countries of Eastern Europe are docu-

---

3. Among the few exceptions are a collection of texts edited by Gisela Ecker, *Feminist Aesthetics* (Boston: Beacon Press, 1986), and Barbara Sichtermann's *Femininity: The Politics of the Personal* (Minneapolis: University of Minnesota Press, 1986).

4. The undiminished significance of this reception is documented in the following volumes, among others: Rosi Braidotti, *Patterns of Dissonance* (Cambridge: Polity Press, 1991); Nancy Fraser and Sandra Lee Bartky, eds., *Revaluing French Feminism* (Bloomington: Indiana University Press, 1992); Carolyn Burke, Naomi Schor, and Margaret Whitford, eds., *Engaging with Irigaray* (New York: Columbia University Press, 1994), in particular, Margaret Whitford, "Reading Irigaray in the Nineties," 15–36.

5. An overview of the development and current state of feminist discussion of the work of Simone de Beauvoir in the English-speaking community can be found in, among others, Toril Moi, *Simone de Beauvoir: The Making of an Intellectual Woman* (Oxford: Basil Blackwell, 1994), and Margaret A. Simons, ed., *Feminist Interpretations of Simone de Beauvoir* (University Park: Pennsylvania State University Press, 1995).

6. The interest in English translations is obviously not limited to Europe. To take only one example, several contributions from Latin America have also been published in the United States. Cf. "Special Cluster on Spanish and Latin American Feminist Philosophy," *Hypatia* (winter 1994): 142–205.

7. Sandra Kemp and Paola Bono, eds., *Italian Feminist Thought: A Reader* (Oxford: Blackwell, 1991) and, by the same editors, *The Lonely Mirror: Italian Perspectives on Feminist Theory* (London: Routledge, 1993).

mented not only by individually translated essays but also by a collection specifically dedicated to these developments.[8]

As for the German community, the situation is somewhat different. Though there is not really a lack of texts available in English translation—there are, on the contrary, more—nevertheless they tend not to be seen as a whole but are scattered in different journals, anthologies, and various book series. Numerous conversations that we have had with colleagues in Canada, England, and the United States have shown us that in general little is known about the development of feminist theory in German-speaking countries. From time to time we have even encountered a lack of awareness that there is any debate going on in this field at all. Though it would certainly be interesting to investigate the reasons for this development, it appears to us to be more pressing to make an effort toward possible change. So with this volume, we would like to make a contribution toward a more accurate picture of the situation, though we are of course in no position to make any claim of completeness.

The general historical background familiar to other Western countries also prevailed in the German-speaking countries. The new women's movement arose around 1968 in conjunction with the student movement, finding its expression not only in diverse political activities but also in a theoretical debate that, since the middle of the 1970s, has increasingly been carried out in academic fields of research. Even though there is still considerable resistance on the part of some institutions, today feminist critique and the discussion of "gender" issues constitute a fundamental element of research in practically all academic disciplines. The number of publications, as well as of themes and theoretical approaches, has grown so much that it is impossible to provide a representative sample in a single volume. It would not even be possible to do this for an individual field.

That is certainly the case in our discipline, philosophy. The history of feminist reflections by German-speaking women philosophers spans three decades, going back to the days of the student movement.[9] One key center of crystallization, the Internationale Assoziation von Philosophinnen (IAPh), was founded in Würzburg in 1974 and modeled after the Society for Women in Philosophy (SWIP).[10] From the beginning, this society empha-

---

8. See Nanette Funk and Magda Mueller, eds., *Gender Politics and Post-Communism: Reflections from Eastern Europe and the Former Soviet Union* (New York: Routledge, 1993).

9. See, for example, an essay by a woman philosopher originally from Vienna, Karin Schrader-Klebert, "Die kulturelle Revolution der Frau," *Kursbuch* 17 (1969).

10. There was also a personal relation to the SWIP: Linda Lopez McAlister, who was doing research in Germany at the time, was a founding member of the Internationale Assoziation von Philosophinnen in Würzburg.

sized publicizing feminist issues in philosophy, and since its founding has, for example, been organizing its own meetings within the congresses of the Allgemeine Gesellschaft für Philosophie in Deutschland.[11] It has also been a regular participant in the World Congress of Philosophy since 1978. Beginning in 1980, the IAPh has held its own symposia every two to three years, the proceedings of which have often appeared in book form. These publications are a testament to growing internationalization: while the first four volumes include only contributions written in German,[12] those since the 1992 Amsterdam Symposium have been multi-lingual.[13] Following this trend, the IAPh today has members in fifteen countries; and the symposium held in Boston in conjunction with the 1998 World Congress for Philosophy was the first to take place outside of Europe.

Another important venue for interaction and presentation has been the journal *Die Philosophin: Forum für feministische Theorie und Philosophie*, which has been published in Tübingen since 1990. Each of its issues are devoted to a particular theme. In addition, several philosophy journals with a more general orientation have published essays on feminist topics. It should be emphasized that on the whole recent years have seen a clear improvement with respect to the publication possibilities for texts on gender-related themes: practically all of the large German publishing houses have included this field in their programs. On the other hand, the situation in academia remains difficult. As in the past, many universities in German-speaking countries neither include feminist theory in their curriculum of philosophy nor offer the possibility for interested students to write their diploma theses and dissertations in this area.[14]

Given this persistent lack of acceptance in the academic arena, it is notable that so many works on feminism have been published in German-speak-

---

11. This society is comparable to the APA, though its sessions do not have the character of a "job market."

12. Manon Maren-Grisebach and Ursula Menzer, eds., *Philosophinnen: Von Wegen ins dritte Jahrtausend* (Mainz: Tamagnini, 1982); Halina Bendkowski and Brigitte Weisshaupt, eds., *Was Philosophinnen denken: Eine Dokumentation* (Zurich: Ammann, 1983); Manon Andreas-Grisebach and Brigitte Weisshaupt, eds., *Was Philosophinnen denken II* (Zurich: Ammann, 1986); Astrid Deuber-Mankowsky, Ulrike Ramming, and E. Walesca Tielsch, eds., *1789/1989—Die Revolution hat nicht stattgefunden* (Tübingen: edition discord, 1989).

13. Maja Pellikaan-Engel, ed., *Against Patriarchal Thinking: A Future Without Discrimination?* (Amsterdam: Free University Press, 1992); Eva Waniek et al., eds., *Krieg/War: Eine philosophische Auseinandersetzung aus feministisches Sicht* (Fribourg: Fink, 1996).

14. For an attempt at an overview of the developments in Vienna, see Herta Nagl-Docekal, "Zwischen Institutionalisierung und Ausgrenzung: Feministische Philosophie an der Universität Wien," *Die Philosophin* 1, no. 1 (1990): 7–17.

ing countries. The themes that have been and are being discussed are very diverse. They correspond in part to the international development of the debate: initially, just as in the Anglo-American context, attempts were made to analyze the gender hierarchy using Marxist categories.[15] Later the writings of French authors oriented around psychoanalysis and deconstruction became the focus of the debate. In sharp contrast to the English-speaking community, there has hardly been any development comparable to "liberal feminism", and for a long time issues concerning the philosophy of law in general were rarely posed. The reason for this peculiarity may have been the fact that the theoretical perspectives of the new women's movement in the German-speaking community were more directly linked to the student movement than had been the case elsewhere. This would explain why feminism here at first "rejected the traditional and institutionalized means of politics and law as thoroughly inappropriate, and attempted rather to practice agitation in defiance of the law. In line with the 'left' critique of the state, of bureaucratization, and of the increasing legalizing of human relations, equal rights were long in disrepute with feminists. In their view, the goal could only be emancipation from but never conformity and alignment with masculine law."[16] Only gradually was this lack of attention paid to legal theory rectified, a process in which the reception of the Anglo-American debate played a significant role.[17]

As we began to plan this volume, we wondered whether, along with the numerous interesting individual studies on a wide variety of issues, there was also something of a characteristic tone within German feminist philosophy, something that would distinguish it from debates in other countries. Although we remain uncertain whether this is the case, it appears to us that there are clearly some specific traits. Philosophical critique is always situated; even where a claim to a radical new beginning is raised thinking is nevertheless codetermined by the preceding situation of discourse—at least negatively, insofar as the new thinking seeks to distance itself from its past. That is also true for women philosophers who have advanced feminist critique since the late 1960s and early 1970s.

15. Cf. Frigga Haug, "Perspektiven eines sozialistischen Feminismus," *Das Argument* 18, no. 159 (1986): 635–50.
16. Ute Gerhard and Jutta Limbach, "Einleitung," in *Rechtsalltag von Frauen*, ed. Ute Gerhard and Jutta Limbach (Frankfurt am Main: Suhrkamp, 1988).
17. Collections with translated essays are characteristic of this, for example, Beate Rössler, ed., *Quotierung und Gerechtigkeit: Eine moralphilosophische Kontroverse* (Frankfurt am Main: Campus, 1993). This book includes contributions from, among others, Virginia Held, Alison Jaggar, and Onora O'Neill.

When one takes into account the differences among philosophical cultures, it is obvious how different the respective starting points were for these women. While university curricula in the Anglo-American community—generally speaking—were predominantly oriented around analytic philosophy, the German community concentrated on the continental European tradition from the Greeks to Heidegger and Critical Theory. (It is only in recent years that the situation on both sides has slowly begun to change.) Against this background, it seems significant to us that so many German-speaking women authors who have been committed to developing feminist approaches in philosophical research have critically counterpoised themselves against the continental European "malestream."[18] Priorities have been set for this project: there is a predominance of work dealing with philosophical developments from the Enlightenment to the present. A number of studies within this time frame offer an overview of broader periods,[19] while others deal in detail with individual "classics."[20] In the end, it was this particular focus of interest that was the decisive factor in our preparation of the present volume. The contributions that follow, taking their point of de-

---

18. An important stimulus was Annegret Stopczyk, ed., *Was Philosophen über Frauen denken* (Munich: Matthes & Seitz, 1980); see also Renate Feyl, ed., "Sein ist das Weib: Denken der Mann," in *Ansichten und Äußerungen für und wider den Intellekt der Frau von Luther bis Weininger* (Darmstadt: Luchterhand, 1984); Cornelia Klinger, "Das Bild der Frau in der Philosophie und die Reflexion von Frauen auf die Philosophie," in *Wie männlich ist die Wissenschaft?* ed. Karin Hausen and Helga Nowotny (Frankfurt am Main: Suhrkamp, 1986), 62–86.

19. Among others, the following books have been particularly innovative: Silvia Bovenschen, *Die imaginierte Weiblichkeit: Exemplarische Untersuchungen zu kulturgeschichtlichen und literarischen Präsentationsformen des Weiblichen* (Frankfurt am Main: Suhrkamp, 1980); Heidemarie Bennent, *Galanterie und Verachtung: Eine philosophiegeschichtliche Untersuchung zur Stellung der Frau in der Gesellschaft und Kultur* (Frankfurt am Main: Campus, 1985).

20. To name just a few: Christine Garbe, *Die "weibliche" List im "männlichen" Text: Jean-Jacques Rousseau in der feministischen Kritik* (Stuttgart: Metzler, 1992); Ursula Pia Jauch, *Immanuel Kant zur Geschlechterdifferenz: Aufklärerische Vorurteilskritik und bürgerliche Geschlechtsvormundschaft* (Vienna: Passagen, 1988); Hannelore Schröder, *Die Rechtlosigkeit der Frau im Rechtsstaat* (Frankfurt am Main: Campus, 1979); Gabriele Neuhäuser, *Familie und Anerkennung: Eine feministische Untersuchung der Familie in Hegels Rechtsphilosophie und in aktualisierenden Anerkennungstheorien* (Frankfurt am Main: Universität-Studientexte zur Sozialwissenschaft, 1994); Christa Rohde-Dachser, *Expedition in den dunklen Kontinent: Weiblichkeit im Diskurs der Psychoanalyse* (Berlin: Springer, 1991); Ursula Menzer, *Subjektive und objektive Kultur: Georg Simmels Philosophie der Geschlechter vor dem Hintergrund seines Kulturbegriffs* (Pfaffenweiler: Centaurus, 1992); Mechthild Rumpf, *Spuren des Mütterlichen: Die widersprüchliche Bedeutung der Mutterrolle für die männliche Identitätsbildung in Kritischer Theorie und feministischer Wissenschaft* (Frankfurt am Main: Materialis Verlag, 1989).

parture from Enlightenment thinking, are exemplary of the feminist reading of the "canon" in the German-speaking community.

The authors of this collection take up diverse methodological approaches to the texts they analyze. In this respect these studies share a characteristic that is typical of feminist research in general: there is definitely no single model of feminist reading. But a certain typology in the development of a feminist approach to the philosophical canon is still recognizable. At the first level, feminist critique discovers and exposes the patent misogyny of the philosophical tradition; it highlights the sexism of many philosophers as well as the impact of this attitude on their work. This was the level at which women, as Ursula Pia Jauch has noted, "questioned the texts of male authors for the amount of misogyny that they might contain and, after a rigorous feminist interrogation, usually reached a little less than friendly verdict."[21] There may be no doubt that much of what has been discovered can help knock the wind out of the false pretensions of philosophers to truth and wisdom. Yet although what this type of critique brings to light is outrageous and hair-raising, it somehow remains unsatisfying; its high-pitched tone of moral indignation soon begins to grow somewhat boring. This is because on this level feminist critique of this kind addresses individual male philosophers rather than the categories and structures of philosophy itself. The charge of sexism is an *argumentum ad hominem* (in the literal sense). The failings that are diagnosed on this level have more to do with the subject than with the content. The subject, the male philosopher, is seen as driven by evil desire and selfish interest in the enslavement women, or at least as blinded by the prejudices of his time and culture, and thus is charged with having strayed from the path of truth and wisdom; yet philosophy itself, the ideas of truth, rationality, humanity, remain untouched. This implies that the element of misogyny can be purged, stripped away, or cleansed from philosophy, as if it were merely an ugly blemish. Yet this is not the way to dismantle the male, gender-specific code of philosophical discourse, a code that plays an important role in constituting the gender relationship as one of domination.

An important step in this direction is made with the second stage in the development of feminist critique. The insight that feminist critique is not limited to overt misogyny but must begin at a level where women, as well as the relations and differences of gender, are not even explicitly at issue, is

---

21. Ursula Pia Jauch, "Schopenhauer or Kant: Gender Difference Between Critique and Spirit of the Age." This volume, 103.

again something that does not pertain to philosophy alone. The fact that for extensive periods of Western history men have dominated the institutional formation of knowledge, that they have stamped it with their vision and shaped it according to their interests, is in no way limited to philosophical knowledge. What feminist critique calls *androcentrism* can be observed in many other scientific disciplines as well, from the human and social sciences to the natural sciences. Androcentrism in various fields of knowledge is defined as the one-sided, uncritical orientation of themes, guidelines, methods, and interpretations around a specifically masculine self-understanding and perspective. Given a society with a strict gender-specific division of labor, this masculine perspective clearly diverges from that of the female sex; yet regardless of this divergence, it sets itself up as the sole authority. While sexism is harmful in its explicit disparagement of women, androcentrism renders gender differences and their problematic as a whole invisible, and for that very reason it is even more pernicious. To a certain extent it is androcentrism, the predominance of the male-centered perspective on reality, that is the reason that the full measure of the gross injustice represented by sexism is simply not perceived.

The discovery of androcentrism is, in all fields, the most difficult and meaningful phase of feminist criticism. Yet it is particularly in philosophy that the exposure of the pretended neutrality and universal human applicability of male thinking and knowledge is of special significance. For it is in philosophy that the question of the essence of human being and of the constitution of the subject of knowledge and action is both posed and answered in a fundamental manner—that is, in a way that claims validity and that provides models for other fields.

Put together, these two stages of the feminist critique of philosophy yield considerable force: the charge of sexism unmasks the illusion of philosophical discourse as an extraterritorial space of thought free of dominance and interest, a realm of pure contemplation beyond social and political relations. The indictment of androcentrism articulates a fundamental critique of the claim to universality in Western thought, showing that it is, on the contrary, determined by cultural, historical, and social conditions. This critique shows, finally, that given the gender specificity of its perspective, Western thought is much less encompassing and valid than had been pretended.

This critique of Western philosophy—the critique that lays bare its complicity with relations of power and dominance, that reveals its functioning as a legitimization discourse in defense of the status quo, that uncovers its presumptions to universality—is in principle not limited to the standpoint of feminism and of women. It is also employed analogously from other discriminated and marginalized perspectives. Moreover, this critical perspective has developed within post-Hegelian philosophy itself and has at the close of the twentieth century practically become the predominant approach. For this reason Rosi Braidotti has justifiably expressed certain reservations: "At a time when the critique of rationality is the dominant theoretical mode, it remains to be seen ... what is specifically feminist about the denunciation of the links between knowledge and power."[22] What is specifically feminist is the insight that the link between knowledge and power is sexed: "The distinctive feature of feminist reflection is its desire to disclose not only the violent power-centered character of rationality, but also the sexed nature of this violence."[23] Seyla Benhabib is right in observing that "gender, and the various practices contributing to its constitution, is one of the most crucial contexts in which to situate the purportedly neutral and universal subject of reason."[24]

It goes without saying that the gender perspective on the relation of knowledge and power only represents one perspective among many others. However, this relativization of feminist criticism is itself relative, for it must be emphasized that historically the discovery and formulation of the gender critique of philosophy has been left up to women and to feminism. The great radical tradition of fundamental philosophical critique and self-critique from Marx to Nietzsche and Freud to the Critical Theory of the Frankfurt School did not fully develop this perspective in a systematic way. It took women to make this happen, and to be sure under particular historical or institutional conditions—namely, on the basis of a comparatively broad and continuing sociopolitical women's movement and the presence of a (somewhat) larger number of women in academia. Their specific experiences and their particular ways of looking at things could only be expressed by women themselves.[25]

This critique of sexual bias is not necessarily a part or a by-product of other forms of critique—just as, vice versa, the critique of gender-specific

---

22. Braidotti, *Patterns of Dissonance*, 175.
23. Ibid.
24. Seyla Benhabib, "Feminism and Postmodernism: An Uneasy Alliance," *Praxis International* 11, no. 2 (1991): 138.
25. Herta Nagl-Docekal, "Von der feministischen Transformation der Philosophie," *Ethik und Sozialwissenschaften: Streitforum für Erwägungskultur* 3, vol. 4 (1992): 530.

relations of dominance revealed by feminist criticism does not automatically constitute an adequate consideration and assessment of every form of social injustice and inequality. In recent years feminist theory has grown more and more aware of this fact by way of extensive internal debate and critique. It is an insight that situates the feminist perspective and relativizes it in the literal and positive sense; that is, it places feminism in context, relating it to a larger field of criticism without thereby diminishing its significance.

The general lesson to be drawn from this is that criticism must be concretely situated, that it must flow from actual experience. The necessary starting point of valid and acute criticism is something that in German would be called *Betroffenheit*—that is, a certain degree of immediate involvement and concern. We use this term with some caution, recognizing that the apparent immediacy it suggests conceals a high degree of complexity and ambivalence. Although concrete concern is a prerequisite for knowledge, the degree to which one is conscious of, and opposed to, injustice and oppression is not directly correlated to the extent of one's suffering. On the one hand, one can be directly affected by injustice, violence, or oppression without reaching an adequate consciousness of it; on the other hand, one may form a sharp sense of injustice and develop a strong desire to fight oppression without a proportionate experience of victimization. Over and above this, it should be emphasized that once it has been discovered and formulated, the validity of the critique both reaches beyond the circle of those immediately concerned and extends beyond the criterion for initially becoming concerned with these matters. With respect to the feminist critique of sexism and androcentrism, this means that the results of this critique are in no way available only to a specific sex, as if they concerned only women. Thus, in spite of our assertion that it was women who, because they were particularly affected by it, submitted gender-specific forms of domination to a systematic critique, nevertheless this critique can also be well understood, accepted, and further pursued by men.

Given these first two levels of critique, and presupposing a kind of symmetry in the dualism of the two genders, the question of the *feminine antithesis* inevitably arises. If all thinking has up to now been dominated by men and thus bears a masculine stamp, then what would a feminine thinking, writing, philosophizing, and so on be like? To be frank, this obvious and apparently logical third step is in fact a misstep, even if it perhaps has some meaning and value. There are two presumptions behind this manner of posing the question, and both are false: first, the dualism of gender is not an immutable reality but an artifact; and second, even given that we accept the gender dualism as established, it is in no way symmetrical. The fact that we can speak of masculine thinking because in the past men have dominated the professional production of theory and philosophy does not admit of the reverse conclusion that there is a yet-to-be-discovered or invented feminine thinking as its counterpart.

In the course of the many years in which we have been occupied with these questions, we have often come across this search for a feminine way of reading, writing, and thinking. It seems to us that this issue is most insistently raised by those men and women who are the least familiar with a feminist point of view. In those rare cases when male colleagues pay some attention to feminist philosophy, it strikes us that they are mostly interested in a quest for a totally alien, exotic vision of feminine alterity. This endeavor is often inspired by idle curiosity, though occasionally also by a deeper desire for a utopian alternative to traditional ways of thinking. As soon as such exaggerated expectations are disappointed (which inevitably must happen) the curiosity is quickly replaced by strong disapproval of such absurdities. This finally results in a rejection of the idea of feminist theory as a whole.[26]

Paradoxically, the vision of a "feminine" thinking operates with the presupposition of complete male dominance of the realm of philosophical thinking. As long as this assumption is in place, the imaginary female counterworld exercises its effect from a mysterious and mythical distance. To invoke it is to embark on a risky adventure at the limits of the male system. When this system is in crisis, it may be deemed necessary to take such a risk in order to save the system from the danger of paralysis—that is, in order to rejuvenate a form that has grown old, to enrich and broaden its scope with an unsettling confrontation with "Otherness."[27] Because of the self-empowerment of women that emerges in the course of the feminist project, now seems to be the time for the great alternative to the male system finally

---

26. This representation corresponds closely to the more general observation of Ute Gerhard: "The assessments of the women's movement vacillates . . . between idealization and denunciation, between overestimation and underestimation, or between being ignored and being overrun" ("Die 'langen Wellen' der Frauenbewegung Traditionslinien und unerledigte Anliegen," in *Das Geschlechterverhältnis als Gegenstand der Sozialwissenschaften*, ed. Regina Becker-Schmidt and Gudrun-Axeli Knapp [Frankfurt am Main: Campus, 1995], 251).

27. Cf. Jacques Derrida, "Sporen: Die Stile Nietzsches," in *Nietzsche aus Frankreich*, ed. W. Hamacher (Frankfurt am Main: Ullstein, 1986), 129–68; Cornelia Klinger, "Eine Fallstudie zum Thema postmoderne Philosophie der Weiblichkeit: Jacques Derrida: 'Sporen: Die Stile Nietzsches,' " in *Theorie Geschlecht Fiktion*, ed. Nathalie Amstutz and Martina Kuoni (Frankfurt am Main: Stroemfeld, 1994), 205–33.

to prevail. What has instead become evident at this point is that the Other belongs to the Same—this is in fact the mechanism behind such projections. At the very moment when the hope appears to have been fulfilled, it proves itself to be an illusion.

We do not deny that women and feminists have also let themselves be seduced by the Fata Morgana of the great female alternative to the male world and to masculine thought. Yet the questions of the essence and place of the feminine as they are posed within feminist theory by and large derive from different motivations and lead in other directions. What is at issue here is less the hopeful prospect of redemption from the predicaments of the masculine system than the question of the ontological status of femininity and gender difference, for these matters have hardly ever figured in the schemes of traditional male-dominated thinking. Gender difference was seen as a contingent factor of the human condition. Whereas masculinity set the standard and norm of what it meant to be human, femininity was denied any autonomous status or value: "woman" was purported to be nothing more than a miscast, failed, stunted man—a "weaker vessel." To be a woman does not entail a particular conception or category but is simply the lack of being male.

There are countless examples from the beginnings of Western thought down to the present that show that woman is not opposed to man as a woman, as a B to an A, or that the two are not placed together under a common concept of a "human" species that would include both. These examples range from Aristotle's theory of reproduction, which traces the creation of the female child back to unfavorable conditions, to Lacan, who opposes the female as "pas-tout," as "not all" against the male "all." As Simone de Beauvoir has noted, "[T]he relation of the two sexes is not quite like that of two electrical poles, for man represents both the positive and the neutral. . . . Humanity is male and man defines woman not in herself but as relative to him; she is not regarded as an autonomous being."[28] It is the resistance against this "phallocentric system of representation"[29] that

---

28. Simone de Beauvoir, *The Second Sex,* trans. and ed. H. M. Parshley (New York: Random House, 1952), xviii.

29. "While the sexes are represented according to a binary structure that reduces n-sexes to two, the binary structure itself reduces one term within the pair to a position definitionally dependent on the other, being defined as its negation, absence or lack. This is a phallocentric representational system in the sense in which women's corporeal specificity is defined and understood only in some relation to men's as men's opposites, their doubles or complements." Elizabeth Grosz, "Inscriptions and Body Maps: Representations and the Corporeal," in *Feminine-Masculine Representation,* ed. Terry Threadgold and Anne Cranny-Francis (London: Allen & Unwin, 1990), 73.

motivates the question that has consumed and deeply divided the feminist theoretical community, namely, whether the category of gender is ontologically viable.[30]

Over the last fifteen to twenty years, this question of a female form of being human has made its way into all branches of philosophy. Is it possible to define a feminine cognitive perspective (including a feminist epistemology) in accordance with a female "essence," which in most cases is deduced from "women's corporeal specificity"?[31] Is there also a women's aesthetics? Perhaps even something like a female logic, as was so often suggested from a deeply misogynist perspective? Lastly, and of particular importance for this type of questioning: Is there a women's ethics and morality?

Not only has there been no unanimity among feminist theorists over positive answers to these questions, but instead we have seen both vehement rejections of all the various attempts to formulate positive answers and even strong resistance to the question as such. The various directions taken up by the critics can be summed up, in simplified form, in the following manner:

First, to an unprejudiced view, the gulf of gender difference proves to be much less deep than the dichotomizing ideology of gender difference would suggest. What counts empirically as gender difference not only remains extremely controversial but is an issue that comes up again and again. This is in particular due to the fact that it intersects and overlaps with a multiplicity of other differences.[32] The fact that the dispute over this issue has been going on for so long without ever being resolved indicates that the question as such is inadequately posed or simply wrong.

Second, under the condition that an essential femininity is assumed, all women are bound to one concept of femininity. Difference feminist positions have been reproached in recent years with particular vehemence precisely because they neglect the cultural and historical differences among women. But the fantasy of a generic, singular Woman is nothing but a relic of the old phallocentric system of representation.

Third, the suspicion has not been completely dispelled that the fruits of

---

30. This does not, by the way, amount to a contradiction between the two concepts of the feminine as wholly alien Other and as a deficient being. Rather, it has to do with two sides of the same coin, or more precisely: the vision of femininity as an alternative form and concept is in general only thinkable on the basis and flip side of the invisibility, unspeakability, and unreality of the feminine. The exclusion of women from the real world forms the presupposition of styling them as the guiding ideal of all possible worlds.

31. Cf. note 29 above.

32. Cf., for example, Cynthia Epstein, *Deceptive Distinctions: Sex, Gender, and the Social Order* (New Haven: Yale University Press, 1988).

feminist efforts to define the essential characteristics of femininity do not fall so far from the tree of patriarchal ascriptions but simply reverse them by placing the traditional characterizations of the feminine in a new, better light. This move to reevaluate long-disparaged feminine qualities is by no means sufficient to nullify the patriarchal view of woman. This is clear for structural reasons and has been well known for a long time. Adorno's opinion is still valid and has not been disproved by difference feminism to this day: "The feminine character and the ideal of femininity according to which it is modeled are products of male society.... The glorification of the female character includes the humiliation of all those who are its bearers."[33] In the same vein, the deduction of feminine qualities from "women's corporeal specificity" must not be trusted, because here the definition of woman is once again deduced from, and reduced to, the body. Finally, the polarizing, dichotomizing contrast of female and male, whether for positive or negative valuation, also raises doubts.

Considered from a philosophical point of view, these and other arguments against the difference position that we have not cited can be summed up in four points: (1) Any recourse to an essential femininity presupposes an ontology, that is, the idea of an order of being. Such a foundation is no longer accepted as universally valid and binding. In the postmetaphysical age in which we undeniably find ourselves, the question of a divine or natural order on which the determination of human being is based has become unviable. As a result, the question of an ontologically or metaphysically grounded determination of gender identity is also obsolete. As Sandra Harding put it, "Once essential and universal man dissolves, so does his hidden companion, woman."[34] There is no longer a heaven that would ordain the laws of human destiny; there is no longer a great book of nature out of which it can be read. The feminist challenge can take on and decisively change the horizon of possibility within philosophy, but it cannot (without doing damage to itself) turn back the wheel of history, in particular the history of thought. It is too "late" for an ontology of gender—just as, by the way, it is also too late for woman to become a subject. The epoch of transcendental philosophy is over as is that of metaphysics.

Now this rejection of the thesis of an ontological viability of the gender

---

33. Theodor W. Adorno, *Minima Moralia: Reflexionen aus dem beschädigten Leben*, in *Gesammelte Schriften* (Frankfurt am Main: Suhrkamp, 1980), 4:105, 106.

34. Sandra Harding, "The Instability of the Analytical Categories of Feminist Theory," in Sandra Harding and J. F. O'Barr, *Sex and Scientific Inquiry* (Chicago: University Press, 1987), 284f.

difference does not lead to the assertion of a gender-neutral humanity as an ontological prius to the gender difference. That would simply result in a retreat from the difference position to the equality position. Rather, the stalemate between these two positions, opposed to one another yet remaining on the same level, must be broken by moving beyond them both.

Given the postmetaphysical condition, neither "gender" nor "human being" can be an absolute source or origin, a firm foundation from which to proceed. Gender is, like any other kind of identity, the effect of a discursive constellation.[35] By *discursive constellation* we understand the totality of social and cultural discourse and practice within which gender identities and roles, along with the binary and polar (dichotomous) structure of their difference, are produced. In other words, the constructed and artificial character of gender identity and gender difference, as well as that of human being in general, is to be understood against the background of the postmetaphysical age.

In its effort to replace masculine ascriptions and proscriptions of femininity by turning to women's own experience and self-descriptions, feminist theory in principle still assumed the parameters of the masculine perspective instead of leaving them behind. It is only with the framework of conceiving of gender identities and differences as *constructions* that it becomes possible to transcend this constellation. This new move brings about a fundamental shift in the outlook of feminist theory, which at this point reaches its fourth level.

Although it may seem as if the debate over (gender) identity as essence versus construction has flared up only in the past few years, nevertheless it should be remembered that the claim that gender identity and difference are produced by society had already been a part of the traditional wisdom of feminist theory. What else is behind the Beauvoirean thesis that nobody is born a woman, but is made one?[36] The idea of construction is already implied by that of gender. In fact, the term *gender* had won considerable popularity in more recent feminist debates because it emphasized the aspect of constructedness in the images of masculinity and femininity. Yet the concept of gender was limited to factors of *social* construction. Whereas economics, politics, socialization, and education were brought into relief as the relevant parameters of the discursive constellation for the production of gender roles

---

35. Cf. Herta Nagl-Docekal, "Weibliche Ästhetik oder 'Utopie des Besonderen'?" *Die Philosophin* 5 (1992): 35.

36. Simone de Beauvoir, *Das andere Geschlecht: Sitte und Sexus der Frau* (Hamburg: Rowohlt, 1951), 265.

and hierarchies, the physical nature of the sexes was left unconsidered. This contrast found expression in the terminological distinction between *sex* and *gender* that had been introduced into the feminist discussion. This distinction reproduced the nature/culture divide; the existence of the natural dimension—biological sex and sex difference—was not denied, but any influence it may have on the social destiny of the person or on the organization of society was rejected. Nature was reduced to the function of the mute substrate of subject, society, and culture.

In the course of the development of feminist theory, this sharp opposition of social and biological sex has proven to be untenable for different reasons and in various respects: First, not only does it not lay to rest the question of the function and meaning of this nature that has been declared to be a passive substrate, but it actually provokes it:

On the one hand, it has not been successful in opposing in a convincing manner the still-vocal antifeminist attempts to defend traditional gender roles by deducing social norms from biological givens. It is more often dismissive and defensive. The assertion that the obviously different physical constitution of the sexes must somehow have some effect on their given psychosocial situation and function is met on this level of debate not with actual arguments, but simply with a drawing of lines and a "moral" injunction to respect them. It is normatively posited that "sex" should have no consequences with respect to social position and roles, but it is not plausibly argued why this could not be the case.

On the other hand, the same constellation gives rise to altogether contrary expectations. A utopian strain of difference feminism still hopes to find resources for a fundamental reform of society in the recourse to an original female nature uncontaminated by social domination and convention. As much as the respective goals of the conservative and feminist-utopian positions may diverge, in a certain sense they are involuntarily on the same side in their mistrust of the sex/gender division and their belief in the significance of the essential biological difference between the sexes. The only difference lies in the negative or positive valuation. From a conservative point of view, sex differences are invoked in order to prove that hopes for social and political change are necessarily thwarted by the iron laws of nature; whereas on the other side, the turn to nature is seen as the bedrock of renewal.

Second, in the course of its development, feminist research and theory has encountered in ever wider contexts and on ever deeper levels the produced and constructed character not only of "gender" but also of "sex" and sexuality.

With respect to uncovering and investigating the ways in which the gender-specific, psychophysical nature of humans is fashioned, feminist theorists were able to take up and further develop the contributions of Freud and Lacan on the one hand and Foucault on the other. Already in psychoanalytic theory one finds the thesis, which has been considerably substantiated by feminism, that "dispositions are not the primary sexual facts, but produced effects of a law imposed by culture."[37]

From another point of view, namely in the context of a feminist critique of the dominant concept of the political, the categories of "public" and "private" have been put into question. The exclusion of women from the political sphere and the relegation of the whole complex of gender relations to the private sphere follows the logic of the nature/culture divide. The distinction between culture/society and nature is meant to mark the differentiation between that which can be produced or at least influenced by human volition and activity and that which lies beyond this scope. To consign the complex of the gender order to the realm of nature thus suggests inviolability. A feminist critique has shown that this differentiation itself is not a fact of nature but an act of cultural and political construction that serves to stabilize the established gender order. Feminism here recognizes that limits belong to the game, and that whoever sets the limits determines the rules, and so dominates the game.

The dichotomy of culture and nature itself is finally recognized as a categorical construction in which the dichotomy of gender is inscribed. The culture/nature distinction, in turn, supports the dichotomy of male and female. In addition, the analogy between the dichotomies culture/nature, male/female, and other dualisms construed as dichotomous (for example, reason and emotion, active and passive) is also recognized.

As a result of these reflections, new doubts are cast on the sex-gender distinction that at an earlier stage of the feminist debate had appeared to be such an important achievement. The differentiation between sex and gender had indeed been an important inroad when seen against the backdrop of the patriarchal tradition that relegated the entire complex of gender relations to the realm of nature, thus placing it out of the reach of political action and

---

37. Judith Butler, *Gender Trouble: Feminism and the Subversion of Identity* (London: Routledge, 1990), 64f.

historical change. Yet this was only a first step. It succeeded in reclaiming one part of this complex for the social terrain, but it did not seriously infringe on the structure itself, in that the sex-gender distinction remained within the conceptual framework of the nature/culture dichotomy. In a certain sense, it can be said to have been a significant move on a given field of play, but it is a far cry from rewriting the rules of the game from a feminist perspective.

This objective comes into view only when we reconsider the differentiation between sex and gender in the manner that has been proposed, for example, by Judith Butler: "Sex, by definition, will be shown to have been gender all along."[38] Taken literally, this formulation of the new position is just as wrong as it is right. It is right insofar as it clearly expresses the constructed, derivative character of "natural" sex. It is (or would be) wrong if it were supposed that it sought to understand the construction of sex through the concept of gender.[39] For the concept of gender is defined as precisely that type of social construction that relies on the juxtaposition with sex. Thus to refer to gender necessarily brings back the question of sex as the mute substrate of the body—or, rather, of nature itself. If the insight of recent feminist theory into the constructed character of (sex) identity and difference—an insight that is not Butler's alone, but which finds in Butler a particularly pregnant formulation—is actually to be fruitful, then a clarification, or rather a more adequate and precise rethinking of the concept of construction is necessary. At issue here is the need for a concept of construction that does not founder on the threshold of nature and culture, but rather reflects it.

This means, in concrete terms, that the idea of *social* construction is to be supplemented by, and expanded into, a cultural or symbolic dimension (nota bene: *supplemented* and *expanded,* not replaced!).[40] This implies both another frame of reference and another notion of construction.

38. Ibid., 8.
39. In a later book, *Bodies That Matter: On the Discursive Limits of Sex* (New York: Routledge, 1993), Judith Butler attempts to settle this misunderstanding: "If gender consists of the social meanings that sex assumes, then sex does not accrue social meanings as additive properties but, rather, is replaced by the social meanings it takes on; sex is relinquished in the course of that assumption, and gender emerges . . . as the term which absorbs and displaces 'sex'" (p. 5). Such a reduction of sex to gender is also insufficient, according to Butler's interpretation. That the concept of gender can be extended in a meaningful manner and, along with social construction, can also include other aspects of construction, is shown by the terminological differentiation introduced by Sandra Harding. See note 40 below.
40. Along these lines, Sandra Harding introduces three levels of the concept of gender: "Gendered social life is produced through three distinct processes: it is the result of assigning dualistic gender metaphors to various perceived dichotomies that rarely have anything to do

Along with the body, the field of cultural or symbolic construction includes the systems of representation and signification: language, art and literature, religion, and philosophy. Thus it involves precisely those spheres that were not explicitly thematized by a concept of social construction that focused on the categories of law, economy, and politics. The symbolic level, not incidentally, relates precisely to those spheres that are conceived as "superstructures" by a materialist perspective that is centered on the social. However, in understanding and clarifying gender relations, they are at least as important, if not of greater relevance. And insofar as the gender order is perhaps more deeply embedded in the foundation of society and culture than other structures (such as social or class structures), the cultural/symbolical structure would almost be the better candidate for the title of "basis" if it were possible to avoid the hierarchical connotations concomitant to architectonic metaphors.

This transition from the level of social construction as it corresponds to the concept of gender to the level of cultural/symbolic construction comprising both gender and sex has been put into a larger context by Julia Kristeva. She interprets this as a paradigm shift from the constellation of the nineteenth to that of the twentieth century, which she in turn relates—however cryptically—to the emergence of questions concerning the gender order, or with the rise of feminism. She describes what we have been calling the cultural or symbolic construct as the "symbolic denominator": "This . . . symbolic common denominator concerns the response that human groupings, united in space and time, have given not to the problems of the production of material goods (i.e., the domain of the economy and of the human relationships it implies, politics, etc.) but rather, to those of reproduction, survival of the species, life and death, the body, sex, and symbol."[41] The gender order is, according to Kristeva, grounded in a symbolic contract,[42] analo-

---

with sex differences; it is the consequence of appealing to these gender dualisms to organize social activity, of dividing necessary social activities between different groups of humans; it is a form of socially constructed individual identity. . . . I shall be referring to these three aspects of gender as gender symbolism (or, borrowing a term from anthropology, 'gender totemism'), gender structure (or the division of labor by gender) and individual gender" (*The Science Question in Feminism* [Ithaca: Cornell University Press, 1986], 17–18).

41. Julia Kristeva, "Le Temps des femmes," in 34/44 *Cahiers de recherche de sciences des textes et documents* 5/1979; "Women's Time," in *Feminist Theory: A Critique of Ideology*, ed. N. O. Keohane, M. Z. Rosaldo, and B. C. Gelpi. (Brighton: Harvester, 1982), 32.

42. The word *contract* should not invite any false associations of equality and justice that would pertain among the contractual parties. That this is a completely erroneous representation already with respect to the "classical" social contract can be gleaned from Marx and Rousseau. The same is true for the gender contract, which Kristeva thus clearly characterizes as also being a victim-contract.

gous to the grounding of the social order in a social contract. Put in another way, the symbolic contract is that type of social contract that regulates not the order of the "production of material goods" but the order of "reproduction, of the survival of the species, of life and death, of the body, of sex, of symbol."

What had appeared only in a postulative and programmatic form in Kristeva's 1979 essay has since been elaborated by feminist research and theory. The cultural/symbolic dimension has become an important field of study in various disciplines from the analysis of religion to film theory. It centers on the question how in each of these discursive constellations the effect of sex is produced, how the gender difference is instituted in its binary and dichotomous form with all its well-known characteristics.[43] In that women were excluded in the past from these activities of discourse production, feminist research must deal with an almost exclusively masculine domain. Jutta Georg-Lauer is right when she states that the real achievement in the establishment of patriarchy was that men were able to secure their command over the production of symbolic systems.[44]

It has become clear that the project of feminist philosophy also belongs in this context. On the level of social construction alone, philosophical discourse may appear to be of rather marginal significance,[45] but in the cultural/symbolic dimension, its importance becomes fully apparent.[46] Thus it

43. For a contemporary overview of the state of research in German, see the collection of essays under the title *Genus: Zur Geschlechterdifferenz in den Kulturwissenschaften*, ed. Hadumod Bußmann and Renate Hof (Stuttgart: Kroener, 1995).
44. Jutta Georg-Lauer, "Postmoderne und Feminismus," in *Postmoderne und Politik*, ed. Georg-Lauer (Tübingen: edition diskord, 1992), 113.
45. Cf. Michèle LeDoeuf, "Cheveux longs, idées courtes," in *Recherches sur l'imaginaire philosophique*, ed. Michèle LeDoeuf (Paris, 1980), 135: ". . . à s'en tenir à une classification des droits refusés aux femmes, . . . il semble clair que s'impose une disproportion entre le droit de disposer de son propre salaire, de décider du destin de sa sexualité, et celui de philosopher, disproportion qui qui ne peut que faire sombrer le droit à la philosophie dans l'anecdotique."
46. As practiced by Genevieve Lloyd, the criticism that a concept of gender exclusively oriented around the social construction of sex is inadequate is of importance to feminist philosophy and philosophical criticism. She also points out that in the area of philosophy, a symbolic gender concept is requisite: "[T]here are aspects of the maleness of reason that are not captured in the idea of socially constructed masculinity. We are here dealing with the content of symbols. That, of course, belongs . . . in the realm of the social. But this maleness, though it does have consequences for the social construction of gender, cannot be equated with socially produced masculinity. . . . The maleness of reason belongs in this category of the symbolic" ("Maleness, Metaphor, and the Crisis of Reason," in *A Mind of One's Own: Feminist Essays in Reason and Objectivity*, ed. Louise M. Antony and Charlotte Witt [Boulder, Colo.: Westview Press, 1973], 71). Cf. Elizabeth Grosz, "A Note on Essentialism and Difference," in *Feminist Knowledge: Critique and Construct*, ed. Sneja Gunew (London: Routledge, 1990), 340: "[N]ot only

Introduction   21

is clear, for example, that one of the most essential and effective instruments in the production of a polar and dichotomous gender difference—namely, a developed system of analogous, mutually defining dichotomy formations—has been at the core of Western philosophy since the Pythagorean table of categories. Rosi Braidotti calls this system of dichotomies "an unacknowledged and camouflaged sexual distinction at the very heart of philosophy."[47] It is clear that the dichotomy of masculinity and femininity is inscribed in the fundamental categorical pairs of the philosophical tradition, pairs such as "form and content," "transcendence and immanence," "reason and emotion," "activity and passivity," and so on. In reverse, the consequence is that in and with its most central categories, philosophy sustains this type of gender difference. Joan Scott's thesis that "politics constructs gender and gender constructs politics"[48] can be translated into "philosophy constructs gender and gender constructs philosophy." Thus Moira Gatens is without a doubt correct when she characterizes the thematization of the connection between the various fundamental dichotomies of Western philosophy and the gender difference to be a decisive step in feminist theory in recent years: "The dichotomies which dominate philosophical thinking are not sexually neutral but are deeply implicated in the politics of sexual difference. It is this realization that constitutes the 'quantum leap' in feminist theorizing. It allows a quite different, and more productive, relation to be posited between feminist theories and philosophical theories."[49]

In this introduction we have been able to do little more than give an overview of the level at which a feminist analysis and critique of the discourse of philosophy must proceed. The issues here include, along with the wide field of dichotomy formations, how and to what extent other symbolic structures, signs, and metaphors are employed within the sphere of philosophy. What remains is concrete work in this field, work that is in full swing from various points of departure. Nevertheless, we have the impression that this work has only just begun, that we are only seeing the tip of the iceberg.

---

must social practices be subjected to feminist critique and reorganization, but also the very structures of representation, meaning, and knowledge must be subjected to a thoroughgoing transformation of their patriarchal alignments."

47. Braidotti, *Patterns of Dissonance*, 193.

48. Joan W. Scott, "Gender: A Useful Category of Historical Analysis," in *Coming to Terms: Feminism, Theory, Politics*, ed. Elizabeth Weed (London: Routledge, 1989), 96.

49. Moira Gatens, *Feminism and Philosophy: Perspectives on Difference and Equality* (Cambridge: Polity Press, 1991), 92. Cf. Ludmilla Jordanova, *Sexual Visions: Images of Gender in Science and Medicine Between the Eighteenth and Twentieth Century* (Madison: University of Wisconsin Press, 1989), 21.

Re-reading the Canon in German

In view of this general background, the editors of the present volume selected essays that are representative of the different approaches to the philosophical canon that have been suggested by feminist authors writing in German. Discussing a number of "classics"—within the time range from the period of the Enlightenment through the present—the following articles introduce an English-speaking readership to the great variety of methods and analytical categories that have been brought to bear on the philosophical tradition.

But this variety of perspectives notwithstanding, the authors of this book also have some intentions in common. One such shared concern is to get beyond the simple notions of "patriarchal thinking" that have informed early feminist critiques of the canon and to disclose some of the more subtle and complex elements of the philosophical constructions of gender that have been elaborated in the given time. Due to this interest, the essays in this book share yet another feature: they challenge—albeit from different angles—some views on the "classics" that have gained the status of received opinions within feminist theory. Arguing along these lines, several authors of the present volume also voice objections against some of the readings of the canon that have been published in English. It may be precisely this aspect of the book that could mark the beginning of intensified discussions on these matters across language boundaries.

The first article suggests itself as a plausible starting point for such an exchange, as *Lieselotte Steinbrügge* contests a thesis commonly accepted in feminist critiques of reason: that the modern concept of reason and the understanding of science and progress based on it, far from banishing the idea of female inferiority to the realm of superstition, ultimately cemented it. Steinbrügge proposes replacing this view with a more differentiated understanding of the Enlightenment conception of reason, which is no more homogenous than Enlightenment images of history. As she shows, it is in particular the often-asserted split between sensibility and rationality that calls for a new reading, since the critique addressing this split is grounded in an inadmissible oversimplification of Enlightenment thought. Using two different positions within the French Enlightenment as an example, Steinbrügge shows how differing conceptions of the "nature of woman" fulfill an essential function in the elaboration of different theoretical systems. While those authors who write in the Cartesian tradition—authors such as Poullain de la Barre and Condorcet—advocate egalitarian gender relations precisely because they exclude the corporeal from their concept of reason, Rousseau, on the basis of his critique of reason, propagates with particular vehemence the inequality of men and women.

The following essay also aims at raising our awareness of the dangers of oversimplification. *Christine Garbe* suggests a reinterpretation of Julie, the protagonist of Rousseau's great novel, which differs decisively from the common feminist understanding. While many authors have seen Julie simply as an object of masculine imagination or as a victim of patriarchal power, Garbe contends that she is to be taken seriously as the subject of her speaking and acting. From this point of view, Garbe explains, it becomes evident that Julie not only experiences and endures the paradoxes of the "amour-passion" that characterize her relationship with her private tutor St. Preux, but that she is also aware of them, whereas neither of the male characters in the novel fully comprehends the situation. Garbe discloses a pattern of ambiguity and disguise that may be read as Julie's form of resistance toward male expectations and attributions. Describing Julie's attempt to overcome those paradoxes through her specific concept of a reasonable and virtuous marriage, which guides her life with her husband Wolmar, Garbe raises the question of why this attempt does not succeed. She holds that Julie's death is to be understood as a sign of failure since the final part of the novel confronts us with a number of striking inconsistencies. It is not unlikely, Garbe concludes, that one of Rousseau's intentions was to show that the bourgeois ideal of marriage is doomed to fail, as its two competing aspects—the aspects of love and economic support—can never be reconciled.

Rousseau is also at the center of the third essay in the volume, which reads his work from the perspective of a more general question. *Herta Nagl-Docekal* discusses the impact of feminist interpretations, examining how our understanding of general philosophical topics changes once "gender" is introduced as a category of analysis. Challenging received opinions on philosophy of history, she presents Rousseau's work as a case in point. While traditional research has hardly considered Rousseau a theorist of historical progress, Nagl-Docekal claims that an interest in precisely this kind of philosophy of history can be traced in his entire work, even in his literary texts, an interest that becomes obvious as we focus on his conception of gender relations. Two features, she explains, are closely related in Rousseau's reflections on mankind's current state of alienation and on how this state could be overcome. As he suggests three changes to be brought about in the future—leading through justice and morality toward the unity of art and nature—Rousseau, at the same time, assigns distinct tasks to the two sexes. Close reading reveals that, according to Rousseau, mankind's future progress depends on men and women accepting and performing well their respective roles. Nagl-Docekal also emphasizes the critical potential of such a feminist approach to the canon, showing that Rousseau's entire concept of history is marked by gender asymmetries.

But what, exactly, does it mean to choose a feminist approach? This methodological question is the core concern of *Ursula Pia Jauch*. Her comparative study of the statement on "the fair sex" in Kant's "Of the Distinction Between the Beautiful and the Sublime" (1764) and Schopenhauer's "Metaphysics of Sexual Love" (1844) is not immediately aimed at producing a new interpretation of these two texts. Instead, Jauch uses this material as an exemplification of her more general reflections on feminist ways of reading traditional philosophy. The author introduces a distinction between what she names the "canonical" and "postcanonical" approaches. According to Jauch, the "canonical" form of feminist criticism is restricted to an investigation into the judgments "on women" made by male philosophers. This kind of endeavor usually ends up lamenting the more or less explicit and insolent misogyny of the mainstream of Western philosophy and does not achieve much more than to replace the traditional male view on women with a feminine or feminist view on male philosophers. Thus Schopenhauer's talk "on women" is substituted by a feminist talk "on Schopenhauer." In contrast, Jauch's plea for a "postcanonical" way of reading proposes to broaden the perspective by way of a feminist self-reflection on its own prejudicial limitations and by redefining the object of interrogation. Not the "other" but gender difference as such should become the focus of a critical and self-critical approach. Jauch goes on to argue that Kant and perhaps to a lesser extent Schopenhauer give some tentative examples of what a postcanonical approach could mean, insofar as they included at least some reflection on the epistemological situatedness of the male subject as it is talking "on women."

The next essay points at yet another way in which a close reading of the "classics" may become relevant for contemporary feminist thought. Providing a careful reconstruction of Hegel's views on gender, *Heidemarie Bennent-Vahle* examines which insights can be gained with regard to the feminist concern to redefine relations between men and women. In her reading of Hegel, she focuses in particular on the way distinct moral principles are assigned to the two sexes. As Bennent-Vahle shows, from the early beginnings of his reflections on this matter in his *Phenomenology of Spirit*,

Hegel's conception implies an asymmetry that means for women to be deprived of power and dependent upon men. Following the further development of Hegel's thinking, Bennent-Vahle observes that expectations with respect to the virtuous conduct of women are increasing in correspondence with a functionalization of the private sphere within the bourgeois social order. This process reaches its climax in the *Philosophy of Right,* where Hegel assigns to femininity a social mission, as he portrays women as smoothing down the potential of conflict in society. While highlighting this instrumentalization of women, Bennent-Vahle stresses that Hegel's conception entails negative effects for men as well. Under the auspices of the subjugation and self-renunciation that is demanded from women, men are prevented from reaching a comprehensive way of self-realization. In this context, Bennent-Vahle views mutual recognition as the only viable alternative to Hegel's dialectic of gender difference.

Central issues of the current feminist debate are the point of departure for *Cornelia Klinger* as well. Specifically, she focuses on and critically examines common ideas on "woman and nature." Very often an analogy is drawn between "woman" and "nature" in general, and in particular between the domination or even destruction of nature and femininity and the values they represent as caused by the process of modernization. In contrast to this view, Klinger contends that an idealization of, as well as a nostalgia for, unspoiled archaic nature and the corresponding symbolization of femininity is only an effect of this very process of modernization. It is only in opposition to rational, artificial/industrial modern "man" that "woman" is imagined as irrational, archaic, and connected to nature. Klinger attempts to understand the development of this kind of sentimental ideology of nature and femininity against the background of the fundamental split between an instrumental and an aesthetic type of reason that took place as a result of the demise of metaphysics in the history of Western thought. While instrumental reason rules in the male-dominated spheres of modern economy, politics, science, law, and so forth, its aesthetic counterpart develops in the private spheres of art and culture, in an individualized religion, and in the idealized home as "haven in a heartless world." The specifically modern form of the division of labor between the sexes that goes together with a strong polarization of essential gender characters runs parallel to the process of the differentiation between value spheres and must be understood as an effort to overcome the disadvantages of modernization by a concept of complementarity.

Käthe Trettin's essay on Frege's logic holds a special position within our collection because it is the only contribution which addresses the field of philosophical logic. Formal logic is perhaps the branch of philosophy least susceptible to a feminist approach. The author intends to sort out viable and nonviable attempts at a feminist critique of logic. In order to achieve this aim, she applies a specific method, investigating the fascination that is created by pure forms and formalization. Referring to Aristotle's syllogistic and to Frege's concept-script, Trettin elucidates the dialectic of "showing" and "silencing" that characterizes formal logic and explains how logic has struggled to become a liberating tool, freeing itself from genus and gender considerations. Her main thesis is that the only legitimate point that can be made with regard to these logical efforts from a feminist perspective is to note their being gender-neutral or gender-indifferent. According to this conclusion, Trettin challenges feminist ways of criticizing formal logic as they have been suggested by authors such as Andrea Nye and Lorraine Code, claiming that such a critique tries anew to "genderize" logic. But Trettin also emphasizes that logic is not settled once and for all—that it is rather, as situational semantics for instance has shown, open to refinement. In view of this openness, Trettin argues, it is indeed desirable to develop a feminist critique of logic, but what is demanded here is an alternative, constructive form of critique that helps to clarify gender concepts.

Whereas the first part of this volume focuses primarily on the Enlightenment and the nineteenth century, the second part approaches the twentieth century with a special emphasis on the turn of the century and the early decades. The time between the 1890s and the 1930s is known as a period of rapid and even violent modernization with far-reaching consequences on the restructuring of gender relations. The essays of *Ursula Menzer, Christa Rohde-Dachser,* and *Ingvild Birkhan* deal with the work of two authors, Georg Simmel and Sigmund Freud, who were not only aware of the deep changes but also contributed in a major way, albeit in different fields, to revolutionizing modern science and consciousness. In spite of this, the three pieces converge in pointing at the long shadow of traditional gender wisdom on the thinking of Simmel as well as of Freud. The ambivalent or negative image of the turn of the century is still aggravated when the work of Otto Weininger is assessed in Birkhan's essay.

Georg Simmel was one of the founders of German sociology and a prominent representative of "Lebensphilosophie." He published a wide range of essays on rather unacademic and unusual topics like fashion, adventure, flirtation, modern city life, and so forth. Among his articles in cultural philosophy are some on femininity, masculinity, gender relations, and the women's movement of his day. Together with much of his writing, these essays had been forgotten for some decades and were rediscovered and republished (both in German and English) only recently in the context of a renewed interest in Simmel. In her contribution to this volume *Ursula Menzer* places Simmel's "philosophy of the sexes" into the larger context of his philosophical and sociological thinking. Although Menzer shares the high esteem which Simmel has earned over the last ten or twenty years for his most insightful analysis of the conditions of modern life, she strongly criticizes his views on gender relations and the role of women in modern society. Combining the methodological tools of hermeneutics and a critique of ideology in her approach to Simmel's philosophy, Menzer diagnoses not only numerous contradictions but also a profound rupture in his thought. For the conditions and interests of women are not only not included when Simmel discusses the positive or negative consequences, the expectations or risks of modern life and society, but Simmel systematically excludes women from the process of modernity and modernization. Following the nineteenth-century ideology of dual spheres, he advocates an ontology of gender difference that polarizes the masculine and feminine principles.

The Freudian portrait of femininity illustrates with rare clarity the role that unconscious fantasies play in generating the myths intrinsic to the construction of psychoanalytic theory. *Christa Rohde-Dachser* conducts a hermeneutical investigation of the unconscious meaning of Freud's theory of femininity and shows how the inferior image of woman portrayed there is transferred in theoretical language. The fantasies described provide an existential security for being male and disguise the male fear of an independent woman (mother) who is able to leave him. The cognitive structure of these fantasies refers to the early childhood where the boy discovers the gender difference and interprets the world along his fantasy of phallic monism. This fantasy has a screen function against much more threatening fantasies of the mother as someone who has a sexual desire of her own. The fantasy of phallic monism is at the same time the basis for a construction of a reality in which woman and man each occupy a predetermined place. Denied is the image of the "Other Woman" as an independent subject. The author shows how through the shaping of an identity of perception and an identity of thought these childlike unconscious fantasies persist in psychoanalytic theory.

Ingvild Birkhan discusses two conceptions of gender identity that are characteristic of the thinking in Fin-de-siècle Vienna and whose impact can be traced into contemporary debates on this issue. Scrutinizing and comparing Otto Weininger's *Geschlecht und Charakter* and Sigmund Freud's *Totem and Taboo,* she detects two distinct theories of female inferiority. Weininger takes "woman" as a symbol of a-logos, instability, and nothingness. Since he constructs the female position in this way, Birkhan argues, his book may be viewed as foreshadowing Lacan's famous theses. With regard to Freud, she highlights the topos of the powerful father and his assassination. Examining the implications of this paternal metaphor, she addresses several issues. One of her concerns is the idea of a contract concluded among men (that is, among the sons) by which they acknowledge one another as equals while women are assigned the status of objects and of gifts in exogamic exchange. Birkhan also discusses Freud's views on religion, pointing out that he is primarily interested in the emergence and significance of patriarchal religion. Due to this restricted focus, she notes, he fails to acknowledge and interpret the manifold presence of female divinities in cultural orders.

With *Astrid Deuber-Mankowsky,* the perspectives are changing, for her article concerns the sphere of gender metaphors and issues of the symbolic meaning of femininity. She traces the question of gender difference in Walter Benjamin's critique of modernity. Benjamin describes the "erosion of inner life" as a consequence of modernization and as a crisis of masculinity, which is exemplified in the work and life of Charles Baudelaire. Deuber-Mankowsky shows how the interest that Benjamin takes in Baudelaire flows from Benjamin's specific approach to history as developed in the *Passagen-Werk*. Centering on his peculiar concept of "presence of mind," Benjamin's historical methodology opens the way to discover Baudelaire as "hero of Modernity." The modern hero is characterized as fetishist, and his fetishism dominates modern gender relations to the detriment of women and femininity. Against this background woman is pictured as prostitute or as masculinized intellectual, as lesbian and as worker in the modern factory, whereas the traditional feminine roles and values are on the wane. The concomitant disappearance of gender difference is taken as paradigmatic of the disappearance of differences in general and finally of the annihilation of life. Deuber-Mankowsky compares the fetishism that Benjamin describes in Baudelaire with Freud's analysis of this phenomenon and with Marx's notion of commodity fetishism. A reversal of life and death is the common denominator in these concepts of fetishism: a perverse fantasy endows the dead object with life while it turns living beings into abstract lifeless objects. This is the point where allegory and commodity come to meet. At the same time, allegory displays a power of destruction that may result in a transgression of the fetishist form of male domination.

The two last essays of this collection focus on the work of two philosophers who are both standing in the tradition of Critical Theory, Max Horkheimer and Jürgen Habermas. *Mechthild Rumpf's* contribution formulates a critique of Critical Theory from a feminist perspective. The author discusses the strikingly numerous references to motherhood and motherliness in the work of Max Horkheimer. She points out the ambivalences and contradictions in his position. On the one hand, the interaction between mother and child is understood as model of a mimetic relationship that reaches beyond the subject-object dualism. Thus the connection of mother and child is not only idealized but is believed to contain a utopian potential for an intact intersubjectivity. On the other hand, in the *Dialectic of Enlightenment* (1947) Horkheimer and Adorno draw a much less favorable picture. Here the authors assume that all memories of the maternal are necessarily wiped out in the process of civilization and of individual socialization, for society demands the denial of "tender family ties." As a consequence, the maternal would lose its potential to serve as a point of resistance to the constraints of society. But Horkheimer stops short of such a conclusion. Rumpf shows that the inconsistency in Horkheimer's position results from his incapacity to fully analyze the situation of women. His utopian vision of the maternal hinges on a gender-specific division of labor that makes the sphere of woman and family appear as an idyllic resort of human values but at the same time as deprived of all power and influence. The male-centeredness of Horkheimer's perspective also finds expression in the fact that the child is exclusively imagined as a male child.

Elisabeth List's essay, as the last contribution to this volume, explicitly addresses the gender implications of modernization and rationality. These topics have been in the background of many other texts and formed the thread through the anthology as a whole. The author approaches Critical Theory with central issues of current feminist theory, in particular the feminist critique of reason, in mind. She challenges the general distrust in reason, as expressed by various representatives of Critical Theory, and argues for a specific reformulation of the notion of reason. This alternative notion should be derived from, and imbedded in, the reality of social life. In her view, the common repression of what is associated with the feminine—feeling, caring, and embodiment—has resulted in a distorted concept of reason. Only from the perspective of a truly human vision of reason and rationality, she asserts, can the gendered constitution of reason be disclosed without repeating the all-too-well-known dichotomies between body and mind, eros and reason, and so forth. And only then will it become possible to overcome the destructive dynamics inherent in the process of rationalization that characterizes Western civilization. List's contribution provides a strong argument for a feminist appropriation of the notion of reason, contrary to a currently widespread tendency among feminists to question and dismiss the notion of reason as ultimately masculine. In the course of her reflections, List not only discusses misconceptions of Critical Theory but also points to an underlying common ground between the feminist project and Critical Theory.

Acknowledgments

The editors of this anthology are very grateful to Iris M. Young, Robin M. Schott, Gerda Postl, and Sanford G. Thatcher, who helped in many ways to bring this book into existence.

1 | FEMININITY AND CRITIQUE OF REASON IN THE FRENCH ENLIGHTENMENT

Lieselotte Steinbrügge

Translated by Stephanie Morgenstern

The Age of Enlightenment, which was already being dubbed "the Age of Reason" by its contemporaries, has fallen into disrepute. Considering the catastrophes that have threatened humanity in the twentieth century, few remain today who have not lost faith in the goddess of Reason, who was worshipped two hundred years ago at the celebrations of the French Revo-

This essay originally appeared under the title "Vernunftkritik und Weiblichkeit in der französischen Aufklärung," in *Die Revolution hat nicht stattgefunden, 1789–1989: Dokumentation des V. Symposions der Internationalen Assoziation von Philosophinnen*, ed. Astrid Deuber-Mankowsky et al. (Tübingen: edition diskord, 1989), 65–79. Also published in *Jahrbuch für Volkskunde*, ed. Wolfgang Brückner and Nikolaus Grass (Würzburg, Innsbruck, and Fribourg: Echter Verlag, 1991), 166–77.

lution in the form of white-robed maidens. More and more female voices are joining the chorus of reason's critics, who not only make rational thought responsible for technological megalomania and the overexploitation of nature but also associate it directly with the oppression of humanity's female half. The feminist critique of reason operates from the premise that the modern concept of reason as well as the understanding of science and of historical progress it inspired have failed to relegate the idea of the inferiority of the female sex to the sphere of myth or religious dogmatism. Ultimately, they have validated it and granted it a certain social currency. The following lines of argument can be discerned in this critique:

1. The alleged universality of reason, the very paradigm of the Enlightenment, has always been a fiction. The rational subject, as conceived by modern thinkers, was always and only the (white) man. Females were excluded from this kind of reason from the very beginning. What was, in fact, male was designated "universally human." Reason was integral to the identity of the male subject alone.[1]

2. The modern conception of reason and science is oriented only to the domination of nature and, by the same token, to the domination of human nature. Given that the woman does not participate in this act of domination, female nature is seen exclusively as the object of a kind of reason practiced by men. Bacon's gendered metaphors are frequently cited as illustrations of this view, and have been invoked by both Evelyn Fox Keller[2] and Geneviève Lloyd.

3. Modern reason, oriented to the domination of nature, functions strictly according to a binary logic: rationality or irrationality, body or spirit, male or female, above or below, master or slave. Any aspects of nature that cannot be slotted into the limited structure of male reason or that cannot be deduced from their primary causes by the standard rules of reason are excluded from this systematized worldview or—more accurately—are mystified. Female nature, in contrast to male reason, stands for the sensual, the unpredictable, the inexplicable; and it is therefore excluded from rational, scientific, and even anthropological discourse. It is, instead, a favored object of the masculine imagination. Nothing is richer than the images cre-

---

1. Cf., for example, Geneviève Lloyd, *The Man of Reason: "Male" and "Female" in Western Philosophy* (London: Methuen, 1984). German: *Das Patriarchat der Vernunft: "Männlich" und "weiblich" in der westlichen Philosophie* (Bielefeld: Daedalus, 1985).

2. Evelyn Fox Keller, *Reflections on Gender and Science* (New Haven: Yale University Press, 1985). German: *Liebe, Macht, und Erkenntnis: Männlich oder weibliche Wissenschaft* (Munich and Vienna: Carl Hanser Verlag, 1986).

ated by the patriarchy, nothing sillier than the "scientific" explanations its thinkers have devised to account for women's nature. "Femininity" was designated the "scientific unknown," the systematic gap, the blind spot of logocentrism.³

Accordingly, modern views of women's nature cannot be explained by reference to models drawn from the sciences; they must be understood, instead, as guided exclusively by patriarchal interests. They are, in other words, ideological. The recurring theme in philosophy about women seems to consist in "legitimating in theory what took place in practice."⁴ In essence, its portrait of women was paradigmatic of philosophical thought's allegiance to the dominant power.⁵

4. Above all, it is the Age of Enlightenment that takes the blame for the birth of this concept of reason and for the dire consequences it has had on the upbringing of women. At the Frankfurt Congress on the Future of the Enlightenment, Friederike Hassauer and Peter Roos characterized the feminist critique of reason as a critique of the Enlightenment itself: "Enlightenment takes a partial reason to be the world's universal reason. This partial reason is the reason of logocentrism, the reason of binary logic, the reason of the patriarchy. All else is dismissed out of hand, all else is liquidated, all else is designated un-reason." They conclude: "The enlightened person was the rational person, and the rational person was the man. Femininity had no place in it."⁶

In what follows, I address a few destabilizing remarks to these familiar claims that have been crystallizing into a paradigm. My doubts about the accuracy of the arguments advanced above stem from the fact that the Enlightenment conception of reason is simply not such a monolithic block. Above all, I hold the supposed separation of sensuality from reason to be an unacceptable oversimplification of Enlightenment thought. It is precisely the critical debate with Descartes's views, and with his division of *res cogitans* from *res extansa,* that characterizes the sensualism of the ideas of the French Enlightenment. The view of history at the time is equally heteroge-

---

3. Luce Irigaray, *Spéculum de l'autre femme* (Paris: Editions de Minuit, 1974).
4. Annegret Stopczyk, *Was Philosophen über Frauen denken* (Munich: Matthes & Seitz, 1980), 344 (trans. by Stephanie Morgan).
5. Cornelia Klinger, "Das Bild der Frau in der Philosophie und die Reflexion von Frauen auf die Philosophie," in *Wie männlich ist die Wissenschaft?* ed. Karin Hausen and Helga Nowotny (Frankfurt am Main: Suhrkamp, 1986), 65.
6. Friederike Hassauer and Peter Roos, "Aufklärung: Futurologie oder Konkurs: Acht Behauptungen," in *Die Zukunft der Aufklärung,* ed. J. Rüsen, E. Lämmert, and P. Glotz (Frankfurt am Main: Suhrkamp, 1988), 40, 42 (trans. by Stephanie Morgan).

neous, and, as Johannes Rohbeck argued in his monograph on the Enlightenment theory of progress, it cannot simply be reduced to the formula of a "feasibility-frenzy."[7]

I draw upon two divergent positions from the French Enlightenment—on the one hand, the ideas of equality formulated in the tradition of Cartesian rationalism by Poulain de la Barre and Condorcet, and on the other hand, Rousseau's views on the differences in gender traits—to show that their views of woman's nature are more than simply normative claims determined by a patriarchal interest in domination; rather, these views fulfill *functions* within the scientific conceptual system of the time, particularly within its anthropology and philosophy of history.[8] It will become clear that equating the domination or exploitation of nature with discrimination against women is based on a false analogy that does not stand up to a scrutiny of these systems' particular views.

In 1673 Poulain de la Barre published his small brochure *The Woman as good as the man; or, the equality of both sexes*.[9] This is by no means the singular work of a possibly eccentric outsider; in fact, it is unthinkable without Descartes's *Discours de la méthode*. The Cartesian postulate of the universality of reason is a prerequisite for Poulain de la Barre's formulation of the equality of the sexes. There had been many apologetics for women before his, but they had sought to "prove" the equality—perhaps even the superiority—of the female sex by means of endless compilations of examples drawn from secular or biblical history. Instead, Poulain—like Descartes—subjects all previous conceptions of female inferiority to methodological scrutiny. The fact that women are not to be found in the arts, sciences, or in public office—which most compiler-apologists had preferred to downplay—is not taken at all by Poulain as a sign that they are by nature incapable of activity in these spheres. He dismisses this common

---

7. Johannes Rohbeck, *Die Fortschrittstheorie der Aufklärung: Französische und Englische Geschichtsphilosophie in der zweiten Hälfte des 18. Jahrhunderts* (Frankfurt am Main: Campus, 1987).

8. In 1983 Christine Garbe had already pointed out the limits of an exclusively ideological critique of Rousseau and had drawn attention to the specific *functions fulfilled by the female* within Rousseau's discourse as a whole. See "Rousseau oder die heimliche Macht der Frauen: Zur Konzeption des Weiblichen bei Jean-Jacques Rousseau," in *Frauen in der Geschichte*, vol. 4, ed. Brehmer et al. (Düsseldorf: Schwann, 1983).

9. François Poulain de la Barre, *De l'égalité des deux sexes: Discours physique et morale où l'on voit l'importance de se défaire des préjugés* (Paris: Jean Du Puis, 1673; reprint, Paris: Fayard, 1984). English edition: *The Equality of the Two Sexes*, trans. with an introduction by Daniel Frankforter (Lewiston, N.Y.: Lampeter E. Mellen, 1989).

conclusion as an example of "prejudice": "We are filled with prejudices, and we must renounce them completely if we are to attain clear and definite knowledge."[10]

Compilation of facts alone does not bring us closer to understanding the nature of something. Following this methodological principle, Poulain seeks to determine the "true nature" of women. According to Cartesian tradition, what is crucial is the intellect, which is made the touchstone of the equality question; Descartes had said, after all, that common sense was the best distributed thing in the world. Descartes had applied the essential equality of the intellect to a sociopolitical argument against feudal hierarchy without considering its application to gender. However, in doing this, he had at least established an epistemological premise that held both genders to be intellectually equal at birth. Now Poulain de la Barre picks up on this premise, and from it builds arguments that are to point the way toward future debate.

His second crucial argument is drawn from the Cartesian distinction between *res cogitans* and *res extensa*. Since the mind is separate from the body, physical traits can have no direct influence on thought. It follows that the specifics of the female body cannot influence her thought, just as the bodily difference between the sexes plays no role whatsoever in the activity of the mind. "Reason has no sex" (*L'esprit n'a point de sexe*): this now famous claim, which encapsulates both the argument for the universality of understanding and its independence in principle from physicality, is the core of Poulain de la Barre's postulate of equality. Thus it is precisely the *separation* of mind and body, of sense and spirit—to which the feminist critics of reason object so strongly—that paved the way for ideas of equality.

Almost 120 years later, on July 5, 1790, Jean Antoine de Condorcet published a newspaper article in the *Journal de la Société de 1789* under the heading "Sur l'admission des femmes au droit de cité" (On the admission of women to the rights of citizenship).[11] In this article he drew attention to an oversight of the national assembly: although it had submitted a robust proposal for human and civil rights, the proposal had failed to include women. "But the rights of men result simply from the fact that they are

---

10. Poulain de la Barre, *De l'égalité des deux sexes*, 9.
11. "The First Essay on the Political Rights of Women: A Translation of Condorcet's Essay 'Sur l'Admission des Femmes au Droit de Cité,' " in Marie Jean Antoine Nicolas Caritat, marquis de Condorcet, *Collected Writings*, trans. Dr. Alice Drusdale Vickery [1790] (Letchworth: Garden City Press, 1893). Reprinted in *Unsung Champions of Women*, ed. Mary Cohart (Albuquerque: University of Mew Mexico Press, 1975), 219–25. Quotations are from this English edition.

rational, sentient beings, susceptible of acquiring ideas of morality, and of reasoning concerning these those ideas. Women having, then, the same qualities, have necessarily the same rights. . . . It would be difficult to prove that women are incapable of exercising the rights of citizenship. Although liable to become mothers of families, and exposed to other passing indispositions, why may they not exercise rights of which it has never been proposed to deprive those persons who periodically suffer from gout, bronchitis, etc.?" (220).

Condorcet presupposes—as does Poulain—a gender-neutral faculty of understanding. But gender neutrality here is not a pretext to legitimate the attribution of a "universally human" quality to what is in fact only male. Quite the reverse: it is an argument to reinstate the woman as equal possessor of both human and civil rights. Condorcet traces all differences between men's and women's mental activity to their different living circumstances and education. In doing this, he is arguing along sophisticated and virtually modern lines. For example, in order to explain a few "typically feminine" ways of behavior, he writes: "Their [women's] interests not being the same (as those of men) by the fault of the law, the same things not having the same importance for them as for men, they may, without failing in rational conduct, govern themselves by different principles, and tend towards a different result. It is as reasonable for a woman to concern herself respecting her personal attractions as it was for Demosthenes to cultivate his voice and his gestures" (222).

Thus here, at the end of the Enlightenment, we are dealing with a view of female emancipation that, although explicitly based on the idea of the universality of reason, applies this concept of universal reason explicitly to *both* sexes.

Admittedly, other views had already been in circulation, and Condorcet's small article could be dismissed as a mere curiosity. Indeed, this could well be warranted as long as his and other views of women are considered only in isolation. But I maintain that his article did not materialize this way by chance, nor because Condorcet was more favorably inclined toward women than were his contemporaries. Rather, it was because the roots of his thought are grounded in a much more comprehensive vision of the philosophy of history. In "Sur l'admission des femmes au droit de cité" he points out one historical development: "Up to this time the manners of all nations have been more or less brutal and corrupt. I only know of one exception, and that is in favour of the Americans of the United States, who are spread, few in number, over a wide territory. Up to this time, among all nations, legal inequality has existed between men and women; and it would not be difficult to show that, in these two phenomena, the second is one of the causes of the first, because inequality necessarily introduces corruption, and is the most common cause of it, if even it be not the sole cause" (224f.).

A few years later, in 1793, Condorcet writes his *Sketch for a Historical Picture of the Progress of the Human Mind*,[12] in which he proves himself to be one of the French Enlightenment's most determined theorists of progress. In it he postulates a direct correlation between economic progress and moral perfection.[13] According to Condorcet, the continuous advancement of the sciences, bringing with it an improvement in living conditions, and above all an increased enlightenment of the individual, leads to a greater equality among people that applies to the sexes as well. "Among the causes of the progress of the human mind that are of the utmost importance to the general happiness, we must number the complete annihilation of the prejudices that have brought about an inequality of rights between the sexes, an inequality fatal even to the party in whose favour it works. It is vain for us to look for a justification of this principle in any differences of physical organization, intellect and moral sensibility between men and women. This inequality has its origin solely in abuse of strength, and all the later sophistical attempts that have been made to excuse it are vain."[14]

Although he only touches upon it peripherally in his *Esquisse,* Condorcet posits a direct connection between increasing social development and the improvement of the woman's situation. His idyllic vision of a peaceful, prosperous world involves the utopia of an emancipated relationship between the sexes that ascribes the same abilities and rights to the woman as it does to the man. While Poulain de la Barre only discusses the woman's capacity for reason in general, for Condorcet the matter takes on historical resonance under the conditions of the social upheaval of 1789. The woman's position is contingent upon the general state of social development. Progress of the human spirit, manifested as progress in the sciences and arts, entails, by the same token, an improvement in interpersonal relations, including those between the sexes. The belief in the inevitable ascent of human reason alongside the simultaneous moral perfection of the human

---

12. *Sketch for a Historical Picture of the Progress of the Human Mind,* trans. by June Barraclough with an introduction by Stuart Hampshire (London: Weidenfeld and Nicolson, 1955). German: *Entwurf einer historischen Darstellung der Fortschritte des menschlichen Geistes,* ed. Wilhelm Alff (Frankfurt am Main: Suhrkamp, 1976).
13. Cf. Rohbeck, *Die Fortschrittstheorie der Aufklärung.*
14. Condorcet, *Sketch for a Historical Picture,* 193.

race makes it possible to contemplate an equality between men and women. Seen this way, the increasing mastery of nature is not understood as an ongoing act of subjugation that also subjugates women; on the contrary, it seems to be a precondition for humans being increasingly able to secure their survival without requiring brute physical force. Survival without the need for force is the necessary condition for the woman—subordinate to the man in physical strength—to assume a position of equal rights to the man's. Condorcet's view on women's rights is therefore genuinely integrated with his philosophical theory of history.

In my view, Condorcet is not an isolated case. It would be worth investigating more thoroughly whether, say, those theorists of progress who postulate a congruence between technical-economic development and social development, and who draw a positive and consistent relationship between these and reason, also develop the conception of an equality between men and women.

This conjecture was supported, for instance, by John Millar's paper, *The Origins of the Distinction of Ranks,* which first appeared in 1771. His work deserves a more thorough treatment on the subject of women than is possible within the scope of this essay. It is of great methodological importance because in it, woman's position in the social hierarchy is considered a criterion of social progress. He bases his natural history of humanity on the changes in women's living conditions, with the premise that change in customs and culture is manifested more conspicuously in relations between the sexes than in any other sphere. "Of all our passions, it should seem that those which unite the sexes are most easily affected by the peculiar circumstances in which we are placed, and most liable to be influenced by the power of habit and education. Upon this account they exhibit the most wonderful variety of appearances, and, in different ages and countries, have produced the greatest diversity of manners and customs."[15]

Of course, the eighteenth century also developed theories of women's nature running completely counter to these. It is well known that an ideal of womanhood was taking shape in this period that confined the woman to the private, domestic sphere and declared the emotional faculties effective in that area to be typically feminine. It is equally well known that this very division of gender traits set the ideological course for women's *exclusion*

---

15. John Millar, *The Origin of the Distinction of Ranks: An Inquiry into the Circumstances Which Give Rise to the Influence and Authority in the Different Members of Society,* reprint of the 4th ed. (Edinburgh, 1806), with an account of the life and writings of the author by John Craig (Aalen: Scientia Verlag, 1986), 14.

from civil rights and was ultimately used to seal the fate of women's cultivation. Though Condorcet's appeal for equal rights for the sexes has fallen into oblivion, his optimistic faith in progress far outlived the eighteenth century. What survived was a belief in differentiated gender traits and in the differences in rights that follow from them. In the history of French thought, this development is strongly associated with the figure of Rousseau, who in his novelized treatise on education, *Emile*,[16] dedicates an entire chapter to the upbringing of girls and elaborates there the all-too-familiar postulates on feminine modesty, deference, self-sacrifice, and so forth. I will limit myself to one aspect of this program of education, though one which I take to be crucial in relation to the current feminist discussion of the critique of reason: the cultivation, or rather the non-cultivation, of the female intellect.

Unlike Poulain de la Barre and Condorcet, Rousseau estimated women's intellectual abilities to be lesser than men's from the very outset; furthermore, he considered the deliberate development and fostering of these abilities to be unnatural. Girls and women should not—indeed, cannot—exceed a particular stage in the development of their thought. Accordingly, their knowledge should be oriented only to the concrete objects important within the confines of their practical lives. It is not a woman's task to reflect upon abstract principles; it is preferable that she remain within the sphere of the tangible. Feminine deficiencies, however, are compensated by other qualities: the man's power to concern himself with "works of the mind" is replaced, in the woman, with the capacity for spontaneous, unreflective observation and feeling. The counterpart to male reason (*raison*) is female taste (*goût*). This opposition provides a clear illustration of the parameters of feminine knowledgeability. Taste applies to both the artistic and moral spheres; it serves equally in judging the beautiful and the good: "Taste is formed partly by industry and partly by talent, and by its means the mind is unconsciously opened to the idea of beauty of every kind, till at length it attains to those moral ideas which are so closely related to beauty. Perhaps this is one reason why ideas of propriety and modesty are acquired earlier by girls than by boys" (338).

By *goût*, Rousseau clearly has in mind a particular kind of knowledge. Taste is by no means arbitrary or merely subjective; rather, it carries with it a certain claim to truth. Taste remains, however, at the level of sensory

---

16. Jean-Jacques Rousseau, *Emile ou de l'éducation*, in *Oeuvres complètes*, vol. 4, ed. Bernard Gagnebin (Paris: Gallimard, 1969). English translation: *Emile*, trans. Barbara Foxley (London: J. M. Dent, 1957). Page references are to the English translation.

knowledge, and is therefore adequate only to making judgments of the particular. Only male reason manages to draw generalizations out of moment-to-moment perception. To develop taste, the girl needs no intensive training or education—on the contrary: its development is natural and immediate. Taste presupposes no acquired knowledge, but natural talent; rational thought is, in fact, detrimental to it. For these reasons, Rousseau expressly discourages any deliberate, artificial cultivation and education for girls. Later, as a woman, the same knowledge-free, spontaneous simplicity she uses in her aesthetic judgment is applied in her social intercourse. She observes and "senses" her environment. Her behavior is not determined by principles but is guided by intuitive empathy. For example, Rousseau describes the host and hostess of a social gathering. The behavior of the man is determined by his knowledge about the individual guests, whereas the woman's is guided by her observation and sensitivity: "The man knowing the assembled guests will place them according to his knowledge; the wife without previous acquaintance, never makes a mistake; their looks and bearing have already shown her what is wanted and every one will find himself where he wishes to be" (346).

This gift of human observation is not the result of upbringing; it is innate to women. It determines their moral judgment and action. Women's social demeanor is not mediated by rational principles, but rather by an unreflective, spontaneous feeling. It is, for this reason, more genuine than men's; in contrast, a man's politeness is deemed "false": "A woman's politeness is less insincere than ours, whatever we may think of her character; for she is only acting upon a fundamental instinct; but when a man professes to put my interests before his own, I detect falsehood, however disguised" (339).

The struggle for advantage, egoism, which impairs the full fruition of the man's sense of taste, seems not to determine the woman's social behavior to the same degree. Unlike in the man, her natural, instinctive politeness is not dominated by an egoist passion. This position of Rousseau's, I believe, is decisive for all further elaborations of his image of women. The category of egoism, which in *Emile* provides the fundamental distinction between masculine and feminine action, is central to his social theory. A closer look at it will provide the key to understanding his principles for Sophie's education and his portrayal of femininity in general.

The history of the advent of egoism is found in *A Discourse on the Origin of Inequality* (hereafter: *Second Discourse*), published in 1755.[17] Self-inter-

---

17. Jean-Jacques Rousseau, *A Discourse on the Origin of Inequality*, in *The Social Contract and Discourses*, trans. G. D. H. Cole, rev. J. H. Brumlett and John C. Hall (London: J. M. Dent, 1973).

est (*amour-propre*) is one of its central concepts. Rousseau associates the origins of egoism with a specific stage of civilization—the invention of agriculture and metalwork—and with the division of labor and emergence of private property that accompany it. This age figures as the third stage in Rousseau's history of humanity. In the original, premoral state of self-sufficient, natural man (the first stage), and in the golden age of communal living (the second stage), natural inequalities in strength, intelligence, and age still had no effect on the life of the collectivity. However, along with the claiming of private land that inevitably accompanies agriculture came competition, rivalry, and "the secret desire of profiting at the expense of others" (87).

From this change in property relations, there followed a change in the motivation for human action. The innate human instinct for self-preservation (*amour de soi*) became perverted into self-interest (*amour propre*). Self-interest is not seen here as natural, as many early social philosophers (Hobbes, Locke, Mandeville) had maintained; Rousseau considers it instead the result of particular social conditions that stifled the basic human instinct of natural pity (*pitié naturelle*). In the early days of socialization, the golden age, the instinct toward self-preservation was still compatible with compassion, or natural pity, because the interests of individuals were united by communal ownership. At this stage, reason existed only in rudimentary form. Humans acquired the ability for conceptual generalization and the faculty for abstract thought only with the arrival of agriculture and metalwork, which coincides with the stage of private property. Abstract reason, therefore, always serves private goals and drives individuals into mutual antagonism. In this third phase of socialization, reason is given an additional task: not only must it tame nature in order to make the earth habitable, but under the new conditions of competition it must also serve to gain an advantage over one's fellow. Reason thus becomes the handmaid of egoism and ultimately becomes fused with it into a single motive.

Rousseau criticizes this, but the fusion of egoism and reason is so striking to him that he equates one with the other. At a developed stage of society, he even sees this relationship as reversed, so that the means ultimately become the cause: "It is reason that engenders *amour-propre*, and reflection that confirms it: it is reason which turns man's mind back upon itself, and divides him from everything that disturbs or afflicts him. It is philosophy that isolates him, and bids him say, at the sight of the misfortune of others: 'Perish if you will, I am secure' " (68).

This critique of reason, as elaborated in the *Second Discourse*, seems to me to be crucial for an appraisal of Rousseau's concept of womanhood. Rousseau does not believe that enlightenment and morality are synonymous, as does Condorcet. For him technical-scientific progress does not entail moral progress; on the contrary, it precipitates moral decline. In Rousseau's understanding, moral sensibility based on reflective reason can function only in human relations on a large scale—that is, in the sphere of public, state morality.[18] But the moment we are dealing with the immediate, interpersonal sphere, moral feeling must ground itself in the original human instinct, in *pitié naturelle*. Calculating, rational thought would only corrupt this instinct.

So if Rousseau wants, at all costs, to curtail the development of rational activity in the girl, what we are dealing with is not merely a "woman's problem." Much more significantly, we are dealing with Rousseau's attempt to rescue, for his conception of history, the notion of a sacred and universal reason that had already lost some of its luster. The Enlightenment, in other words, already comes equipped with its own critique of reason. In sensualistic moral philosophy, reason had overtones of purposive rationality, of egoism, of cold, calculating inhumanity. The compassion-free attitude—which Rousseau portrays in its most chilling colors—functions well in the competitive, cut-throat business life of men; it is practically a prerequisite for its efficiency. But immediate interpersonal relationships, most clearly embodied within the family, would collapse if the principle of calculating reason were to prevail. From this comes the call for a private morality that would be founded upon a counterauthority: the principle of genuine feeling. What was a general tendency in moral philosophy becomes heightened in Rousseau with a gender-specific emphasis. The general tendency was to relegate direct human contact and mutuality to an area outside the sphere of calculating, rational thought. Rousseau does the same and, to a great extent, ascribes those moral qualities required within the interpersonal sphere to the woman because she is closer to it, according to her biological and social function. The woman becomes the moral sex.

If the females of the human species are to become aware of this function at all, their innate human perfectibility—which is also, as Rousseau shows in his *Second Discourse,* the precondition for human corruption—must be stifled in their development. Women must be left in an almost primitive condition—more specifically, at the phylogenetic stage of the golden age, when human reason, still at an early point in its development, had not yet

---

18. I am not pursuing here the likewise developed *moral reason*, which makes it possible for the corrupted person of civilized society to act within the sphere of public morality, and which, in my view, defines the moral behavior of the man in opposition to that of the woman. See Steinbrügge, *The Moral Sex: Woman's Nature in the French Enlightenment*, trans. Pamela Selwyn (Oxford: Oxford University Press, 1995), 63–70.

entered into a conflict of interest with instinctual interpersonal action. With Sophie, Rousseau brings the lost golden age back into the harsh world of competitive individuals. When Emile and his tutor leave Paris for the provinces "like true knights errant" to seek out a suitable helpmeet, it is just as much a voyage into the past of humanity in search of as-yet-uncorrupted human nature. Only in this sanctuary, far from the civilized city, can feminine nature flourish.

The corruption of the human race was carried out by a dynamic inherent in its very perfectibility. To forbid this development would seem a difficult task. The guiding principle to "desire mediocrity in all things," which underlies Rousseau's view of Sophie's apprenticeship toward womanhood, represents an effort to stifle a development; and this, it seems, can only be carried out by compulsion. Hence the innumerable tips, in the fifth book of *Emile,* on how to seize the means of compulsion early in the girl's education.

In conclusion, I would like to draw out some consequences of this discussion. If feminist critics of reason declare Enlightenment thought to be bankrupt because it excluded the feminine in declaring itself to be the universal discourse of reason, they should at least be aware of the following dilemma: the most emancipated views on feminine nature (the famous exceptions one does not know what to make of) were advocated by the very thinkers whose concept of reason excluded the sensual and the physical. I maintain that the Cartesian concept of reason was, in fact, the very first that allowed for an inclusion of women in the society of thinking people. Furthermore, as shown by Condorcet's case, equality between the sexes was championed even by those theorists of progress who must be numbered among the greatest offenders in their devout faith in instrumental reason, and who best match the negative image of "blind optimists of progress" that today's critics of reason rightly denounce. Women do make an appearance in these theories and are not simply absorbed into the general category of "human." Poulain's writings, as well as Condorcet's response to the proposal for human and civil rights, clearly illustrate the awareness that there was a specific kind of personhood embodied by women, and that, even in the context of a "hard" theory of progress, the utopian vision of a life shared between the sexes involved a vision of equal rights.

The reverse is also true: the idea of men and women's inequality, the insistence on the differences between them, the polarization of gender traits, the view that reason can be integral to the identity of the male individual alone—all these should become arguments strongly supporting the practice of social discrimination against women. Yet they stemmed from that very faction of the Enlightenment that harbored the greatest skepticism—as do today's critics of reason—about the "progress of the human spirit" and the "gender-neutrality" of understanding. The figure of the woman as moral authority performs a necessary function within an anthropological system that presupposes that the human race was originally good but has since been corrupted by the effects of civilization. This much is true: women were excluded from the society of thinking individuals—that is, the society of individuals whose thought was abstract and therefore cold. Nevertheless, they had a clearly defined place in the anthropological system as a whole and were not, as has often been argued, denied their humanity.

The Enlightenment's repressive image of women, founded upon inequality and elaborated most extensively by Rousseau, does not arise out of an arrogant faith in the perfectibility and universality of reason. In the Enlightenment, reason's limits were clearly acknowledged. Its leading thinkers responded to the crisis of reason with moral philosophies that withdrew this admittedly partial reason from certain spheres of life in favor of what was taken to be a more natural feeling. Feeling was set apart as a corrective counterpart to reason, and this expression of the critique of reason was itself integrated into the anthropological definition of the feminine. Feminine nature became the place from which reason could be put to question. The "moral sex" is the critique of Enlightenment reason.

2

JULIE, OR THE FEMININE DIFFERENCE
A New Reading of Rousseau's *Nouvelle Héloïse*

Christine Garbe

Translated by Melanie Richter-Bernburg

> Love is the realm of women.
> It is they who necessarily give the law in it, because, according to the order of nature, resistance belongs to them, and men can conquer this resistance only at the expense of their liberty.
> —Rousseau, *Letter to M. d'Alembert on the Theatre*

Until now, most feminist interpretations of Jean-Jacques Rousseau's *Julie, ou, La Nouvelle Héloïse* have seen the novel as a story of sacrifice: in giving

---

This essay originally appeared under the title "Die Verfehlung der Geschlechter in der Liebe: Julie oder die neue Héloïse," in Christine Garbe's *Die "weibliche" List im "männlichen" Text: Jean-Jacques Rousseau in der feministischen Kritik* (Stuttgart: Metzler, 1992), 157–81. Translator's note: *Julie, ou, La Nouvelle Héloïse* is cited as *NH* in references to the text. Passages quoted in English are from the only complete English translation of the work to appear since its original publication. In William Kenrick's four-volume *Eloisa, or a Series of Original Letters* edition of 1803 (facsimile reprint 1989), the translator undertook a renumbering of the letters that make up the novel; here, to avoid confusion, references to the translation are to the volume and page number in Kenrick. These references are followed by the page number of the French edition (see References).

up her deeply loved tutor, Saint-Preux, Julie, the novel's protagonist, sacrifices her "female desire" and acquiesces in the patriarchal order of her father and the husband who was chosen for her by her father.[1] However, even as the wife of an unloved husband and the mother of two sons, she is not able to satisfy this order; only her death at the end of the novel brings about the complete negation of woman pursued by Rousseau.[2]

I would argue, on the contrary, that Julie has a voice of her own in this novel and that it is a voice that deserves to be heard and taken seriously. It may be that the widespread feminist habit of perceiving the female literary figure primarily as a victim and as the object of male imagination or repression leads to a reproduction of precisely the status of victim and object. If, for example, we assume that Julie has bowed to her father's dictates, then we can only read as a cover-up her letter to Saint-Preux in which she acknowledges her accountability and details her rejection of passionate love.[3] In this case Julie does not have, or does not seem to have, any self-awareness. But what if this letter also contains an element of insight? What if Julie is thus acting as a (literary) subject? In other words, what if we take the female literary figure seriously, even when she says things that are unacceptable to feminism? My reading will focus on the two major constellations in which Julie seeks her happiness: the passionate love (*amour-passion*) for Saint-Preux in the first part of the novel; and a sensible, virtuous marriage and family life in the second part. Julie is not by chance the heroine; for it is in this figure, and only in this one, that Rousseau stages the two competing discourses of love of the eighteenth century. And in this light, her death takes on new significance.

---

1. Peggy Kamuf presented a particularly interesting version of this interpretation in her study *Fictions of Feminine Desire: Disclosures of Héloïse* (1982). There she inquires into the traces of the "excessive desire" of a woman that is obliterated by the phallocentric reduction of the difference between the sexes (p. xiv). Kamuf's reading, which investigates the intertextual relationships between the "new" Héloïse and her historic model, sees in Rousseau's version of the story a dialectic negation of the "old Héloïse." While the latter would have insisted on her "unconverted" sexual desire, Julie's inner turn (her "conversion" at the end of the third part of the *Nouvelle Héloïse*) ultimately means the "voluntary" renunciation of her own desire. Julie, like the historic Héloïse, is caught between two different orders: the old, represented by her father; and the new, represented by her husband. Her desire for the tutor Saint-Preux fits into neither of these orders and must therefore be sacrificed. According to Kamuf (97–122), Julie truly does undergo "conversion" in the end—in contrast to the historic Héloïse—and therefore creates the conditions for the *new* order of Clarens.

2. This is the view of Montet-Clavié (1984), 64ff. I will return to her interpretation of the *Nouvelle Héloïse* below, in my discussion of Julie's death.

3. Part 3, letter 18, of the *Nouvelle Héloïse* (II, 233–81/340–65).

The Paradox of *Amour-Passion*

Love is, as we know, one of the greatest metaphors for becoming one. Love develops its harmonizing power in complete union, in the symbiosis of two souls—the elimination of the difference between the I and the you, the self and the other. Saint-Preux allows himself to be blinded by that power: "I am sometimes inclined to flatter myself that as there is a parity in our years, and a similitude in our taste, there is also a secret sympathy in our affections. We are both so young that our nature can hitherto have received no false bias from any thing adventitious, and all our inclinations seem to coincide. Before we have imbibed the uniform prejudices of the world, our general perceptions seem uniform; and why may I not suppose the same concord in our hearts, which in our judgment is so strikingly apparent?" (I, 46/32).

The concept of passionate love expressed here did not always exist. Only in the eighteenth century does that which we call love take on a separate existence from the traditional, external criteria of being worthy of love. You no longer love someone primarily for her beauty, virtue, or merits. You love someone because you understand her or, to be more exact, because you get along with her. In a conversation with a loved one, the issue is not primarily to understand things and processes—it is to recognize that the other understands those things just as you do. And if this hope is fulfilled, you feel this as the happiness of love. Understanding becomes self-reflexive.[4]

But understanding another, or being understood by him, is more than the cumulative result of a continuing series of actions or statements. That would still touch only the outside of a figure that has also been much discussed since the eighteenth century—the individual. What is essential is to understand the individual—his way of thinking and feeling, an entire complex system of unique behaviors, opinions, and feelings—in short, the individual's innermost being or "heart." Passionate love appears to be the answer to what is basically the hopeless situation of this new figure. The more complex and unique the individual, the more demanding, and therefore the more improbable, the concept of understanding. Who can understand this complicated, complex individual? And how can anyone understand an individual's innermost being if it can never reveal itself in its totality?

Since the innermost being of an individual manifests itself only in externals, the feeling of love, the feeling of being "one heart and one soul," must

---

4. See the discussion in Luhmann 1982.

infer a hidden agreement from the existence of a visible agreement. It must infer the internal from the external. If Saint-Preux and Julie think the same way, feel and judge the same way, then this agreement must also apply to their hearts, their souls, the inner core of their personalities. If, on the basis of the discourse of sensibility, we are inclined to understand the heart as the hidden whole of a personality, then the inference of the inner from the outer reveals that its fundamental rhetorical figure is one of synecdoche. The new discourse of love that was forming in the eighteenth century takes a visible part (*pars*) for the imaginary whole (*pro toto*) and strives unceasingly to assure itself of agreement. This is precisely the reason for the totalist presumptuousness of love and for its continuing error. The figure of synecdoche structures the yearning of lovers and produces their forever inconclusive dialogue—vain labor in search of perfect concord.

In keeping with this totalist claim, intimate love also brings passionate discourse under its sway in the eighteenth century. This discourse, which in centuries before had concentrated on admiring, honoring, and adoring—that is, on the articulation of distance—is now committed to "nearness." To be precise, it is committed to the communication of individuality. Intimacy and passion appear to have become one under love's roof. But what we take for granted today turns out to be problematic on closer examination. For not only does passion—which thrives on change and the charm of the unfulfilled—have a difficult time surviving continuous, fulfilled intimacy, but there is a fundamental collision between passion and intimacy when lovers try to reach an understanding about their passion in intimate discussion. The lover is then both the object of desire and the source of understanding, both the subject of, and a partner to, the discussion. The lover is supposed to be understanding without losing attractiveness. But trying to combine passion and intimacy is like trying to undertake a paradoxical journey on which the most dependable companion possible is, at the same time, the journey's exotic goal.

Discourses of love have concerned themselves with this paradox since the eighteenth century, with well-known consequences. Lovers in world literature no longer fail because of external hindrances (the animosity of fathers or the arbitrariness of narrow-minded aristocrats). They fail, above all, because of themselves, because of the totalist claim of synecdoche. In vain, lovers swear by the highest authorities to reassure themselves about their feelings. Saint-Preux implores his lover: "No, be assured, my Eloisa, that the irresistible decree of heaven has designed us for each other. This is the first great law we are to obey, and it is the greatest business of life to calm, sooth, and sweeten it while we are here" (I, 145/92).

Saint-Preux needs a higher authority—heaven, providence, God, the laws of nature—as guarantor of the certainty he avers. One of these absolute authorities must shore up the audaciousness of the synecdoche. We will see that Julie, in her accounting to Saint-Preux, also calls on one of these authorities—the laws of nature—but with a different intent. She expresses doubt about a recourse to metaphysics.

Analysis of the first sequence of love letters in the *Nouvelle Héloïse* (part I, letters 1–15) provides confirmation of the thesis that external barriers (in particular, differences in social standing) have played an increasingly peripheral role since the eighteenth century.[5] Antagonism expresses itself here primarily in terms associated with love and guilt. Saint-Preux does not feel guilty because of their *social difference* but because of Julie's *decency:* "I hope I shall never so far forget myself, as to . . . fail in that respect which is due to your *virtue,* even more than to your *birth* or personal charms" (I, 43/31).[6] Julie articulates her "guilt" in analogous terms:

> [T]here was not in my soul one vicious inclination. My virtue and innocence were inexpressibly dear to me; and I pleased myself with the hopes of cherishing them in a life of industrious simplicity. . . . The very first day we met, I imbibed the poison which now infects my senses and my reason. . . . Every thing [feeds the passion that consumes me]—every circumstance combines to abandon me to myself, or rather cruelly to deliver me up to thee. . . . No; that first false step plunged me into the abyss, and now my degree of misery is entirely in thy power. (I, 57–58/39–40)

When these individuals, burning with love, try to understand their feelings in terms of virtue and guilt, it is only superficially a question of the conflict between chastity and sexuality. To reduce moral discourse to its apparent material core—the repression of sexual desire—is a misunderstanding (and not only in feminist criticism); for the eighteenth century, it seems to me, sexualized virtually the entire realm of intimate discourse. Sexuality became the metaphor for successful or unsuccessful intimate commu-

---

5. See also Gallas 1990, 68: "Anders als oft beschrieben ist die Trennung der Liebenden bei Rousseau nicht durch äußere Hindernisse erzwungen."
6. Author's emphasis in all Rousseau citations.

nication and thus a meta-metaphor for the internal condition of the individual. The degree of intimacy appears to be measurable only in sexual terms. Therefore, it is not surprising that particularly in the form of taboos and in whispers, talk is always only of "it."[7]

Instead of suspecting that the virtuous discourse of love between Julie and Saint-Preux is charged with sexual animosity, it is important to analyze it for its semantic content, for its projections. What does the sensitive soul mean when it speaks of "poison," "consuming passion," "abyss," and being "delivered up"? It is a mistake to examine the terms of virtue and guilt only for their moral implications. Structurally, virtue is comparable to the idea of the denotation since it refers to the same rhetorical figure (just as the idea of the denotate assumes a signification identical to it). The virtuous individual is in possession of herself, something that cannot be asserted for vice. Only in this sense can we understand Julie's description of the end of her passionate love as liberation: "This tie, which I dreaded so much, [marriage to an unloved husband] has *extricated* me from a slavery much more dreadful; and my husband becomes dearer to me for having restored me to myself" (II, 279/364–65).

Virtue is being-with-oneself, the inner concord of duty and inclination. Vice, on the other hand, is the unrestrained desire of the subject, which is consumed by poison and flame, and which dissolves, surrenders, and fuses. The unfolding of the paradoxes of passion and intimacy are experienced by the subject only in a state of vice. Against this background, every temporary state of balance between lovers is a fleeting moment on the way to the next loss of balance. In Julie's words:

> And yet a strange foreboding whispers to my heart, that these are the only days of happiness allotted us by heaven. Our future prospect presents nothing to my view, but absence, anxiety, dangers and difficulties. The least change in our present situation must necessarily be for the worse. . . .
> I conjure thee, my kind, my only friend, to endeavour to calm the turbulence of those vain desires which are always followed by regret, repentance and sorrow. Let us peaceably enjoy our present felicity. (I, 78/51–52)

But this is an impossible undertaking, for her friend experiences not enjoyment but suffering. Julie comments on her decisive error—the loss of her

---

7. Here, I have adopted the analysis of Foucault 1976.

innocence—as follows: "Innocence and love were equally requisite to my peace: as I could not preserve them both, and was witness to your distraction, I consulted your interest alone in the choice I made; and to save you, ruined myself" (II, 240–41/344).

In her admission to Saint-Preux, Julie presents herself as a self-sacrificing woman. Because the inner struggle between virtue and passion threatened to destroy him, she gave in to him. She confuses, as it were, the position of the self and the other. Because the other is more important to her than herself, she places him above her. In order to save him, she gives herself up as lost. But the matter is more complicated, for Julie earlier made a different confession to her cousin Clara:

> Love alone might perhaps have been my security; but compassion . . . has fatally undone me.
>
> Thus, *my unhappy passion* assumed the form of humanity, the more easily to deprive me of the assistance of virtue. . . . Without knowing what I did, I resolved on [my ruin], and forgetting every thing else, thought only of my love. Thus one unguarded minute has betrayed me to endless misery. (I, 152–53/96)

Here Julie's virtuous compassion is far more ambiguous. Is it conceivable that even her compassion is merely an offshoot of her unhappy passion? Is it conceivable that vice is masquerading as virtue? The line between them no longer seems at all clear. Analytic logic collapses under the weight of passion. It gives way to a totalism that recognizes contradiction only in the form of paradox—as the unity of opposites, not as their logical incompatibility. The individual, supposedly at one with herself, subjects herself to a whole that reproduces the contradictions within her. It is a whole full of internal ambivalence. Though the discourse of synecdoche attempts to absorb the individual into a whole, it obviously radicalizes the differences and tends decidedly toward a rhetorical figure of contradiction par excellence— the oxymoron. The beloved being is at once feared, detested—and desired. He or she becomes the object of the greatest pleasure and the most profound suffering. Saint-Preux begins his first declaration of love to Julie with the hint of a curse: "I must fly from you, Eloisa; I feel I must. I ought not to have stayed with you so long; or rather, I ought never to have beheld you."[8] His admission of love therefore logically takes the form of a request that

---

8. *NH*, I, 43/31.

she reject him: "There seems but one method to extricate me from this embarrassment: the hand which involved me in it must also relieve me. As you are the cause of my offence, you must inflict my punishment: out of compassion, at least deign to banish me from your presence" (I, 44–45/32).

The paradoxes of passion have been thought for a long time to include the contradiction between desire and fulfillment. For structural reasons, *amour-passion* can articulate itself only at a distance from the beloved being. Though it urges rapturous union, it becomes tangled in ambivalence and complications. It tends toward catastrophe. And it would appear that this passion is "one with itself" only in the "happy catastrophe." It is at home only at a distance. Rousseau himself gave theoretical articulation to this structure both through the tutor in *Emile*[9] and through Julie:

> We enjoy less that which we obtain, than that which we hope for, and are *seldom happy but in expectation*. In fact, man, . . . of boundless avarice, yet narrow capacity, has received of Heaven a consolatory aid, which brings to him in idea every thing he desires, displays to his imagination, represents it to his view, and in one sense makes it his own. . . . But this shadow vanishes the moment the real object appears; the imagination can no longer magnify that which we actually possess; the charms of illusion cease where those of enjoyment begin. *The world of fancy, therefore, the land of chimeras, is the only world worthy to be inhabited*. (IV, 192–93/693)

If lovers are only happy *before* they are happy, the paradox of passion unfolds here in its temporal dimension. Lovers see themselves involved in catastrophes that, upon sober examination, are found not to exist. They feel themselves to be shaken by ambivalent feelings that a cooler head would be able to distinguish. And they attribute to one another a perfection that no one but themselves can see. In short, those who love live in a different world. But if Rousseau stresses the moment of illusion, he also insists that without such illusion love is not possible: those who remain within the sober discourse of the denotation are inaccessible to the strong feelings of passionate love. Those who love appear to live, above all, in metaphors. Rousseau writes in the "Dialogue" conceived as a second preface to the *Nouvelle Héloïse:* "Love is nothing more than an illusion . . . it is surrounded with

---

9. "Before tasting the pleasures of life you have plumbed the depths of its happiness. . . . You have tasted greater joys through hope than you will ever enjoy in reality. The imagination which adorns what we long for, deserts its possession" (*Emile*, 411/821).

objects which have no existence but in imagination, and its language is always figurative" (I, xviii/15).

Yet lovers ignore the figurative nature of their own self-reflection, and they are lovers only insofar as they take the metaphors literally. They experience the truth of the metaphors and are disappointed. Love had a long life in metaphoric speech; however, in the eighteenth century it begins to take its metaphors literally. It thus rebels against the difference that first constituted its existence and that again makes its appearance as self-deception and mutual misjudgment where it is ignored. In an age of gallantry, the figurativeness of the passions was probably still consciously recognized. Under the dictates of intimate and individual discourse, however, figurative existence becomes subject to the demands of ultimate truth and authentic communication. Its potential for paradox therefore increases. It must be asked, however, whether a woman—who makes the laws in the "realm of love"—is as taken in by the paradoxes of *amour-passion* as a man who, in Rousseau's discourse, does not understand differences.[10]

Julie's Difference in the Discourse of Love

Julie only *appears* to be caught up in the paradoxes of passionate discourse in the same way as Saint-Preux. Not only is she the one who formulates a late rejection of *amour-passion,* but she also practices a certain dishonesty from the beginning and thus introduces a degree of ambivalence into the emotional discourse of love. Contrary to her own declarations,[11] she is in no way open with her lover. Instead, she is constantly keeping something from him; she is constantly leaving him in the dark about her own wishes, feelings, and motives. Though she later admits this to Saint-Preux, she still keeps some of her secrets. She admits to him the reasons why she sent him away after their first kiss and why she then gave herself to him after all, although she was promised to another man (which she had also kept from him). She reveals to her former lover her pregnancy and later miscarriage. But there is something about which she will continue to leave Saint-Preux in the dark: her desire and her pleasure.

---

10. See Garbe 1992, chap. 3 ("Die Genese der männlichen 'Freiheit' ") and chap. 5 ("Die Schleier der Schamhaftigkeit—Rousseaus Theorie der Weiblichkeit").

11. See *NH,* I, 57/40.

The difference between the language of Saint-Preux and that of Julie is perhaps most readily recognizable in the exchange following their night together in Julie's chamber. Saint-Preux, who had made no secret of his burning desire even before this meeting,[12] gives himself up completely to the transport of his feelings in the letters that follow: "Oh! let us die, my sweet friend! let us die, thou best beloved of my heart! How shall we hereafter support an insipid life, whose pleasures we have already exhausted? Tell me, if thou canst, what I experienced last night!" (I, 245/147–48).

Saint-Preux writes of his physical pleasure—his joy, his delight, his bliss. For him there can be no doubt. He has exhausted the "entire delight" of love and is now trying to recall to mind, as he writes, what constitutes his utter bliss. For Saint-Preux, the real pleasure begins only after the pleasure; it is not the satisfaction of sensuous desire that is the bliss of this experience but the "close union of souls" in the hour after pleasure:

> I was tranquil, and yet was near my Eloisa. I adored her, but my desires were calm. I did not even think of any other felicity than to perceive your face close to mine, to feel your breath on my cheek, and your arm about my neck. What a pleasing tranquillity prevailed over all my senses! How refined, how lasting, how constant the delight! The mind possessed all the pleasure of enjoyment, not momentary, but durable. What a difference is there between the impetuous follies of appetite, and a situation so calm and delightful! It is the first time I have experienced it in your presence. . . . That hour I shall ever think the happiest of my life, as it is the only one which I could wish should have been prolonged to eternity. (I, 247/148–49)

What more could Saint-Preux expect from love and sensual pleasure? He has savored all the stages of pleasure. Sensual love has been replaced by the merging of souls. Saint-Preux appears to have found his way to the unity and totality he has always said was the goal of his and Julie's love. His only desire now is to extend this state indefinitely. But this means dissolving the difference between the momentary and the lasting, between the I and the you: "Take from me all that remains of mine, and give me a soul entirely yours."[13]

---

12. See *NH*, I, 243–45/146–47, as well as the interpretation of this letter in Starobinski 1984, 86–87.
13. *NH*, I, 249/150.

The following letter initiates their separation. For Julie, the night of love so emphatically praised by Saint-Preux has a different meaning. Quite apart from the fact that she does not say a word about this (second) night, her confession of the first night to Clara was far more ambiguous than is the description by Saint-Preux. Julie apparently needs an apology for her sensuous desire, an excuse that she admittedly first hides from her lover.[14] While Julie presents herself to Saint-Preux as filled with desire ("this evening, I will perform my promises, and discharge at once all the obligations of love"),[15] this is not the way she sees herself. In retrospect she indicates that she arranged the dangerous tryst because she wanted a child. On the other hand, she alludes, at least, to the possibility that the motives she has advanced for her willingness to make love are a pretext and could therefore be (self-)deceptive: the virtue of sympathy may merely have masked her "fateful passion,"[16] and the audacity of the nighttime rendezvous veiled her "fond love" in a "gentle palliation."[17] Not only are the woman's actions unclear, but her desire remains hidden by an indecipherable ambiguity.

The nature of passionate love would appear to consist of precisely this tangled web of deceptions and self-deceptions; Julie expresses this insight in her famous letter of accounting to Saint-Preux following her marriage to Wolmar. Just two months previously she had still believed, she writes, that only human caprice could prevent her happiness with Saint-Preux: "*Blind love* (said I) was in the right; we were made for each other, if human events do not interrupt the affinity of nature" (II, 234/340).

But as she once again calls to mind the story of their love, Julie recognizes that there was an immanent necessity to its failure. She writes that the sense of unity is to be felt only within one's self, not in the other; and she says that there will therefore never be absolute certainty about whether the unity of two souls is actually perfect or whether the other actually feels exactly the same way as one does oneself. Julie's accounting articulates this insight almost exclusively in terms of appearance and illusion: "It is now near six years since I first saw you. . . . My heart surrendered itself to you on the first interview. I *imagined* that I saw in your countenance the traces of a soul which seemed the counterpart of mine. I *thought* that my senses only served as organs to more refined sentiments; and I loved in you not so much what I saw, as what I *imagined* I felt within myself" (II, 234/340).

14. See *NH*, I, 240–43/144–46.
15. *NH*, I, 240/145.
16. *NH*, I, 153/96.
17. *NH*, II, 243/345.

Though the lovers gave themselves up to this illusion because external obstacles appeared to be responsible for their unhappiness (their difference in status, the prohibition of her father), Julie recognizes in retrospect that the fallacy lay within their passion. Passion, she writes, pretends to something that is never attainable. Their love therefore seems to her to have been a chain of delusions and disappointments:

> What led me into a mistake, and what perhaps still misleads you, is the opinion, that love is necessary to make the married state happy. My good friend, this is a vulgar error; honour, virtue, a certain conformity, not so much of age and condition as of temper and inclination, are the requisites in the conjugal state; nevertheless, it must not be inferred from hence, that this union does not produce an affectionate attachment, which, though it does not amount to love, is not less agreeable, and is much more permanent. Love is attended with a continual inquietude of jealousy, or the dread of separation, by no means suitable with a married life, which should be a state of peace and tranquillity. The intent of matrimony is not for man and wife to be always taken up with each other, but jointly to discharge the duties of civil society, to govern their family with prudence, and educate their children with discretion. Lovers attend to nothing but each other; they are incessantly engaged with each other; and all that they regard, is how to show their mutual affection. But this is not enough for a married pair, who have so many other objects to engage their attention. *There is no passion whatever which exposes us to such delusion as that of love.*—We take its violence for a symptom of its duration. . . . But on the contrary, it is consumed by its own ardour. (II, 293–94/372)

Though Julie makes use here of the vocabulary of placid enlightenment, it would be too simple to deny her letter any insight, to charge it with capitulation to patriarchal values. For her words do, in fact, allude to the paradoxes of love, to the dramatic link between passion and intimacy outlined above. Julie distances herself from, and takes leave of, the deceptive promises of synecdoche; and she appears to do so in that she falls back on the well-known discourse of the Enlightenment. I will examine this assumption in more detail below. For now it should be noted that to Julie the fulfillment of love can consist only in the renunciation of fulfillment—even if this is, as we will see, no lasting solution:

(Julie) Yes, my dear and worthy friend, to keep our love inviolable, we must renounce each other. (II, 278/364)

(Saint-Preux) . . . you never were my Eloisa more perfectly than at this moment in which you renounce me. Alas! I regain my Eloisa, by losing her for ever. (II, 281/366)

The Order of the Sexes in Clarens

In that which follows, we will examine the nature of Julie's new, second happiness as wife of Wolmar, as mother, and as good soul in the community of Clarens. For the suspicion lies close at hand that Julie's only aim is to make herself comfortable now in a genteel, bourgeois existence. At first this suspicion seems to be borne out when Julie writes: "As to M. Wolmar, no delusion is the foundation of our mutual liking: *we see each other in a true light;* the sentiment which unites us is not the blind transport of passionate desire, but a constant and invariable attachment between two rational people, who being destined to pass the remainder of their lives together, are content with their lot, and endeavour to make themselves mutually agreeable" (II, 295/373).

Here, Rousseau seems to present his readers with the Enlightenment option: the sensible marriage is based not on passion but on the harmonious complementarity of different abilities and traits of character, as well as on a friendly, unimpassioned tone. It may be irritating in this context that Julie describes her marriage to Wolmar, in part at least, in the same metaphorical terms she used to describe her relationship with Saint-Preux—as the unity or union of two souls: "It seems as if we could not have suited each other better, had we been formed on purpose for our *union*. . . . We are each of us exactly made for the other; he instructs me, I enliven him; the value of both is increased by our union, and we seem destined to form but *one soul* between us; to which he gives intelligence, and I direct the will" (II, 295–96/ 373–74).

The difference between the unity of the lovers and the unity of the married partners would seem at first to consist in the fact that the former is based on misjudgment and blindness, while the latter came about without self-deception. But we should remember that passion under the sign of synecdoche meant the union of souls as *identity,* as congruence. The unity of a married couple, on the other hand, is based on the *complementarity* of souls ("We are each of us exactly made for the other"). The totalist claims of passionate love are therefore also rejected from a structural point of view.

Let us examine, then, whether the model of sensible marriage is more workable than that of passionate love. Does Rousseau's presentation of marriage suggest a preference, a plea for this second model? Did Rousseau, the sentimental enthusiast, change camps, recognize his error, and return penitently to the lap of reason? Let us see where the second half of the *Nouvelle Héloïse* leads us.

At first glance, it would seem that the new life Julie lives at Clarens following her marriage is the literary realization of an ideal type called by feminist discourse the "complementarity theory of the sexes."[18] In contrast to Emile and Sophie, who move to a big city where their relationship is dashed against the cliffs of urban customs and treacherous seductions,[19] Julie and Wolmar remain in the country, where they create a functioning estate at Clarens. The harmonious complementarity of the sexes unfolds here as a gender-specific division of labor. M. de Wolmar takes on the role of the sensible master of the house and father of the family; he oversees farming on the estate and supervises the servants. Julie characterizes him as sensible and unemotional.[20] Moreover, he has always led a "well-ordered and proper life," which is why he is healthy and youthful, despite his advanced age (he is nearly fifty years old). He brings only the advantages of age—experience and wisdom—to their marriage. Even the "passion" he feels for Julie is "so even and temperate, that one would conclude he had power to limit the degree of his passion, and that he had determined not to love beyond the bounds of discretion."[21]

Thus, while Wolmar supervises the running of the estate, Julie is in charge of the distribution and consumption of the goods the estate produces.[22] This means not only supplying the community with what is useful and necessary but also seeing to its comforts and organizing its pleasures. Julie tends to the art of enjoyment[23] by carefully meting out those pleasures and comforts.[24] Clara describes Julie's principle of action as follows: "Abstinence

18. See Bovenschen 1979, 24ff.
19. See *Emile et Sophie, ou, Les solitaires,* the fragmentary continuation of *Emile,* 881ff.
20. See NH, II, 288/369.
21. NH, II, 289–90/370.
22. See Saint-Preux's report, NH, III, 235–36/530.
23. NH, III, 256/541.
24. The best example of this is the Apollo Room in Clarens, which is used as a dining room only rarely. The reason Julie gives is that the "trouble of being always at ease is the greatest [trouble] in the world" (*NH,* III, 261/544).

from what we delight in is a tenet of your philosophy; it is, indeed, the Epicureanism of reason."²⁵ Above all, however, Julie is the emotional center of Clarens, the social link in the community. Her emotional ties extend far beyond the narrow circle of husband and children; every inhabitant of Clarens becomes, in principle, her *"child."* Rousseau's protagonist appears now in the form of a *"great mother"*: "Labourers, domestics, all who serve her, if it be but for a day, become her children; she takes part in their pleasures, their cares, and their fortune; she inquires into their affairs; and makes their interest her own; she engages in a thousand concerns for them, she gives them her advice, she composes their differences, and does not show the affability of her disposition in smooth and fruitless speeches, but in real services, and continual acts of benevolence" (III, 83/444).²⁶

It is the wife, therefore, who creates the emotional ties within the extended family, not only between father and children, but also between all the other members of the community. Rousseau leaves no doubt that Wolmar is the head and Julie the heart of the community. He also shows that Julie's warmth and influence are ever so much greater than those of Wolmar, who prepares, as it were, the ground upon which her influence radiates. It seems that Julie's "conversion" (Peggy Kamuf) has returned her to a state of innocence, so that she incorporates more or less freely and without reflection all the good that her husband can only acquire through reason and experience.²⁷ This is the interpretation of Lieselotte Steinbrügge: "The wife is the center of virtue. She lives out, in her person, the philosophy of Clarens. She can do this because the process of moral insight is, in her, neither an act of reason [as is the case with Wolmar] nor a struggle between two conflicting souls [as is the case with Saint-Preux]. It takes place, rather, as an act of spontaneous empathy with the moral climate of Clarens. Her virtue is not the result of exertion but is the realization, the unfolding of her nature. . . . Clarens is, as it were, the materialization of her inner nature."²⁸

But if this were the case, the question we posed earlier would have to be

---

25. *NH*, IV, 137/662. The economy of Clarens and Julie's special function there is described in detail in the second letter of part 5, Saint-Preux to Mylord B.; here there are also further comments on Julie's "sensible Epicureanism." See *NH*, III, 236/531 and 256/541.

26. I cannot discuss the economic function of this "motherly love" in greater detail here, but see the detailed study by Steinbrügge 1987, chap. 5, secs. 4 and 5.

27. This corresponds to the construction of Immanuel Kant (1968) in "Observations on the Feeling of the Beautiful and Sublime" ("Beobachtungen über das Gefühl des Schönen und Erhabenen," 850ff.). In Kant's opinion, the virtue of women is "beautiful"; that of men is "sublime" because it is attained only through inner struggle.

28. Steinbrügge 1987, 94 [trans. MR-B].

answered with yes: Rousseau would then indeed have conceived the sensible marriage as the ideal worth striving for, passionate love as an unworkable model. He would clearly have taken sides with one of the alternatives and would have put calm friendship in place of raging passion as the model of interpersonal relations. But the solution Rousseau offers us is not that simple. And here too we must decipher the "feminine text." Indeed, the entire second half of the novel is permeated by a profound ambiguity, beginning with the last letter before a long period of silence in the epistolary dialogue between Julie and Saint-Preux. Even here Julie's answer to his concerned question about whether she is at least happy in her new life[29] is anything but simple and clear. Julie writes: "I am happy in all respects, and nothing is wanting to complete my felicity but yours."[30] This statement contains an inner contradiction: You cannot be happy in "all respects" if something is "wanting." And her confession that she cannot be happy if Saint-Preux stops loving her seems almost to confront him with a classic double-bind situation—for did she not, on the other hand, insist that he give her up? Julie makes her own happiness doubly dependent on that of Saint-Preux and relativizes it in a way that will find closer explanation only in the farewell letters written as she is dying.

But even before this, the text gives indication enough that perfect unity and harmony are a deception, a mere illusion that hides a secret deficiency.[31] The metaphor frequently used for this ambiguity in the second half of the novel is the veil, which in effect denies entry to Julie's most innermost being. Her husband formulates it most suggestively when he writes of Julie: "A *veil of wisdom and honour* make so many folds about her heart, that it is impenetrable to human eyes, even to her own" (III, 199/509).[32]

Peggy Kamuf, in her reading of the *Nouvelle Héloïse*, stresses that Julie's inner turn ("conversion") during the marriage ceremony is the condition for the "new order at Clarens"; that is, in this "almost mystic scene," Julie

29. See *NH*, II, 283/367.
30. *NH*, [MR-B]/369.
31. Even at the beginning of part 4 of the *Nouvelle Héloïse*, which is set off from the first half of the book by a distance of six years, Julie's sense of deficiency is clearly described: it is an unanswered yearning for an all-encompassing love. Julie complains in her letter to Clara about the loss of her mother and of her lover; and she hints that neither love for her children nor for her husband is enough to fill this gap. (See *NH*, III, 3–4/399.)
32. It would be worth doing a separate study of the motif of the veil in all its facets in the *Nouvelle Héloïse*. We need think only of Saint-Preux's dream of a veiled Julie on her deathbed—a dream that anticipates her actual death—or of the veil brought back from India by Saint-Preux and used by Clara to cover the face of the dead Julie. See Pelckmans 1981/82.

has eradicated every possible difference between her outward behavior and her inner desires.³³ From now on her husband, as Rousseau demands, can function as the "inspector" with regard to her virtue.³⁴ But may we conclude from this that all possibilities for deception (and self-deception) have been eliminated once and for all? Julie's particular place in Clarens, her "Elysium," will give us greater clarity on this point.

The "Female Place" in Clarens: Elysium

Elysium, the garden in Clarens that Julie creates on her own, is the "female place" in the community, the metaphor for the wife in the sensible and virtuous marriage and family. Interpretations of the *Nouvelle Héloïse* generally see in Elysium the symbolic center of the novel, the most intense representation of Julie's virtue and integrity. They take as their own, as we shall see, the male perspective of Saint-Preux and Wolmar. At first glance, Elysium would seem to confirm Rousseau's preference for the Enlightenment option. According to Peggy Kamuf, Elysium presents itself as the most obvious sign of Julie's successful "conversion": "What Saint-Preux is given to see [in Elysium] is the concrete result of Julie's conversion, a place in which a hidden, interior space of potential deception was laid bare and thus renewed. The garden is a spatial representation of the moment when Julie became Mme. de Wolmar, which is to say, the new Julie—and the new Heloise" (Kamuf 1982, 116).

Wolmar himself points toward this interpretation when he explains to Saint-Preux that Julie laid out Elysium as a substitute for the woods in Clarens, the place where the passionate love between Julie and her tutor found its first "immoral" expression in their first kiss:³⁵ "My wife has never set her foot in those groves since she has been married. I know the reason, though she has always kept it a secret from me. You, who are no stranger to it, learn to respect the spot where you are; *it has been planted by the hands of virtue*" (III, 157/485).

Saint-Preux also appears to undergo his "conversion" from lover to friend in this place. For the first time he succeeds in seeing in Wolmar not

---

33. See Kamuf 1982, 106.
34. Kamuf 1982, 105.
35. See *NH*, part 1, letters 13 and 14.

the victorious rival, but the fatherly friend.[36] Saint-Preux enters Elysium in order to call to mind the charms of his former lover, but he sees everywhere only the signs of her virtue. He apparently accepts Wolmar's interpretation of the garden:

> As I entered Elysium . . . I suddenly recollected the last word which M. Wolmar said to me yesterday very near the same spot. The recollection of that single word instantly changed my whole frame of mind. I thought that I beheld the *image of virtue,* where I expected to find *that of pleasure.* That image intruded on my imagination with the charms of Mrs. Wolmar, and for the first time since my return, I saw Eloisa in her absence; not such as she appeared to me formerly, and as I still love to represent her, but such as she appears to my eyes every day. (III, 159/486)

Elysium contains the first signs of the success of a therapy chosen by the wise M. de Wolmar. He is the one who speaks of a "cure"[37] for Saint-Preux—who is still threatened by his own passion. Saint-Preux must replace the image of his former lover (Julie d'Etange) with that of the wife and mother (Mme. de Wolmar). The danger to his passion comes from memory and the power of recall that Wolmar intends to turn "in another direction"—successfully, as it would seem.[38] Like Wolmar, Saint-Preux now also reads Elysium as a symbol of the *innermost* being of the woman who set it as a sign: "The word Elysium seemed to me an *emblem* of the purity of her *mind* who adopted it. . . . 'Peace (said I), reigns in the inmost recesses of her soul, as in this asylum which she has named' " (III, 160–61/487).

Saint-Preux insists on the simple correspondence of exterior (garden) and interior (heart, soul). His own relationship to the landscape as the mirror of the soul is transferred by means of this assumption to Julie. It is true for

---

36. See the scene in Elysium in which Julie and Wolmar invite Saint-Preux to participate in "paternal affection" (*NH*, III, 143/477). Montet-Clavié (1984, 70–71) interprets this scene as a foreshadowing of Julie's death, which serves to unite the two men in their function as representatives of a "paternal order" that must obliterate the feminine (i.e., the motherly) function. In my opinion, Montet-Clavié arrives at this conclusion through an over-interpretation of the term "paternal love." After all, Saint-Preux embraces both Wolmar *and* Julie when he assures them that their children are as dear to him as they are.

37. *NH*, III, 202/510.

38. He writes to Clara: "I compel him always to look at the wife of his friend, and the mother of my children; I efface one picture by another, and hide the past with the present" (*NH*, III, 230/511).

A New Reading of Rousseau's *Nouvelle Héloïse* | 63

Saint-Preux that his perception of the landscape is a projection of the state of his soul onto external nature, as the town of Meillerie readily reveals.[39] In his perception of Elysium, therefore, we reencounter the basic pattern of synecdoche that I have analyzed with respect to Saint-Preux's and Julie's declarations of love. The pattern makes its appearance, ironically, just as Saint-Preux declares with utter conviction that he has now overcome his former ill-fated passion. This should be a warning to us.

It would seem that Wolmar and Saint-Preux are the first defenders of the theory that has accompanied Rousseau research from the beginning and that has also been taken over by feminist interpretations. According to this theory, Elysium is the perfect symbolic representation of Julie's virtuousness and, in its capacity as the feminine, of her superior morality.[40] What distin-

39. In part 1 of the novel, Saint-Preux had waited in desperation in Meillerie (on the opposite shore of Lake Geneva, from which he could see Julie's residence) for Julie's permission to return (see *NH*, I, 138ff./88ff.). He writes of Meillerie: "Perhaps too, this is heightened by the nature of the place I live in; it is dark, it is dreadful; *but then it suits the habit of my soul.* ... While my mind is distracted with such continual agitations, my body too is moving as it were in sympathy with those emotions. I ... find every thing as horrible without as I experience it within" (*NH*, I, 140–41/90). In part 4, a thunderstorm on Lake Geneva during a boat outing forces the two former lovers to take shelter in a place where Saint-Preux recalls for Julie all of the torments he had once experienced there. Even now this place becomes the location of a last great temptation (see *NH*, III, 215ff./517ff.). With regard to this passage, de Man (1983, 200–201) has called attention to the correspondence between the description of the landscape (lonely, wild, deserted) and the theme of the letter (the temptation to fall back into their old passion). He points out, however, that the symbolic relationship between the landscape and the soul that can be seen here can in no way be argued for the *Nouvelle Héloïse* as a whole; it does not apply to the supposed symbolic heart of the novel, Julie's Elysium.

40. There is agreement in this respect between the analyses of Steinbrügge and Kamuf. For Steinbrügge, the "wilderness of nature" has been reconstructed in Elysium—thanks to Julie: "Only here is the complete harmony of the human and of nature to be found. The peaceful atmosphere of the estate finds its most perfect expression in the part that Julie has 'cultivated.' What has taken Wolmar years to accomplish through discipline and planning she achieves easily, without effort, in accordance with nature and unconsciously. ... Julie's activities are like a natural force—similar to the vegetation of Elysium" [Erst hier findet sich die vollkommene Harmonie von Mensch und Natur. Die friedliche Atmosphäre des Gutes findet ihre vollkommenste Ausprägung in dem von Julie "bewirtschafteten" Teil. Sie vollbringt mühelos, ohne Anstrengung, naturwüchsig und unbewußt, was Wolmar nur kraft jahrelanger Disziplin und Planung erreicht hat. ... Julies Tätigkeit gleicht—ähnlich wie die Vegetation des Elysée—einer Naturkraft] (Steinbrügge 1987, 95). The historical, philosophical connection of Elysium to what was referred to by Rousseau as the "golden age," between a state of nature and society, seems to me to be an important and meaningful reference; however, Steinbrügge overlooks the implications of appearance, of artificiality in the layout of Elysium. Steinbrügge reads it literally, as it were, as nature (and therefore also as the nature of woman), although its artificial character is emphasized. On this point, see also de Man (1983, 202), who objects to Mornet's historic, naturalistic commentary as follows: "But this 'natural' look of the garden is by no means the main theme of the passage. From the beginning we are told that the natural aspect

guishes feminist from traditional interpretations is the differing assessment of one single aspect: for feminists, the virtue of the wife equals the subjection of female desire to an ideological figure of the patriarchy. However, the problem may be that some feminists are taken in all too easily by the readings of their male colleagues.

The "natural," modest woman is already the product of a double cover-up in Rousseau's theoretical construct,[41] and the literary representation of woman in her Elysium is quite in keeping with that. The naturalness of the garden is nothing but mere appearance. The novel in no way makes a secret of this. On the contrary—Julie hurries to enlighten her guest, who feels that he is in the middle of a wilderness or even on a deserted South Sea island. But Saint-Preux is mistaken in another respect in this wonder of a garden. Because he still holds fast to the myth of the identity of woman and nature, he cannot believe that Elysium is the embodiment of human planning and labor. He therefore explains to Julie:

> In truth . . . it has cost you nothing but inattention. It is indeed a delightful spot, but wild and rustic; and *I can discover no marks of human industry.* You have concealed the door; the water springs I know not whence; Nature alone has done all the rest, and even you could not have mended her work. (III, 133–34/472)

Julie's labor is apparently invisible to Saint-Preux; she corrects him immediately:

It is true . . . that Nature has done every thing, *but under my direction,* and you see nothing but what has been done under my orders. (III, 134/472)

The mode of female activity repeatedly postulated by Rousseau is realized most fully in Julie's Elysium: woman has someone else act for her (*faire quelqu'un faire quelque chose*).[42] Julie allows nature to go into action for

---

of the site is in fact the result of extreme artifice, that in this bower of bliss . . . we are entirely in the realm of art and not that of nature."

41. I have discussed this at length by way of Rousseau's theory of feminine modesty; see Garbe 1992, 82ff., esp. 98–103.

42. See Rousseau's remarks in *Emile:* "Woman . . . perceives and judges the forces at her disposal to supplement [*suppléer*] her weakness, and those forces are the passions of man. Her own mechanism is more powerful than ours; she has many levers which may set the human heart in motion. *She must find a way to make us desire* [faire vouloir] *what she cannot achieve unaided and what she considers necessary or pleasing*" (*Emile,* 350/737). See also my discussion in "Die Frau und das Zeichen" (Woman and the sign), in Garbe 1992, 82ff.

her purposes by installing a clever irrigation system that turns the formerly sparse and dry orchard into a paradise. The underground and therefore invisible system fed by diverting the water of two springs is the work of woman;[43] and it is the perfect expression of the fact that she does everything by appearing to do nothing. Woman is the master of indirectness (the "diversion" of the water) and of disguise (the underground installation of a system of canals). What does it mean that Julie reveals this secret to her now former lover? She calls on him expressly to take leave of his mystifications: "I could not comprehend this riddle; but Eloisa . . . said to me . . . 'Go, and you will understand it. Farewell Tinian! Farewell Juan Fernandez! Farewell all enchantment! In a few minutes you will find your way back from the end of the world' " (III, 134–35/472).

Julie shows and explains all of Elysium to Saint-Preux; she explains the secret of its irrigation system and leads him deep into the interior of the garden where no stranger has ever been. Finally, she even gives him one of the four keys that permit entry to her "paradise." It is as if, with "her place" (Elysium), Julie wanted to give her former lover a sign, a hint, of how things look inside her. Saint-Preux could learn from this demonstration that what presents itself as pure nature is not in the least natural: Julie has laid it all out artificially and at the same time has carefully erased all traces of artificiality:[44]

> (Saint-Preux) Still there is one thing here . . . which I cannot conceive, which is, that though a place so different from what it was can never have been altered to its present state but by great care and culture, *yet I can no where discover the least trace of cultivation.* . . .
>
> (Wolmar) O, . . . it is because they have taken great pains to efface them. . . .
>
> (Julie) Besides, nature seems desirous of hiding her real charms from the sight of men, because they are too little sensible of them, and disfigure them when they are within their reach. . . . They who

---

43. Kamuf (1982, 114ff.) has subjected the secret of Elysium—its irrigation system—to a detailed and enlightening analysis. In particular, she points out that the two springs—diverted by woman—that now flow together in Elysium represent the old (paternal) and the new (Wolmar's) order. On the one hand, there is the fountain that Julie's father had built, under the sign of aristocratic magnificence, that now has no place at Clarens; and on the other, there is the water from the public fountain, which Julie diverts through Elysium and which runs down into Lake Geneva.

44. See Lechte 1982.

are in love with her, and cannot go so far in pursuit of her, are forced *to do her violence,* by *obliging* her, in some measure, to come and dwell with them, and all this cannot be effected without some degree of *illusion.* (III, 146–47/479–80)

The vocabulary of Julie's explanations must come as a surprise. In contrast to Saint-Preux and Wolmar, who deny the evidence of human labor, Julie is very direct. Nature here, supposedly unspoiled and intoxicating—above all for the male observer (Saint-Preux, Wolmar, Julie's father)—is the result of violence, force, and illusion. It is Julie who notes the difference between her garden and true nature by pointing out that true nature "flees closely settled areas": "It is in the tops of mountains, in the midst of forests, in desert islands, that she displays her most affecting charms."[45]

It seems reasonable to relate Julie's comments to her own nature. Seen in this light, even the supposedly natural virtuousness of woman would be the result of a metamorphosis brought about by force and violence, one whose artificial character is obliterated by a second artful intervention, a deception that makes the illusion appear natural. If we accept this reading, Julie would have given her lover—and the reader—the "key" to deciphering her "nature" in the form of Elysium. The *spatial representation* of woman would not be a mere representation of the natural (or rather, of the "converted" woman who has returned to her nature); it would also be its own *deconstruction*. For Elysium makes clear the doubly deceptive effect by which the "nature" created by woman comes into being.[46]

---

45. *NH,* III, 147/479.
46. A point made by de Man (1983, 201–4) also speaks for this interpretation. Using Elysium as an example, de Man discusses the question of whether there is a symbolic or allegorical relationship between the landscape and the "landscape of the soul." In contrast to the example of Saint-Preux/Meillerie (see note 39 above), for which de Man finds a symbolic interpretation fitting, de Man insists that Elysium has an allegorical meaning. In spite of the relationship of the surface text to the actual art of the garden at the time (English versus French gardens, for example), de Man considers attention to the literary sources of Elysium to be indispensable to its interpretation. This includes in particular the parallels between Elysium and the medieval garden of love as found in the *Roman de la rose* (which is alluded to just a few pages earlier by Saint-Preux and which is the earliest source for the love story of Héloïse and Abélard); and the numerous allusions to the island of Robinson Crusoe (which, as we know, was the young Emile's only reading matter). If we take both of these literary models into consideration, Julie's garden already has an unmistakable double meaning at this level: as erotic pleasure garden (*Roman de la rose*), and as Protestant garden of virtue and duty (*Robinson Crusoe*). De Man confirms that the novel employs two different modes—"the allegorical language of a scene such as Julie's Elysium and the symbolic language of passages such as the Meillerie episode" (204). De Man also underscores the priority of allegorical over symbolic

Admittedly, Saint-Preux is as little able as Wolmar to read Julie's "text." A man understands little about deciphering the ambiguities of feminine discourse, so the two gentlemen subsequently engage in enlightened discussions of the art of French, English, and Chinese gardens, giving themselves up to the illusion that Julie's garden is exactly what it pretends to be: the image of the virtuous woman and mother, a "charming image of respectability and innocence," as Saint-Preux says.

Julie's Death

If feminist interpretations are to be believed, it becomes clear at the end of Rousseau's great narrative—at the latest—that women are done a bad turn. His heroines do not enjoy a happy fate: both Sophie and Julie must die before the narrator can be at peace. According to a widespread feminist reading, they are objects of fatal desire[47] or victims of a patriarchal system that destroys nature along with the feminine.[48] Such an interpretive approach reads the death of the literary heroine according to a theory of reflection: literary death portrays the factual or symbolic status of women in society. Even less mimetically oriented interpretive approaches tend to take the literary death of a female figure literally. Though they may not make the author himself or his "fatal desire" or a destructive social system responsible for a woman's death, they do consider her death as essential in constituting the phallocentric "symbolic order." In this reading, Julie's death is an indication that woman has no place in the male order. Julie's acquiescence in marrying a husband chosen by her father therefore appears to be the sacrifice of the desires of the woman, if not the sacrifice of the woman herself. For Danielle Montet-Clavié, Julie's death sends a clear message— Rousseau's theoretical economy functions only on condition of the death of

---

diction in the novel, but he devotes no attention to the gender-specific distribution of these two modes, which is, in my opinion, quite clear and which finds its explanation in Rousseau's construction of differences in the sexes.

47. This is the argument of Renate Berger and Inge Stephan in the introduction to their anthology, *Weiblichkeit und Tod in der Literatur* (1987, 2).

48. "In the aesthetic coupling of femininity and death, the aggressive potential of a system made up of isolation and subjection finds its expression [In der ästhetischen Koppelung von Weiblichkeit und Tod kommen die aggressiven Potentiale eines Systems zum Ausdruck, das auf Ausgrenzung und Unterwerfung besteht]" (Berger and Stephan 1987, 3).

the woman:[49] "Julie is exemplary only insofar as she occupies an impossible position: loyal wife at the cost of her life, true mother in ceding her place to the father. The order of virtue and morality, which has already demanded sacrifice of the lover, prescribes for the wife and mother a place that death alone allows her to fill. Julie can only realize herself, can only be a woman of value [*femme de valeur*], by effacing herself before an economy in which she has no place but that she supports even to the point of disappearing."[50]

In these comments we encounter a thesis that is common in poststructuralist-inspired feminist interpretations: The symbolic order of the patriarchate constitutes itself through the exclusion of the feminine, that is, through the death of the woman. Elisabeth Bronfen, for example, writes about the "beautiful corpse" as a constant among literary motifs since the eighteenth century: "There are many examples that support the theory that society regenerates itself through the corpse of the woman—through the gift of her body, her blood, her life."[51] Bronfen adds: "In the dead body of the woman, the semiotic other is given a signifier. It is all the same whether it refers to the dangerously chaotic, the innocently pure, or fear of loss of a privileged object of desire. These are all values that are linked with the feminine. The other is translated into the normative order through this act; in fact, it is made the privileged signifier of the certainty of this order."[52]

I cannot discuss this theory at length in the present context;[53] rather, I will limit myself to the question of whether the literary staging of female death in the *Nouvelle Héloïse* lends itself to the social or poststructural approaches outlined above.

Let us first recall our starting point. Julie renounced her passionate love for Saint-Preux because she thought she recognized its deceptive nature. She married Wolmar and now lives a virtuous life with him and their two sons in the country. She has "taught" Saint-Preux something about the ambiguities of this idyll in the tour of her Elysium. But Saint-Preux did not know

---

49. See Montet-Clavié 1984, 64: "L'économie théorique de Rousseau fonctionne à partir de la mort nécessaire d'une femme, seule réalisation possible de sa valeur."

50. "Julie n'est exemplaire qu'à tenir une place impossible, épouse fidèle au prix de sa vie, véritablement mère à laisser la place au père. L'ordre de la vertu, de la moralité qui a exigé le sacrifice de l'amante prescrit à la mère une place que la mort seule permet de remplir. Julie ne se réalise, n'est femme de valeur qu'à s'effacer devant une économie où elle n'a pas sa place mais qu'elle cimente à disparaître" (Montet-Clavié 1984, 66 [trans. MR-B]).

51. Bronfen 1987, 101 [trans. MR-B].

52. Bronfen 1987, 106 [trans. MR-B].

53. See Garbe 1992, chap. 10 ("Der kulturkonstitutive Ausschluß des Weiblichen" [The culturally constitutive exclusion of women]).

how to read the woman's signs. If readers of the novel were to adopt the point of view of Saint-Preux or Wolmar, they would have to assume that Julie has reached the pinnacle of happiness. Everything seems to be well ordered as the novel moves toward its dramatic finale and Julie's death. Shortly before the conclusion of this sentimental idyll—that is, at a point where Rousseau's novel almost seems to stand still—the author pauses for a moment of magnanimous self-reflection on the preceding narrative, allowing events to pass once again in review. The condition for this is the death of Julie, who falls ill after saving one of her children from drowning in Lake Geneva. Suddenly, Rousseau's novel is once again full of drama and significance. A minister approaches Julie's deathbed and elevates her to a symbol of motherhood: "Your death, madam, is as exemplary as your life: you have lived to exercise your charity to mankind, and die a martyr to maternal tenderness."[54]

Julie's death appears to be less unambiguous for her husband. Her cheerful composure in the face of death awakens fears that she has kept something from him: "I have penetrated your sentiments; you are glad to die, you rejoice to leave me. . . . Have I deserved on your part so cruel a desire?"[55]

It is Julie herself who contradicts Wolmar: "Can I rejoice to leave you? You, the business of whose life it has been to instruct and make me happy! you, who of all the men in the world, were the most capable to make me so; you, with whom only perhaps I could have lived within the bounds of discretion and virtue! No! believe me, if I could set any value upon life, it would be that I might spend it with you" (IV, 240/720–21).

The image of the martyr to maternal love is thus joined by the image of the death of a perfect wife. But as we see, Julie's confession contains an inconspicuous "perhaps." Wolmar was "perhaps" the only one with whom she could have had a good marriage. Perhaps, however, there might have been another possibility. Julie herself hands Wolmar the letter to Saint-Preux in which she admits to him the love that never ended: "Long have I indulged myself in the salutary *delusion,* that my passion was extinguished; the delusion is now vanished, when it can be no longer useful. . . . In vain, alas! I endeavoured to stifle that passion which inspired me with life; it was impossible; it was interwoven with my heart strings. It now expands itself, when it is no longer to be dreaded; it supports me now my strength fails me; it cheers my soul even in death" (IV, 277/740–41).

54. *NH,* IV, 233/717.
55. *NH,* IV, 240/719.

Julie makes this confession, as she says, without regret. She regrets neither that she married Wolmar (for this made possible her life in virtue), nor that she has always loved Saint-Preux in her innermost heart (for this makes her an honorable woman). Death appears to be the necessary condition for reconciling virtue and love—at the price, to be sure, of projecting them into the beyond. It would seem that the novel treats virtue as an earthly matter, while love can renew itself in the eternal realm. It is only from this perspective that Julie can give her farewell letter to Saint-Preux a final consolatory note: "That virtue, which separated us on earth, will unite us for ever in the mansions of the blessed. I die in that peaceful hope; too happy to purchase at the expense of my life the privilege of loving you without a crime, and of telling you so once more" (IV, 281/743).

Here, Julie seems to speak with complete openness for the first time; here she seems to reveal herself. She leaves it to her interpreters to define her death as a reassuring utopia of love, as an indictment of the cold law of virtue, or as a sacrifice in favor of the laws of the patriarchate. For all their differences, these interpretations agree in reading Julie's words as, first, authentic, and second, as the bearer of the message of the entire novel (a view Rousseau himself may have shared). The novel's message appears to be compressed in these lines.

But after all the deceptions, does this ending present us with Julie's real voice? And is Julie, after all the uncertainties of this love, now sure of herself? The fact that she is on her deathbed would seem to speak for this interpretation; the nearness of death does not seem to allow for any ambivalence. Or does it? "I foresee, I feel your affliction: I know too well you will be left to mourn; the thoughts of your sorrow cause my greatest uneasiness: but reflect on the consolation I leave with you."[56] What if these last lines, the last letter to Saint-Preux, has perhaps only this one function—to provide consolation, to reunite all the things that cannot be reunited?

This does not have to be interpreted as consciously intended by the author or the protagonist. Rather, it seems to be a question of the possibilities of narration. We are familiar with death as a metaphor that urges us toward clarity: "This was Julie's life." We might assume that Rousseau now introduces death—after weaving a long tale of pretense and deception—in order to force himself to clarity, or to allow himself clarity. It is as if he wanted to help his unresolved story arrive at a balance. Just this once he wants to say what really *is*. But to see a clear message in Julie's death means subjecting a

---

56. *NH*, IV, 278/741.

complex and ambiguous story to a telos, means resolving it in retrospect. It is apparently difficult, not only for feminist Rousseau reception, but for the reception of Rousseau as a whole, to break free of a teleological reading and to release the individual voices in the novel once again to their individuality (for which the conception of the work as an epistolary novel would speak). Nevertheless, Julie's death escapes clear and definite interpretation. The dying Julie herself paves the way for two quite contrary interpretations of her death. There is, on the one hand, the balance of her life drawn for Clara and Wolmar, in which she stresses the degree of her happiness:

> Thus . . . you see to what *felicity* I was arrived. I enjoyed a considerable share of happiness, and had still more in view. The increasing prosperity of my family, the virtuous education of my children, all that I held dear in the world assembled, or ready to be assembled around me. The time present and the future equally flattering; enjoyment and hope united to complete my happiness. Thus raised to the pinnacle of earthly *bliss,* I could not but descend; as it came before it was expected, it would have taken its flight while I was delighted in the thoughts of its duration. (IV, 250/726)

Here Julie presents herself as one who has nothing more to wish for in this world and who can calmly wait for death in the middle of a fulfilled life. "I live at once in all that I love," she writes in her next-to-last letter to Saint-Preux; "I am replete with happiness, and satisfied with life; come, death, when thou wilt! I no longer dread thy power."[57] But this self-interpretation contradicts another that Julie sets down in a different context—that of religious conviction—in the same letter to Saint-Preux. Here she admits to her former lover that, inwardly, she is in quite a different state: "Every thing around me gives me cause of content, and yet I am not contented. A secret languor steals into the bottom of my heart: I find it puffed up and void, as you formerly said was the case with yours: all my attachments are not sufficient to fill it. This disquietude, I confess, is strange: but it is nevertheless true" (IV, 194/694).

Julie is not happy about the happiness that has been hers; indeed, she feels her happiness is a "burden" to her.[58] It is too much of a good thing—or, to put it differently, she lacks the sense of insufficiency that represents

---

57. *NH*, IV, 185/689.
58. *NH*, IV, 194/694.

the potential for desiring something she does not have: "[T]hose who have no desires must be very unhappy; they are deprived, if I may be allowed the expression, of all they possess. . . . To live without pain is incompatible with our state of mortality: it would be in fact to die.—He who has every thing in his power, if a creature, must be miserable, as he would be deprived of the pleasure of desiring; than which every other want would be more supportable" (IV, 192–93/693–94). Julie says clearly: Desire drives life; it keeps life alive. Those who have nothing more to desire because they have everything are, as it were, already dead. Or they desire, like Julie, the possibility to desire: "And yet . . . I am constantly uneasy: my heart sighs after something of which it is entirely ignorant."[59]

Even if Julie's sense of insufficiency in this letter finds apparent pacification in her turn to God,[60] her farewell letter to Saint-Preux suggests a different interpretation. How easily could her old passion have flamed up once again to replace that vague sense of insufficiency—that secret emptiness of the heart—in the constant company of the man who had been the object of her first grand feelings. In any case, Julie indicates to Saint-Preux in this last letter that she had been mistaken about the tranquility of her feelings: "You imagined me cured of my love; I thought so too. Let us thank Heaven that the deception hath lasted as long as it could be of service to us. In vain, alas! I endeavoured to stifle that passion which inspired me with life" (IV, 277/740–41).

There is yet another respect in which her view appears to be dimmed again by passion. Instead of a clear ability to distinguish between I and you, there is an inescapable projection: Julie's concern that Saint-Preux could suffer a "relapse" in her constant presence was in truth not directed at him but at herself.[61] Julie's death forestalls a relapse that is dangerously close, a relapse into the old antagonism of passion and virtue. From a hermeneutic point of view, her death might appear to be the last definitive sacrifice of virtue to passion: "Have I not lived long enough to be happy and virtuous? In taking me hence Heaven deprives me of nothing which I ought to regret [and secures my honor. . . . After so many sacrifices, I consider those I must

---

59. Ibid.
60. In this confession, Julie reveals the basis for her religiosity: "Therefore, finding nothing in this globe capable of giving it satisfaction, my desiring soul seeks an object in another world . . ." (IV, 195/694). The theological turn in Julie's desire deserves discussion of its own, but for reasons of space, I cannot undertake that discussion here. In de Man's study of the novel, he emphasizes that the very errors that structured the relationship between Julie and Saint-Preux recur in Julie's relationship to God. See de Man 1979, chap. 9, 188ff.
61. "The fears I thought I felt for you I undoubtedly felt for myself" (*NH*, [MR-B]/278).

still make to be inconsiderable. It means dying only one more time.]" (IV, 277–78; [MR-B]/741).

Was Julie at the pinnacle of happiness or in the abyss of passion? Or was the pinnacle of her happiness *simultaneously* the edge of the abyss? Is her death a happy farewell to a harmonious and well-ordered community or a hurried flight from an eruption of fateful passion? What was the quality of this "happiness" of virtue if Julie can say, almost with relief, that she has lived long enough and made sacrifices enough for it? Which of Julie's voices should we believe, the one she uses with Wolmar, Clara, and her children, or the one that confesses unfailing love to Saint-Preux?

The novel provides no unambiguous answers to these questions. Julie quite clearly presents us with two different interpretations of her death and therefore leaves us with an irreducible ambiguity. This woman does not speak "clearly" even in the face of death. She thus disappoints not only those she leaves behind but her readers and those who would interpret her as well. For in the face of death, we expect clear confessions.

Nevertheless, one conclusion can be drawn. Julie's ambivalent messages undermine the interpretation that sees a victory of virtue over passion; and they contradict the assertion that with the *Nouvelle Héloïse,* Rousseau has ruefully returned to the Enlightenment camp. Julie's death does *not* lead to general reconciliation and the reunion of sensitive souls; and this is underscored by the final letter in the novel. Julie's last wish, that Saint-Preux and Clara come together, will not be fulfilled, as that letter from Clara makes clear. Instead, Clara ends her letter, and thus the novel, with dark forebodings of her own approaching death. Julie's ability to create ties between all those she loves and to keep those ties alive is evidently limited. The community at Clarens makes an absolutely desolate impression at the end of the novel. Clara writes: "I am solitary in the midst of company; a mournful silence prevails around me; and in the stupidity of my affliction, I speak to nobody, having but just life enough in me to feel the horrors of death. . . . [Julie's] children are growing up apace, her father is insensibly wasting, her husband is in continual agitation of mind: in vain he strives to think her annihilated" (IV, 282–83/744).

Rousseau refrains from creating a sentimental reconciliation. And scarcely anyone would maintain, with regard to the darkness of the final picture, that the death of his protagonist functions as what Bronfen called a "privileged signifier of the certainty of this order." A different notion appears to lie nearer at hand. If it is true that Rousseau has played out the two competing discourses of love of his (and our?) times in the person of Julie, then her death could be read as an indirect admission that *both* of these ideas have failed and thus as an indication of the *unlivability* of the bourgeois relationship between the sexes that forces women into the straitjacket of a role as housewife, wife, and mother. Rousseau, as we know, played a significant role in conceptualizing this relationship (see, for example, the fifth book of his *Emile*). But even the marriage of Emile and Sophie—which appears to be a happy synthesis of passionate love and the reasonable/natural complementarity of the sexes—leads to failure, as shown by the fragmentary continuation titled *Emile et Sophie, ou les solitaires*. In *both* grand conceptions of the relations of the sexes (and therefore also of femininity), Rousseau provides the grounds for calling those conceptions into question. Looking back at Rousseau's texts from a distance of more than two hundred years, the literary fiction emerges as far more complex and far-sighted than the theoretical, conceptual discourse that has been devoted to it.

REFERENCES

Berger, Renate, and Inge Stephan, eds. 1987. *Weiblichkeit und Tod in der Literatur*. Cologne.

Bovenschen, Silvia. 1979. *Die imaginierte Weiblichkeit: Exemplarische Untersuchungen zu kulturgeschichtlichen und literarischen Präsentationsformen des Weiblichen*. Frankfurt am Main.

Bronfen, Elisabeth. 1987. "Die schöne Leiche: Weiblicher Tod als motivische Konstante von der Mitte des 18. Jahrhunderts bis in die Moderne." In Berger and Stephan 1987.

Foucault, Michel. 1976. *Histoire de la sexualité*. Vol. 1, *La volonté de savoir*. Paris.

Gallas, Helga. 1990. "Ehe als Instrument des Masochismus oder 'Glückseligkeits-Triangel' als Aufrechterhaltung des Begehrens? Zur Trennung von Liebe und Sexualität im deutschen Frauenroman des 18. Jahrhunderts." In *Untersuchungen zum Roman von Frauen um 1800*, ed. Helga Gallas and Magdalene Heuser. Tübingen.

Garbe, Christine. 1992. *Die "weibliche" List im "männlichen" Text: Jean-Jacques Rousseau in der feministischen Kritik*. Stuttgart.

Kamuf, Peggy. 1982. *Fictions of Feminine Desire: Disclosures of Heloise*. Lincoln, Neb.

Kant, Immanuel. 1968. "Beobachtungen über das Gefühl des Schönen und Erhabenen." In Immanuel Kant, *Werke,* vol. 2, ed. Wilhelm Weischedel. Frankfurt am Main. (Trans. as *Observations on the Feeling of the Beautiful and Sublime* by John T. Goldthwait. Berkeley, 1960.)

Lechte, John. 1982. "Fiction and Woman in 'La Nouvelle Heloise' and the Heritage of '1789.' " In *1789—Reading, Writing, Revolution,* ed. Francis Barker. Colchester.

Luhmann, Niklas. 1982. *Liebe als Passion: Zur Codierung von Intimität.* Frankfurt am Main.

Man, Paul de. 1979. *Allegories of Reading: Figural Language in Rousseau, Nietzsche, Rilke, and Proust.* New Haven.

———. 1983. "The Rhetoric of Temporality." In *Blindness and Insight.* 2nd ed. Minneapolis.

Montet-Clavié, Danielle. 1984. "La femme comme nature morte dans l'oeuvre de J.-J. Rousseau." In Jeanine Garrisson et al., *G.R.I.E.F.—La femme et la mort.* Toulouse.

Pelckmans, Paul. 1981/82. "Le rêve du voile dans La Nouvelle Héloïse." *Révue Romane* 16–17.

Rousseau, Jean-Jacques. 1948. *Lettre à d'Alembert sur les spectacles,* ed. M. Fuchs. Lille and Geneva. (*Letter to M. d'Alembert on the Theatre,* trans. Allan Bloom. In *Politics and the Arts.* Glencoe, Ill., 1960.)

———. 1961. *Oeuvres complètes,* ed. Bernard Gagnebin and Marcel Raymond. Vol. 2, *La Nouvelle Héloïse; Théâtre—Poésies—Essais Littéraires.* Paris. (*Eloisa, or a Series of Original Letters,* trans. William Kenrick. 2 vols. London, 1803 [facsimile reprint, Woodstock Books, Oxford, 1989].)

———. 1969. *Oeuvres complètes,* ed. Bernard Gagnebin and Marcel Raymond. Vol. 4, *Emile; Education—Morale—Botanique.* Paris. (*Emile, or, Education,* trans. Barbara Foxley. London 1911. For a translation of the fragmentary continuation of Book V, see *Emilius and Sophia; or, The Solitaries,* in *Emilius and Sophia; or, a New System of Education,* trans. William Kenrick. 4 vols. London, 1783.)

Starobinski, Jean. 1984. "Jean-Jacques Rousseau und die Gefahren der Reflexion." In *Das Leben der Augen.* Frankfurt am Main. [Original title: *L'oeil vivant.* Paris, 1961.]

Steinbrügge, Lieselotte. 1987. *Das moralische Geschlecht: Theorien und literarische Entwürfe über die Natur der Frau in der französischen Aufklärung.* Weinheim. (2nd ed., Stuttgart, 1992.)

3

PHILOSOPHY OF HISTORY AS A THEORY OF GENDER DIFFERENCE
The Case of Rousseau

Herta Nagl-Docekal

Translated by Sabrina Völz

Was Rousseau a philosopher of history? The results of research on the history of this term speak against it. The expression "philosophie de l'histoire" can be traced back to Voltaire's review of Hume's *Complete History of England,* which appeared in 1764. Shortly after that, in 1765, Voltaire published his *Philosophie de l'histoire.*[1] Both dates follow the years in which Rousseau's principal writings had appeared.

With regard to the subject itself, however, the matter turns out to be

---

This essay originally appeared under the title "Rousseaus Geschichtsphilosophie als Theorie der Geschlechterdifferenz," in *Deutsche Zeitschrift für Philosophie* 42, no. 4 (1994): 571–89.

1. Cf. "Geschichtsphilosophie," in *Historisches Wörterbuch der Philosophie,* ed. Joachim Ritter, vol. 2 (Darmstadt, 1974), col. 415f.

more complex. Everything depends on how the term "philosophy of history" is defined. A negative conclusion—the thesis that Rousseau's work does not include any reflections in the field of philosophy of history—seems justified only if the notion "philosophy of history" refers exclusively to theories that interpret the history of humanity in terms of a uniform model suggesting either a cyclical pattern or some form of progress. Presumably, the fact that this reading of the notion is quite common explains why Rousseau is usually not taken into consideration when the development of philosophy of history is reconstructed. This widely shared definition does not, however, provide a comprehensive account of the original intentions of philosophy of history.

The starting point for philosophy of history was a rejection of teleological concepts, which in most cases were of theological provenance. Whereas, for example, Bossuet in his *Discours sur l'histoire universelle* (1681) still attributed historical processes to direct interventions of God, the thinking of the Enlightenment introduced the intention to understand history solely with reference to humanity. In order to achieve this, attention was first of all given to the question of the specific features of the human being, of the emerging of humans from nature. Thus it is no mere coincidence that philosophy of history evolved at the same time as philosophical anthropology. A further focal point of this new project was the present. Now perceived as the result of processes generated by human beings, the present could also be viewed from the perspective of practical changeability. In this way, the beginnings of philosophy of history involved an impulse for political and moral renewal and covered elements of utopian thinking. If the term *philosophy of history* is defined with regard to these subject matters, it may without question be applied to Rousseau. Now, Rousseau appears as a philosopher of history *avant la lettre*. And this characterization is valid not only in view of some of his writings, but can be traced in his entire work, even in his literary texts.

This essay does not claim, however, to provide a comprehensive survey of Rousseau's philosophy of history. Instead, it highlights elements that have received little attention until now. The starting point will be Rousseau's diagnosis that the present is marked by a pervasive alienation of human beings resulting from the antagonism of their selfish interests. In outlining how this alienation can be overcome, Rousseau assigns different tasks to both sexes. Thus a sensible development in the future of humanity depends, according to him, on men and women accepting and performing well their respective roles. It is this element of a gender theory in Rousseau's philosophy of history that will be examined here more closely.

A Program for the Overcoming of Alienation

First, the framework of Rousseau's reflections needs to be examined. Alienation is not thought of as the *conditio humana,* but as the result of the formation of society and the division of labor.[2] In his considerations regarding the beginnings of the history of humanity—Rousseau, by the way, classifies these thoughts as "hypothetical and conditional reasonings, better fitted to clarify the nature of things than to expose their actual origin"[3]—he assumes that prior to the inner developments of civilization, there was a period in which human beings did not live in an alienated way but lived in accordance with their original nature.[4] Rousseau characterizes the "natural state" as a phase not yet marked by dependence—either by hierarchic relationships among individuals or groups, or by a dependence of individuals on their own passions. Desires are developed no further than the possibilities for the satisfaction of basic needs.[5] (Even this phase is not conceived as completely lacking history. As Iring Fetscher correctly observes, one can differentiate between at least two periods in Rousseau's considerations on the "natural state."[6] However, this cannot be dealt with here.)

In characterizing the process of civilization as a history of losses, Rous-

---

2. For Hans Barth, the term *alienation* appropriately allows recognition of the inner connectedness of all of Rousseau's writings as well as the aspect that became relevant for Kant's, Schiller's, Hegel's, and Marx's philosophies of history. Cf. Hans Barth, "Über die Idee der Selbstentfremdung des Menschen bei Rousseau," *Zeitschrift für philosophische Forschung* 13 (1959): 16–36.

3. Jean-Jacques Rousseau, *A Discourse on Inequality* (London 1984), 78. For considerations regarding hypothetical constructions of history, see Friedrich Engel-Janosi, "Bemerkungen über hypothetische Geschichtsschreibung," in *Die Wahrheit der Geschichte, Versuche zur Geschichtsschreibung in der Neuzeit* (Vienna, 1973), 29–40.

4. For a detailed examination of the differences in Rousseau's and Hobbes's views, cf. Leo Strauss, *Natural Right and History,* chap. 6.

5. "Since the savage desires nothing other than the things which he knows, and since he only knows things which to posses lies in his power, or which are easy to acquire, nothing can be more limited than his intellect" (Rousseau, *A Discourse on Inequality,* 89).

6. Iring Fetscher, *Rousseaus politische Philosophie: Zur Geschichte des demokratischen Freiheitsbegriffs,* 3rd ed. (Frankfurt am Main, 1975), esp. 35ff.

seau subsequently saw himself confronted with multiple accusations of promoting a return to the way of life at the beginnings of the history of humanity. Rousseau, of course, rejected this interpretation in his second discourse: "What now? Does one have to destroy societies, to do away with mine and yours, to go back to life with the bears in the forest? That is a conclusion like those of my opponents. On the one hand, I would like it to happen, but on the other hand, I do not want to save them from the disgrace of taking the logical step. O you, to whom the divine voices have not yet spoken, and who know no other call of your genus than the peaceful perfection of this short life, . . . go into the forest . . . and do not fear you would lower your genus, when you forego knowledge, in order to forego your vices."[7]

Rousseau emphasizes, in this context, that the process of civilization is irreversible and, moreover, that a mere return to the earliest living conditions is not desirable either. He turns to "people like me . . . , for whom their passions have for once and for all undermined their original simplicity, who can no longer sustain themselves on grass and acorns, and who cannot do without laws and their superiors . . . all, who are convinced, that the divine voice called the entire human race to insight and to the happiness of the heavenly spirits."[8] Thus, Rousseau does not advocate a "dropping out," but a new way of dealing with the present condition as it evolved historically.

In characterizing the competence for this renewal, Rousseau draws upon the Christian concept of conscience. Hence, one element of the specific make-up of human beings is to have heard "the divine voices," that is, to be gifted with an impulse to act in a just and moral manner, and with the expectation of eventually participating, by virtue of this way of acting, in the "happiness of the heavenly spirits." Human beings can thus "endeavor to practice virtues—which they are obliged to follow, after gaining knowledge of them—in order to earn the eternal prize, with which they can expect to be rewarded."[9]

If it is indeed important to transform present living conditions on the

---

7. Rousseau, *A Discourse on Inequality*. This passage is not found in the English edition used here. It is quoted from the French/German edition: Jean-Jacques Rousseau, "Diskurs über den Ursprung und die Grundlagen der Ungleichheit zwischen den Menschen," in *Schriften zur Kulturkritik: Die zwei Diskurse von 1750 und 1755* (Hamburg, 1978), 125–27; trans. by Sabrina Völz.
8. Ibid.
9. Ibid.

basis of this moral competence, it is necessary to proceed in a step-by-step fashion. Rousseau's individual works may be interpreted as each bringing out another aspect of this transformation. The following comments will illustrate this. But before doing that, let us take another look at the objective of the suggested renewal. Here the term *autonomy* forms the central determining factor. According to Rousseau, heteronomy—which is the cause of all the sufferings of the civilized individual—has to be overcome in both of its variants—dependence on other people as well as on one's own passions. With regard to this freedom from dependence, the anticipated future shaping of life is analogous to the "state of nature." Nevertheless, there exists a decisive difference: the projected freedom from damages induced by society is brought about by human beings, not predetermined by nature. Thus, the anticipated autonomy is thought of as a *second nature* mediated through criticism and action. Therefore, Rousseau, in the dispute with his opponents quoted above, underscores that the human genus has a different call than to return to a mere "peaceful perfection of this short life."

This concept of a second nature was viewed by Kant—justifiably so, as should become evident in the following reflections—as the actual point of Rousseau's thinking on philosophy of history. In the course of his own considerations regarding this subject in his essay "*Speculative Beginning of Human History,*" Kant notes that Rousseau is searching "to answer this more difficult question: how must culture progress so as to develop the capacities belonging to mankind's vocation as a *moral* species and thus end the conflict within himself as [a member of both a] moral species and a natural species?"[10] Like Rousseau, Kant also thinks that all human efforts have to be concentrated "until art so perfects itself as to be a second nature, which is the final goal of the human species' moral vocation."[11] For Peter Horak, the agreement goes so far that it seems justified to regard Rousseau's and Kant's considerations on these matters "as two variants of a single philosophy of history."[12]

---

10. Immanuel Kant, "Speculative Beginning of Human History," in *Perpetual Peace and Other Essays on Politics, History, and Morals* (Indianapolis, 1983), 54. Georg Krainer illustrates the importance of the reception of Rousseau's work for Kant. He states that "to know Rousseau's idea of cultural criticism is to know the leitmotif of Kant's entire critical work." He further notes, "The main critical works . . . are only the methodically prepared and secured form of that idea" ("Beitrag zur Analyse der Kritischen Philosophie: Kultur—Zivilisation—ethisches Gemeinwesen," Ph.D. diss., University of Vienna, 1980).

11. Kant, *Speculative Beginning of Human History*, 55.

12. Peter Horak, "Jean-Jacques Rousseau und Immanuel Kant: Die Parallelen und Gegensätze einer Geschichtsphilosophie," *Wissenschaftliche Zeitschrift* 33, no. 1 (1984): 46.

From the Misery of Civilization to the Autonomy of Citizens

The establishment of freedom for citizens is the first task on this route outlined by Rousseau. He holds that the states that have developed throughout history are based on a contract between unequal individuals, and that this inequality has increased during the course of time. "If we follow the progress of inequality in these different revolutions, we shall find that the establishment of law and the right of property was the first stage, the institution of magistrates the second, and the transformation of legitimate into arbitrary power the third and last stage. Thus, the status of rich and poor was authorized by the first epoch, that of strong and weak by the second, and by the third that of master and slave, which is the last degree of inequality, and the stage to which all the others finally lead until new revolutions dissolve the government altogether or bring it back to legitimacy."[13]

The "legitimacy" Rousseau has in mind here should be brought about by replacing the old unjust contract with a new one.[14] In his study on the social contract, Rousseau specifies his concept of this new contract. Its underlying idea is that individuals should not only be subjects of the state—and in this way subject, as equals, to its laws—but also parts of the sovereign. This means that "each, uniting with all, nevertheless obeys only himself, and remains as free as before."[15] The concept of autonomy that Rousseau formulates here is not limited to the area of civic freedoms. Rousseau also applies it to the overcoming of the second type of dependence, that is, to the control of passions. Thus, in his work on the social contract, he speaks of "the moral freedom which alone renders man truly master of himself; for the impulsion of mere appetite is slavery, and obedience to the law one prescribes to oneself is freedom."[16] I will return later to this point.

It is noteworthy that Rousseau applies his concept of freedom for citizens only to men. In his outline of an ideal society, women have their place exclusively within the family. They find themselves in a situation of twofold subordination. On the one hand, they are subject to state legislation without

---

13. Rousseau, *A Discourse on Inequality*, 131.
14. Emmanuel Hirsch examines how this new contract relates to the old one. He characterizes it as "the proper determination of the original basis of each truly existing government" ("Rousseaus Geschichtsphilosophie: Ein Beitrag zum Verständnis des Contrat social," in *Rechtsidee und Staatsgedanke: Festgabe für Binder* [Berlin, 1930], 241).
15. Jean-Jacques Rousseau, "Of the Social Contract or Principles of Political Right," in *Of the Social Contract and Discourse on Political Economy* (New York, 1984), 14.
16. Ibid., 19.

being part of the sovereign; on the other hand, within the sphere of the family, wives are subordinate to the rule of their husbands. Rousseau notes in his study on the social contract that "the family is then, if you will, the primitive model of political societies; the chief is the image of the father, while the people are the image of the children."[17] In *Emile* this comparison is expanded with regard to the situation of the wife: "She ought to reign in the home as a minister does in a state." This means that the wife is subject to her husband's legislative rule, and Rousseau goes on to underline the subordinate character of this situation: "When she fails to recognize the voice of the head of the house, when she wants to usurp his rights and be in command herself, the result of this disorder is never anything but misery, scandal, and dishonor."[18] Consequently, the aforementioned principle of justice, which emphasizes obedience to "the law, which one prescribes to oneself" does not apply to women. Here Rousseau breaks with his own concept of a legitimate institution; with regard to the family he does not confront the historically developed form with a new, just principle of coexistence. Heidemarie Bennent has pointed out this rupture in Rousseau's argumentation: "The cancellation of the contract of rule with regard to marriage conceives of no new contractual form free of subordination."[19]

According to Rousseau's own categories, denying someone's autonomy means not viewing a person as a human being: "To renounce one's liberty is to renounce one's quality as a man, the rights of humanity and even one's duties. . . . Such renunciation is incompatible with human nature."[20] Apparently Rousseau does not perceive the contradiction of not applying the principle of political autonomy to women.[21] Moreover, he modifies his anthropological concept at this point. Now he departs from assuming a single type of human nature and writes: "Woman is made to yield to man and to endure even his injustice."[22] Thus, Rousseau ascribes to women a particular nature manifesting itself in a disposition toward obedience. (Furthermore, he defines this specific nature by sham—but more to that later.) Correspondingly, the education of girls should differ from that of male chil-

---

17. Ibid., 5.
18. Jean-Jacques Rousseau, *Emile or On Education* (New York, 1979), 408.
19. Heidemarie Bennent, *Galanterie und Verachtung: Eine philosophiegeschichtliche Untersuchung zur Stellung der Frau in Gesellschaft und Kultur* (Frankfurt am Main, 1985), 92.
20. Rousseau, *Of the Social Contract*, 9.
21. This contradiction is also discussed by Susan Moller Okin, *Women in Western Political Thought* (London, 1980), 99.
22. Rousseau, *Emile*, 396.

dren.²³ As Rousseau recommends, "They ought to be constrained very early. This misfortune, if it is one for them, is inseparable from their sex."²⁴ And he goes on to note, "from this habitual constraint comes a docility which women need all their lives, since they never cease to be subjected either to a man or to the judgments of men and they are never permitted to put themselves above these judgments."²⁵

Rousseau's concept of nature becomes inconsistent at this point. In the state of nature that he hypothetically assumes, women as well as men live in autarchy, and there are yet no circumstances of subordination. Thus, what kind of nature does he have in mind when an inclination toward obedience is assigned to women? Rousseau arbitrarily calls nature here, what has evolved only in the state of society. Seyla Benhabib and Linda Nicholson, among others, have called attention to this inconsistency: "The ambivalence in Rousseau's conception of nature leads to what he describes as 'sexual differences,' yet what in reality are carefully cultivated, shaped, learned differences in the behavior, thinking, feeling, and perception of men and women."²⁶ Rousseau's way of proceeding is certainly paradigmatic of a tradition of thought continuing up until the present. Attempts are made to this very day to legitimate norms that are directed at establishing and supporting hierarchical gender relations by asserting that they are grounded in nature. Yet as just shown, a *petitio principii* is to be detected here: these norms, which are claimed to be deduced from nature, have first been projected into it.

This blur in Rousseau's concept of nature points to a fundamental problem. In hypothetically outlining the development of humankind—the way from the natural state through the different phases of inequality—he is not concerned with the history of *all* human beings, but deals solely with the history of men. The subordination of women is not viewed as a component of historical change. In this context, it is striking that in Rousseau's study

---

23. A grave misinterpretation is found in the article "Emile ou de l'éducation," in *Kindlers Literaturlexikon*, which says, "The novel concludes with his [Emile's] marriage—one has supplied him with a young girl, who was educated according to the same principles" (Munich, 1988–92), 8:3076.

24. Rousseau, *Emile*, 369.

25. Ibid., 370.

26. Seyla Benhabib and Linda Nicholson, "Politische Philosophie und die Frauenfrage," in *Pipers Handbuch der politischen Ideen*, ed. Iring Fetscher and Herfried Münkler (Munich, 1985–88), 5:537. Cf. also Silvia Bovenschen, *Die imaginäre Weiblichkeit: Exemplarische Untersuchungen zu kulturgeschichtlichen und literarischen Präsentationsformen des Weiblichen* (Frankfurt am Main, 1980), 169.

on the origins of inequality, the genesis of the family is not treated under the aspect of gender hierarchy. Heidemarie Bennent accurately remarks, "While . . . the whole history of human civilization is seen as the increasing depravation of the autarchic archetype, strictly speaking, the emerging of gender difference would also have to be seen as a characteristic of deterioration."[27] Yet for Rousseau, women are excluded from history, since their subordination is understood as given by nature. As Silvia Bovenschen critically observes, "The 'female nature' cannot exist by itself, it is not conveyed with the central categories of philosophy of history, it is only indirectly distinguishable from male precepts."[28] In the course of such criticism, it should not be overlooked, however, that in its anticipatory components, Rousseau's philosophy of history nevertheless does refer to women. (This will be examined more closely in the ensuing remarks.)

The hierarchy of genders appears to Rousseau as a necessity with regard to the task assigned to women in the ideal order. To use an expression taken from Marxist terminology and widely employed in feminist theory, it is the task of reproduction. Male children need to be educated by their mothers in a way that allows them to become proper citizens; male citizens need the emotional support and the personal care provided by their wives: "The good constitution of children initially depends on that of their mothers. The first education of men depends on the care of women. Men's morals, their passions, their tastes, their pleasures, their very happiness also depend on women. Thus the whole education of women ought to relate to men. To please men, to be useful to them, to make herself loved and honored by them, to raise them when young, to care for them when grown, to counsel them, to console them, to make their lives agreeable and sweet—these are the duties of women at all times."[29]

It has been repeatedly stressed in feminist studies that the theoretical foundations of the modern state imply a concept of women's exploitation. Diana Coole illustrates this point: "If women were active in the polity, the differentiations without which justice and liberty could not endure for Rousseau, would collapse. . . . The family provides a place where particular-

---

27. Bennent, *Galanterie und Verachtung*, 86.
28. Christine Garbe points out that Bovenschen herself presupposes the women's lack of history: "In an attempt not to play down the complete power of the patriarchy, emphasizing the exclusion of women from history, she unexpectedly arrived at merely once again confirming the 'omnipotence of patriarchy,' thus unwillingly reproducing the women's lack of history" (*Die "weibliche" List im "männlichen" Text: Jean-Jacques Rousseau in der feministischen Kritik* [Stuttgart, 1992], 121f.).
29. Rousseau, *Emile*, 365.

ity and passion can be safely expressed because they are defused there. The wife who services her husband encourages such expressions but then safeguards them so that they never cross the domestic threshold."[30] In a similar consideration, Lynda Lange concluded that it is not possible to correct Rousseau's political philosophy by simply including women when speaking of citizens. "With regard to the question of universal citizenship, it is apparent that the social role of women as 'natural' reproductive workers is incompatible with participation in the general will."[31]

This kind of feminist criticism of the concept of gender differences characteristic of the late Enlightenment—similar ideas can be found in Kant's, Fichte's, and Hegel's work—is frequently challenged with the thesis that this concept is merely a reflection of the living conditions of that time. Such a line of argumentation has not, however, considered that Rousseau again and again declares his concept as a contrastive model to the reality he observed. Furthermore, the background of intellectual history has to be kept in mind. Numerous writings published in France during the time of early Enlightenment explained—under the influence of Descartes's philosophy—that both sexes are equal with regard to their intellectual capabilities.[32] In other words, as an element of his philosophy of history, Rousseau's model of gender relations also has an anticipatory character.

Above all, Rousseau looks critically at the urban forms of life during his time. His investigation of this subject can be read as a theory of the modern life world in which some features agree with Max Weber's analysis. It is clear to Rousseau that urban living conditions do not embrace his shaping of the family without further qualification, but instead involve an isolation of individuals: "Unfortunately, domestic education no longer exists in our larger cities. Society has penetrated everything and is so disordered, that . . . one lives in his house like at the market place. When one only lives in society, one naturally no longer has a family. One hardly still knows his or her parents. They are viewed as strangers."[33] This alienation is shown in partic-

30. Diana H. Coole, *Women in Political Theory: From Ancient Misogyny to Contemporary Feminism* (Sussex, 1988), 118.
31. Lynda Lange, "Rousseau: Women and the General Will," in *The Sexism of Social and Political Theory: Women and Reproduction from Plato to Nietzsche*, ed. Lorenne M. G. Clark and Lynda Lange (Toronto, 1979), 48.
32. Margit Hauser confronts Rousseau's considerations with this tradition of women's apology, in particular with François Poulain de la Barre's work entitled *L'egalité des deux sexes* from 1673 (reprinted in the English language under the title *The Equality of the Sexes* [Manchester, 1980]). Cf. Margit Hauser, *Gesellschaftsbild und Frauenrolle in der Aufklärung* (Vienna, 1992).
33. Rousseau, *Emile*, 388.

ular in the continuation of *Emile* published under the title *Emile and Sophie or The Solitary*.[34] This fragmentary text reports that the two pupils with whose wedding the book *Emile* ends move into the city and experience the failing of their marriage. Sophie dies thereafter. For Rousseau, there is no place for the woman outside of the family.[35]

At this point, the limitations of Rousseau's project when put into practice are obvious. The renewal that Rousseau intends cannot be achieved within the scope of modern living conditions. When Rousseau's ideal features a patriarchally structured family life in the country as documented in the novel *La Nouvelle Héloïse*,[36] its unrealistic character is apparent.[37]

Current feminist theory, in its critique of such models of social structure, has made clear that all depends on a rethinking of the public as well as the private sphere. First of all, the principle of self-determination must also be applied to women. Women need to participate in the public processes of decision making in the same way as men, and in addition, they have to have the same chances in the professional world. Equal rights and equal treatment in a formal sense are not fully sufficient measures, however, as experience has shown. Women are at a disadvantage even when they are no longer legally discriminated against. One essential cause for this asymmetry seems to be that women are still viewed as primarily responsible for housework and raising the children and hence as not being totally available for the

34. Quotations are taken from the German edition: Jean-Jacques Rousseau, "Emile und Sophie oder Die Einsamen," in *Gesammelte Werke* (Munich, 1979), 13:645–90.

35. This is documented also by Rousseau's devaluative remarks about the ability of women to learn. Rousseau writes about the woman as a blue-stocking and aesthete: "Outside her home she is always ridiculous and very justly criticized; this is the inevitable result as soon as one leaves one's station and is not fit for the station one wants to adopt. All these women of great talent never impress anyone but fools" (*Emile*, 409.) An educated woman from Paris, speaking from her own experience, expressed her objection to this passage in a letter to Rousseau. (Wishing to remain anonymous, she signed the letter with "Henriette.") For an analysis of the correspondence beginning with this letter, see Claudia Honegger, *Die Ordnung der Geschlechter: Die Wissenschaften vom Menschen und das Weib* (Frankfurt am Main, 1991), 19–29.

36. Jean-Jacques Rousseau, *Julie or The New Eloïse: Letters of Two Lovers, Inhabitants of a Small Town at the Foot of the Alps* (University Park, Pa., 1968).

37. Rousseau's economic considerations are also debated in this context. His ideal is the autarchy of rural housekeeping. Robert Spaemann writes, "Rousseau confronts the developing bourgeois society which estranges humans to the same extent as it combines their interests with one another with a society not based on material relationships. The Marxist concept to renew the human community through removing the moment of material dependence from it, presents itself as a consequent continuation of Rousseau's thought" ("Von der Polis zur Natur: Die Kontroverse um Rousseaus ersten Diskurs," *Deutsche Vierteljahresschrift für Literatur* 47 [1973]: 595).

public sphere.[38] Therefore, the conception of a gender-specific division of labor must be questioned in principle. Belonging to a particular gender does not mean being qualified for a certain occupation.[39] Where this is not kept in mind and the division of labor is designed by appealing to the natural differences between the sexes, the problems of biological determinism result.

From Justice to Morality

All of these considerations only concern the first step of the renewal process advocated in Rousseau's work. One has to notice here that in Rousseau's outline for the future, the establishment of a just state is not the ultimate objective. In this respect, the fragmentary text entitled *Emile and Sophie, or The Solitary* is again significant. After the failure of his marriage, Emile flees from his native country and falls into Arabic slavery. Nevertheless, his life there is organized according to principles of justice, in part through his own commitment, in part due to the principles of his masters. And now Emile experiences that a form of living altogether based on the idea of law has its limitations. While the Arabic sense of justice is praised, it is simultaneously also criticized for a lack of compassion, mildness, and generosity: "These humans are without compassion; however, they are just. While one cannot expect either mildness or compassion, one does not need to fear arbitrariness or malice."[40] Even under just conditions, Emile remains a "solitary man."[41] (The thought that an order of life following the rules of reason is

---

38. Cf. Susan Moller Okin, *Justice, Gender, and the Family* (New York, 1989).

39. A detailed exposition of this argument can be found in Michael Walzer, *Spheres of Justice* (New York: Basic Books, 1983). For a feminist commentary on Walzer, see Herta Nagl-Docekal, "Die Kunst der Grenzziehung und die Familie," *Deutsche Zeitschrift für Philosophie* 41, no. 6 (1993): 1021–33.

40. Rousseau, *Emile*, 683.

41. Seyla Benhabib and Linda Nicholson interpret this text to mean that Emile actually attains the true objective of his education: "Finally through reflection on his own education, he becomes the autonomous human whom Jean-Jacques wanted to form. Does Rousseau ultimately admit that his idea of male autonomy and family life are incompatible? That the man, in order to become a 'natural human,' has to renounce all claims to the woman and has to leave her his son?" ("Politische Philosophie und die Frauenfrage," 540). This reading seems to disregard the fact that the entire text is written in the form of a complaint about the loss of the closest relationships.

not entirely satisfying appears several times in Rousseau's writings and will be taken up in the following comments.)

The order based on the new and just social contract appears limited in its scope also insofar as it is not necessarily adopted as an obligation. "Indeed, each individual may, as a man, have a particular will contrary to, or divergent from, the general will which he has as a citizen. His private interest may speak to him quite differently from the common interest."[42] Rousseau notes that the "private will naturally tends to preferences,"[43] so that there exists a constant threat of violations of the law and of corruption.[44] "For the vices, which make social institutions necessary, are the same vices which make the abuse of those institutions inevitable. Leaving aside the unique case of Sparta . . . laws, being in general less strong than passions, restrain men without changing them; so that it would be easy to prove that any government which, without being corrupted or degenerate, worked perfectly according to the ends of its institution, would have been instituted unnecessarily, and that a country where nobody evaded the laws or exploited the magistracy would need neither laws nor magistrates."[45]

Already at this point, Rousseau indirectly formulates his actual ideal. He endeavors to show that human beings have to change themselves. In the end, one should no longer have to be forced into obeying the laws, but should abide of one's own free will, that is, out of duty. At this point, Rousseau's philosophy of history becomes a theory of morality. In the consequence of this move, the central question is, how is it possible to overcome the second form of dependence, the dependence from one's own passions. In order to solve the problem, Rousseau applies the principle of autonomy to the individuals. "It is only when the voice of duty succeeds physical impulsion, and right succeeds appetite, that man, who till then had only looked after himself, sees that he is forced to act on other principles, and to consult his reason before listening to his inclinations."[46] Only by adopting moral principles can human beings become truly human. Rousseau notes shortly after the passage just quoted that the human being should praise the moment that saved him forever and "transformed him from a stupid and ignorant animal into an intellectual being and a man."[47]

42. Rousseau, *Of the Social Contract*, 17.
43. Ibid., 23.
44. Ibid., 81–84.
45. Rousseau, *A Discourse on Inequality*, 131.
46. Rousseau, *Of the Social Contract*, 18.
47. Ibid., 18.

With regard to philosophy of history, these considerations lead to the objective of creating a society that is based on morality to such an extent that external laws become superfluous. Here the question arises whether Rousseau views such a form of coexistence as an ideal that must be striven for but can never fully be realized, or whether he thinks that it can indeed be achieved at some point in the future. In his texts, one finds evidence that would seem to support both positions. While Rousseau's statements about the intensity of particular interests point in the direction of the first opinion, his interpretation of Sparta presupposes at least a partial realization of this ideal. Rousseau speaks about "the unique case of Sparta, where . . . Lycurgus established morals so well that it was almost unnecessary to add laws."[48]

In any case, it appears to Rousseau, as this passage demonstrates, that a renewal of education is necessary. The pedagogical program developed in *Emile* is derived from Rousseau's philosophy of history. How Rousseau defines the character of this book seems noteworthy: "It makes very little difference to me if I have written a romance. . . . This ought to be the history of my species."[49] His reflections on education are based on the assumption that each newly born individual is in the "natural state." The upbringing, then, ought to be oriented at the historical development of humanity. The core of this task lies in seeing to it that in the course of the development of the individual only those elements of the history of mankind that promote meaningful coexistence are repeated. In particular, this involves preventing the emergence of competitive behavior, which Rousseau sees as the ultimate root of civilization's misery. As Günter Buck noted, Rousseau creates in *Emile*, "an account of the future development, taking place within the bosom of society, but free from its entanglements, an account of the future natural history of humanity which can be brought about through experiment . . . and has to be devised in a philosophical manner."[50] The predominant goal of this education lies in enabling the development of a moral attitude.

In this context, Rousseau's view of gender difference is again of great importance. The development of morality depends on women. They appear, as Lieselotte Steinbrügge has underlined, as the "moral gender."[51] In charac-

48. Rousseau, *A Discourse on Inequality*, 153.
49. Rousseau, *Emile*, 416.
50. Günter Buck, "Über die systematische Stellung des 'Emile' im Werk Rousseaus," *Allgemeine Zeitschrift für Philosophie* 5, no. 1 (1980): 6.
51. Cf. Lieselotte Steinbrügge, *Das moralische Geschlecht: Theorien und literarische Entwürfe über die Natur der Frau in der französischen Aufklärung* (Weinheim, 1987). As Friederike Hassauer underscores, the women in Rousseau's work behave towards men as the "beauti-

terizing this specific competence of women, Rousseau is not thinking primarily of the educational relationship between mothers and children, but of the relationship between the sexes. Here the background once again is an anthropological assumption, namely, that women have a natural inclination toward shame: "The Supreme Being wanted to do honor to the human species in everything. . . . While abandoning woman to unlimited desires, He joins modesty to these desires in order to constrain them."[52] The education of girls ought to cultivate this inclination and to watch their decency. "Chastity must be a delicious virtue for a beautiful woman, who has an elevated soul."[53] Through her restraint, a woman shall finally govern over the desires of the man. "Although her attractions have hardly developed, she already reigns by the sweetness of her character and makes her modesty imposing. What insensitive and barbarous man does not soften his pride and adopt more attentive manners near a sixteen-year-old girl who is lovable and pure, who speaks little, who listens, whose bearing is seemly and whose conversation is decent, whose beauty dos not make her forget either her sex or her youth, who knows how to inspire interest by her very timidity and to gain for herself the respect she gives to everyone?"[54]

The woman must make sure that she is not merely perceived as an object of desire. By means of her modesty, she can gain respect as a person, and only on this basis can the relationship between man and woman be shaped as a relationship between humans. Rousseau shifts this subject to the foreground at the end of his novel, *La Nouvelle Héloïse*. There Rousseau tells about the destiny of Lord Bomstone, a supporting character in this novel. A prostitute, Laura, is led to Lord Bomstone, but she resists his advances, even when he tries to use force. Laura loves the lord and can only express it by refusing him. Only through this refusal does her individual fate become visible to Bomstone. He begins to respect her, and finally asks her to marry him, however, she declines his proposal (/).[55]

In this way, the relationship between the sexes is the place of transition from physical nature to morality. Rousseau defines the term *love* on the basis of this thought. In his *Discourse on Inequality*, he already calls for a

---

ful preacheresses" ("Die alte und die neue Heloïsa: Weibliche Zugänge zur Schrift," in *Auf der Suche nach der Frau im Mittelalter: Fragen, Quellen, Antworten*, ed. Bea Lundt [Munich, 1991], 299).

52. Rousseau, *Emile*, 359.
53. Ibid., 391.
54. Ibid., 390.
55. This appendix is not included in the English translation used here. Cf. Rousseau, *Julie oder Die neue Héloïse: Briefe zweier Liebenden aus einer kleinen Stadt am Fuße der Alpen* (Munich, 1988), 783–95.

distinction of this kind: "Let us begin by distinguishing the moral from the physical in the sentiment of love."[56] As a feeling, love is part of nature, but feelings can only develop where lasting commitments are found. At first a feeling for the beautiful begins to develop, and as this means that an interest in perfection is evolving, morality will eventually emerge:

> There is no true love without enthusiasm, and no enthusiasm without an object of perfection, real or chimerical, but always existing in the imagination. What will enflame lovers for whom this perfection no longer exists and who see in what they love only the object of sensual pleasure? . . . In love everything is only illusion. I admit it. But what is real are the sentiments for the truly beautiful with which love animates us and which it makes us love. This beauty is not in the object one loves; it is the work of our errors. So, what of it? Does the lover any the less sacrifice all of his low sentiments to this imaginary model? Does he any the less suffuse his heart with the virtues he attributes to what he holds dear? Does he detach himself any the less from the baseness of the human *I*?[57]

In his study entitled *Speculative Beginning of Human History,* Kant will represent the relevance of modesty for the development of a moral attitude in a very similar way. There one can read in a reflection on the "fig leaf" in *Genesis,*

> [M]aking a propensity become more internal and obdurate by removing the objects of the senses [from view] already displays consciousness of a certain mastery of reason over the impulses, and not merely, as in the first step, an ability to pay obeisance to them within smaller or greater boundaries. *Refusal* was the feat whereby man passed over from mere sensual to idealistic attractions, from mere animal desires eventually to love and, with the latter, from the feeling for the merely pleasant to the taste for beauty, at first only human beauty, but then also the beauty found in nature. In addition, *decency*—a propensity to influence others' respect for us by assuming good manners (by concealing whatever could arouse the low opinions of others), as the proper foundation of all true socia-

---

56. Rousseau, *A Discourse on Inequality,* 102.
57. Rousseau, *Emile,* 391.

bility—gave the first hint of man's formation into a moral creature.⁵⁸

Where Rousseau focuses on the development of morality, he repeatedly speaks about the power women have over men and the "authority of the beloved."⁵⁹ This could give rise to the impression that at this point the above-mentioned relationship of subordination between the sexes would be turned upside down. However, appearances are deceptive. The woman serves the man in this context as well by initiating his moral development. Rousseau's actual interest lies in the moral education of men, and women are again in a position of being instrumentalized. This is also documented in the way *Emile* is constructed: attention is not devoted equally to the education of male and female children; girls are not discussed, aside from very sporadic remarks, until the point at which Emile needs to form his feelings and at which he has to become the head of a family and, consequently, a citizen.⁶⁰

Furthermore, in this context it should be considered that the moral task of women is established through the anthropological thesis attributing to them a specific disposition toward modesty so that here again the above-mentioned problem arises.⁶¹ Sarah Kofman, who examines the "economy of

---

58. Kant, *Speculative Beginning of Human History*, 52.
59. Rousseau, *Emile*, 391.
60. Sarah Kofman wrote, "In this theatrical fiction represented by Emile, only one single act of the play is devoted solely to the women, the last. Symbolic expression of the subordination of women—this weak sex, this second sex—to the stronger sex, which always and solely serves as the point of reference. A gesture which repeats the one of the divine creation, as the first woman was formed as a derivative from the rib of the first man and for the purpose of helping him. 'It is not good for man to be alone. I will make a helper suitable for him' (Genesis 2:18). It is not good for man to be alone, Emile is a man. We have promised him a companion. She has to be given to him (*Emile*, 357)." See Sarah Kofmann, *Rousseau und die Frauen* (Tübingen, 1986), 15.
61. For Steinbrügge, the problem lies in a "biologization": "The woman is defined to a larger extent than the man by drives. Drives which Rousseau views as being close to animal instincts. . . . Because of her biological functions and the social role which is derived from them, the woman is at first placed closer to the area of nature than the man" (*Das moralische Geschlecht*, 82). According to my reading, one has to consider, however, that in Rousseau's work, reason—which is predominantly attributed to man—is also given by nature. Thus, Rousseau writes in a passage quoted previously, "The Supreme Being wanted to do honor to the human species in everything. While giving man inclinations without limit, He gives him at the same time the law which regulates them in order that he may be free and in command of himself. While abandoning man to immoderate passions, He joins reason to these passions in order to govern them" (*Emile*, 359). The accent of this reflection is not placed on the biological constitution of human beings, but on the abilities that distinguish them from animals. Accord-

modesty"[62] in Rousseau's work, characterizes the thesis asserting its natural origin as a *petitio principii* that has its roots in patriarchal interests: "Nothing legitimizes the natural character of modesty . . . , except Rousseau's phallocratic view."[63]

Feminist analysis does not fully acknowledge all the aspects of Rousseau's considerations, however, when it emphasizes only this structure of subordination. One has to keep in mind that the woman, in comparison to the man, is depicted as being capable of greater subtlety, and that this image has its source precisely in entrusting to her the development and the differentiation of feelings. To give but one example, when Rousseau characterizes the virtue of women, it is not about asceticism, as many authors have accused him, but rather the woman must learn to express her desires in a different, indirect way. "Her fate would be too cruel if, even in the case of legitimate desires, she did not have a language equivalent to the one she dare not use. Must her modesty make her unhappy: Must she not have an art of communicating her inclinations without laying them bare?"[64] In consequence of this thought, a more complex language is ascribed to women as well as the ability to perceive nuances, in particular nonverbal ones.[65]

That Rousseau lends larger subtlety to women in this way leads him to present the actual, final objective of the future historical developments in a literary female character. This will be explained in the following section.

The Utopia of the Unity of Art and Nature

As for the just state, so also for morality, Rousseau develops in his outline for the future yet another more far-reaching perspective. This is true in particular with regard to his book *La Nouvelle Héloïse*. (As he did in referring

---

ing to that line of thought, Rousseau also interprets the woman's shame as a substitute for the "instinct of beasts" of the female animal (ibid.). This is not the place to reproach Rousseau for reducing women, in contrast to men, to their biology; the problem lies rather in the fact that modesty is ascribed to them as a specific and constant characteristic that is independent from history.

62. Kofmann, *Rousseau und die Frauen*, 20.
63. Ibid., 26.
64. Rousseau, *Emile*, 385.
65. Ibid., 383f. For a more complex analysis of men's and women's language in Rousseau's work, see Garbe, *Die "weibliche" List*, 108–13.

to *Emile,* Rousseau could also say about this book that its actual subject is history.)

Rousseau shows that perfection is not necessarily achieved with morality, that morality remains limited as long as it solely bases action on reason. Rousseau demonstrates this in the figure of Monsieur de Wolmar, the man Julie, in order to go along with her father's wish, chooses to marry although she loves her former private tutor.[66] In a letter from Julie, Wolmar is characterized in detail. On the one hand, there is no doubt that to act on the basis of reason represents a legitimate ideal. Thus one reads, "With all the trouble that I have taken to observe him, I have not been able to find passion of any kind in him except that which he has for me. Yet this passion is so even and so temperate that one would say that he loves only as much as he wishes to and that he wishes to only as much as reason permits. . . . In this respect, I find him much superior to all our men of feeling whom we ourselves admire so much, for our hearts deceive us in a thousand ways and act only according to an always secret principle; but the reason has no other end except that which is good, its rules are sure, clear, practicable in the conduct of life."[67] But at the same time, the boundaries of such an attitude also become clear; in the same letter Julie states, "I have never seen him either gay or sad. . . . He does not laugh; he is serious."[68] And further, "If I were as calm as he, too much coldness would reign between us and would make our union less agreeable and less sweet."[69] The similarity with Emile, the solitary one, who experiences the limits of justice, seems obvious.

Julie represents an ideal that goes beyond mere reason. It has to do with a different way of dealing with passions. Indeed, the passions should be

---

66. The meaning of the fatherly law in this novel is examined by Ingvild Birkhan. "In the beginning of the novel *La Nouvelle Héloïse,* one finds the erotic inflammation, but also the 'no' of Julie's father is located almost in the same way in the beginning. Instantly, love is also found as knowing about its violation against the patriarchal order illustrated here by the specific fatherly will. I believe this will stands symptomatically and principally for the dominion of the father that the woman is not supposed to leave" ("Die Psyche der Frau im Schatten der Mutter: Gedanken zur Strukturierung der bürgerlichen Liebe," in *Das Weib existiert nicht für sich: Geschlechterbeziehungen in der bürgerlichen Gesellschaft,* ed. Heide Dienst and Edith Saurer [Vienna, 1990], 89).
67. Rousseau, *La Nouvelle Héloïse,* 260.
68. Ibid.
69. Ibid., 262. Also for Klaus Dirscherl, "it becomes clear, Wolmar is not that perfect, as he at first seems. . . . The difference between Wolmar and Julie is immense. Wolmar acts entirely rationally, and Julie heroically changes her former *amour passion* into an *amour sagesse*" ("Der Roman der Philosophen: Diderot—Rousseau—Voltaire," *Romanica Monacensia* 23 [1985]: 112).

controlled, but at the same time they should remain present. Reason should not replace feelings but should rather be connected to them in a harmonious whole. Ernst Cassirer locates the actual core of Rousseau's philosophy here: "From the beginning, his entire thinking is concerned with the problem of 'bliss.' It searches for a unity, a harmony between virtue and bliss."[70] Cassirer relates this search to the "eudaemonism, which dominates the entire ethics of the eighteenth century."[71] It also seems worth regarding that Rousseau anticipates here essential elements of Schiller's concept of the *schöne Seele* (beautiful soul).

What does it mean, that this ideal in Rousseau's work (and not only in his) is personified by a female character? The dichotomous design of the characteristics of genders discussed above needs to be considered here once more. As has already been mentioned, it is constructed in a way that the woman has no place within the framework of the modern life. This creates the opportunity for men to project that dimension of life which they miss in their sphere onto the woman. In this way, the feminine becomes the utopia of the modern age.[72] It should not be overlooked, however, that the fact that women are excluded from modern life is not changed by that, but rather it is strengthened.

In one of her letters Julie writes, "Isn't it very unworthy for a human, when he cannot live together with himself in harmony, when he has one guiding principle for his actions and another for his feelings, when he thinks as if he has no body, and acts as if he has no soul, and when he is unable to fully appropriate anything of what he does during his entire life?"[73] This topic, the mediation of reason and feeling, is above all explained in the last part of the novel (in an abundance of nuances that cannot be examined in entirety here). The relationship between Julie and St. Preux, her former private tutor, does not break off with Julie's marriage. Julie endeavors rather to bring both commitments into harmony. In a letter to St. Preux written shortly after her wedding, she initially voices her criticism about adulterers,

70. Ernst Cassirer, *Das Problem Jean-Jacques Rousseau* (Darmstadt, 1975), 28.
71. Ibid.
72. Cf. Herta Nagl-Docekal, "Von der feministischen Transformation der Philosophie," in *Ethik und Sozialwissenschaften: Streitforum für Erwägungskultur* 3, vol. 4 (1992), in particular the section entitled, "Die Frau als Utopie der Moderne," 528f. The process of idealizing the feminine is pursued in detail by Cornelia Klinger as well; "Woman—Landscape—Artwork: Alternative Realms or Patriarchal Reserves?" Chapter 6 in this book.
73. This passage is not found in the English edition used here. It is quoted from the German edition: Jean-Jacques Rousseau, *Julie oder Die neue Héloïse: Briefe zweier Liebenden aus einer keinen Stadt am Fuße der Alpen* (Munich, 1988), 378.

and then she outlines her perspective: "Love is nothing for them but a shameful relationship, and they lose honor without finding happiness. . . . Is it not better to purify so dear a sentiment to make it lasting? Is it not better to save of it at least that part which can concur with innocence? Is that not to save all of it that was most charming? . . . I shall love you always, do not doubt it. The sentiment which attaches me to you is still so tender and so lively that another woman would perhaps be alarmed by it."[74] Only with regard to the perspective of harmonization that is aspired to here is it justified to interpret Rousseau's philosophy of history by means of the postulate "back to nature"—although one has to keep in mind that even in this case it has actually nothing to do with a return. Rather, morality should be practiced in such a manner that it can provide room for feelings to develop as natural inclinations.

This thought is presented first of all in metaphorical form. The metaphor is Julie's garden, of which a letter from St. Preux gives a detailed account. This garden was laid out by Julie in such a way that the observer is under the impression that it is nature in its original form. St. Preux reports, "At the same time I thought I saw the wildest, the most solitary place in nature, and it seemed I was the first mortal who had ever penetrated into this desert island. Surprised, impressed, ecstatic over a sight so little expected, I remained motionless for a moment, and cried out with involuntary enthusiasm, 'Oh Tinian! Oh Juan Fernandez! Julie, the world's end is at your threshold' " (492). St. Preux let himself be set right by Julie, " 'It is true,' she said, 'that nature has done everything, but under my direction, and there is nothing here which I have not ordered. . . . Go farther within, and you will understand. Adieu Tinian, adieu Juan Fernandez . . . !' "(492). However, although the artificiality of the garden is repeatedly pointed out in this manner to St. Preux, his original impression always is renewed.

Julie calls her garden "Elysium," and in this name an ambivalence is announced. St. Preux reports the relevant part of the conversation with Julie in the garden: " 'Well, what do you think of it?' she said to me as we were returning. 'Are you still at the world's end?' 'No,' I said, 'Here I am completely out of the world, and you have in fact transported me into Elysium.' "(310). This passage alludes to the problem that the desired reconciliation of reason and feeling cannot be achieved in reality, but only can be thought of as happening "out of the world." This tension remains decisive for the rest of the novel.

---

74. Rousseau, *La Nouvelle Héloïse*, 255.

If one follows how the individuals are depicted in this conversation, it is noticeable that for Julie, although the impression of naturalness seems perfect, the efforts behind it cannot be made to disappear. For example, she says "Those who love nature and cannot go seek it so far away are reduced to doing it violence, to forcing it in some manner to come dwell with them, and all this cannot be effected without a little illusion"(312). In other words, for Julie, virtue retains a background of coercion and of violence against nature.[75]

This tension becomes an open ambivalence in connection with Julie's death. As Christine Garbe pointed out, Julie interprets her forthcoming death for various people in different ways. She speaks to Wolmar and to her cousin and confidante Clara about the extent of her happiness: "My happiness, that had gradually increased, had now reached the highest summit."[76] But in her last letter to St. Preux, she emphasizes that virtue never belonged to her as a kind of a second nature: "You had thought me cured of my love for you, and I thought I was too. Let us give thanks to the One who made that delusion last as long as it was useful. Who knows whether, seeing that I was so close to the abyss, I might not have lost my head?"[77] From this point, Julie views her death in another light. "Haven't I lived long enough for happiness and virtue? . . . After so many sacrifices, I consider the last one that I have to make as insignificant. It only means to have to die one more time."[78] Garbe seems justified in asking, "Was Julie at the peak of happiness or at the abyss of passions? Or was the peak of her happiness at the same time the edge of the abyss?"[79] At the end of the book, Rousseau works out the topic of ambiguity with great sophistication. The report of Julie's death contains a series of Christological motives, which at the same time are taken back. Thus, some persons present see Julie as raised from the dead, and the family has to dispel this false perception. Furthermore, on her deathbed, Julie speaks words unmistakably reminiscent of the New Testament: "I am not actually leaving you. I shall be with you. By

---

75. Lieselotte Steinbrügge does not go into this element of the text. She comments on Julie, that "her virtuous behavior is not the result of effort, but the realization, the unfolding of her nature." Cf. Steinbrügge, *Das moralische Geschlecht*, 49. For Steinbrügge, the "Elysée" has no ambivalent features for that reason. "Rather, it embodies the world of the woman, in which . . . the utopian program of social harmony in Rousseau's work is realized in a perfect way." Cf. ibid., 95f.
76. Rousseau, *Julie oder Die neue Héloïse*, 763 (cf. note 73).
77. Rousseau, *La Nouvelle Héloïse*, 405.
78. Rousseau, *Julie oder Die neue Héloïse*, 778 (cf. note 73).
79. Garbe, *Die "weibliche" List*, 179.

leaving you united, my spirit and my heart will remain with you. You will always feel that I am with you."[80] However, her expectation is not fulfilled. The circle of her loved ones gives the impression of hopelessness after Julie's death.[81]

In this way Rousseau reaches a culmination in which philosophy of history points beyond itself. The project for human praxis that he outlines leads in its final consequence to an ideal that is unachievable within the course of history. Thus it seems that Rousseau ultimately intends to draw our attention, albeit in an indirect manner, to eschatological issues.

80. Rousseau, *Julie oder Die neue Héloïse*, 763 (cf. note 73).
81. Tony Tanner paid particular attention to this failure: "At the end, all bonds have snapped: father, husband, cousin, lover, children, thrown back or turned in upon themselves, wandering around in a daze of misery without communication. . . . There is a glimpse here of that unspeakable solitude at the heart of all relationships which every other page of the book works to transcend or to conceal or to deny" ("Julie and 'La Maison Paternelle': Another Look at Rousseau's *La Nouvelle Héloïse*," in *The Family in Political Thought*, ed. Jean Bethke Elshtain [Brighton, 1982], 124).

4 SCHOPENHAUER OR KANT
Gender Difference Between Critique and Spirit of the Age

Ursula Pia Jauch

Translated by James Dodd

Kant, that otherwise fruitful and treasured source of Schopenhauer's thought, appears to have been a complete failure with respect to particular knowledge of a metaphysical object—namely, the gender difference. At any rate, Schopenhauer in 1844 was critical: "Kant's discussion of the subject in the third section of the essay 'On the Feeling of the Beautiful and the Sublime' . . . is very superficial and without special knowledge; thus it is also

This essay originally appeared under the title "Schopenhauer oder Kant: Geschlechterdifferenz zwischen Zeitkritik und Zeitgeist," in *Schopenhauer in der Postmoderne: Jahrbuch der Internationalen Schopenhauer-Vereinigung,* ed. Wolfgang Schirmacher (= Schopenhauer-Studien vol. 3) (Vienna, 1989), 49–58.

partly incorrect."[1] The familiar title of the discourse in which Schopenhauer introduces gender difference as a particular metaphysical object is "Metaphysics of Sexual Love." The title of the criticized Kantian treatise that deals with the object under consideration, "Of the Distinction Between the Beautiful and the Sublime in the Interrelations of the Two Sexes,"[2] has a somewhat more aesthetic than metaphysical connotation. Both investigations, Kant's of 1764 and Schopenhauer's of 1844, claim that they have recognized something essential with respect to the vinculum of the genders. And both authors, Kant and Schopenhauer, have a similarly tangled relationship with one another, and not only with respect to gender difference.

Moreover, since I have given my contribution the slightly eccentric title "Schopenhauer or Kant: Gender Difference Between Critique and Spirit of the Age," I will, for the sake of clarity, begin with an outline of what I have in mind. I first show by way of two examples what in fact I do *not* have in mind—namely, the further perpetuation of canonical feminism. I then attempt to show in two points how this nevertheless could be done in relating Kant and Schopenhauer with respect to gender difference. Thus, along with the two versions of methodological prelude, there will be two points with the following titles: 1. Feminist epistemology as critique of the age, with the example of Schopenhauer and Kant; and 2. *Zeitgeist* as manifestation of an ethics of sexual difference.

Toward a Methodological Prelude

The theme—Kant, Schopenhauer, and gender difference—is enticing; and to be sure, a comparison of only a few passages from Kant's "Of the Distinction Between the Beautiful and the Sublime in the Interrelations of the Two Sexes" and from Schopenhauer's "Metaphysics of Sexual Love" illuminates the assessment of gender difference as it had been part of the prevailing spirit of the age. This had, of course, also been the old position of the women's movement which, with the sharp vision of the injured, and being in fact

---

1. Arthur Schopenhauer, *The World as Will and Representation,* vol. 2, trans. E. F. J. Payne (New York: Dover, 1966), 533; *Die Welt als Wille und Vorstellung* [= WWV], II, in *Sämtliche Werke* II, ed. Löhneysen (Stuttgart: Cotta-Insel, 1976), 681.

2. Cf. Immanuel Kant, *Observations on the Feeling of the Beautiful and the Sublime,* trans. John T. Goldthwait (Berkeley and Los Angeles: University of California Press, 1960); Akademieausgabe [= Ak] II:205ff.

on the losing side in the history of philosophy, questioned the texts of male authors concerning their degree of misogyny and, after rigorous feminist interrogation, reached more often than not a smashing verdict. As an exercise, I will once more play out this classical-feminist procedure with respect to the passages from Kant and Schopenhauer. It runs something like the following:

At the beginning of his "Observations" on the relation of the genders, Kant reflects on the strange practice of giving women, *pars pro toto,* the title of "the fair sex." According to Kant, he who "first conceived of woman under the name of the *fair sex*" had perhaps intended to be flattering, yet he was closer to the mark than he himself would have believed. For, according to Kant, "without taking into consideration that her figure in general is finer, her features more delicate and gentler, and her mien more engaging and more expressive of friendliness, pleasantry, and kindness than the male sex"—Kant, the distinguished ladies' man—"even so, certain specific traits lie especially in the personality of this sex which distinguish it clearly from our own and chiefly result in making her known by the mark of the beautiful."[3] So far Kant. Now Schopenhauer, almost eighty-seven years later, supposedly taking up the discussion with Kant on the aesthetic of the "fair sex" directly: "Only a male intellect clouded by the sexual drive could call the stunted, narrow-shouldered, broad-hipped and short-legged sex the fair sex: for it is with this drive that all its beauty is bound up. More fittingly than the fair sex, women could be called the *unaesthetic* sex."[4] So far Schopenhauer. The feminist judgment in the dispute between Kant and Schopenhauer concerning the "fair sex" should fall in favor of Kant's superior charm, even if he is not free of all canonical doubt. Schopenhauer, on the other hand, was and is cast as a churlish misogynist.

For another example, one that is incendiary in the context of the current debate over equality and gender difference, take the following remark of Schopenhauer's: "Woman in the Occident, that is to say the 'lady,' finds herself in a false position: for woman (justifiably called by the ancients *sexus sequior*) is by no means fitted . . . to hold her head higher than the man or to enjoy equal rights with him. The consequences of this false position are equally obvious. . . . (The Salic law, a superfluous truism, should not be

---

3. Kant, *Observations,* 76; Ak II:228.
4. Schopenhauer, "On Women," in *Essays and Aphorisms,* trans. R. J. Hollingdale (New York: Penguin, 1976), 85; *Parerga und Paralipomena: Kleine philosophische Schriften* [= PuP] II, in *Sämtliche Werke* V, ed. Löhneysen (Stuttgart: Cotta-Insel, 1965), § 369, p. 725f.

necessary.) The European lady is a creature which ought not to exist at all."[5] Contrast this with a statement by Kant on equality and the gender difference. In §26 of the *Metaphysics of Morals,* the "Rechtslehre," Kant defines the "relation of marrieds" as one of "equality of ownership, both as the mutual ownership of persons . . . as well as goods."[6] Even feminine gregariousness, which Schopenhauer finds so reprehensible in what he describes as the monstrous construct of the European lady, finds a positive assessment in Kant, for whom "woman is the best proof that humanity is made to be, in the joys of life, well disposed, neither weighed down nor anxious. After they [i.e., women] are brought into society, everything becomes convivial"[7] Here too the canonical feminist indictment could denounce Schopenhauer as misogynist; Kant demonstrates an evident sensibility to the necessity of equal conditions in the conscientious formation of gender-specific living arrangements.

Enough with what I *don't* want to do. Is there another, nonorthodox possibility of talking about the different valuations of gender difference given by Kant and Schopenhauer? Can extending the Schopenhauerian "On Women" with unimaginative pronouncements "On Schopenhauer" that are just as dependent on, as they are uncritical of, the prevailing *Zeitgeist* be avoided? I believe that there is such a possibility, and I propose to replace the classical, orthodox discourse about the "other" gender (sometimes the "false" gender, more recently the "different" gender)—with a discourse as differently gendered subjects, on the object of gender difference. This brings me to my first additional point:

Feminist Epistemology as Critique of the Age, with the Example of Schopenhauer and Kant

In order to elaborate this, I propose the following working thesis: feminist self-critique as critique of the age has brought the orthodox discussion—thus the emphasis on male prejudices against women—to a discourse on gender difference *as such,* one that is both modest and hesitant. This means that it is the sexual being of the judging and knowledge-seeking subject that

---

5. Schopenhauer, "On Women," 87; PuP II, § 369, p. 728f.
6. Cf. Kant, Ak VI:278.
7. Cf. Kant Ak XV/2:569, Reflexion 1287.

accounts for the epistemological distortions of its power of judgment. It appears to me that, supported in this way both epistemologically and self-critically, a comparison between Schopenhauer and Kant could yet be ventured. A Schopenhauerian speculation "On Women" would thus be replaced by a reflection on the unity of human nature and the difference between the sexes, whereby philosophy (and this I take to be incontestable) can best secure the ever-dangerous path of a science (i.e., a *minimally prejudicial* science) in areas of sexual difference. Here, I believe, lies the essential difference between canonical and postcanonical critique.

To show this by using the example of Kant or Schopenhauer, postcanonical critique would first of all have to be a feminist critique of the *Zeitgeist*-relative discourse either of "On Women" or of the "Interrelations of the Two Sexes." Postdogmatic feminism as critique of the age makes the modest demand that the philosophical gaze does not treat these strange natural entities that fall under the names of woman, female, "fair sex," ladies, and other rubrics of feminine existence as exotic objects of investigation. Freed from essentialist and biological classifications as gendered subjects, we can begin to reflect on gender difference as such. That holds precisely for the contemporary attempts to overturn the classical male perspective in the history of philosophy, that is, the displacement of the "male" view with the "feminine" view: feminist judgment must also account for its own prejudicial limitedness. It would, in fact, prove the intellectual poverty of feminist critique of the age if it were to merely displace "On Women" talk with "On Schopenhauer" talk.

With respect to the reflection on one's own prejudices and those of the age, Kant and Schopenhauer have themselves occasionally paved the way for us, insofar as they made a certain type of view, that of the "other" gender, an object of their reflections. This is precisely what Schopenhauer means when he identifies the male intellect *clouded* by sexual desire as the origin of the beauty of the feminine sex. Sexual appetite obscures; thus for Schopenhauer it also reduces the possibility of "objective" knowledge. The discussion of the male intellect clouded by sexual desire corresponds in epistemological content to the argument that as sexual beings the possibility of our achieving insights that would hold universally for sexual subjects is conditioned. In this way Schopenhauer may well have contributed to a gendered critique of metaphysics *avant la lettre*.

In Kant one also occasionally finds something like a reflection on a genuine unclarity with respect to knowledge of the thing in itself that is relative to the sex of the subject who desires to know. Even in "Observations on the Feeling of the Beautiful and the Sublime," Kant introduces, relatively uncritically, the totality of all men with the plural "we," the male "we" that is entitled to judge feminine forms of life. The advantages of femininity are formulated within a blatantly male perspective.[8] By contrast, in his *Anthropology from a Practical Point of View,* one can discern what is at least a certain sensibility for the fact that what is understood by femininity is relative to the male perspective. For Kant the inquiry into femininity suddenly has to do with "characterizing the feminine sex" by using "the principle which served as Nature's end in the creation of femininity, and not what we have devised ourselves as its end."[9] Yet the idea that there may actually be epistemological unclarities caused by gender appears to have occurred to Kant only in the 1790s. In a letter to Schiller from 1795, Kant affirms the jurisdiction of critical reason for the reflection on the gender difference. The fact that not unity but difference is necessary for the reproduction of the human species, as it is in the realm of organic nature, had "always" struck Kant as "amazing and as a sort of chasm of thought" for reason.[10] In my opinion, this "chasm of thought," an exceptionally enigmatic formulation for an otherwise meticulous critic of reason, points more toward the epistemological consequences of gender difference than to some sort of fear that Kant had of the different, "other" gender.

Let us take another example from Kant, this time from 1764—and here I would like to point to an initial difference between Kant and Schopenhauer—where he supplies what is at least a modest epistemological metareflection on the position of the analysis vis-à-vis its object, the "Interrelations of the Sexes." For at the beginning of his observations, Kant cautiously states that "here it is not enough to keep in mind that we are dealing with human beings." Rather, one needs to take care at the same time not to leave out of consideration that "they are not all alike"[11] and that he, Kant, precisely because of the epistemological distortion of the male perspective, will not proceed in this case as a philosopher in possession of the truth, but as an "observer," one who is implicated in the possibility of knowing the matter itself.

By contrast, in 1844 this epistemologically relevant position of the phi-

---

8. Cf. Kant, *Observations,* 76ff; Ak II:228ff.

9. Kant, *Anthropology from a Pragmatic Point of View,* trans. V. L. Dowdell (Carbondale: Southern Illinois University Press, 1996), 219; Ak VII:305.

10. Kant, *Philosophical Correspondence, 1759–99,* trans. Arnulf Zweig (Chicago: University of Chicago Press, 1967), 221; Ak XII:11.

11. Kant, *Observations,* 77; Ak II:228.

losopher who is always at the same time a gendered subject can barely be teased out of Schopenhauer, even if while speculating on the "metaphysics of sexual love" he all the while ascribes his reflections on the meaning and status of femininity within the tension of gender relations. Yet in his 1851 "On Women," that literary product of a crippled faculty of self criticism, prejudice, and knowledge, the "women" mentioned in the title still appear only as singular, isolated objects of a metaphysical reflection that places itself squarely on the other side of the tension between the unity of human nature and the difference of sex.

Now whereas in Schopenhauer the discussion only deals with the damage done by sexual desire to the male ability to know, that is, exclusively with respect to the female other objectified by this desire, the same does not hold for women. The feminine power of judgment is generally disqualified because of gender specificity; women are "everywhere stuck in the subjective"; they lack "all objectivity of mind." By contrast, the exposition of objectivity in the male intellect occurs, according to Schopenhauer, only in the contingent case of precisely the active male sexual drive.[12]

Back to Kant, trembling before the chasm threatening to devour reason that had suddenly yawned before him in the guise of the gender difference. Kant expressed—*contre coeur,* so to speak—the issue of contemporary feminist epistemological critique insofar as he began to recognize an abyss for reason in the fact of gender difference, while up to then reason had been hypostatized as objective, capable of truth, and gender neutral. Kant was seldom in his epistemology so close to a questioning rationality; that is, to considering if reason, which for the most part has been (unjustifiably) represented in the history of philosophy as gender neutral, were nevertheless dependent on a conception of reason mediated by the masculinity of traditional thinkers. Here—trailing along behind the *Critique of Pure Reason*—we have the problem of unity and plurality casting a shadow over Kant's earlier exclusion of gender difference from the efforts of critical reason to reflect upon its possibilities and limits.

What I mean is that these undertakings of both Kant and Schopenhauer cannot, if they intend to be a critique of metaphysics, get by without proving their own indetermination, understood here as a nondetermination by gendered perspective.

Now what does all this have to do with *Zeitkritik* and *Zeitgeist?* To conclude and sum up this step, I would like to formulate my first point in the

12. Cf. Schopenhauer, "On Women," 86; PuP II, § 369, p. 727.

following fashion: Feminist critique of the age has at least led from a discourse about women that is dependent on the spirit of the age, to a discourse about gender difference as such. For the moment I will leave open whether this new manner of discourse is not just as dependent on the spirit of our age as "On Women" had been in its own time.

Any critique of an age, however, has at least one presupposition: the ability to think against the dominant spirit of the age, its *Zeitgeist*. Critique presupposes the ability to relate both to the other and to the self in a way that is critical of prejudice. Feminist critique of the age as epistemological critique is enlightened feminism, which means that the subject speculating, arguing, and conjecturing about the other sex is in turn conscious of itself as gendered. The discussion of the gender difference at least means that the gender that had, for the most part with the connotation of a negative anthropology, traditionally been designated as the "other" sex (also as the "false sex," thus "women") will no longer be the only element to be raised to the level of a metaphysical object, but instead the object will be gender difference itself as incarnation of ontological difference. In keeping with the tradition of the schools, ontological difference, as difference, demands first of all the "correct" approach to the differing other; that is, an approach that bases itself on an ethical theory. With this I come to:

The Ethics of Sexual Difference as Manifestation of *Zeitgeist*

As is already known, Schopenhauer gives his reflections on the relation of the sexes the eloquent title "Metaphysics of Sexual Love." Of course in Schopenhauer this can only be meant polemically: the relations between the sexes are neither moral nor metaphysical in that they require neither morality nor metaphysics. Now there is, to be sure, in Schopenhauer no *meta ta fusika;* what dominates is *fusis,* the pure mechanics of drive that is at play beyond the individuated intentions of the will of apparent agents. Without any metaphysics, sexual love, the putative desire of love, dangles on the apron strings of a blindly driving preservation of the species independent of human comprehension. When Schopenhauer describes male genitalia as the "focus of the will," this is—though striking—nothing more than a *façon de parler.* The reproduction-driven male is just as shrouded in desire as he was before with respect to his ability to know. The pure mechanics of the drive to propagate, which arises as the goal of the species, undermines any attempt to ground a "metaphysics of sexual love"; in particular, it undermines any serious attempt to shore up the steep terrain between the sexes with the trusses of a sexual ethics.

Here Schopenhauer expresses the pure sexual pessimism of the nineteenth century; he underwrites the bourgeois sexual morality that culminates in the idea of bourgeois marriage. It is a marital or legal-positivistic climax that is related to the omnipotent right to dispose of the female body, including the practical legal permissibility of marital rape. It is also a sexual pessimism insofar as there can be no mediation between desire and a moral theory of action. As if by remote control, the goal of the species fills men with desire, the modalities of this goal being inaccessible to the subject wandering about in his individuation.

Whoever would wish to object that, nevertheless, the Schopenhauerian ethics of compassion have something to add here, would again be disappointed. For precisely here the "silencing of all and every willing [das Quietiv alles und jedes Wollens]"—which Schopenhauer, in order to moderate an all-too-egotistical dynamic of the pure will, proposes in § 68 of the fourth book of *The World as Will and Representation*—fails. Though compassion may very well include that ability in certain moments to extend the intensity of the bodily experience of the will beyond one's own corporeal limitation to fellow human beings, nevertheless Schopenhauerian compassion-ethics bears little similarity to an insight into a moral counterbalance or a quasi-rational moral law. For Schopenhauer, compassion does not lead to any type of compassion *ethics*, because in general it lacks the power of, for example, a Kantian or a deontological moral rationality. It is not the rational human being in accordance with the moral law (i.e., the human being that wills to act morally) that stands behind the silencing of every willing, but the pure mechanics of the will that "now" turns humans away "from life": it is the will, not humans, that "shudder[s] at the pleasures in which it recognizes the affirmation of life." Thus it is beyond moral reason that the human attains "the state of voluntary renunciation, resignation, true composure, and complete will-lessness."[13] With that, sexual desire in Schopenhauer falls within the paradigm of the transcendentally controlling will independent of individuated human desires, even when it is to be moderated by the silencer of every willing.

---

13. Schopenhauer, *The World as Will and Representation*, vol. 1, § 68, p. 379; WWV I, bk. 4, § 68, p. 515.

Yet Schopenhauer is uncertain: freedom or necessity? Moral law or pure mechanics of desire? Even in the margin, where Schopenhauer confesses that the "effect of the silencing" is in the end "an act of freedom of the will," Schopenhauerian sexual pessimism remains as a consequence of the pure desire-mechanics of the will. Against all Kantianizing appropriations and attempts at system amalgamation, desire follows the model of instinctive act, the consequence of which is that the individual person is not to be held accountable; desire is inaccessible for the modalities of an ethical ought.

Under his own suffocating sexual pessimism, Schopenhauer, in my opinion, succumbs uncritically to the shameful spirit of the nineteenth century. This spirit, by help of an equalizing mechanism under the guise of sexual ethics, had completely wiped away the needs of the female sex, which had found itself in a weaker position anyway in the pursuit of its interests within the mechanics of desire.

With Kant it is different. In his precritical phase, Kant was also sexually pessimistic with respect to the coincidence of the natural necessity of desire with the freedom of the will. Sexuality, understood as the natural desire of humans, has for Kant, first of all, only the connotation of a distortion of the idea of humanity. This is somewhat evident in the following remark from the *Ethik Menzer:*[14] "The affection that one has for a woman does not have to do with her as a human being, but because she is a woman, accordingly a man is indifferent to the humanity of woman, only the sex is the object of his affection" (206). What for contemporary eyes may appear as quasi-protofeminist content of this quotation does not really, in my view, amount to a feminist conception—that is, one tied to female-emancipative interests—but rather only manifests the proximity of feminist argumentation in the history of ideas to the prejudice-critical Enlightenment.

In Kant's 1798 *Anthropology,* which has since been branded by canonical feminism as the most misogynist, there occurs a remark that can—*avant la lettre,* so to speak—be justifiably called an insight into the commodity character of sexuality. It has to do with the object of a marital sexual ethics: "Eccentric thinking along this line would only have bad consequences on the whole feminine sex, because it would degrade the woman to a mere means of satisfying the desires of the other sex."[15] Sexuality, although its

---

14. Kant, *Ethik Menzer*. This lecture transcript comprises Kant's moral-philosophical lectures of the years 1775–80.

15. Kant, *Anthropology,* 223; Ak VII:309.

resemblance to commodities and means is recognized as a mirror image of the early bourgeois relations that surround it, should be neither marginalized nor driven out, and certainly not deproblematized with a pessimistic *laissez-faire laissez-aller*. Sexuality is understood by Kant as *a necessitas naturalis* that does not, as philosophy had done up to that point, suggest the shamefulness of sexual desire, but that at most calls for an inquiry into the conditions under which sexuality is morally possible.

The Kantian program of sexual ethics runs thus: "Accordingly, conditions must be possible under which alone the employment of the *facultatum sexualium* corresponds to morality. There must be a reason [*Grund*] that restrains our freedom with respect to the employment of our inclinations, such that they are congruent with morality."[16] Thus Kant is searching for the place where sexuality and morality are congruent against the backdrop of gender difference.

Now whether Kant himself carried out this astonishingly "modern" program of sexual difference ethics is doubtful. But at any rate he outlines—and this is worth noting within the perspective of the contemporary discussion about gender difference as a mode of *Zeitkritik*—the foundation of a sexual ethics that remains to be established concretely, that is, one understood as an ethics of sexual difference in which the needs and satisfactions of different genders have a place.

Schopenhauer or Kant—or: Schopenhauerian or Kantian *Zeitgeist?* It appears to me sensible for contemporary feminist critique of the age to appropriate, in an undogmatic sense, the Enlightenment critique of prejudice as it was represented by Kant, even with respect to the gender difference, instead of continuing to insist on questions of the discourse on the "other" gender as represented by Schopenhauer, whether negative or positive. Schopenhauer, in questions of sexual difference, is completely obsessed with the polarizing and crude misogynous spirit of the nineteenth century. He is a too-comfortable, too-easy adversary for an intelligent feminist critique. If today there is talk of a renaissance of Schopenhauer as a fundamental critic of the age, at least in this case this is not so. In fact, as epistemology and critique of prejudice, feminist theory has better things to do than once more celebrating in Schopenhauer the old sentimentality and self-pity of feminine existence in the history of philosophy.

One can be convinced that Schopenhauer should be put through the mill

---

16. Kant, *Ethik Menzer*, 207.

of a postcanonical critique and thereby, however much contrary to expectations, experience something of the same fate he had in canonical feminism.

I will leave it to the reader to reach such a conclusion. Rather, in closing I would like to invoke the title of this essay, which in retrospect I could easily revise as *Neither Schopenhauer nor Kant*. Feminist critique of the age, as epistemology, can finally come of age, be content, and in *friendly* and *honest* indebtedness detach itself from the apron strings of the history of philosophy.

Nevertheless, let us put forward one last contentious word to Schopenhauer: he criticizes the Western tradition of metaphysics—and justifiably so—for its formidable effort to make the body disappear in thinking. But the way in which Schopenhauer himself brings the body back is by no means accidental, the body that can signify gender-differentiated being. Thus Schopenhauer places the body at the center of his metaphysics; yet in his hands, the body irreconcilably falls apart into the set pieces of gender difference.

5 THE FEMALE AS ETHICAL RESOURCE IN THE PHILOSOPHY OF HEGEL

Heidemarie Bennent-Vahle

Translated by Christine M. Manteghi

The Family as a Natural Moral Community

Fichte's concept of marriage, which on the surface seems to embrace the ideal of liberal, individualized love, upon closer scrutiny shows distinct signs of a moralization of the reinforcement of marriage as an institution. In the concept of feminine love, which implies an unconditional subordination of the wife to her husband, not only is all the inconstancy of feelings substan-

This essay originally appeared under the title "Das Weibliche als Reserveinstanz des Sittlichen und das 'andere' Recht der Familie in der Philosophie Hegels," in *Galanterie und Verachtung— Eine philosophiegeschichtliche Untersuchung zur Stellung der Frau in Gesellschaft und Kultur*, ed. Heidemarie Bennent (Frankfurt and New York: Campus Verlag, 1985), 138–70.

tially diminished, but also all sources of friction that could potentially threaten the peace of the marriage and the stability of the familial order are avoided from the outset. In Fichte's philosophy, the conception of a naturally, organically harmonious familial unit, whose private life is to be protected from interference by the law, does not constitute an antagonistic position toward public authority as it did in the minds of the early Romantics. Fichte rather seeks to establish the family as a sphere of private intimacy within the apparatus of the state, which maintains the state's ability to function by actually invalidating its laws.

The fact that, in comparison with Hegel, Fichte attaches a rather marginal importance to the legally immune family realm can, in my opinion, be explained by his optimistic view of the relationship between the individual and the established social order. His political philosophy is based on the belief that individual citizens can develop a positive relationship toward the legal system that governs them; that is, it is based on the idea of a reason-based decision on the part of all citizens to willingly accept the legislative authority. Insofar as the state does function as a restrictive authority but as such is developed according to the ideal of the social contract out of the needs of the individuals and their desire for freedom, its restrictive, rigid order takes on a positive, rational value. Because the objective, controlling authority of the state is empirically rooted in the general will of all, and in principle the individual is therefore positively preserved within the law, the opposing familial sphere can be given a place at the margin of society for the free self-development of the individual, although it is important in itself as well.

As will be demonstrated here, it is first in Hegel's writings that the family attains its full significance as a counterpart to public life and as its educational preparatory institution. Here the family is rescued from the periphery of society and elevated to the status of a fundamental building block of the established system of government. This rise in the political value of the family appears in the context of a new political theory of Hegel's, in which he noticeably distances himself from a political philosophy that is founded in contract law. Since the basis of Hegel's political theory can not be addressed here in broad terms, only some of the essential criteria will be summarized.

Hegel's philosophy of law no longer traces the universality of the state back to that which the multitude of individual wills has in common, but it rather grants the state an absolute objectivity that is detached from all social empiricism. The sovereign authority of the state is then only guaranteed when it is classified as a metaphysical dimension that reaches beyond all actually completed development: "In any case, however, it is absolutely essential that the constitution should not be regarded as something made, even though it has come into being in time. It must be treated rather as something simply existent in and by itself, as divine therefore, and constant, and so as exalted above the sphere of things that are made."[1]

In criticizing Kant's view of civil society, Hegel exposes the problem inherent in this universality that is built on a system of private needs; he draws attention to the conflicts that will inevitably emerge and will no longer be able to be controlled according to this society's principles. In order to guarantee the preservation of the social order, the state's governing power must be made independent from the private interests of its individual citizens.[2] According to Herbert Marcuse, "*Hegel's* illuminating critique of Kant's ethics is intended among other things to demonstrate the practical impossibility of the social universality proclaimed by *Kant* and to present a different, no longer social one as the basis of authority and as the realm where individual freedom is preserved."[3] As Marcuse explains, Hegel develops a definition of freedom in which every conflict between individual will and the objective potential to realize it is abandoned in favor of a "demarcation of freedom as reality."[4] Since an absolute claim forms its basis, the sustained orientation of this concept of freedom toward everyday life means a complete dissolution of the conflict between the individual and the living conditions of his social environment. Finally, it implies a voluntary conformity to the objective necessities and conditions in which these lose their arbitrary quality for the individual. The state itself represents the highest and most perfect embodiment of freedom, but only in an advanced stage of Western history: "The state is the Divine Idea as it exists on Earth. We have in it, therefore, the object of History in a more definite shape than before; that in which Freedom obtains objectivity, and lives in the enjoyment of this objectivity."[5] The integration into the state, which has an absolute worth, forms the basis

---

1. Georg Wilhelm Friedrich Hegel, *Hegel's Philosophy of Right*, trans. Knox (Oxford: Clarendon Press, 1942), 178. German: *Grundlinien der Philosophie des Rechts oder Naturrecht und Staatswissenschaft im Grundrisse*, vol. 7 of *Werke in zwanzig Bänden: Theorie Werkausgabe* (Frankfurt am Main, 1970), § 273, 439.

2. On the sovereignty of the state that is represented in the person of the monarch, see especially Franz Xaver von Baader, *Sätze aus der erotischen Philosophie*, vol. 4b of *Sämtliche Werke*, ed. Franz Hoffmann et al. (Aalen, 1963), § 278f., 442–49.

3. Herbert Marcuse, *Theoretische Entwürfe über Autorität und Familie, Studie über Autorität und Familie: Forschungsberichte aus dem Institut für Sozialforschung* (Paris, 1936), 179.

4. Ibid., 180.

5. Hegel, *The Philosophy of History*, trans. Sibree (New York: Dover, 1946), 39. German: *Vorlesungen über die Philosophie der Geschichte*, vol. 12 of *Werke*, 57.

of individual independence in the world: "For the Law is the objectivity of Spirit; volition in its true form. Only that will which obeys law is free, for it obeys itself—it is independent and so free."[6]

Because Hegel elevates the existing state to the embodiment of the rational essence of the human being, it then remains for the individual to subordinate himself unconditionally to the dominant norm. Freedom is achieved in the act of subordination. As Hegel explains, individuals must be educated by the various institutions of the state so that they develop the fundamental attitude necessary for a "spontaneous" integration into the existing order. The family is entrusted with significant obligations in this educational process, for it must provide for the moralization of the individual that makes his civic existence first possible.

If the principal function of the family lies in subsuming the immediate self-interest of the individual in a more general interest, as will be argued later in detail, then the family itself must have a strictly objective value that is superordinate to the individual emotional states of its members. Consequently, Hegel protests vehemently against the individual's claim to the unrestricted development of his emotional domain as propagated by the Romantics. He considers the Romantic coupling of love and marriage to be an unstable foundation for the private collective, and stresses instead the ethical quality of the family unit with which the individual should coalesce: "A third view of marriage is that which bases it on love alone, but this must be rejected like the other two, since love is only a feeling and so is exposed in every respect to contingency, a guise which ethical life may not assume. Marriage, therefore, is to be more precisely characterized as ethico-legal love, and this eliminates from marriage the transient, fickle, and purely subjective aspects of love."[7]

For Hegel, the public wedding ceremony is a necessary precondition for the ethical understanding of marriage. Similarly, in the case of the intention to separate, individual whims should not be given free reign, but rather an exact investigation of the situation based on the moral status of the marriage should be conducted by official agencies. The bond of matrimony was conceived for eternity and may be dissolved only in extremely exceptional cases:

> But it is on this account, too, that marriage must be regarded as in principle indissoluble, for the end of marriage is an ethical end, an

---

6. Ibid.
7. *Hegel's Philosophy of Right*, 262. German: *Grundlinien der Philosophie des Rechts*, § 161, 310.

end so lofty that everything else is manifestly powerless against it and made subject to it.... But it is not indissoluble except in principle, since as Christ says, only "for the hardness of your heart" is divorce established. Since marriage has feeling for one of its moments, it is not absolute but weak and potentially dissoluble. Legislators, however, must make its dissolution as difficult as possible and uphold the right of the ethical order against caprice.[8]

Although Hegel more strongly supports marriage and family as institutions than does Fichte, while at the same time granting an increased authority to the state supervising agency to have a say in cases of marital breakdown, he too generally rejects the interference of public authorities in private affairs.[9] Like Fichte, he sees man and woman (as well as the future children) as a single entity before the law. The relationships of family members to one another are a private matter and can be organized according to natural instinct into a harmonious whole without the interference of the state—as such, it is the immediate expression of a morality that stems from nature. Special entitlement to rights within the family is legally unfounded: "The *Family Relationship* is the natural union of individuals. The bond of this natural society is love and trust, the knowledge of this original union and of action in accordance with it. According to their particular relationships, the individuals composing this society possess particular rights; if these rights were asserted in the form of legal rights the moral bond of this society would be destroyed, that bond in which each receives what intrinsically belongs to him out of the sentiment of love."[10]

The love that holds the family circle together has a great moral significance in Hegel's philosophy of law. Thus, the erotic element of the marital relationship is substantially reduced, since this too obviously accommodates only the individual and, what is more, also attaches the stigma of instability to the marriage. The concept of morality once again takes on a strictly objective quality, after the early Romantics had defined it in a manner rebel-

---

8. Ibid., 263; § 163, 314.
9. He expressly objects to the concept of contractual marriages: "The union of persons of opposite sex which **Marriage** is, is not merely a *natural*, animal union, nor, at the other extreme, is it a mere *civil contract*, rather it is essentially a moral union of sentiment (Gesinnung) in reciprocal love and confidence which constitutes them one person" (Hegel, *The Philosophical Propaedeutic*, trans. Miller [Oxford: Blackwell, 1986], par. 51, p. 46. German: "Rechts-, Pflichten- und Religionslehre für die Unterklasse," in Hegel, *Texte zur Philosophischen Propädeutik*, vol. 4c of *Werke*, § 51, 265).
10. Ibid., par. 192, p. 164; § 192, 62.

liously opposed to the normative law. While it was maintained in the *Athenäum* fragments that "[t]he first inkling of morality appears in opposition to positive law and conventional right, and indicates an unlimited sensitivity of feeling,"[11] Hegel demands that "the law of morality" must be upheld "against caprice" or "in the face of individual desires."[12]

The unity of the family members, which is grounded in ethical love, is characterized in real life by the subordination of all members to the authority of the father: "Natural obedience within the family is based on the existence of a *single* will in this entity, which is namely that of the head of the family. In so far the family constitutes only *one* person."[13] On the basis of such a hierarchical internal family structure, Hegel's postulate of the ascendancy of the family principle over individual interests must have quite varied results for each family member. While the sacredness of the family unit—as will be shown—demands obedience and assimilation on the part of its members, it allows the father, who functions outside the family as its representative and within the family as its head, a relative development of his personality. This explains an apparent contradiction in Hegel's ideas: he designates the family, on the one hand, as the domain of individual freedom; and on the other hand, he stresses its objective, moral validity, which is completely detached from the personal interest of the individual.

The rigid concepts of marriage and family, which are oriented toward the absolute conception of the state, specifically, as they are presented in Hegel's philosophy of law, form a marked contrast to the seemingly revolutionary tone of his earlier writings. There, in exactly the manner of the Romantic rebellion, he attacks social institutions that, because they rest on the division between duty and inclination, are alienating, and that stand in conflict with love as a model of "reconciliation in the mutual understanding of the other."[14] Love symbolizes the possibility of a universally developed form of human existence within society that is not hindered by an unwieldy order. Ulrike Prokop remarks on the young Hegel's understanding of love: "This is how he interprets the concept of Christian love. The continual flow of social needs and interests requires no regulating legal institution due to the

---

11. Friedrich Schlegel, *Athenäums-Fragmente: Charakteristiken und Kritiken I*, ed. Hans Eichner, vol. 2 of *Kritische Friedrich-Schlegel-Ausgabe*, ed. Ernst Behler (Munich, 1967), fragment 425, 248. Trans. Manteghi.

12. *Hegel's Philosophy of Right*, 263; *Grundlinien der Philosophie des Rechts*, § 163, 314.

13. *The Philosophical Propaedeutic*, par. 23, p. 32; "Rechts-, Pflichten- und Religionslehre," § 23, 246.

14. Ulrike Prokop, *Weiblicher Lebenszusammenhang: Von der Beschränktheit der Strategien und der Unangemessenheit der Wünsche* (Frankfurt am Main, 1976), 163.

spontaneous harmony of all involved."[15] In his early period, Hegel develops an alternative to the fossilized duality established by society between individual desires and an order that denies their fulfillment. He designs a republic in which the social institutions are repeatedly changed and/or overcome by the realization of individual thinking and feeling within them. He sees Ancient Greece as the model for this republic[16]—there is "no definitive objectivity, no fixed objectivity that is defined for all eternity."[17]

Here the love in which the perfected human society is symbolized is not yet limited to personal relationships in the private sphere. It was in the light of growing skepticism toward the idealistically exaggerated and thus unrealizable Romantic position that a turning point in Hegel's thinking first emerged, in the course of which the difference between the subjective ethical love of the private family unit and the objective ethical order of the state is gradually established. However, before family life can join in peaceful harmony with the public sphere, as his philosophy of law or other later works depict, a long history of persistent struggles occurs in which the spirit of contradiction present in the familial principle becomes apparent.

The *Phänomenologie des Geistes* [Phenomenology of the Spirit] pays tribute to the very earliest separation of morality into a divine (familial) and a human (political) law—two sides, whose conflict with one another provides the impetus for the dialectical progression of history starting with the fall of the Greeks. The beginning stages of this struggle will be analyzed as precisely as possible in what follows, in order to examine the fundamental principle of a dialectic that reflects the relationship between the sexes. Only one thing will be revealed in advance—that the picture of the family in ancient society presented in the *Phänomenologie* is in stark contrast to the strict organization of the nuclear family of Hegel's time. The originally loving bond among blood-related family members that stands opposite to the iron supremacy of the state has little in common with the educational drill of civil child rearing, whose function is "to break down the child's self-will, and thereby eradicate his purely natural and sensuous self."[18] With refer-

---

15. Ibid., 162.
16. Georg Lukács, *The Young Hegel*, trans. Livingsone (London: Merlin Press, 1975), 84. German: *Der junge Hegel: Über die Beziehungen von Dialektik und Ökonomie*, vol. 8 of *Werke* (Neuwied, 1967), 128f.
17. Prokop, *Weiblicher Lebenszusammenhang*, 164. On the dialectical concept of life and love of the young Hegel, see Petra Christian, *Einheit und Zwiespalt: Zum hegelianisierenden Denken in der Philosophie und Soziologie Georg Simmels*, Soziologische Schriften 27 (Berlin, n.d.), chap. 3.
18. *Hegel's Philosophy of Right*, 265; *Grundlinien der Philosophie des Rechts*, § 174, 327.

ence to this, Bloch notes the gradual transformation of what is originally the music to a love song into "the virtuous life of the model family."[19] Why nothing of the hints of matriarchy that are present in the *Phänomenologie* remain in Hegel's later works will be dealt with later.

Brief Predeliberations on the *Phänomenologie des Geistes*

While several additional remarks on Hegel's gender theory appear throughout his entire body of works, the basic elements of it are developed in his *Phänomenologie des Geistes*. Since Hegel deals with the gender problem in a key section of his first important work, it can be assumed that he ascribes a significant status to it within the entire context of his text. Therefore, the viewpoint contained in the chapter on the interrelation of gender-specific moral forms will be briefly outlined in terms of the general context of the *Phänomenologie*. It goes without saying that this work's complexity and degree of difficulty make gross overgeneralizations inevitable.

The distinctive characteristic of Hegel's philosophy lies in his understanding of the dialectic no longer only as a form of human thinking, but rather as an ontological and/or metaphysical principle according to which concrete reality develops. This philosophy is also concerned with demonstrating that the self-progression of the spirit and that of reality describe one and the same process. Human reason is no longer seen as being independent from history and as a preexisting store of intellectual structures, but rather as something that has developed as the result of a long process. Based on the fundamental conviction that everyday practice and the realm of ideas are in a state of permanent interaction with one another, the central objective of Hegel's *Phänomenologie* is to depict the course of consciousness formation and re-formation in its most significant stages and to relate it to the material processes of human development. It is also his goal, in looking retrospectively at the historical development of reason, to make the experience of humanity gained over the centuries available to the individual consciousness, so that it may advance from being an ordinary to a philosophical consciousness.

The dialectic forms the foundation upon which history can be rationally

---

19. Ernst Bloch, *Natural Law and Human Dignity*, trans. Schmidt (Cambridge: MIT Press, 1986), 122. German: *Naturrecht und menschliche Würde* (Frankfurt am Main, 1977), 142.

understood as a continual process of growth. The dialectical historical process is meanwhile guided by a superordinate principle whose own progression is represented by history; that is to say, the individual forms of philosophical worldviews correspond in their historical succession to different stages in the development of world reason, which in itself is only one form. Thus, the successive forms of consciousness that crystallize temporarily in the dialogical play of opposites form only transitory stages in the dialectical process of self-discovery of an absolute spirit. Wrested from its predualistic harmony into *consciousness*, the world spirit must undergo several phases of alienated realization in order finally to truly become self-aware in conscious, conciliatory unity with objectivity: "Ariadne's thread is also the main connecting thread in the historical dialectic, by means of which the world spirit finds its way out of the darkness of its uncertain origin or essence into the light. It finds its way from the initial *immediate* identification of subject and object through its separations and alienations to the final *mediated* identity of subject and object."[20]

Indeed, a reconciliation (which cannot be discussed in detail here) occurs in the *Phänomenologie* solely on the theoretical level of absolute knowledge. Hegel could hardly allow a real situation to correspond to this theoretical reconciliation, considering the unstable and explosive contemporary historical situation. According to Georg Lukács, the fact that Hegel permits the reconciliation of social life to occur in a utopian sphere shows the "integrity" of the philosopher, who "prefers to leave vacant in thought a place that was vacant in reality, rather than to fill it with figments of the imagination."[21] Only years later did Hegel progress to a comprehensive reconciliation in the sphere of reality by recognizing, as has already been mentioned, the Prussian state apparatus as an objectification of the absolute.

In order to adequately introduce the basic concept of a gradual perfection of the human consciousness in its interaction with real human lives, (i.e., just like the dialectical course of consciousness itself) Hegel undertakes a threefold look at history from a subjective, an objective, and finally from an absolute perspective.[22] After he leads the reader from the immediate, ordinary consciousness, which stands in contrast to the external circumstances of nature and of social life as a foreign objectivity, through all stages of the subjective spirit to the realization of spiritual objectivity—that is, after that

20. Ibid., 69.
21. Lukács, *The Young Hegel*, 505; *Der junge Hegel*, 619f.
22. The brief, by no means exhaustive remarks on the structure of the *Phänomenologie* refer primarily to the work's structure as it is outlined by Lukács, ibid., 466–518; 572–635.

which is real is presented as something produced by the spirit—history must once again be traversed to illustrate this insight. This time real history, the concrete activity of society, is the point of interest. While the consciousness is already delivered from a total alienation from things here, and in Hegel's terminology has become self-consciousness, actual perfection on the level of absolute awareness still remains to be achieved. This goal is reached when the historical process itself comes to a standstill and the realization of the spirit can not be advanced any further. Looking once again through the historical manifestations of the spirit at the end of history, this last look back draws the individual stages of the process together in the context of their completion, toward which all preceding stages have unconsciously navigated. "The novelty at this stage is that the laws and the interconnections that have accompanied and determined the struggles of history but which had hitherto not been recognized by the heroes in the drama, now enter their consciousness and are illuminated by the light of absolute knowledge."[23]

Hegel's treatment of the subject of gender distinction appears at the beginning of the second major part of the *Phänomenologie*, that is, at the beginning of the section that deals with the laws of actual history and after the previously purely subjective consciousness was followed to that end of its course, where its own relationship to objectivity became apparent to it. At exactly this point, the consciousness comprehends its own historicity. It is in the concrete ethical collective forms of the family and of society that the previously immaterial forms of consciousness—or the "abstract good," as Hegel deems it elsewhere—are given an objective meaning. Above all else, the now objective consciousness is able to comprehend social reality as its own product: "What observation knew as a given object in which the self had no part, is here a given custom, but a reality which is at the same time the deed and the work of the subject finding it."[24] Before the spirit can adequately develop its immanent truth in the real world, it must undergo several stages of alienated realization. The three subdivisions of the chapter on the spirit indicate the phases of the dialectical historical development that the spirit must experience in order to become cognizant of itself in its newly achieved morality—a morality, whose realization is then no longer anticipated.

23. Ibid., 508; 624.
24. G. W. F. Hegel, *Hegel's Phenomenology of Spirit*, trans. Miller (Oxford: Clarendon Press, 1977), 276. German: *Phänomenologie des Geistes*, vol. 3 of *Werke*, 339. In text references are to the English edition, abbreviated *PS*.

The Separation of the Different Ethical Worlds

In the very earliest stage of ethical life, individual reasoning finds itself in immediate harmony with the world; that is, the individual is automatically linked to the morals and customs of his society. But the dissolution of this paradisiacal condition is already heralded in this initial stage, for the moral essence exists here as a duality. "It thus splits itself up into distinct ethical substances, into a human and a divine law. Similarly, the self-consciousness confronting the substance assigns to itself according to its nature one of these powers" (PS 266). The balanced coexistence of the divine and the human spirit in the "beauty of ethical life" (PS 265) of ancient society, according to Hegel's design, functions only as long as the individual makes no claims to a personality which he then strives to achieve in a directed act. This complete absence of individual goals gives the original state in which the balance of the different powers is preserved an extremely hypothetical quality. Additionally, the balance of the ethical worlds that complement and keep each other in check seems fragile. Everything appears to be construed in terms of the conflict that is supposed to set history in motion. Hegel reveals, then, that the destruction of the natural harmony between the individual and society is inevitable insofar as the "seed of destruction" is inherent in this unity, "for this immediacy has the contradictory meaning of being the unconscious tranquillity of Nature, and also the self-conscious restless tranquillity of Spirit" (PS 289). As this formulation expresses, the presence of the spiritual in the natural state already preordains its own destruction, for the tendency to strive beyond that which is merely natural is inherent in the spirit.

In the domain of social life, the spirit brings about its objectification by acting. The diversity of moral referential forms that first unveil themselves to the acting person soon reduces itself to "the duality of a law of individuality and a law of universality" (PS 267). Here, Hegel is concerned with the two different kinds of moral existence in the human and divine law, which he more precisely defines as "real, self-conscious action" in the community or as the "immediate or existent" morality in the family. Although the family is "the *unconscious,* still inner Notion [of the ethical order]" of morality, it inherently carries the "element of self-consciousness" (PS 268) within it, whereby is meant that the moral essence also seeks to actively exert itself over the individual here within the family, for the consciousness "brings into existence the unity of its self and substance as its own work, and thus as an actual existence" (*PS* 266). More will be said on this point later after the various principles of morality have been more precisely defined.

The relationship of humankind to the divine and/or human law is predetermined by gender; therefore, it is completely independent from free will and from social influences. Men and women are instead permanently linked to one of the two moral powers whose realization they must aspire to: "Nature, not the accident of circumstances or choice, assigns one sex to one law, the other to the other law; or conversely, the two ethical powers themselves give themselves an individual existence and actualize themselves in the two sexes" (*PS* 280). Nevertheless—and this is essential—the two forms of moral imperative that govern real, active life derive from one and the same undying essence that, as a result of the interaction of these forces, gravitates toward the final and highest consciousness of itself. "The difference of the sexes and their ethical content remains, however, in the unity of the substance, and its movement is just the constant becoming of that substance" (*PS* 276).

Insofar as the individual behaves in a specifically ethical way, he is forced, on the basis of his gender-specific disposition, to a one-sidedness. As a result of this bias, he necessarily acts in violation of the opposite law and becomes guilty of transgressing it. Since he is unable to attain an awareness of the inherent interrelation between both sides of morality, which discloses itself to the objective view of the "modern"[25] observer, he painfully experiences in every concrete action the "contradiction between its knowledge of the ethical character of its action, and what is in its own proper nature ethical" (*PS* 266). But only by acting, which forces a breakdown of the intact moral order of ancient society, can the progression to consciousness be fulfilled.

> What there appears as order and harmony of its two essences, each of which authenticates and completes the other, becomes through the deed a translation of opposites in which each proves itself to be the non-reality, rather than the authentication, of itself and the other. It becomes the negative movement, or the eternal necessity of a dreadful fate which engulfs in the abyss of its single nature divine and human law alike, as well as the two self-consciousnesses in which these powers have their existence—and for us passes over

---

25. Here, the term "modern" refers to the reader of the *Phänomenologie* who has achieved an objective viewpoint.

into the absolute being-for-self of the purely individual self-consciousness. (*PS* 279)

The act that causes the conflict occurs, as Hegel illustrates using the example of the Antigone tragedy, in the community's violation of the natural divinity of the individual. Also, when the political authority can succeed in suppressing the original rights of the individual, it is soon revisited by compensatory justice on the part of the opposing force, which favors the natural individual. A struggle takes place in which the antagonistic forces are finally both defeated and then experience a first alliance in a new form of community having a positive tendency that more decidedly includes the rights of the individual. "What in the world of the ethical order was called the hidden divine law, has in fact emerged from its inward state into actuality; in the former state the individual was actual, and counted as such, merely as a blood relation of the family. As this particular individual, he was the departed spirit devoid of a self; now, however, he has emerged from his real existence. Because the ethical substance is only the true Spirit, the individual therefore withdraws into the certainty of his own self; he is that substance as the positive universal, but his actuality consists in his being a negative universal self" (*PS* 290).

The objective realization of individual rights leads first to the formal universality of a political form of justice before which all are equal as human beings without at the same time meaning something as individual persons. What from an "objective" standpoint is the first step in the process of realizing a moral basis is in reality experienced as foreign rule by an arbitrary authority: "Consciousness of right, therefore, in the very fact of being recognized as having validity, experiences rather the loss of its reality and its complete inessentiality; and to describe an individual as a 'person' is an expression of contempt" (*PS* 292). Morality achieves objectivity only at the cost of a complete self-alienation. So while the moral seed is deprived of its immediate truth at the level of the community, this is preserved in an opposing realm of belief. Here, the despised individual maintains his natural integrity. The shift to a conscious realization of morality occurs by means of a division of morality into the domains of a belief withdrawn from reality and an education oriented toward reality, which are foreign to or even hostile toward one another (*PS* 265).

Corresponding to this division of the moral essence is a lasting break between the family and the community; that is, the spheres of divine and human right that first existed in a preconscious harmony come in stark contrast with one another. The individual experiences this as an alienation of his innermost being from the rules of the social norm. The sacrifice of the original state of happiness is the price that humanity must pay for its advancement. At the end of the long journey through the icy coldness of unfamiliar realities, Hegel expects a complete reconciliation of the divided worlds, according to his model, through the influence of enlightened reason: "[A]nd the realm which was divided and expanded into this world and the beyond, returns into self-consciousness which now, in the form of morality, grasps itself as the essentiality and essence as the actual self; it no longer places its world and its ground outside of itself, but lets everything fade into itself, and, as conscience, is Spirit that is certain of itself " (*PS* 265). Until this is attained, during the long progressive period of advancing realization, the indestructible, eternal truth of the spirit remains at the base of the changing social reality as something immanent but nevertheless real, for its true place is within the family.

This exalted function of the familial principle now must be more precisely illustrated. It primarily deals with the real opportunities that exist for the female consciousness that falls under this principle. The investigation focuses at length upon the dialectical processes of a remote, mythical prehistoric time, since according to Hegel the course of gender relations is determined in this distant past. The first dawning of self-consciousness already initiates an exclusion of the female from the stage of public life and her restriction to the emotional interior of the family realm, where she must lead a secluded, formless existence.

The gender dialectic that emerged with the fall of the mythological world is paradigmatic in character. But it refers not only to an immutable opposition of the sexes, but at the same time to an internal disunity of the male individual, who in the discrepancy between his "perceived essence" and his "true, active self-existence" must continually annihilate and advance himself. The self-alienation of the world spirit, which influences the historical destiny of the man, is rooted in a gender-related division of the world, which Hegel prescribes to all of history. Thereby, the seemingly trivial gender problem, which incidentally is never explained in the course of the *Phänomenologie*, takes on a key role in the Hegelian system.

The strict division of the world into a feminine/private and a masculine/public sphere, which, as we have seen, is *civil* in origin, is classified by Hegel as a natural law and is made the starting point of the dialectical development of history. This must be explained in greater detail, because without actually intending to do so, Hegel exposed modern gender-role standards as the key elements of a society that is based on denial and alienation.

The Ethical Function of the Family Within the State

Reality is organized according to the dichotomy of the moral essence: on the male side, there is the community, in which the moral spirit takes on a precisely defined and clearly visible form. "In the form of universality, it is the known law, and the prevailing custom; in the form of individuality it is the actual certainty of itself in the individual as such, and the certainty of itself as a simple individuality is that Spirit as government. Its truth is the authority which is openly accepted and manifest to all; a concrete existence which appears for immediate certainty in the form [of] an existence that has freely issued forth" (PS 267–68). Having been hypostatized and made manifest in this manner, morality provides concrete directives for the practical action of the state's citizens. On the other hand, the divine law that governs on the familial, female side does not attain a concretization in exactly formulated behavioral directives. It remains in the "realm of immediacy" (PS 268) and expresses itself only in the "feeling" of a blood-related, natural unity and alliance of the family members. Insofar as the natural, hereditary right of the individual is expressed here, so to speak, the morality that is sealed in immanence forms an antipode to the officially binding law of the community, in which the individual counts only as a subordinate. "For the ethical power of the state, being the movement of self-conscious action, finds its antithesis in the simple and immediate essence of the ethical sphere; as actual universality it is a force actively opposed to individual being-for-self; and as actuality in general it finds in that inner essence something other than the ethical power of the state" (PS 268).

The generalizing power of the political authority is an affront to the spontaneous, natural rights of the individual, which form the immediate heart of morality. This moral seed that escapes an objectification in constitutional law is preserved and nurtured by the family—it represents a deep-seated connection of individuals at the very source of morality, namely, the inalienability of its natural rights: "The individual who seeks the pleasures of enjoying his individuality finds it in the Family, and the necessity in which that pleasure passes away is his own self-consciousness as a citizen of his nation" (*PS* 276–77). Since the fading of this pleasure is apparently an inevitable price of entering into society, while at the same time in Hegel's mind everything leads toward this entrance into society, which is an objectification of morality (*PS* 370),[26] the family alone must prepare one for it. Its interest in the individual may therefore not become lost in personal affection or even erotic attraction; it may not affect the individual in his unique existence, but rather as "a universal being freed from his sensuous, i.e., individual reality" (*PS* 270). Because spiritual morality does not permit the devotion to a specific, sensory being, the moral action of the family can never be directed toward a living incarnate individual, but rather only toward the "*unreal*, powerless shadow," the dead one, "who, after a long succession of separate disconnected experiences, concentrates himself into a single completed shape, and has raised himself out of the unrest of the accidents of life into the calm of simple universality" (*PS* 270). It must be the goal and purpose of the family not to allow base natural forces to take control over the dead one(s), but rather to make sure that "the right of [the] consciousness be asserted in it" (*PS* 270). It is the duty of the family to give death its spiritual dignity by not simply abandoning the dead one to the anarchistic powers of a usurping nature, but rather by joining him with the earth, which is "elementary, imperishable individuality" (*Ps* 271). The earth holds back the unregulated chaos of inferior energies that threaten to dishonor the corpse. In the symbolic act of burial, death becomes "*something done*" (*PS* 270); it is no longer natural, but rational.

The family as a blood-related and thus natural organization of individuals is also ethical, because in counteracting the disorderly dynamics of matter, it asserts the unifying potential of the spirit. Driven by the muffled ethical impulse according to which a member of the blood-related community rediscovers himself in another, in its service to the dead, the family fulfills the spirit's need to combine everything isolated into a single unity. But in real life, this moral law that never loses sight of generality calls for the priority of the family over the needs and interest of the individual. Only in this way can the family function as the basis of the state apparatus that has to protect itself against self-interest and hedonism: "It seems, then, that the ethical principle must be placed in the relation of the individual member of the Family to the whole Family as the Substance, so that End and content of what he does and actually is, is solely the Family" (*PS* 269). Upon closer

---

26. For according to Hegel, the human being is "only real and substantial in his role as citizen."

examination, however, this concern for the family unit that is directed at "the acquisition and maintenance of power and wealth" (*PS* 269), is in itself a particular end because it is driven by desire; it is an end, however, that can only be achieved by means of an integration into the universality. The (male) individual, who functions as the point of integration, must leave the protection of the family and join the community, where he is forced "to subdu[e] the natural aspect and separateness of his existence" (*PS* 269). Such an erosion of the individual is understood by Hegel now as "a negative relation to the family" (*PS* 269), although it occurs, as he had just indicated, for the purpose of securing family property. It already becomes discernible here that the family takes on an ambivalent function. On the one hand, it forms the true point of origin of the civic ethos, in that it binds and obligates the head of the family: the father is strongly motivated by responsibility for others to conform to the community. On the other hand, the family functions as an oppositional reservoir of that which is purely human and that is clearly differentiated from the state: "The positive End peculiar to the Family is the individual as such" (*PS* 269).

Later, in his reflections on the philosophy of law, Hegel lays particular emphasis on the moralizing effect of the family, while its antagonistic side is largely disregarded. Hereby, the special interconnection of the family with property plays a central role. Insofar as the head of the family must recognize the property that he is assigned to manage as "in principle common," that is, protected by inheritance rights,[27] his egoistic desire for personal profit is largely neutralized. But the enduring containment of selfish whims within the context of the family serves to further a positive integration of private property into the sociopolitical order.[28] "It is not merely property which a family possesses; as a universal and enduring unit, it requires possessions specifically determined as permanent and secure, i.e., it requires capital. The arbitrariness of a singular owner's particular needs is one moment in property taken abstractly; but this moment, together with the selfishness of desire, is here transformed into something ethical, into labor and care for a common possession."[29]

Although the *Phänomenologie* identifies the family as a protective domain in which the "law of the heart" rules,[30] it outlines a basic principle of the private sphere, according to which the individual is completely inconse-

---

27. Hegel, *Philosophy of Right*, 119; *Grundlinien der Philosophie des Rechts*, § 178, 330.
28. Marcuse, *Theoretische Entwürfe*, 184.
29. Hegel, *Philosophy of Right*, 116; *Grundlinien der Philosophie des Rechts*, § 170, 323.
30. Hegel, *Phenomenology of Spirit*, 273; *Phänomenologie des Geistes*, 339.

quential in his real trials and tribulations. The family organization thus appears from the start to be oriented toward a state in which the individual irrevocably *serves* as the "representative of an economic function."[31] According to the moral law, the domestic collective must be free from all immediately personal affection, and especially free from the troublesome sources of friction caused by natural desire. The brother-sister relationship, in which all sensuality is set aside, is characterized by Hegel as the most noble of all family relationships. As far as possible pure of all physical attraction and pleasurable contact between individuals, the family forms the essential pillar of state institutions: "The negative essence shows itself to be the real power of the community and the force of its self-preservation. The community therefore possesses the truth and the confirmation of its power in the essence of the Divine Law and in the realm of the nether world."[32]

The protagonist of the divine law in the family is the woman. It will now be explained in the context of the specific definition of female morality, to what extent the family is significant in two respects: as the domain of individual development, and as the point of induction into society.

The Specific Influence of Female Morality on the Family

The *Phänomenologie* assumes the woman's natural predetermination for the family sphere without argumentatively supporting his presupposition in some way. The exclusion of the female gender from that sphere which lends morality its objective contours, is an unspoken premise that requires no further discussion. A harmony of the matriarchal and patriarchal dimensions of morality assumed to be true of Greek society gives the impression of an initial equality of the sexes, but this deals only with the distant, bygone world of mythology, and the male advantage was secured already with the first progressive movement into history. The natural human right claimed by the female side sinks as mythology itself, "into the waters of forgetfulness."[33] "It is obviously only a natural law of mythology, and Hegel, under-

---

31. Max Horkheimer, "Theoretische Entwürfe über Autorität und Familie," sec. 1 of *Studien über Autorität und Familie: Forschungsberichte aus dem Institut für Sozialforschung* (Paris, 1936), 65.
32. Hegel, *Phenomenology of Spirit*, 273; *Phänomenologie des Geistes*, 335.
33. Ibid., 287; 351.

lining the absence of consciousness in it, separates it from every possible reappropriation by later times."[34]

The second-class status of the woman and the domain that she governs in the gigantic project of history was unmistakably expressed by Hegel in his later works. The historical mission of women lies, not in action, but rather in sacrifice: "[T]hey are characterized not indeed as something evil, but as something imperfect; not as something indifferent, but as representing a state in which we are not to remain permanently, since they are themselves to be sacrificed, and must not in any way injuriously affect that absolute tendency and unity which belong to Spirit."[35] He justifies the primarily intellectual weakness of the woman, whom he accuses of having a capricious, unprincipled "childish nature,"[36] by referring to anatomy. He already sees in biological processes proof of the woman's inability to objectivize and thus to act toward specific goals. The analogy of biological processes and intellectual abilities appears to be wholly unproblematic for Hegel.

> Just as in the male the uterus is reduced to a mere gland, so, on the other hand, the male testicle remains enclosed in the ovary in the female, does not emerge into opposition, does not develop on its own account into active brain; and the clitoris is inactive feeling in general. In the male, on the other hand, we have instead active feeling, the swelling heart, the effusion of blood into the corpora cavernosa and the meshes of the spongy tissue of the urethra; to this male effusion of blood correspond the female menses. In this way, the reception [Empfangen] by the uterus, as a simple retention is, in the male, split into the productive brain and the external heart. Through this difference, therefore, the male is the active principle, and the female is the receptive, because she remains in her undeveloped unity.[37]

---

34. Bloch, *Natural Law*, 121; *Naturrecht*, 141.

35. Hegel, *Lectures on the Philosophy of Religion*, vol. 3, trans. Spiers (London: Kegan Paul, 1895), 106. German: *Vorlesungen über die Beweise vom Dasein Gottes*, vol. 17 of *Werke*, 304.

36. Hegel, *Grundlinien der Philosophie des Rechts*, § 165, 318. (Note: the remarks from which this passage comes are strangely not included in the English translation *Philosophy of Right*.)

37. Hegel, *Hegel's Philosophy of Nature*, trans. Miller (Oxford: Clarendon Press, 1970), 413. German: *Die Naturphilosophie: Mit den mündlichen Zusätzen*, part 2 of *Enzyklopädie der philosophischen Wissenschaften im Grundrisse*, vol. 9 of *Werke*, § 369, 518f.

Based on this interpretation of the female nature, everything else that has been said about the woman can to a certain extent be linked together: her unsuitability for higher sciences as well as for intelligent reasoning in general, her lack of talent in the political sphere, and thus her fixation on the family[38]—qualities of the female that are no longer anything novel. Nevertheless, Hegel does not linger at these purely external definitions of the cliché female figure, but rather links the female essence, as has already been outlined, in a specific manner to the historical undertakings of the world spirit.

Standing in the way of this moral self-consciousness is above all human sexual and emotional life. The female love that reigns within the family sphere must therefore prove its moral quality by being addressed not toward a specific person or several individuals who are unique and irreplaceable to her, but by globally advancing the cause of the familial principle. "In the ethical household, it is not a question of this particular husband, this particular child, but simply of husband and children generally; the relationships of the woman are based, not on feeling, but on the universal."[39] If the woman must remain vague and purposeless in order to maintain the morality of her feelings, the possibility of her seeing herself reflected and acknowledged in a concrete opposite is therefore ruled out. So long as her feelings are specifically aimed at a certain individual, however, subjective emotions dominate and morality is corrupted: "Since, then, in this relationship of the wife there is an admixture of particularity, her ethical life is not pure; but insofar as it is ethical, the particularity is a matter of indifference, and the wife is without the moment of knowing herself as this particular self in the other partner."[40]

---

38. Interestingly enough, Hegel explains that the intellectual maturity of the man (i.e., his rational self-distancing and his attitude of social responsibility) are products of a thorough scientific education. The very psychological division that enables objectivity first appears as a result of the separation from his parents and of his integration into strict educational institutions—institutions from which girls were systematically kept at great distance. Nevertheless, the inferiority of the female intellect is still considered to be a natural condition: "This very ability is the one that is developed through scientific education; for this form of education exercises the understanding of relationships and is an enduring transitional phase in the elimination of individuality from general points of view, and conversely in the application of the general to the individual. Scientific education generally has the effect of separating the spirit from itself, of extricating it from its immediate, natural existence, from its unfree sphere of feeling and instinct, and placing it in the realm of reason" (cited in "Gymnasialreden," in Hegel, *Nürnberger und Heidelberger Schriften*, vol. 4a of *Werke*, 348f). See also Hegel, *Philosophy of Right*, par. 166, p. 114–14; *Grundlinien der Philosophie des Rechts*, § 166, 319.

39. Hegel, *Phenomenology of Spirit*, 274; *Phänomenologie des Geistes*, 337.

40. Ibid., 275; 337.

The ego attains self-consciousness—as Hegel explains in his philosophy of law—solely by means of "a renunciation of independence" on the basis of moral love; that is, the ego no longer sees itself as an isolated, autonomous being, but knows of itself only as the unity of itself with another and of the other with him.[41] The binding element is not a conscious and rational law as in the state, but solely the instinctive certainty "that I do not wish to be a self-subsistent and independent person and that, if I were, then I would feel defective and incomplete."[42] Consequently, a moral self-consciousness in a strict sense is not possible for the woman, whose existence is rooted in love.[43] Only in the relationship to the brother, which is pure of all desires of the flesh, is her individuality liberated to a degree that she experiences "an intuitive awareness of what is ethical."[44] But the "equilibrium of the blood-relations" that makes the mutuality of egos between the sexes possible belongs in the paradisiacal stage of childhood, just as Hegel projects it into humanity's age of childhood. And just as the equality of the matriarch and patriarch is phylogenetically destroyed in the emergence of history, so the siblings' state of suspension breaks ontogenetically with the entry into adulthood. Now the brother enters into public life and turns his back to the family, while the woman is permanently fused by marriage into the private sphere. "In this way, the two sexes overcome their [merely] natural being and appear in their ethical significance, as diverse beings who share between them the two distinctions belonging to the ethical substance."[45]

Hegel explains here with remarkable openness that in the establishment of the patriarchal matrimonial order or in the entry into it, the potential for self-consciousness that indeed also initially exists in the woman is stifled before it can ever begin to develop. After an ephemeral self-contact by means of spiritual interaction with her brother, she is driven back into the confinement of the familial sphere before progressing to a real and complete self-consciousness, where she, bound by the functions of her gender, is restricted to relationships that are less moral because they are "mixed . . . with feeling."[46]

Karen Böhme, who reflects on the possibilities of female self-awareness with respect to Hegel's dialectic of master and servant, comes to the conclu-

---

41. Hegel, *Philosophy of Right*, 261; *Grundlinien der Philosophie des Rechts*, § 158, 307.
42. Ibid., 261; 308.
43. Ibid., 263; 317f.
44. Hegel, *Phenomenology of Spirit*, 274; *Phänomenologie des Geistes*, 336.
45. Ibid., 275; 338.
46. Ibid., 273; 336.

sion that the female self-consciousness more than that of a servant is based on the dependency on a "master." Consequently, in the end the woman is only able to comprehend herself and her purpose in life in her function as an object: "Just as the servant's consciousness dissolves in the process of recognizing his master as such, the woman lost herself in a similar manner in the man. She is no longer identical with herself as a self-consciousness; she can no longer find herself as an individual."[47]

According to the gender dialectic developed by Hegel, the woman must be completely oriented toward the personality of her mate. Essentially incompatible with this concrete directive, however, is a governing moral ideal that guides the existence of the woman according to which "in her vocation as an individual and in her pleasure, her interest is centered on the universal and remains alienated to the particularity of her desire."[48] Such a twofold demand on the woman, who is on the one hand supposed to unconditionally surrender herself to her husband and who on the other hand may not desire him as a unique being, has to unleash irresolvable conflicts within the woman. Even if the ambitious principle of female morality inevitably conflicts with reality, however, it still possesses a regulative effectiveness as an aspired goal. The woman attempting to attain a moral identity will accordingly try to make herself largely immune to the personality of her husband and as far as possible to obey his commands and needs without resistance. The woman to whom the concept of "the particularity of desire" remains foreign will try to suppress all sexual feelings and still also be at her husband's disposal, for the man, who "possesses as a citizen the self-conscious power of universality, [and] thereby acquires the right of desire and, at the same time, preserves his freedom in regard to it."[49] The indifferent, passive, tolerant attitude of the woman allows the man a relative realization of his individuality in the private sphere; whereas in the official social domain he is, on the contrary, nothing more than a number.

The dissection of the integral reality into the opposing spheres of state and family, as well as the splitting of the male ego into the extreme poles of desireless consciousness and conscious desire, is the goal of the Hegelian progression of history from the very beginning. But the entry into the *"predefined"* social world brings, in the end, only negative results for both sexes:

47. Karen Böhme, *Zum Selbstverständnis der Frau* (Meisenheim, 1973), 39.
48. Hegel, *Phenomenology of Spirit*, 275; *Phänomenologie des Geistes*, 337.
49. Ibid.

A "self-discovery" is allowed the man, on the one hand, within the impersonal universality of the laws whose network, while indeed stifling his individuality, can never really completely take it over; and on the other hand, in the blind desire of the "purely natural," which because it has no true opposite also can not affect his ego. The woman suffers on the one side a loss of her civil rights, which could at least provide her an existence as a number. On the other hand, in the private domain, she must effect a complete self-relinquishment, which reaches into the innermost depths of her being. The possibility of a communicative exchange between the sexes is excluded. In his role as citizen, the man becomes a stranger to himself; and in the family he finds only a selfless opposite who is completely submissive to him. But here he is ultimately denied a true encounter with himself, which can only be based on a conscious and voluntary acknowledgment by the other.

The woman, whose intentions remain global and nonspecific, is general enough as a personality to represent everything that is imposed upon her from the outside. Having failed, like her own essence, to find a form of expression, she is just as unable to acknowledge the individuality of her husband other than only through superficial reflexes. Her reactions to the spouse, whether approbative or rejective, can never bridge the abysmal gap that results from the inequality of the sexes. On this point, Karen Böhme notes: "She admires him, she envies him, sees him as advantaged in life, resents his freedom or remains in silent resignation, but she always sees him from the outside; what he actually *is* is usually foreign to her."[50]

The relationship of the sexes in unfolded moral objectivity as Hegel perceives it in his *Phänomenologie* leaves no room for real communication and drives both the man and woman into profound loneliness. In the detachment of the ethical spirit of the family from all immediate chaos of feelings and the senses, which also affect the isolated person, the vitality of those who love degenerates and decays. They no longer have any real contact with one another: "The perfected human society radically excludes the anarchy of the senses, it denies its natural principle, denies its actual basis and acknowledges only the room of a clean house, the well-ordered household, through which respected persons move, naive and yet invulnerable, affectionate yet unapproachable.[51]

50. Böhme, *Zum Selbstverständnis*, 42.
51. Georges Bataille, *Der heilige Eros* (Darmstadt, 1974), 214. (English: *Eroticism*, trans. Dalwood [San Francisco: City Lights Books, 1986]).

The Philosophical Instrumentalization of Women and Possibilities for Women in the Real World

Even when the interaction of the sexes, as we have seen, essentially does not allow a true self-development for either sex, by far the greater disadvantage lies with the woman. The woman's generosity, which in the original, natural state affects all blood-related individuals, degenerates in the course of history and in the crystallization of the separate worlds of state and family into a passive one-dimensionality and uninterested willingness of the woman, who could, so to speak, attach herself to any man with the same indifferent self-abandonment. What counts about the spouse is at the most his social status, upon which the well-being of the family unit depends: "A strong economic, even physiological interest joins the woman with the ambition of the man. Above all, however, she is concerned with her own economic security and that of her children."[52] The real qualities of the man's being remain beyond the limited scope of the reverent, passionless woman. Nevertheless, that component of tolerant humanity that allows him a protective and supportive refuge within a rigid state apparatus is preserved precisely as a result of the woman's indolence in the private sphere. But, to reiterate once more, even this niche of happiness ultimately lacks a sensibility for individuality.

The divine law, "whose origin no man knows,"[53] remains in an abstract and illusionary nonreality. It contains absolutely no objective behavioral instructions apart from the exceptional case of burying the dead. "The content of ethical action must be substantial or whole and universal . . ."[54] The woman who conforms to this law appears almost unavoidably in an unfavorable light. Since no concrete standard for her actions is available, all attempts to actively fulfill the ethical obligation are subject to failure. Compared with the obscure general female who allows all desires free reign, the real woman must be a disappointment. The distinct quality of women that escapes definition is outlined by Simone de Beauvoir as follows:

> And if it is so difficult to say anything specific about her, that is because [the] man seeks the whole of himself in her and because she is All. She is All, that is, on the plane of the inessential; she is

---

52. Horkheimer, "Theoretische Entwürfe," 68.
53. Hegel, *Philosophy of Right*, 115; *Grundlinien der Philosophie des Rechts*, § 166, 319.
54. Hegel, *Phenomenology of Spirit*, 269; *Phänomenologie des Geistes*, 331.

all the Other. And, as the other, she is other than herself, other than what is expected of her. Being all, she is never quite this which she should be; she is everlasting deception, the very deception of that existence which is never successfully attained nor fully reconciled with the totality of existence.⁵⁵

Since, according to Hegel's views on female love of the family, only a feeling that is free from all sensuality is acceptable, the ethical dignity of the woman can even be reduced in the normal interaction she has with her relatives. A contemptible remnant of the material persists in all of these family relationships. Morality and feeling are in principle incompatible, and the woman who is guided by her feelings is by virtue of her own actions constantly in danger of sinking from the feeling of moral universality to a mere lowly feeling. Despite her supposedly deeply rooted moral instinct, the woman is never completely free from episodes of emotionality. Hegel poetically described the imponderable, almost prophetic nature of a femininity that is simultaneously sinful and pure:

> The secret is—women's
> Power over the hearts of us men
> This secret is buried deep
> Within them, even impenetrable
> I believe, to God himself. (Not really.)
>
> When on that great day
> Set aside for seeking out all blemishes
> God inspects the hearts of women
> *He'll find them either all*
> Guilty or all innocent;
> So interwoven are their hearts.⁵⁶

How negative the extreme into which Hegel's concept of women is able to degenerate is shown in the following extract in which a supposedly historical stage of female regency is depicted. The cruelty and even bloodthirstiness

---

55. Simone de Beauvoir, *The Second Sex*, trans. Parshley (New York: Vintage Books, 1989), 197–98. German: *Das andere Geschlecht: Sitte und Sexus der Frau* (Hamburg, 1968), 205.

56. Hegel, *Grundlinien der Philosophie des Rechts*, § 165, 318. (This poem is not in the authorized English translation.)

of women in public offices is in no way reminiscent of the reverent, charitable compassion and the basic moral instincts of the woman that are described in the *Phänomenologie:*

> Tradition alleges that in former times a state composed of women made itself famous by its conquests: it was a state at whose head was a woman. She is said to have pounded her own son in a mortar, to have besmeared herself with the blood, and to have had the blood of pounded children constantly at hand. She is said to have driven away or put to death all the males, and commanded the death of all male children. These furies destroyed everything in the neighborhood, and were driven to constant plunderings, because they did not cultivate the land. Captives in war were taken as husbands: pregnant women had to betake themselves outside the encampment; and if they had born a son, put him out of the way.[57]

The remote unreality of the female principle, which makes the failure of women inevitable, has a relevance for the moral development of humanity that should not be underestimated. Which function is given to the female law is to be more clearly explained below. This law possesses, as will be shown, no intrinsic value and autonomy at all, not even when the seemingly powerful goddesses of revenge claim their right. Hegel's intricate thought progression leads to a struggle in which the female paradoxically loses even in her victories.

Let's once again briefly outline the interrelation of the two different ethical forms. The female embodies the moral law in its immanent truth; that is, it preserves the still-undeveloped moral core, "the mute unconscious substance of all,"[58] within the positive legal organization of the state. History is the process of the dawning of consciousness of this moral truth, which was always present and persistently survives the progression of time. It occurs through a transcendence into objectivity. The separation of the moral essence into a male and female law that occurs at the beginning of history is understood by Hegel as an alienation of the objectively formed world of morality from its innermost substance. Neither of the two laws can exist in isolation: "Neither of the two is by itself absolutely valid; human law proceeds in its living process from the divine, the law valid on earth from that

---

57. Hegel, *Lectures on the Philosophy of History,* 97; *Vorlesungen über die Philosophie der Geschichte,* 127.
58. Hegel, *Phenomenology of Spirit,* 287; *Phänomenologie des Geistes,* 351.

of the nether world, the conscious from the unconscious, mediation from immediacy—and equally returns whence it came. The power of the nether world, on the other hand, has its actual existence on earth; through consciousness, it becomes existence and activity" (PS 276).

The historical development represents a gradual fusion of the two laws; the final goal is their true reconciliation, accompanied by the ultimate recognition of the sameness of the seeming opposites in their essence. Within the dialectical process, however, the principles are in no way as equal as Hegel first tries to assert. The man and woman as the protagonists of the divorced worlds are given completely different functions in serving morality. The man links the unequal realms through directed action, while the woman functions solely as a passive medium. The individual man connects the creative consciousness as an inherently void power of hypostasis with the fundamental moral truth. His frequent return to the bosom of the family reconnects him with the unconscious sources of morality that the woman generates by virtue of her existence, without herself being admitted to the official public sphere. Active self-realization does not belong to the woman's essence; she lingers at the margins of society as the guardian of the absolute, from which perspective she inspires the man in his objective plans. While the man therefore acts as a synthesizing element of both sides of morality and thus also carries the divine principle deep within himself, the woman, from the perspective of her dull ignorance, has no other function than to guarantee an indistinct realization of morality. She is supposed to prove, solely by means of her passive existence, that the moral spirit can ascend from being an unworldly immanence to reality. "The one extreme, the universal self-conscious Spirit becomes, through the individuality of the man, united with its other extreme, its force and element, with unconscious Spirit. On the other hand, the divine law has its individualization—or the unconscious Spirit of the individual its real existence—in the woman, through whom as the middle term, the unconscious Spirit rises out of its unreality into actual existence, out of a state in which it is unknowing and unconscious into the realm of conscious Spirit" (PS 278). The unification of morality with reality in the woman helps the man out of the depths of mere feeling to intellectual clarity. He thus actively makes a contribution to that historical project that can be characterized on the whole as "the forcible appropriation by the subject of the wealth of substance."[59] This corresponds, as we will see, to a "depletion" of the female by the male.

59. Lukács, *The Young Hegel*, 491; *Der junge Hegel*, 603.

Since the shift from the divine principle to the human law can only succeed within the context of the essential sameness of both, the gender-specific differentiation turns out to be only an apparent difference—the "law that is manifest to it is linked in the essence with its opposite; the essence is the unity of both."[60] When a reconciling light is shed on gender relations from the perspective of the suprahistorical philosophical observer, then real life seems indeed to be influenced by the antagonistic interests of both sides over long periods of time. As has already been mentioned, the conflict manifests itself on the occasion of a conscious and decisive moral act of the individual, by virtue of which this individual unavoidably makes himself guilty of violating the opposing law. The inequality of opportunity that becomes apparent on a real level in the two separate forms of laws can be illustrated in this problem of guilt.

Whoever acts toward the fulfillment of communal obligations violates the divine law without even the possibility of being aware of it when carrying out the act, for the divine still remains hidden. Only after the act, when the Erinyes take the underworldly power from him, does he realize his crime. Conversely, whoever attempts to assert the divine law stands in violation of a clearly articulated, conspicuously governing law. In this act lies the strange self-contradiction, with the desire on the one hand to oppose the legitimacy of reality in accordance with a "chthonic ur-power," and at the same time, on the other hand, to verify the law as something real by means of this act, which itself aims toward an objectification of morality. "The accomplished deed completely alters its point of view; the very performance of it declares that what is ethical must be actual; for the realization of the purpose is the purpose of the action" (*PS* 284).

A clear responsibility results from the recognition of that which is objective, against which the woman specifically acts, especially since the emergence from immanence that is specific to the divine in principle signifies a recognition of objectivity. Antigone serves as an example of such rebellion, for she respects her obligations in her conscious disobedience toward Creon. Her offense is—Hegel must be understood here in this manner—her very turn to conscious activity; for as soon as the divine law is robbed of its immediacy and is more precisely defined in a concrete goal, it loses its authenticity and degenerates into an attitude (*PS* 284). Although Hegel characterizes the moral consciousness of the woman as a self-degeneration—"thereby surrender[ing] his *[sic]* own character and the real-

---

60. Hegel, *Phenomenology of Spirit*, 283; *Phänomenologie des Geistes*, 347.

ity of his *[sic]* self, and [is] ruined" (*PS* 284)—it is at least granted her in the realm of possibility. The exhaustion of this possibility is meanwhile an obligation—one that the woman (Antigone) takes upon herself because she must actively realize the lawfulness of reality. In her abandonment of protest, and in suffering the punishment, the woman confirms the supremacy of the human law—Hegel quotes here the last words of Sophocles' tragedy: "Because we suffer, we acknowledge that we have erred" (*PS* 284). The anguished acknowledgment itself is a betrayal of the divine, and Antigone must be destroyed. She returns irretrievably into the earth's bosom; the feminine sinks into the darkness. "Even in her live burial, in her descent into unreality and pure pathos, the female must recognize the extent of her obligation."[61] The guiding principle of the woman's life can hardly be understood in a more negative light.

The radical expulsion of the female from the official stage of historical life that is symbolized in the fate of Antigone corresponds to the overthrow of the matriarchy that Engels termed "the world historical defeat of the female sex."[62] If Hegel is proposing that the vengeance of the underworldly power also cast doubt on the male law and that as a consequence it must take on a new form, then the man still remains free to construct reality solely according to his own standards. The woman's status as an object in the struggle between the sexes is constant.

But as long as worldly power violates the natural right of the individual, it will find an opponent in the woman, who furtively schemes against it: "Since the community only gets an existence through its interference with the happiness of the Family, and by dissolving [individual] self-consciousness into the universal, it creates for itself in what it suppresses and what is at the same time essential to it an eternal enemy—womankind in general."[63] The inventory of female strategies of aggression that follows explains how the woman calculatingly tries to draw personal advantage from the social institutions. The enthusiasm and interest of the woman, apparently far removed from all those general moral sentiments, leads now toward that which is individual, youthful, and vital. In this negative function of the female gender that undermines objective ethical forms by stimulating individ-

---

61. Luce Irigaray, *Das Geschlecht, das nicht eins ist* (Berlin, 1979), 277. (*The Sex Which is Not One*, trans. Porter [Ithaca: Cornell University Press, 1985]).

62. Friedrich Engels, *The Origin of the Family*, trans. West (revised) (New York: International Publishers, 1972), 120. German: *Der Ursprung der Familie, des Privateigentums und des Staats* (Berlin, 1977), 66.

63. Hegel, *Phenomenology of Spirit*, 288; *Phänomenologie des Geistes*, 352.

ual egoism, Hegel sees only a superficial obstacle to the general intentions of the moral spirit. He resolves the contradiction in his evaluations of the female by means of a dialectical scheme. On an internal level, the moral principle has a quasi-immoral appearance that is directed toward the particular; the "substance that is sealed within" appears "in its outer existence . . . as the will of an isolated individual" (*PS* 280). Female subversiveness, which Hegel's historical process can not do without, thus loses its causticity. Even with protests and resistance, the woman still subconsciously achieves that which is idealistic from the male point of view.

But if the individual revolt goes too far, the community must intervene with force. In order to put an end to the unruliness of particular interests within the state order, the state possesses the instrument of war, which bestows "the negative power to feel" (*PS* 280).

> In order not to let them [particular interests] to become rooted and set in this isolation, thereby breaking up the whole and letting the [communal] spirit evaporate, government has from time to time to shake them to their core by war. By this means the government upsets their established order, and violates their right to independence, while the individuals who, absorbed in their own way of life, break loose from the whole and strive after the inviolable independence and security of the person are made to feel in the task laid on them their lord and master, death. (*PS* 272–73)

Intrigue and war, shrewd plots, and brutal force are the tools of a dialectic that forges a course toward the objectification of the ethical. Hegel's depiction of the gender struggle allows it to become clear that the development of human rights propelled forward by female subversion in no way means a gradual fulfillment of female demands. Humanity's ascent consists much more in the increasing ability to subdue the remaining remnants of a spirit of dissent and to contain them within the objective provisions of the law. The idea of reconciliation that is the goal of Hegel's gender dialectic hardly gets to the heart of the matter. This, incidentally, becomes clear from many of his statements: "Human law . . . *is, moves* and *maintains* itself by consuming and absorbing into itself the separation of the Penates, or the separation into independent families presided over by womankind, and by keeping them dissolved in the fluid continuity of its own nature" (*PS* 287–88).

The subversive spirit of the family, which threatens to destroy the community if it becomes stronger, is tamed in the ideal state of Prussian design. Here it is united with public authority into a very deliberate system: the family trains the individual for social success and offers him both order and relaxation in well-portioned dosages. Important tasks of the family are the basic raising of the children to a civic way of thinking, the channeling of physical desires, the moralization of property, and the obligation of the individual to a greater whole—but also a certain freedom of movement, a temporary disburdenment and liberation of the working male citizen. In the female citizen around whom such a family is centered, the feminine appears henceforth in a domesticated, distorted form. Not infrequently the dutiful wife becomes the most zealous advocate of social obedience and sexual moderation. It is exactly she who will see to forming the sphere given her as reputably as possible, to raising the children to be respectable and diligent members of society, and to encouraging the man to voluntarily subordinate himself to the principle of economic achievement. "Being dependent on the position and income of the man, the woman has to rely on the father's adaptation to circumstances, and on the expectation that he under no circumstance rebels against the ruling power, but that he instead invokes all means in order to progress in the present."[64] Thus, in the nuclear, civic-minded family, the female loses her aggressiveness and degenerates into an authority-strengthening element. As if to prove that the divine became truth, the woman has to identify with the male order. While the right of the individual still has a place in the family and in the woman, its most avid champion, according to Hegel's social theory, it should henceforth be given room to develop insofar as it neither attacks nor undermines the existing state apparatus. The human law "embraced" the divine within itself; it reformed the family into a constitutive part of itself and thus neutralized the family's historical self-centeredness.

Such a result was foreseeable, for the "other" form of law, the female law, naturally has no autonomy from the very beginning. Hegel already projects the principle of the civic society into the origin and "natural essence" of humanity, in which the woman exists only in a complete dependence on her husband. His attempts to subsume everything in a unified, rigid principle of the spirit precludes from the very outset any possibility of a true gender differentiation in his way of thinking. "In actuality, dialectics does not liberate differences; it guarantees, on the contrary, that they can always be recaptured. The dialectical sovereignty of similarity consists in

---

64. Horkheimer, "Theoretische Entwürfe," 68.

permitting differences to exist, but always under the rule of the negative, as an instance of non-being. They may appear as the successful subversion of the Other, but contradiction secretly assists in the salvation of identities."[65]

The woman as the other can not really be different; she can not have an independent guiding life principle, but must eternally preserve the male ideal of truth. Traces of a matriarchal world, a hint of which is imparted in the *Phänomenologie,* are recast by Hegel before they can take shape into a pre-stage of patriarchal law. The unconscious, which Hegel discovered long before Freud's research on the basis of manifest reality, can for Hegel unproblematically be described in terms of the language of the Logos. Aware of the historicity of the rational self-consciousness, he gives reason absolute supremacy over nature from which it emerges chronologically: "Nature is the first point of time, but the absolute prius is the Idea; this absolute prius is the last, the true beginning, Alpha is Omega."[66]

This high-flown idealism had broader consequences for the real woman than for anyone else. She is still identified with nature, but is no longer considered to be a purely material, spiritless being; instead she has to represent the presence of the spiritual in its natural state. Since she is supposed to symbolize the moral law in its transhistorical, static truth, the step into consciousness is denied her. If she participated in the official activities of society, then she would lose her ethereal flair and that existential balance that allows her to become symbolic of both the cradle and endpoint of humanity. But thereby the highest end of the process of history would have no reassurance in that which presently exists. Historical movement would even come to a standstill if the woman, as the "everlasting irony of the community,"[67] did not provoke the spirit of individuality with her moral impulses. Thus, society establishes the legitimacy of its goals in the image of the female, "store [of] substance for the sublation of self,"[68] who is herself deprived of all power of prediction. "[T]he masculine will be able to retrace the path of his discursive law, but it is also the role of the masculine to

---

65. Michel Foucault, "Theatrum Philosophicum," in *Language, Counter-Memory, Practice,* trans. Bouchard and Simon (Ithaca: Cornell University Press, 1977), 184–85. German: *Der Faden ist gerissen,* ed. Gilles Deleuze and Michel Foucault (Berlin, 1977), 43. See also Julia Kristeva, *Die Revolution der poetischen Sprache* (Frankfurt am Main, 1978), 140.
66. Hegel, *Hegel's Philosophy of Nature,* 19; *Naturphilosophie,* § 248, 30.
67. Hegel, *Phenomenology of the Spirit,* 288; *Phänomenologie des Geistes,* 352.
68. Luce Irigaray, *Speculum of the Other Woman,* trans. Gill (Ithaca: Cornell University Press, 1985), 224. German: *Speculum: Spiegel des anderen Geschlechts* (Frankfurt am Main, 1980), 278.

prescribe the law for the female, since she can have no knowledge [of it] for herself."[69]

The woman must always remain the same in order to symbolize indestructible, original intactness, whereby she both confirms and corrects male reason in its undertakings. The individual is thereby largely denied the development of a personal identity. "She ensures the Erinnerung of the consciousness of self by forgetting herself."[70] She becomes the willing instrument of the man; her silence in all intellectual matters elevates his speech to an unchallenged truth.

It appears that in the course of Hegel's reasoning no substantial difference between the sexes is established. The difference in the sexes corresponds to a difference between harmony and disunity, as was already the case in Schelling's concepts, whereby the female in practice always signifies an intellectually incompetent, passive figure. Thus the woman, who now advances to being the executing organ of the highest ends, is indeed elevated substantially; but in actuality, nevertheless, she remains completely subordinate. She is that which the man also is, only in another form, which is unconscious and altered. It is a form that fails to explain the intense strife in the social world. Designated as the symbol of that which the man most ardently strives to attain, the woman is separated from that which is discursive and is equated with objectivity. She guarantees that the world of objects does not remain something hopelessly foreign to the male intellect but rather can be gradually comprehended and penetrated.

> In thinking an object, I make it into thought and deprive it of its sensuous aspect; I make it into something which is directly and essentially mine. Since it is in thought that I am first by myself, I do not penetrate an object until I understand it; it then ceases to stand over against me and I have taken from it the character of its own which it had in opposition to me. Just as Adam said to Eve: "Thou art flesh of my flesh and bone of my bone," so mind says: "This is mind of my mind and its foreign character has disappeared."[71]

For a subject, as Hegel describes here, intimacy only begins when the perception and individuality of the other is extinguished. With regard to a human opposite, the consequences are fatal: the ego only encounters itself;

69. Ibid.
70. Ibid., 225; 280.
71. Hegel, *Philosophy of Right*, 226; *Grundlinien der Philosophie des Rechts*, § 4, 47.

all world experiences become an unending process of self-reflection. It has already been pointed out how dismal the relationship between the sexes would look according to Hegel's views. The unlimited receptiveness of the woman can indeed lend the man a feeling of immeasurable freedom and importance, but it thwarts every interpersonal closeness. According to their ideal roles, the sexes must increasingly grow apart. The more the man distinguishes his abilities in his work for society, the more foreign the women who stands outside official life will appear to him.

The isolation that comes from pursuing one's own wishes in another becomes apparent in Hegel's gender theory. These desires are always disappointed because no opposite, not even a very elastic female, is empty enough not to bring about the feeling of something foreign that one does not want to adapt to. Hegel also speaks of the disillusionment that trivial everyday life necessarily brings about, and of the disillusionment with which one sees the ideal woman transformed into an uninteresting, discontented housewife: "The woman takes charge of the household management; children arrive; the adored wife, at first unique, an angel, behaves pretty much as all other wives do; the man's profession provides work and vexations, marriage brings domestic affliction—so here we have all the headaches of the rest of married folk."[72]

---

72. Hegel, *Lectures on Aesthetics*, vol. 1, trans. Knox (Oxford: Clarendon Press, 1975), 593. German: *Vorlesungen über die Ästhetik II*, vol. 14 of *Werke*, 220.

6 | WOMAN—LANDSCAPE—ARTWORK
Alternative Realms or Patriarchal Reserves?

Cornelia Klinger

Translated by James Dodd

I

In recent years the analogy between nature and woman[1] (or the feminine), or rather their affinity and relatedness,[2] has received much attention in femi-

---

This essay originally appeared under the title "Frau—Landschaft—Kunstwerk: Gegenwelten oder Reservoire des Patriarchats?" in *Feministische Philosophie* (= Wiener Reihe zur Philosophie, vol. 4), ed. Herta Nagl-Docekal (Munich and Vienna: Olenbourg, 1990), 63–94.

1. With this theme we will be predominantly dealing with ideas and ideologies of the feminine and not with real women and their history. The fact that we will thus be moving primarily on a symbolic level justifies speaking of "woman" or "the feminine" in an abstract sense.

2. That the disdain and oppression of woman and nature is not just about similarity, but about sameness, is explicitly emphasized by Luce Irigaray: "The exploitation of nature is not

nist debates and research. On the level of description, the negative aspects have been particularly at the forefront. Here the contempt for woman/femininity is related to the rejection of nature, the connection being the greater proximity of woman and nature. Whether merely purported or factual, this proximity is, in any case, established in Western patriarchal culture; and on this level, the destruction of nature and the oppression of woman/femininity are also directly related.

This assertion of a correspondence between the feminine and nature is extended to include a parallel in the dynamic of historical development. Though formulated much earlier in Western thought, rationalism, which culminated in the age of capitalism and industrialization, is blamed for both the exploitation of nature and the suppression of the feminine in an intensified form. The structural change that male domination underwent in the process of modernity is interpreted as an intensification and expansion of this type of domination and suppression.

There are so many examples of this interpretation in feminist literature that the ones cited below represent only a small selection:

> Nature-culture dualism is a key factor in Western civilization's advance at the expense of nature. As the unifying bonds of the older hierarchical cosmos were severed, European culture set itself above and apart from all that was symbolized by nature.³

> An organically oriented mentality in which the female principles played an important role was undermined and replaced by a mechanically oriented mentality that either eliminated or used female principles in an exploitative manner.⁴

> With the unfolding of a mathematical-calculating bourgeois mentality a qualitative new phase of the subjection of nature began, to which the once cherished—and, during the entire middle ages, still recognized—natural creative power of woman fell victim. The biological productivity of woman, as well as specifically feminine practices of a magic-mimetic approach to nature, must have been

---

a parallel, it is the same [as the exploitation of woman]" (*Zur Geschlechterdifferenz: Interviews und Vorträge* [Vienna, 1987], 77).

3. Carolyn Merchant, *The Death of Nature: Women, Ecology, and the Scientific Revolution* (San Francisco: Harper & Row, 1983), 143.

4. Ibid., 2.

an outrage to the advocates of the new scientific ways of appropriating nature.⁵

The "new human" of the industrial age was the man. The magical-mythical image of the woman remained preserved in the bourgeois age, but hereafter she did not count in any way as the subject of the appropriation of nature, but as object of nature domination; like the desire for the reconciliation with nature, the fear of the vengeance of nature was fixed in her image as an integral part of exploited nature. Women did not take part in the "subjugation of nature," they were themselves placed in this context of subjugation. The witch stands at that point of the historical development where the exploitation of nature takes on its systematic character.⁶

Above all, what has been conspicuous in the feminist discussion in recent years is that most of the arguments are no longer intended to reject or even cast doubt on the patriarchal identification of nature and the feminine. Instead, a strong tendency has developed to consider this as a given, and then to reinterpret it within a critique of civilization. In this sense, not only is it claimed that humans in general are natural beings, but that in addition there is a special affinity between nature and femininity.⁷ Woman simultaneously identifies herself with nature, sets herself up as the champion of all that has been suppressed in the name of male culture, and prepares to submit to a radical critique of the opposition between nature and culture as a specifically male myth of rationality:

> A stubborn myth of male society expresses itself in the principle of rationality. It is a way of thinking that no longer understands reason as a capacity of humans as *natural* beings . . . but that views rationality as supernatural, as cleansed of materiality and of the transitoriness of natural processes, as abstract and thus as capable of dominating natural processes. . . . The dispassionate logic of the

---

5. Heidemarie Bennent, *Galanterie und Verachtung: Eine philosophiegeschichtliche Untersuchung zur Stellung der Frau in Gesellschaft und Kultur* (Frankfurt am Main, 1985), 36.

6. Silvia Bovenschen, "Die aktuelle Hexe, die historische Hexe und der Hexenmythos," in G. Becker, Silvia Bovenschen, H. Brackert, et al., *Aus der Zeit der Verzweiflung: Zur Genese und Aktualität des Hexenbildes* (Frankfurt am Main, 1977), 292.

7. The most consistent approach to date of a self-identification of femininity and nature has been presented by Susan Griffen in *Woman and Nature: The Roaring Inside Her* (New York: Harper & Row, 1978).

modern way of thought is the power of the principle of rationality over nature, natural processes, and everything which is, in accordance with male interests, ascribed to it: women, children, animals, vegetation, and foreign peoples.[8]

To be sure, there are also objections to the construction sketched here of a sort of fateful, parallel intensification of the contempt for nature and for women at the onset of the bourgeois age. For example, Maurice and Jean Bloch represent, with plausible arguments, the interpretation that precisely in this age, in the thought of the Enlightenment, the traditional contempt for nature was overcome for the first time: "Nature is no longer something to be despised as low; it is rather to be cherished, and, above all, it is the source whereby society, morals, education, even medicine, are to be reformed and purified. The radical implication of such an idea for a society where legitimacy was supposed to come from God through monarch and church can hardly be over-emphasized."[9] The Blochs claim that the more significant break is rather the one that runs between the newly emerging admiration of nature and the persistent contempt of feminine nature, a contempt that, in sharp contrast to the above-cited authors, they hold to be characteristic of traditional and primitive societies (in explicit agreement with the anthropological researches of Sherry Ortner[10]): "What is striking at first sight is the extent to which the eighteenth-century representation of women, as being in certain fundamental ways more bound by nature or closer to nature, is once again reminiscent of that reported from many other parts of the world. . . . One might almost say that the eighteenth-century philosophers had a New Guinean view of woman as dangerous because of her uncontrolled power and as potentially polluting and disruptive."[11]

---

8. Renate Genth, "Patriarchale Naturbeherrschung: Weiblichkeit und phallokratische Naturzerstörung," in *Rationalität und sinnliche Vernunft: Frauen in der patriarchalen Realität*, ed. Christine Kulke (Berlin, 1985), 130f.

9. Maurice Bloch and Jean H. Bloch, "Women and the Dialectics of Nature in Eighteenth-Century French Thought," in *Nature, Culture, and Gender*, ed. C. P. MacCormack and M. Strathern (Cambridge: Cambridge University Press, 1980), 31.

10. Sherry B. Ortner, "Is Female to Male as Nature is to Culture?" in *Women, Culture, and Society*, ed. M. Z. Rosaldo and L. Lamphere (Stanford: Stanford University Press, 1974), 67–87.

11. Bloch and Bloch, "Women and the Dialectics of Nature," 40. For a discussion of the contrasting positions, cf. Brita Rang, "Zur Geschichte des dualistischen Denkens über Mann und Frau," in *Frauenmacht in der Geschichte: Beiträge des Historikerinnentreffens 1985 zur Frauengeschichtsforschung*, ed. J. Dalhoff, U. Frey, and I. Schöll (Düsseldorf, 1986), 194–204. Referring to the American research initiated by Sherry Ortner's essay, where the contempt and

Subject and Thesis

The reflections that follow in a sense contradict both interpretive approaches. On the one hand, I show that the concept of the nature of woman undergoes a transformation in the development of the modern conception of the world and comprehension of nature. This contradicts the interpretation that would claim that an archaic remnant is preserved in modern thought with respect to the nature of woman. This would appear at first glance to be in agreement with the interpretation set out at the beginning that claims that a strong intensification of the opposition between nature and culture comes about in conjunction with the processes of modernity. Yet in departure from this view, I will show that the exacerbation of the suppression and exploitation of the feminine and of nature are not the only consequences of the changes that emerge in the wake of the process of modernity. For these changes also give rise to a new type of liberation bound up with the veneration of nature and femininity.

In sum, my thesis runs thus: The correspondence of femininity and nature involves not only negative aspects, that is, parallel suppression and contempt, but is also related to striking similarities with respect to "positive" aspects ascribed to femininity and to nature that have, to date, received less attention.

The transition from the traditional to the modern understanding of nature and the feminine is often described, in a simplifying way, as the transition from a two-sided and contradictory image of nature and the feminine that moves between the poles of fear and adulation to an understanding that is wholly, or even linearly—that is, exclusively—oriented around manipulation. On the same level of simplification, I would juxtapose to this another interpretation: in the process of imposing the principle of rationality, the original dualism set out in Western thought disappears, but not in favor of the dominance of rationality as a unified principle; rather, the dualism is exacerbated and its character transformed.

The issue is not exhausted by ascertaining in patriarchal ideology the similar content of a "positive" image of the feminine and a "positive" concept of nature. In addition, there is a convergence of the positive concepts

---

discrimination of woman based on her proximity to nature is considered an archaic relic, Rang criticizes the thesis of an intensification, since the end of the eighteenth century, of the dualism nature/culture and femininity/maleness. She considers this interpretation to be a peculiarity of the German debate (since Karin Hausens' widely received essay on the polarization of gender character).

of nature and femininity in a third concept: the idea of the beautiful. For reasons that will be explained later, the positive idea of nature falls wholly under the concept of landscape, or the *beautiful* in nature. This yields the transition from the concept of landscape to the third concept in the title I have given to these reflections. This is the transition from landscape to the theme of the work of art, in particular the connection between natural and artistic beauty in classical aesthetics. In the latter there is also maintained a particularly close relation between the idea of the beautiful and the idea of the feminine, not least through the polarization of the female and the male in the categories of the beautiful and the sublime.

But first, two preliminary remarks:

The first concerns terminology. When I set forth the thesis that, in the patriarchal ideology of modernity, there is a correspondence between a "positive" image of the feminine and a "positive" image of nature, just as there is a correspondence between woman and nature with respect to the negative developmental dynamic, the adjective *positive* certainly does not carry with it any valuation on my part. It merely has to do with a variant of patriarchal ideology that explicitly raises and idealizes the feminine, or rather nature, and does not debase or denounce it in a direct way. Whether this ideology has had positive effects, what such effects consist of, what their limits are, and whether they are sufficient for us to make a positive valuation—these are difficult questions that demand separate, more detailed investigation (cf. part III). In order not to be constantly anticipating such an investigation, or to avoid any misunderstandings with the suggestive adjective *positive*, I will rather speak of a "sentimental" concept of femininity and nature.

My second preliminary remark concerns the question of why, in general, the object of these considerations is being taken up here. Has not everything that there is to say about it already been said? The fact that the contempt for woman corresponds to an adulation and idealization of the feminine, even the strong relationship between the intensity of both attitudes, is sufficiently known. The same is true of the alternating relationship between the exploitation and destruction of nature and the yearning for nature. Nothing should be more obvious than the assertion that there is a similarity in argument and structure between the idealization of the feminine and the yearning for a reconciliation with nature, just as there is a connection between the negative aspects, between the contempt for nature and the discrimination against women. Yet if I am correct in my claim that, nevertheless, this point has never really been sufficiently established, or in any case not in a form that goes beyond a passing remark,[12] then this is something that needs further explanation.

First, to answer this question with respect to the theme of femininity, it is to be expected that the reasons for this lack of attention lie in the assessment of the sentimental conception. Insofar as this assessment is very much divided between (at least) two sides, the reasons for the relative lack of attention also point in different directions. With respect to those who critically oppose the sentimental concept of the feminine (which among feminists may always remain the majority), such reasons are readily available: the positive-sentimental characteristics of the patriarchal concept of the feminine possess no importance or substance of their own. In the face of the overwhelming emphasis on the discrimination, exploitation, debasement, and contempt that constitutes patriarchal reality, particular sentimental impulses appear either to be merely illusory or, considered functionally, to be whitewash for the purpose of stabilizing the status quo by way of obfuscation. The contempt for, and debasement of, woman form the primary characteristics of the patriarchal order; to idealize the oppressed simply represents its advancement by other means. These other means come down to nothing more than their function; they not only possess no value themselves, but they also do not appear to have their own rules or any specific structure or dynamic that would call for special consideration.

On the other hand, there is certainly no lack of feminists who—to formulate it as generally as possible—have a very positive relationship to some elements of the sentimental concept of femininity. I have already referred at the beginning to the growing tendency in recent years to accept the identification of the feminine and nature, to turn it into something positive, and to use it as a lever in a comprehensive critique of culture or modernity. These approaches focus on the context of female life, on the historical social character of woman, or even unabashedly on feminine nature. The question of the connection to patriarchal ideology is here preferably avoided—to pose it amounts to a challenge to this type of feminist game, for the question is often posed with polemical intent, which of course hinders an unbiased response.

In sum, the idealizing aspects of the patriarchal ideology of femininity strangely remain in the shadows. Either any importance they may have is contested due to the patriarchal context into which they are set, or they are

---

12. "[L]ike the desire for the reconciliation with nature, the fear of the vengeance of nature was fixed in her image [= the image of woman]" (Bovenschen, "Die aktuelle Hexe," 5).

recognized only because the patriarchal context has been pushed into the background. Our approach rejects both variants. On the one hand, I have no doubt that the sentimental concept of femininity and the sentimental comprehension of nature are products of patriarchal ideology. On the other hand, precisely such products make apparent the necessity of opposing patriarchal ideology in a way that is not limited to the proof of its harmfulness and offensiveness, but that recognizes, and in turn analyses, the historical effectiveness of the representations that it has developed. Feminism and the women's movement have put patriarchal ideology on trial. It is a moral and political trial, and as such is undoubtedly justified. It was, and will remain for some time necessary.

Nevertheless, we are involved not only in a moral and political trial *against* patriarchal ideology, but also in a historical trial *with* it. That means that we must recognize that we are, both individually and as a collective, under its influence as our immediate, cultural world; and also, vice versa, we must recognize that we have influenced *it*, that it is changeable and has changed. In a moral and political perspective, patriarchal ideology stands against us as our opponent. But in the historical and cultural perspective, both sides stand next to one another in a context, both find themselves in a situation in which mutual influence is possible. It is from this perspective that a different, perhaps more precise sort of assessment of patriarchal ideology is requisite—without letting this be misunderstood as a realignment or even retreat from the political and moral confrontation.

Finally, the sentimental concept of nature also receives relatively little attention for reasons that are not dissimilar. When the question of the modern conception of nature is posed, the aspects of the domination, oppression, and exploitation of nature come to the fore as the most important, and here interest is primarily directed to the conception of nature developed by the modern sciences. The fact is rarely considered that, at the beginning of the modern age, the metaphysical concept of nature is superseded by not only *one*, but *two* new conceptions. It is superseded not only by the rationalistic, mechanistic concept of the natural sciences but, complementary to that, also by an aesthetic concept of nature.[13] Yet today alternative

13. Cf. Jörg Zimmermann, "Zur Geschichte des ästhetischen Naturbegriffs," in *Das Naturbild des Menschen*, ed. Jörg Zimmermann (Munich, 1982), 129–30. The understanding of nature is fundamentally transformed in the "mechanization of the world picture," in the displacement of the interpretation of signs and intuition of ideas by experimental observation and theoretical construction. "The end point of this development forms that sober concept of nature of Kant's critical philosophy, which determines the material side of nature as the 'sum total of all objects of experience' and its formal side as the 'regularity of all objects of experi-

interpretations of nature are developed, or the question of their possibility is posed, with the pretense or desire to provide an alternative to the prevailing conception. Given the lack of a full awareness of the existence of past countermovements to the dominant rationalism of modernity, one gets the impression that only now are alternatives to the dominating, rationalistic-scientific concept of nature being set forth—as if there were no oppositional tradition, no models, no predecessors.

II

The Analogies Between Femininity and Nature

When inquiring into the common characteristics of the sentimental ideals of the feminine and of nature, the first characteristic that should be pointed out is the historical conditions of their emergence. Not only did both developments occur around the same time historically, but there was no other time in which they could have occurred. Both the sentimental concept of femininity and the "positive" understanding of nature presuppose the modern process of rationalization. That is, both temporally and logically, their appearance is predicated on the break with nature that characterizes modernity and the modern age. To put it still more bluntly: patriarchal Western thought develops a "positive" idea of the feminine[14] and nature only in the course of, and as a result of, the consistent self-imposition of power over woman and nature.

---

ence.' The correlate of objective knowledge is nature alone as object of empirical science." To this process there corresponds, on the other side, an entirely new mode in which the aesthetic concept of nature emerges: "The displacement of the metaphysical by the scientific concept of nature leaves behind an empty place which, from now on, is the express possession of a differently developed, aesthetic concept of nature" (130). Zimmermann even characterizes the transformation of the metaphysical concept of nature into the aesthetic concept as one of the most significant events in the cultural history of the eighteenth century, an event which, as such, should be given its due, though which nevertheless has received less consideration as a whole in comparison to the dissolution of the metaphysical concept of nature in the mechanistic picture of the world in modern natural science.

14. This is not to say that before the onset of the modern age there was no idealization of femininity. The most obvious case in this respect is the cult of the Virgin Mary in the Middle Ages. Mary was venerated for qualities that essentially distinguished her from other women, so that a kind of contradiction existed between her as an apparent exception and the normal woman, whereas modern idealization pertains to a veneration of femininity as such.

In the beginning I referred to the connection between the transformation of the ideology of femininity and the beginning of the modern age—namely, that very often this connection is seen, though only in a one-sidedly negative sense, as an intensification of the exploitation and oppression of the female sex, as a relative degradation of the social status of woman. The ambivalence of the new concept of nature is, by contrast, more clearly apparent in the diagnosis of the connection between the transformation of the concept of nature and the rise of the industrial age. The connection between the domination and the idealization of nature is without question diagnosed and basically accepted to be both unavoidable and unproblematic. Take for example the following statements:

> [T]he sensitivity for the particular phenomenon of "landscape" emerged only at a late stage of Western history precisely because it presupposes the loss of the unitary feeling for the whole of nature. It is only the process of individuation of inner and outer forms of existence, the dissolution of the original bonds and ties into differentiated spheres—this great formula of the post-medieval world—that first lets us see landscape in nature. No wonder antiquity and the Middle Ages had no feeling for landscape; the object itself had not even come into existence in the mental distinctiveness of perception and in the developed independence of its form.[15]

> The pleasure in nature, and the aesthetic turning to nature, presuppose . . . the social domination of nature. Where nature becomes powerful, breaking her chains, sweeping away humans thus rendered helpless, there the blind horror holds sway in dread. Freedom is existence over harnessed nature. Thus there can be nature as landscape only on the condition of freedom and on the basis of modern society.[16]

The basic assumption of the Western philosophical tradition that freedom is only possible as existence over harnessed nature is repeated unquestioningly not only in conservative thinkers like Joachim Ritter. The following remark of Adorno, whose thought was so strongly determined by

---

15. Georg Simmel, "Philosophie der Landschaft," in *Brücke und Tor*, ed. M. Landmann (Stuttgart, 1957), 143.

16. Joachim Ritter, "Landschaft: Zur Funktion des Ästhetischen in der modernen Gesellschaft," in *Subjektivität* (Frankfurt am Main, 1974), 162.

the yearning for the nonidentical, shows agreement—at least as far as the assessment of the past goes—with Ritter: "Times in which nature confronts man overpoweringly allow no room for natural beauty; as is well known, agricultural occupations, in which nature as it appears is an immediate object of action, allow little appreciation for landscape. Natural beauty, purportedly ahistorical, is at its core historical; this legitimates at the same time that it relativizes the concept. Wherever nature was not actually mastered, the image of its untamed condition terrified."[17]

It would be an oversimplification, along the lines of a critique of ideology, to dispose with the idealization of nature by referring to the prior, underlying subjugation of nature, dismissing the idealization as mere illusion. Nor can it be a matter of focusing solely on the side of idealization, with the intent of forgetting the powerlessness that accompanies it. Both belong together and are not reducible to one another.

For a more appropriate understanding of the sentimental conception of femininity and nature, it is necessary to distinguish between "closeness" and "yearning." The modern idealization of woman and nature should never be misunderstood as an immediate closeness or bond—it is rather based precisely on the opposite. This is why it is characterized as sentimental. A sentimental turn to something presupposes distance between the subject and the object toward which the subject turns—whether the distance is actively contrived as a break, passively borne as a loss, or both simultaneously. This distance assures that there is no threat from the other side. After its destruction or subjugation, or at least its being put at a distance, the object of fear returns in an opposite form: as an object of yearning. In this sense the sentimental ideal of femininity and nature not only happens to develop more or less at the same time as the intensifying process of subjugation cited at the beginning, but it is in the most tightly knit causal connection with it.

Just as little as a positive or even an enthusiastic turn to femininity or nature should be confused with a factual closeness, so vice versa, the bond with nature in traditional or primitive societies, or even their reliance on woman, should not be taken as proof of a more positive assessment (inspired by yearning) of woman or nature. I consider false all approaches that, from the closeness of premodern societies to nature, go on to deduce an esteem for the feminine or even a real improvement in the status of women. This is true at least as far as Western culture is concerned, for here the

---

17. Theodor W. Adorno, *Aesthetic Theory*, trans. Hullot-Kentor (Minneapolis: University of Minnesota Press, 1997), 65. German: *Ästhetische Theorie* (Frankfurt am Main, 1970), 102.

dependency on, and bond with, nature is always (or, more cautiously, has always been since the imposition of patriarchal structures) interpreted as subjugation, and is opposed with all means available.[18] Differences between various epochs of European history have much more to do with differences in the quantity and quality of available means than with the goal.

The further development of the sentimental conception of nature and femininity must be seen in light of those processes that have had the most decisive impact on modern development: the advancing differentiation and separation of various spheres of value and life. With respect to our theme, this differentiation concerns (*a*) the further division of female and male activities (that is, over and above the natural or traditional division of labor between the sexes); (*b*) the sharper division between the spheres of production and reproduction/recreation/consumption; (*c*) transformations in the allocation of the tasks of the public and private spheres; and, finally, with respect to the theme of nature, (*d*) the further progressive differentiation between city and country.

We turn first to the question of the relations between the sexes. In the feminist research of recent years, the effects of the processes outlined above have been overwhelmingly represented as negative and disadvantageous to women. The most important arguments to this effect are those that point to the decline in the importance of the family[19] and the reduction of the female contribution in the sphere of production[20]—in short, the reduction of woman to the realm of the home, which on its part is also reduced in eco-

---

18. I agree on this point with the above-mentioned approaches of J. and M. Bloch and S. Ortner. Cf. notes 9–11.

19. Cf., for example, Joan B. Landes, "Hegel's Conception of the Family," in *The Family in Political Thought*, ed. J. B. Elshtain (Brighton: Harvester Press, 1982), 132: "The new family, unlike the old, is dependent, subordinate and contingent. Alone, it can no longer provide for the economic livelihood of its members"; cf. also Bennent, *Galanterie und Verachtung*, 40: "The family *reduced* itself from an economic unity of ends to an association *limited* to consumption and regeneration" (my emphasis).

20. Cf., for example, Beverly W. Harrison, "The Effect of Industrialization on the Role of Women in Society," in *Making the Connections: Essays in Feminist Social Ethics* (Boston: Beacon Press, 1985), 42: "[A]dvanced industrial technological systems of production, developed under the aegis of private capital, weaken women's social role"; the improved position of women in traditional societies is tied to their participation in production: "As Margaret Mead and other anthropologists have observed, in rural societies the functions of production and consumption are closely conjoined, and both men and women are producers" (45). Barbara Duden makes the same claim with respect to European history: We see "the women in the lower and middle classes in the 18th century as true creatures of work, crude beings, slaving away . . . ; yet for that their work is also equal to the work of men, and is also considered as such" ("Das schöne Eigentum: Zur Herausbildung des bürgerlichen Frauenbildes an der Wende vom 18. zum 19. Jahrhundert," *Kursbuch* 47 [1977]: 131).

nomic importance. It is mainly these factors that lie behind the assertion that the social position of woman has deteriorated in the modern age.

We must start from the fact that the process of differentiation reinforced the consignment of woman to the realm of the family—what is more, to a family that had been restructured as a nuclear family. The sphere ascribed to the feminine—that of privacy, of the house, of the family, which first comes into being as the product of a rigid gender-specific division of labor and a process of differentiation—is, virtually in defiance of its origin, advanced as the representative of the lost wholeness, unity, and completeness of society. It is almost as if the ongoing process of the division of labor between the sexes, the result of which is the house as the sole arena of woman's activity, had been forgotten. It is as if the exclusion of this realm had suppressed all of that, so that the activity of woman could appear to be nonwork; and the house, the family, could appear to have a nondifferentiated, nonspecialized status.

Of course, it is in this way that the aim of keeping women out of the public sphere, thus preventing them from having an active influence on social and political interests, is pursued, in fact successfully. In addition, women are denied recognition of their work as work, which means that they are (in more than a material sense) deprived of the "fruits" of their labor. In other words, the old traditional discrimination and exploitation is successfully continued under the conditions of a new age. However, along with these age-old efforts of patriarchy, wholly new types of demands emerge.

The process of modernity is accompanied by the (likewise progressive) consciousness of its attendant costs. The atomization of society and the alienation and division of labor are increasingly experienced as hardships. The disappearance of the traditional order in the process of modernity results in a profound loss of meaning and security. In the face of the dark aspects of the process of rationalization, a bright light is cast on the realm it touches the least: in the special, ever more isolated sphere of the family, and in woman at its center, what had otherwise been lost is again found.

With the onset of the bourgeois age, a significant shift occurs in the distribution of prestige between the public and private spheres. Since the ancient beginnings of Western culture, the public space had been in one way or another the place of self-realization (of the man), the place where one proved oneself as well as realized the values of a given society and culture.[21]

---

21. Naturally, such an assertion is abominably careless. In the course of Western history, ideas as to what realm and what type of life are the best in achieving social esteem and personal happiness have changed in varied and profound ways. It is a long way from the political life of

In sum, the public sphere was the space of true human being, while the realm of the household was devoted to the mere fulfillment of material needs necessary for life. In the bourgeois age an almost complete reversal occurs. While the fulfillment of material needs (now rapidly expanding) becomes a matter for the public sphere (or rather the market), the private sphere becomes the place of individual self-realization (again, exclusively of the man); it is also the refuge for traditional values and virtues. Whereas in premodern times woman had been barred from politics and society because she was, to put it crudely, "too base"—that is, irresponsible, incapable of raising herself to the values, virtues, and ideals that transcend the individual—now it is the exclusion of woman from the business of society that lies behind her being "too good" for this world—that is, beyond the instrumental reason and egoism that rules it.

The most important characteristic of this exclusion of woman and the private sphere from the process of modernity in the new epoch is not only the exemption from work and production. It also implies an exclusion from historical development in general. Given that the family is understood as a retreat for the traditional (and that means natural) order, it is almost inevitable that woman appears to be a historyless being. It is in this sense that Hegel, for example, speaks of piety as the "law of woman," the law determining the family, and characterizes it "as the law of the ancient gods, 'the gods of the underworld'; as 'an everlasting law, and no man knows at what time it was put forth.' "[22]

The more there is a tendency to interpret the course of history as a process of tragic separation or even ruin, the more bright the light surrounding woman, who had been excluded from this course of events. With a look to Rousseau, Paul Hoffmann writes: "Woman remains close to the primitive goodness of her nature. . . . The condition of woman, precisely because she is situated outside of history in the same timeless sphere as the state of nature, coincides with the highest values which are the most necessary to the life of the species as well as its spiritual recovery."[23]

---

the Greek citizen of the polis to the exemplariness of the hermit existence of a medieval monk. But whatever the place had been in which the realization of the best of humanity (= male) was to be established, it was always—and it is with this point that I am concerned—far away from the family, from household life. To lay the realization of virtue and humanity in the lap of the family is reserved for modern bourgeois society.

22. G. W. F. Hegel, *Hegel's Philosophy of Right*, trans. Knox (Oxford: Clarendon Press, 1942), 115. German: *Grundlinien der Philosophie des Rechts*, vol. 7 of *Werke in zwanzig Bänden* (Frankfurt am Main, 1970), § 166, p. 319.

23. Paul Hoffmann, *La femme dans la pensée des Lumières* (Paris, 1977), 378f.

The core of the analogy between the sentimental conception of femininity and the concept of landscape is modernity's idealization of the excluded as a relic and representative of the lost wholeness. Thus what is common here is not only this being outside of society and history, but also the strange displacement of this exclusion, which makes possible the "ascent" of the excluded into a representation of wholeness. There is thoroughgoing agreement that, through the use of the landscape ideal, that which had otherwise been lost in the process of modernity is to be saved:

> Aesthetic nature as landscape . . . , in a countermove to the object domain of the natural sciences which is extracted from the metaphysical concept, has taken over the function of presenting the whole of nature in "intuitive" images and of keeping aesthetically present to humans the "harmonic unison in the cosmos."[24]

> While . . . in the social, the technical, the spiritual, and in the moral there are countless struggles and inner conflicts, this same form [i.e., of culture, C.K.] establishes over against nature the reconciled richness of landscape, which is individual, closed, content in itself and thus remaining attached, without contradiction, to the whole of nature and its unity.[25]

Just as with the conception of femininity, the most important presupposition of the landscape ideal is also its exclusion—perhaps here it would be

---

24. Ritter, "Landschaft," 153.
25. Simmel, "Philosophie der Landschaft," 143. While in both Ritter and Simmel the function of nature and landscape is taken to be compensatory, Helmut J. Schneider proposes another interpretation in the essay "Utopie und Landschaft im 18. Jahrhundert." The aesthetic perspective on nature is neither fundamentally different from the scientific-instrumental nor compensating for it. Rather, it has to do with promoting the claim to dominate nature by other, specifically aesthetic means. The aesthetic image of nature "is the anticipation of the perfect domination of nature in which the subject enjoys its power over nature precisely by setting it free. The landscape in the Enlightenment is to be understood as the aesthetic emergence of the controllable manifold of the world of experience in which modern humanity sets eyes upon its own limitless desire for discovery and potential for development. . . . If that is so, then the relation between scientific-economic objectification of nature and the aesthetic representation of nature would come together on the basis of the image of the landscape itself; it would then not only be a question of a compensatory but also of a dialectical relation" (in *Utopieforschung: Interdisziplinäre Studien zur neuzeitlichen Utopie,* ed. Wilhelm Voßkamp [Frankfurt am Main, 1985], 3:175). This position is interesting insofar as—similarly with the reflections presented here—it casts doubt on the dogma of the complementarity of the different spheres.

more appropriate to say exemption—from productivity and work. The experience of the beautiful in nature "has to do with nature only as appearance, never as material for work and reproduction of life."[26]

Perhaps I am mistaken, but what for me stands out the most is that which in the end is precisely true for woman: that is, that the sentimental conception is concerned less with the reality of woman or of nature than with a particular way of perceiving them. There can not for a moment be a doubt that nature is and always will remain "material for work and the reproduction of life," and that the idealization of nature as landscape does nothing to release it from this fate. A sentimental concept of nature is simply another perspective on nature, a perspective in which the rationalistic-instrumental perspective is neither subsumed nor overcome. The sentimental principle of reality does not revolutionize the rationalistic-instrumental principle (nor, nota bene, vice versa).

Likewise, women are by no means exempted from work and from its accompanying hardships. Such exemption is only the case—if at all—for a small minority of bourgeois women, and even for them only insofar as their multifaceted duties and activities are not recognized as work. These aspects of feminine existence are simply obliterated; but not only, as feminist criticism objects, in order to withhold recognition of female work in the form of money, power, and respect, but also in order to retain an alternative to the rationalistic-male-bourgeois world of work, alienation, and competition—an alternative model this world urgently needs for its continued existence.

It is almost superfluous to point out that femininity and landscape not only structurally correspond to one another but also that at the same time that they gravitate toward one another, that they appear to belong together. It is not for nothing that Rousseau has his Emile search for Sophie precisely in the country and not in the city. The concept of rural innocence that is thus brought to mind goes far beyond Biedermeier morality, but rather refers to a utopian alternative realm of femininity and landscape: "Nature, which remains for Rousseau an ideal realm, primitive yet undefiled and authentic, is associated with the family and woman."[27] The woman is closer to nature, and not only nature in the temporal sense (as an original state of nature), but also in the spatial sense (nature as landscape).

In the essay "Landscape with Figures," Leonore Davidoff, Jean L'Espera-

---

26. Adorno, *Ästhetische Theorie*, 103. Trans.: Dodd.
27. Diana Coole, *Women in Political Theory: From Ancient Misogyny to Contemporary Feminism* (Brighton, Sussex: Wheatsheaf Books, 1988), 114.

nce, and Howard Newby delve more deeply than can be done here into the close association of woman with nature, in particular in Anglo-Saxon bourgeois family ideology. After comparing landscape and family ideologies, they come to the following conclusion: "The rural and domestic idylls had many features in common. Territorially, these two areas merged together in the symbolism of the garden where nature could be enjoyed but was also tamed and controlled."[28] In the essay "The Family as Utopian Retreat from the City," Kirk Jeffrey comes to the same conclusion. He characterizes the family as the "outpost of the country . . . within city walls."[29] Both the country and the realm of the household represent sanctuaries in which the (male) individual can seek refuge from the threatening reality of the city and industry. "Ideally the family ought to be rural; and a later generation . . . would discover that it was possible to commute to the city while still enjoying a home life far removed from its terrors, in houses surrounded by a few hundred square feet of welltrimmed grass."[30] Jeffrey and Davidoff and their colleagues lay great importance on the fact that this connection survived into the twentieth century and up to the immediate present:

> The more that the wider society grows in centralized corporate and state power, in size of institutions and in alienating work environment, the more the home becomes fantasized as a countering haven. Home-baked bread, French farmhouse cookery, wine making, organic gardening—the whole gamut of "creative homemaking" have become the suburban substitutes for the fully fledged return to the self-sufficient small holding. . . . In their suburban homes, wives are still expected to create a miniature version of the domestic idyll, set in suburban pseudo-rural estate surroundings while their male counterparts swarm into central city offices and factories.[31]

The Analogies Between Woman, Landscape, and Artwork

The ideals both of femininity and of nature sketched here lead to a third concept: that of the beautiful,[32] or of art. The countermovement to the proc-

28. Leonore Davidoff, Jean L'Esperance, and Howard Newby, "Landscape with Figures: Home and Community in English Society," in *The Rights and Wrongs of Women*, ed. J. Mitchell (Harmondsworth, Middlesex: Penguin, 1976), 160.
29. Kirk Jeffrey, "The Family as Utopian Retreat from the City: The Nineteenth-Century Contribution," *Soundings: An Interdisciplinary Journal* 55, no. 1 (1972): 28.
30. Ibid.
31. Davidoff, L'Esperance, and Newby, "Landscape with Figures," 172f., 175.
32. Incidentally, Davidoff and her colleagues speak of the "*Beau* Ideal" in order to indicate the bond between rural and domestic idyll.

ess of the rationalization of modernity, which until now has been described as a process of sentimentalization, can also be placed under the heading of aestheticization.

The term *landscape* is almost unavoidably connected to the beautiful or to art. I probably would even have done better to employ the more general concept of natural beauty, of which landscape represents a particularly important case in point. On its part, natural beauty is almost exclusively a subject of art—again only since, and on the basis of, the processes of modernity. "Just as nature began gradually to vanish from human life as *experience* and as the (active and feeling) *subjectivity*, so we see it emerge in the world of the poet as an idea and as subject-matter."[33] Landscape painting is infused with the modern way of thinking right down to its technique: "[T]he view of nature in landscape painting is dependent on the representation of space, on the perspective, the subjective choice of selection; and although with that only the artistic conditions that make nature in general representable are indicated, nevertheless everything else is very strongly dependent on the 'perspectivity' of modernity."[34]

The presentation of nature or landscape in art fulfills the same function as the actual landscape or beauty of nature. More precisely, even the task ascribed to landscape, the substitution for the lost unity and wholeness of a *Weltbild* (world picture), finds its realization only in art because the represented landscape, to an even greater extent than the actual landscape, is in the position to transmit the impression of unity. The represented landscape refers more to the human subject than does the real landscape that is first constituted as something perceived, in that the represented landscape refers to the subject, the artist, who first produced it. "As standing in for the observer or reader, the painter or poet achieves this fusion of the individual part with a whole. To create, as beautiful appearance, this unity of nature and humanity, and to let this be aesthetically experienced, is the function of the artistically formed landscape and, at the same time, the cause of its coming into existence."[35]

Art never merely represents landscape; it actually creates it. The artist becomes a creator of worlds. "Nature comes to itself as such in the artist.

---

33. Friedrich Schiller, *On the Naive and Sentimental in Literature*, trans. Watanabe-O'Kelly (Manchester: Carcanet New Press, 1981), 34.
34. Hans Holländer, "Weltentwürfe neuzeitlicher Landschaftsmalerei," in *Das Naturbild des Menschen*, ed. Zimmermann, 188.
35. Mathias Eberle, *Individuum und Landschaft: Zur Entstehung und Entwicklung der Landschaftsmalerei*, 2nd ed. (Gießen, 1984), 38.

In his work it reaches, as appearance, the real, essential bond with human beings and history. What no longer comes about in social praxis is achieved in art—namely, the realized bond, the unison of human being and nature, nature and history."[36]

Of central importance for the possibility of the representation of landscape in art is again the exclusion or, even more precisely, the disregarding of work and production. Hans Holländer speaks of an "increasing sensibility to the purposeless view of nature's own regularities"[37] as the necessary presupposition for the art of landscape: "The views of nature and forms of space in landscape painting follow, first of all, from the distance from landscape as natural or something worked. . . . It is evident that landscape painting . . . was a result of the culture of the city. At least this is where the spark came from, after which there were many painters who 'lived in the country' but not off the land."[38]

To be sure, the connection between woman and beauty is "as old as the world," but it is only in the context of modern thought that it takes on a systematic meaning, as it does, for example, in the polarization of the beautiful and the sublime in Kant—which was not explicitly conceived with reference to the gender relation, but was applied to it. The same is true for Schiller's distinction between grace and dignity. Kant ascribed to woman the "beautiful virtues"; Schiller considered his concept of the "beautiful soul" as something that was primarily realized in the female sex.

"It is in a beautiful soul, therefore, where sensibility and reason, duty and affection harmonize."[39] The sense of the beautiful lies in the conservation of the unity, of the harmony that is broken asunder in the male, modern order. The yearning for Greece in the whole of German classicism turns on this point. In the concept of the beautiful soul, a faint glimmer of this utopia is carried over to woman. The invocation of Greece again recalls the archaic character of the sentimental conception of the feminine. At the end of the eighteenth century, there is a strong sense that the process of modernity has irrevocably banished into the past the presuppositions for an order of thinking and society grounded in a harmony of nature and culture. That which is past is still, in a certain sense, felt within the nostalgic return to Greek art and culture, or in the idea of femininity.

36. Ibid., 59.
37. Holländer, "Weltentwürfe neuzeitlicher Landschaftsmalerei," 189.
38. Ibid. Cf. Eberle, *Individuum und Landschaft*, 57.
39. Friedrich Schiller, *Über Anmut und Würde*, in *Schillers Werke, im sechs Haupt- und vier Ergänzungsbänden*, ed. Paul Merker (Leipzig, n.d.), 6:94.

Yet it should not be overlooked that there is an ambivalence in this nostalgic idealization of the past, even with respect to the yearning for Greece. It is not seldom that the grief over the irrevocable loss of the past is accompanied by an arrogance that, regardless of the criticisms of its darker side, nevertheless regards the current age to be superior, and for which the beautiful harmony of Greece carries with it the odium of primitivity. With respect to femininity, yearning is even more unambiguously mixed with contempt. Despite all the nostalgia, this beautiful unity and totality of a past order not only fails to amount to a realistic goal, but it is not even truly a goal at all.

The ease, the effortlessness, the originality, the lack of compulsion (which Schiller so strongly stresses as characteristic of the dignity identified with the male sex: "With dignity thus arises the spirit in the body as master")[40]—all of these qualities of the beautiful soul again refer to the exemption from work: "The beautiful soul has no other merit beyond that it is. With an ease, as if in it only instinct were acting, it carries out the most painful duties of humanity, and the most heroic sacrifice that it wins from natural drive strikes even this drive as a voluntary effect. For it itself knows nothing of the beauty of its acts."[41]

More than a century later, but still in the same tradition and, in a way, intensifying and completing it, Georg Simmel drew the analogy between femininity and the work of art (note: *not* between woman and artist—which would have been more suggestive or even obvious!). The fact that both woman and artwork represent unity and wholeness in a self-differentiating, male-dominated world, a world plagued by such differentiation as its inner tension and alienation, also constitutes, according to Simmel, their *tertium comparationis*:

> As women became the bearers of the culture of the household, there accrued to them that psychic being, the symbol of which is the house as distinct from those demands pulling from all sides: constancy, completeness, unity in which the complexity and conflicts of life on the outside come to a rest. . . . This unity, which relegates the cultural role of the woman to her inwardness, or which had fashioned it from the former—gives her . . . something of the character of the artwork. The essence of this is nevertheless

---

40. Ibid., 103.
41. Ibid., 94.

the self-contented unity, the self-satisfaction not achieved by any natural image.[42]

The artwork alone is a whole in the way that the world-unity is a oneness; its borders set it inviolably apart from all the multifarious confusion of things. The woman represents such a unity in contrast to the man, who is bound up with the dispersed multiplicity of inestimable life.[43]

Lou Andreas-Salomé, in the same year and in the same spirit as Simmel, arrived at similar opinions; but she drew the parallel not between woman and artwork as object, but between woman and the artist/genius as subject.[44]

Independent of its direct relation to landscape and femininity, art, in the conceptual determination given to it by classical aesthetics at the end of the eighteenth century, also bears characteristics similar to those that we have demonstrated with respect to the other motifs. This is something that cannot be detailed further here, but only summarized thematically:

- The sphere of art arises as autonomous, thanks to the same process of modernity with its differentiation of spheres that had brought about the formation of the private sphere or the constitution of nature as landscape; that is, art in the contemporary-modern sense also presupposes the separation of art and life (and from that point on labors on many levels to overcome this separation).
- The division of art from "life" results in the appearance that art is not subject to the conceptions of value and laws of the modern world. In particular, artistic production and productivity do not appear to be "work" in the modern sense; that is, art does not succumb to the conditions of the division of labor and the market. Artistic production appears to preserve a preindustrial, handicraftlike mode of production (i.e., little division of labor, nonalienating); furthermore, it is felt to spring from nature and to exist as a whole. Of course, contrary to the work of woman, who is disparaged for her naturalness, here it is nevertheless naturalness,

---

42. Georg Simmel, "Bruchstücke aus einer Psychologie der Frauen (1904)," reprinted in *Georg Simmel: Schriften zur Philosophie und Soziologie der Geschlechter,* ed. H.-J. Dahme and Klaus Christian Köhnke (Frankfurt am Main, 1985), 178.
43. Ibid., 177f.
44. Lou Andreas Salomé, *Die Erotik: Vier Aufsätze,* ed. E. Pfeiffer (Munich, 1979), 22.

even the (putative) unconsciousness and unreflecting quality of artistic activity, that is the object of sheer boundless wonder (concept of genius).
- By being excluded from the modern, bourgeois-male industrial society, the sphere of fine arts becomes representative of a lost wholeness and harmony. It is even differentiated and specialized precisely in order to allow for this very differentiation and specialization to be denied and forgotten. This makes up the illusory character of art.
- Just as with the familial, private sphere, the aesthetic sphere fulfills important functions in the reproduction of the bourgeois-male individual. In order to compensate for the sorrows of alienation, one-sidedness, and so forth, a temporary or long-term refuge is found in the isolated and sheltered realms of art and privacy.

The parallel drawn here between the sphere of art and the sphere of privacy is in partial agreement with Max Weber's theory of modernization. According to Weber, art and the erotic constitute spheres of the inner-worldly powers of life, "the essence of which, from the ground up, is of an a-rational or anti-rational character."[45] With that, art and the erotic are, on the one hand, modern (they form the so-called third value sphere complex, along with the complex of natural science and technology as the first, and rational natural law and the Protestant ethic as the second). On the other hand, they are, at the same time, considered to be opposed to the process of rationalization.

Yet to interpret, as I have done here, not only the erotic or erotic love but also the familial, private sphere in a broader sense as analogous to the aesthetic, and to juxtapose it to moral-legal and natural-scientific technological rationality, must appear dubious. The family betrays far too unambiguously the characteristics of a moral-legal institution; its economic functions are all too important—in sum, there cannot be any doubt that the family has ties with the rational structures of state and society.[46] Although it is true that love and the erotic are the core of the antirationalistic impulse of the private

---

45. Max Weber, *Gesammelte Aufsätze zur Religionssoziologie* (Tübingen, 1978), 1:554.

46. The bourgeois nuclear family figures consistently in Habermas's schematic presentation of the Weberian theory as a social form of expression ("social agency") of the Protestant ethic. It therefore belongs wholly to the second of the three spheres of value. It is distinguished by a clear line of demarcation from the third sphere of value represented by autonomous art. (Characteristically, the corresponding place for it on this level in the third realm is left empty in Habermas's schema.) Cf. Jürgen Habermas, *Theory of Communicative Action*, trans. McCarthy (Boston: Beacon Press, 1984). German: *Theorie des kommunikativen Handelns*, 2nd ed. (Frankfurt am Main, 1982), 1:237.

sphere, it is a characteristic peculiarity of modernity to establish bond between love and the erotic on the one side, and marriage and family on the other—a feat that had not been achieved in any other age, and one that no other age would even have had attempted. It seems to me that this fact speaks—not exclusively, but also not unimportantly—for seeing the familial, private sphere as a phenomenon that should be understood as on the one hand a legal, moral, and economic institution, but on the other hand as also a part of the alternative realm of the aesthetic-sentimental. If, in addition, we take into consideration that it is, above all, the quasi-countercultural aspects that to this day preserve or result in a certain attractiveness of marriage and family,[47] then the question arises whether with respect to the long development of the family we should not speak of a gradual transformation of this legal-moral institution into a sentimental, alternative world.

III

What I have described is the structure of an ideal type, which in this particular form had been in effect—if at all—only for a brief, fleeting moment in history, somewhere around the turn from the eighteenth to the nineteenth century. The ideal of fine art as the substitute for lost metaphysical or religious instances of a sense of totality disappeared with the decline of the great philosophical systems in the era after German Idealism.[48] The sentimental landscape ideal fades at the latest around the middle of the nineteenth century.[49] The validity of the sentimental conception of femininity does not lend itself to such a precise "end date." On the one hand, it remained in effect for a longer period; on the other hand, from the beginning its effectiveness had already been exposed to much stronger resistance—

---

47. Cf., for example, Christopher Lasch, *Haven in a Heartless World: The Family Besieged* (New York: Basic Books, 1977).

48. Cf. Joachim Ritter, "Ästhetik," in *Historisches Wörterbuch der Philosophie*, ed. Joachim Ritter (Darmstadt, 1971), vol. A–D, 555–80.

49. Cf. Eberle, *Individuum und Landschaft*, 25f; also Hans Sedlmayr, *Verlust der Mitte: Die bildende Kunst des 19. und 20. Jahrhunderts als Symbol der Zeit* (Salzburg, 1948). On the landscape garden, the appearance of which Sedlmayr dates at around 1720 and to which he had attributed the "new leading tasks" of art: "Around 1830 is the beginning of the end: the park becomes like a museum, a type of nature museum. . . . The experience is emptied of genuineness, of the all-feeling and the religious" (24).

namely in its competition with the egalitarian principle as the foundation for a new ordering of the relations between the sexes.

In contrast to what are at first glance narrow limits to its validity as well as to its brief duration, in all three realms the sentimental—or, better, the aesthetic—conception has had an aftereffect. It has, strictly speaking, led an afterlife up to the present day, so that in the end it appears to be little justified to speak of a demise of the sentimental or aesthetic conception. What disappeared was simply its initial historical expression.

The later development, in part, took on the character of a process of trivialization. This is true above all for the aesthetic idea of nature, which as an independent conception has been almost completely disavowed[50] and has instead found its way into almost all branches of culture, leisure, and advertising industries.[51] Yet insofar as it exercises an even more lasting hold on the imagination of countless people in this way, we would do well to avoid dismissing it with educated conceit and ideological-critical enthusiasm.

That the conceptions of femininity and art were better able to defend themselves against the process of trivialization (though without wholly escaping it) may lie in the fact that, more than in the case of landscape and nature, they are more directly connected to human subjects who resist their own trivialization. With respect to the realms of art and the family, their functional connections with other, very differently structured areas of society have in many cases been analyzed and criticized. Artists and women (not everyone, just those who reflect the most on their situation) have attempted to make clear to themselves and to others that, as products of the processes of modernity, the spheres ascribed to them are just as subject to the laws of these processes as the realms of economy and industry, law and the state, and so on. Despite their apparent withdrawnness, they are nevertheless subject to the rationalistic and capitalistic logic on which they depend and which they serve. The real problem, of course, consists in the fact that the realms of art and privacy are useful to rationalistic logic not (only) *in spite of* but *because* they appear to be withdrawn from it. That is, the problem lies less in the illusoriness attached to the otherness of the aesthetic and the

---

50. There are nevertheless some indications that in the twentieth century the landscape ideal is not completely dead or disavowed; cf., for example, Robert Rosenblum, *Die moderne Malerei und die Tradition der Romantik: Von C. D. Friedrich bis Mark Rothko* (Munich, 1981); also Hugh Cumming, "Post-Modern Landscape," in *The Post-Avant-Garde Painting in the Eighties: An Art and Design Profile* (London, 1987), 77–80.

51. Adorno, *Aesthetic Theory*, 64. "With the collapse of romanticism, that hybrid domain, cultural landscape, deteriorated into an advertising gimmick."

private than in its functionality. From this it follows that any attempt to back away from this functionality on the way toward an insistence on the otherness of "true" art or "true" femininity does not and cannot step out of this functional connection with the other spheres; for even the most worthwhile contribution of those spheres, which are taken to be alternative models, nevertheless preserves the dominant principle of reality in their very opposition and otherness.

Nevertheless, both the sentimental concept of femininity and the aesthetic ideal of art have survived. For the hope has never been abandoned, either with respect to art or femininity, that there is yet a subversive potential, a utopian reserve against the dominant principle of rationality. In innumerable guises the idea has been entertained that the appearance of the "other" could be, or could at least someday become, the herald of something better. What Adorno says about natural beauty is likewise true for artistic beauty even after its feminist revision—even for the ideal of the feminine, and even for the age where art is no longer beautiful: the sentimental or aesthetic conceptions "share the weakness of every promise with that promise's inextinguishability."[52]

To this day in discussions about art as well as about femininity, these weaknesses and indelibility of promises are led again and again into the field and played out against one another. All the arguments about the question whether femininity, nature, and art are reserves in the service of the dominant order or whether, despite their "weaknesses," they represent alternative utopias and thus remain the bearers of an indelible promise have been in circulation for a long time. If in spite of this a convincing argument has not been made, then we must consider whether what we have taken to be obvious presuppositions are in fact mistaken. If a pressing and important question cannot be answered, the possibility must be considered that it has been incorrectly posed. To state it concretely: it is plausible that a certain one-sidedness in our understanding of the processes of modernization could be responsible for the fact that this back-and-forth between the arguments of weakness and promise repeats itself almost cyclically.

Although for a long time the connection between the process of rationalization and the unfolding of antirational counterconceptions has been recognized,[53] still in many cases modernity—or, better, modernization—is often

52. Ibid., 73.
53. So, for example, Henri Lefebvre observes: "The flip side to the objectivity of the technical process is a corresponding release of subjectivity. . . . Subjectivity seizes hold of that which is left to it. It feels itself to be simultaneously abandoned and freed—for private life, for aesthet-

identified all too one-sidedly with rationality or rationalization.[54] This can happen in two ways. First, the processes of rationalization and modernization are *completely* posited together as one. The consequence is that all phenomena that are opposed to ends-rational and value-rational thinking appear as alien and external to modernity. They appear, on the one hand, as survivals of a premodern order, leftovers from tradition that are gradually but irreversibly wiped out by the dynamic of the rationalization process. Or, on the other hand, they are interpreted as the harbingers of another order of things beyond the principle of reality that is currently dominant, in that the complete identification of modernity and rationality understands any opposition against the latter to be a declaration of war on the former. Second, rationality and modernity are *partially* identified with one another, even to the extent to which the process of rationalization does not represent the only—though certainly the dominant—characteristic of the process of modernization. By contrast to the first variant, all other phenomena are recognized as also belonging to modernity, but they are understood to be of secondary importance and subordinate to the dominant rationality. Thus the connection between the rational and the arational or antirational aspects of modernity are only seen in their dependence and utility for the latter.

---

icism, for moralism" (*Einführung in die Modernität: Zwölf Präludien* [Frankfurt am Main, 1978], 246). Jürgen Habermas also refers to the close connection between the progress of the process of rationalization and the development of contrary tendencies: "On the one hand, a decentered understanding of the world opens up the possibility of dealing with the world of facts in a cognitively objectified [*versachlicht*] manner and with the world of interpersonal relations in a legally and morally objectified manner; on the other hand, it offers the possibility of a subjectivism freed from imperatives of objectification in dealing with individualized needs, desires, and feelings [*Bedürfnisnatur*]" (*The Theory of Communicative Action*. vol. 1, *Reason and the Rationalization of Society*, trans. McCarthy [Boston: Beacon Press, 1984], 216).

54. The one-sidedness of the concept of rationality is also true of Habermas's objection to Weber's theory of modernity: "From Weber's sociology of the economy, state, and law, one gets the impression that in modern societies, rationalization processes attach only to empirical-theoretical knowledge and to the instrumental and strategic aspects of action, whereas practical rationality cannot be institutionalized independently, that is, with an inner logic specific to a subsystem" (*The Theory of Communicative Action*, 1:254). Habermas makes a significant shift of emphasis from ends-rational to value-rational systems of action. He reclaims the importance of practical reason for modernity, in contrast to the priority that instrumental reason had had in Weber. But the third group of value spheres remains almost as unconsidered as it had been previously. The spheres oriented against reason receive just as much mention in Habermas's reconstruction of the Weberian approach as they had received in Weber himself. Habermas explains: "Aesthetically imbued counterculture belongs, together with science and technology on the one hand, and with *modern legal and moral representations* on the other, to the whole of rationalized culture" (161–62; cf. note 53). Yet practical reason remains unambiguously the focus of his interest.

Neither view corresponds to reality. On the one hand, no one can seriously assert that the utopian potential of the alternative realms of the private sphere or the aesthetic has, to date, hindered instrumental rationality. On the other hand, there can be just as little talk of the victory of the process of rationalization over the phenomena that oppose it. On the contrary: the more rigid the forms adopted by the process of rationalization in some areas, the greater the need for compensation in others. This means that the relation between the opposing spheres of modern culture cannot be interpreted as a zero sum game; one side never wins solely at the expense of the other.

Finally, it seems to me that the assumption that the alternatives of the aesthetic and the private promote and aid the progressive rationalization of other spheres has more to do with a one-sidedness of perspective than with reality. We could just as well make the contrary observation: the progressive process of rationalization quantitatively and qualitatively strengthens the process of sentimentalization. This state of affairs makes it explicable why, in spite of doubts, an assertive avowal of an aesthetic understanding of the world and of nature, as well as a feminine utopia, is always possible. This is the case not so much as a way of overcoming existing structures of thinking and valuing (for which it often mistakes itself), but is rather a possible way of creating a space within this structure—something that in the long run may even prove to be a path toward a substantial modification of this structure.

Whether in the future the relation between the processes of rationalization and sentimentalization retains the form it has had up to now; whether one day the dynamic of development will nevertheless change in favor of one over the other; or even whether, as some expect, only in the future will there perhaps be the real revolution of the aesthetic and the emergence of feminine values[55]—all this seems to me to be difficult to predict. One thing can be said with some certainty: whatever direction future developments may take, they will not have had their beginning in today nor even tomorrow but will have had a long history that led up to them. To cast some light on this history was the goal of these reflections.

---

55. Cf., for example, Jean-Marc Ferry, "Modernisation et consensus," in *Esprit: Changer la culture et la politique, Revue mensuelle* no. 101 (May 1985). Also beginning with Weber's theory, Ferry deals principally with the third realm of aesthetics and culture, claiming that even if in the past its importance was second to the scientific-technical and legal-moral spheres, in the present the point has been reached where it can take over the leading role in the process of modernity: "It is very possible that 'aesthetic reason' will one day be called on to play a historical role of the first importance in modernization, that our environment will one day be transfigured by an aesthetic revolution" (24).

7 | IS A FEMINIST CRITIQUE OF LOGIC POSSIBLE?

Käthe Trettin

Translated by George Matthews

Women and Formalism

"I am a woman reading logic," writes Andrea Nye in the introduction to her book *Words of Power: A Feminist Reading of the History of Logic*.[1] What can this explicit expression, "a woman reading logic" mean? At first glance this is easy to understand: logic seems to be something masculine if, on the one hand, we consider the few female students enrolled in logic courses and if, on the other hand, we look at the history of logic—Philo

---

This essay has been written specifically for the present collection.
1. Andrea Nye, *Words of Power: A Feminist Reading of the History of Logic* (New York: Routledge, 1990), 5.

of Megara, Zeno, Aristotle, Ockham, Frege, Russell, Wittgenstein, Quine. "Apparently there are no women in the history of logic,"[2] says Nye. To decide "as a woman" to step into this scene—"the history of logic"—is thus somewhat comparable to a field researcher or an ethnologist entering into the terrain of a foreign yet somehow interesting society in order to see whether their signs and symbols and their encoded ritual activities can be decoded and translated.

Nye's statement, however, becomes problematic if one (a) looks more closely at the predicate "am a woman" and asks whether this ascription can be taken as self-evidently meaningful, as it is in ordinary spoken usage, or if one (b) considers what "reading logic" could mean. The first question seems to Nye not to be a question. A woman is precisely a woman. This is an unshakable identity, and if we find ourselves forced to half-concede even one example of what this means, a whole slew of the most current stereotypes will follow in order. According to these, a woman is to be characterized as follows: "uncomfortable in the world of men, involved in the physical details of family life, births, marriages, the keeping of houses, a woman too intent on emotional commitments to be capable of purely abstract thought."[3] Disregarding the fact that I am not so sure that these typifying features continue to have a sound empirical basis today, I have my doubts about their validity in the realm of the scientific professions. Just as not every (male) grocer, (male) manual laborer, or (male) bank president is, or must be, a logician, neither is every (female) housekeeper, (female) biochemist, or (female) doctor a philosopher of logic. That is, the concepts "being a woman" and "being a man" might not be graspable as sharply delimited, logically dichotomous classes, least of all if the elements of being a woman, considered unproblematically as a class, are construed as opposed to logic.

The lacking problematization of the first question thus has an influence on the second, since the desire to "read" logic, as Andrea Nye would like to read it, can only be possible as a project of a woman characterized in this way. Thus, "Logic is a human invention . . . and it must speak *of* something, speak of ambitions, fears, hopes, disappointments, despairs. . . . Not only must it speak of something but it must speak *to* someone and thereby institute the relations in which communication is possible."[4]

2. Ibid., 2.
3. Ibid., 5.
4. Ibid., 4. The author herself believes that the status of "being a woman" clearly does have something to do with the project of reading logic: "Perhaps *only* a woman would undertake such a project, would do such a thing as try to read logic" (ibid., 5).

The observation that logic is a human invention, and that this invention was also accompanied by hopes and intentions, is doubtless correct. But on the other hand, the characterization of logic as a communicative medium is extremely dubious. Not only is it not the case that logic "speaks" of hopes, disappointments, and fears, but in a certain sense it does not speak at all; it has no communicative function, at least as long as by "logic" we mean classical deductive logic (and Andrea Nye means just this as well).[5] It should be remembered, to put it as Wolfgang Stegmüller does, that logic can "be defined, in a first approximation, as the *doctrine of the principles of correct argumentation.*"[6] The ideal of "correct" argumentation itself turns on the concept of "logical entailment," that is, on the fact that the interrelation of diverse propositions can be generated out of the analysis of their logical meaning and that this can be demonstrated in a verifiable, intersubjective—that is, *formal*—manner. The history of logic presents various attempts to attain this ideal by means of a progressive formalization. This project is moreover not restricted in its field of application to natural languages and the argumentation implemented in them. It can be applied in connection with other formal languages, especially that of mathematics, or it can, qua formalization, render the structure of dynamic systems—that is, "processes," "events," and "activities"—intersubjectively demonstrable.[7]

It is thus one thing to accept the noncommunicative character of logic and thus to think through the specific symbolic and demonstrative character of this formalizing, analytic praxis and the collection of truth-preservative rules of entailment that result from it. It is something entirely different to attempt a reading of the history of logic as if it were readable in narrative terms. However one should judge such an attempt, in my view it is not at all clear why it should be labeled "feminist." Are women "naturally" storytellers and men "naturally" logicians? Nye forgets that logicians do nothing but "communicate" day in and day out *about* their logics and those

---

5. Nonclassical logics, such as epistemic logic, nonmonotonic deduction, or paraconsistent logics, are more strictly oriented toward the communicative functions of language, which is replete with belief statements, bivalent undecidable arguments, and contradictions. But even these logics are not *per se* communicative; they are analytic.

6. Wolfgang Stegmüller, *Probleme und Resultate der Wissenschaftstheorie und analytischen Philosophie*, vol. 1, *Erklärung, Begründung, Kausalität (Studienausgabe, Teil A)* (Berlin: Springer-Verlag, 1983), 40.

7. For a historical survey of "the logic of action," see Krister Segerberg, "Getting Started: Beginnings in the Logic of Action," *Studia Logica* 51 (1992): 347–48. For what is an assuredly subjectively colored, but nevertheless informative and problem-oriented account of the state of "relevant theory and logics," see Richard Sylvan, "Process and Action: Relevant Theory and Logics," *Studia Logica* 51 (1992): 379–473.

of others, both in writing and in speech; that within the philosophical community they foster a regular exchange about the objects that populate their metalogics (propositions, truth functions, operators, etc.); that they entertain ontological thoughts about their abstractions and ask as Quine, for example, does: "Whither classes?"[8] Logical objects are thus copiously written and spoken of.

Because of all of this, I believe that a "feminist" engagement with logic should not take its departure from an unreflective pair of concepts, namely those of "nature versus artifact," and then apply analogs of these oppositional concepts to the objects of its investigation. An analogy of oppositional pairs construed in this way, *woman versus man : natural language versus artificial language*, would generate two correlations that would once again stand in opposition: *woman/natural language versus man/artificial language*. Leaving out of account the fact that in the history of logic we find, and continue to find, not only analytic philosophy but also the prefeminist current of *Ordinary Language Philosophy,* to which Andrea Nye oddly enough does not refer, feminist studies have in the meantime advanced adequate, detailed critiques of the correlation between woman and nature as a mere projection.[9]

It thus seems to me that a potential feminist engagement with logic, if it is to have a point, would have to concentrate on the formal or formalistic character of logic. This thesis nevertheless immediately generates the question of whether a philosophical encounter with a formal science from a *feminist* perspective can be at all meaningful and advantageous. Is there any reason at all for a feminist critique? Are not logical abstractions and constructions far removed, on the one hand, from all sexual phenomena and, on the other hand, from all cultural and social gender attributes? And this, to the extent that my question about whether logic is criticizable from a feminist perspective, may possibly prove itself to be a false question.

In this chapter I will show that logic provides a fitting terrain for the very *heuristic of suspicion* that has been so well tested in feminist analytic praxis. The heuristic of suspicion in this case would show that logic, like all neutralistic conceptions claiming universal validity, is suspect of being determined

---

8. Willard Van Orman Quine, *Word and Object* (Cambridge, Mass.: MIT Press, 1980), sec. 55.
9. From Silvia Bovenschen's *Die imaginierte Weiblichkeit: Exemplarische Untersuchungen zu kulturgeschichtlichen und literarischen Präsentationsformen der Weiblichkeit* (Frankfurt am Main: Suhrkamp, 1979) to Judith Butler's *Gender Trouble: Feminism and the Subversion of Identity* (New York: Routledge, 1990).

by tacit androcentric particularities. Certainly there are two points to be aware of in this undertaking:

1. A heuristic is naturally not a distinctive method. As a feminist investigation, it develops out of the heightened attentiveness of empirical persons, whom we usually label "women," to certain asymmetries between linguistic-symbolic and social realities; thus it is realized in what might be called the detective's technique of investigation. As such it has already been successful, for example, in disentangling the fact that although certain types of grammatically masculine substantives and professional titles, which seem not to exclude women (*"der Philosoph,"* "the scientist," *"l'écrivain"*), are revealed in their corresponding personal and relative pronouns (*"ein Philosoph, der . . . ,"* "the scientist . . . he," *"l'écrivain . . . il"*) to indicate—as if this were self-evident—a person of the masculine gender. As a result, an alternative convention for such designations could be straightforwardly introduced in certain institutional and discursive domains (*"Philosoph/Philosophin,"* "the scientist—she or he"). This heuristic was also successful in the analysis of the politically and the ethico-juridically important concept "man." If the language in question has a neutral generic term available, such as German *Mensch,* the androcentrism can manifest itself in the usage of this term. (A prime example of this is the fact that human rights and civil law since the French Revolution did not, until the present century, include women.) If the language in question does not have a gender neutral term available ("man," *"homme," "uomo"*), a neutralization in the direction of nondiscrimination has been advanced; and as a result, in almost all international conferences today, discussion is led not by "chairmen" but by "chairpersons."

2. While a feminist heuristic of suspicion has been successful, through socially and politically motivated linguistic analysis, in changing some conventional language games, the extension of such a heuristic to the analysis of logical formalization is not as plausible. Why should feminist philosophers be suspicious of, for example, bivalent propositional logic or the quantified predicate calculus? What could possibly motivate them to criticize the formal true/false dichotomy? Why should they bring gender concepts to bear on a system that has developed an extraordinary degree of *indifference* or *disinterestedness* toward gender differences? To the contrary, is not this disinterestedness toward gender a positive point from a feminist perspective?

In the next section I present a metatheoretical position that I have developed elsewhere, which I call *fascination analysis.* To give an example of how it works, I then use it to analyze the perfect figure of the Aristotelian syllogism. In the third section I discuss, by considering the case of Frege's conceptual notation (*Begriffsschrift*), how useful the fascination-analytical perspective can be for a feminist critique. In the final section, I develop my thesis that feminist critique of logic implies a logical critique of gender concepts and their employment.

The Method of Fascination Analysis

What is it that is so fascinating about logical formalizations? With this simultaneously unusual and simple question begins a metatheoretical analysis of logical constructions that I call *fascination analysis*. This question is distinct from the usual kinds of questions asked in the philosophy of logic—such as those about what logical formalization in general, or some particular calculus, accomplish—in that it brings into play an affective surplus that does not seem to be immediately justified. Thus one may well ask what such surplus there could possibly be. Can logical formalization at all be described with the adjective "fascinating?" Is this not just a senseless attribution? Or if it is not completely senseless, is it nevertheless not a particularly convincing expression? We shall see.

The question about the fascinating character of logical symbolization[10] takes on a certain plausibility if we consider one of Wittgenstein's provocative statements from the *Tractatus,* sentence 5.5563: "In fact, all the propositions of our everyday language, just as they stand, are in perfect logical order."[11] This is provocative because the question that at once foists itself upon us is why a logical analysis that makes use of an artificial symbolic language must be carried out at all. Why is it necessary to formulate "elementary propositions" and then to formalize them? After all, section 5.5563 is an extensive commentary on the central point 5: "A proposition is a truth-function of elementary propositions." Furthermore, even in his late essay

10. In what follows, I use the expressions "logical formalism" and "formalism," and "logical symbolization" and "symbolization" as synonyms, respectively. What is meant are arbitrarily chosen written signs to which a logical meaning is assigned. Signs interpreted in this way can then be operated (ideally) without further interpretation.
11. Ludwig Wittgenstein, *Tractatus Logico-philosophicus,* trans. D. F. Pears and B. F. McGuinness (New York: Routledge, 1974).

On Certainty, Wittgenstein notes: "Am I not getting closer and closer to saying that in the end logic cannot be described? You must look at the practice of language, then you will see it."[12] Logic, so Wittgenstein's claim can be read, is always at work whenever I speak or write any normal sentence. One need not worry oneself about it further. Oddly enough, one has worried oneself about it since ancient times, has tried to describe logical form as such, to separate it out, to disentangle it from the fabric of the text and the practice of language. But why, exactly?

At first glance, therefore, my initial fascination-analytical question is only the expression of a certain philosophical wonder: there must be something particularly auspicious, something especially attractive in the formal itself, a *fascination,* a *liberating* moment. Otherwise the history of formalization in our cultural tradition would not be sufficiently explainable. The supposition of such a *fascination with form* immediately generates the hypothesis: *logical formalization is a technique of liberation.* This hypothesis, of course, immediately suggests the further question: *From what does logic free us?*

The question of the fascinating character of logical formalization is thus not only a question about the functions of logical artifacts, the questions of how they in fact arose and how they relate to other systems of symbolization such as natural languages. In contrast to most investigations in the philosophy of logic, which relate themselves in a positive way to logical constructions and evaluate their particular efficacity, I have turned my attention to what falls by the wayside in the establishment of the formal, to that from which it "liberates" us, what is cordoned off—or as I put it—passed over in silence. I thus employ, with methodological intent, a term that is absent in most accounts of the philosophy of logic but that is, in contrast to "fascination," one that, thanks to Wittgenstein, possesses a certain dignity, "silence." However, and in a way different from that of the Wittgenstein of the *Tractatus,* I aim my question not at a realm beyond the logical and the enunciable, but directly in the midst of formalism. The concept "silence/silencing" (*Schweigen/Verschweigen*) as an alternative concept to psychic repression makes possible a critical investigation of, among other things, "logical visibility" or "logical evidence," that is, the evidence that in the form of logical notation shows and only shows. The question of what is fascinating in logical formalization is thus also a question about the *silence*

---

12. Ludwig Wittgenstein, *On Certainty,* ed. G. E. M. Anscombe and G. H. von Wright, trans. Denis Paul and G. E. M. Anscombe (New York: Harper & Row, 1969), no. 501.

in logic. It asks about what logic is capable of silencing.[13] The three key concepts with which I attempt a meta-analysis of formal logic are thus *fascination, liberation,* and *silence/silencing.* This vocabulary and its methodological application will be clarified in what follows.

"In that which is fascinating throughout real history," writes the philosopher of religion Klaus Heinrich, "there are unresolved conflicts, unsettled tensions; unresolved problems are always present. The history of fascination is one of symptoms, and it has a generic substrate."[14] But is it not the case that in formal systems like that of logic problems are solved, symptoms cleared up, conflicts settled? Was not the program of logic the most successful "anti-fascination enterprise" of our cultural history, so that one must in fact say that although conflicts may be everywhere apparent, they are completely absent from formal logic?

The category developed by Heinrich and employed by him in his religious, philosophical, and mythological investigations, that of the "history of fascination" (*Faszinationsgeschichte*), allows for the analysis of cultural history in terms of its symptomatology. Just as a psychoanalyst begins with symptoms and then follows them to traces of concealed psychic conflicts, Heinrich investigates moments of fascination as symptoms of repressed real conflicts. As I have already mentioned, I have added to this another terminology, that of silence and silencing, because I believe that fascination with logic is not to be accounted for in terms of a history of drives, which is incapable of accounting for the fact that something silenced is not necessarily also repressed.

I understand the concept of *fascination,* which includes as well the lexical meaning, "to be under a spell, to be captivated by something," as a composite concept, by definition part of an oscillatory semantics. It is a term that indicates emotive and affective situations that are difficult to see through. Even from an analytic perspective, and put in a thoroughly simplified way, a mixture of attraction and repulsion, of anxiety and liberation, generally

---

13. For a detailed account of this issue, see Käthe Trettin, *Die Logik und das Schweigen: Zur antiken und modernen Epistemotechnik* (Weinheim: VCH [Acta Humaniora] 1991); on "logical evidence," see also Käthe Trettin, "Logische Formalisierungen und Evidenz," in *Analyomen 1: Proceedings of the First Conference "Perspectives in Analytical Philosophy,"* ed. George Meggle and Ulla Wessels (Berlin: de Gruyter, 1994), 259–65.

14. Klaus Heinrich, "Das Floß der Medusa," in *Faszination des Mythos,* ed. Renate Schlesier (Basel: Stroemfeld/Roter Stern, 1985), 340. See also Klaus Heinrich, *Eine religionsphilosophische Einführung in die Logik* (Basel: Stroemfeld/Roter Stern, 1981).

lies here. Situations where fascination holds sway can thus be described as tense situations, whose structure is agonal, conflictual, ambiguous.

Fascination analysis is a procedure applied to the constructions, rules, and notations of a logical calculus—that is, to radically written symbols—which seeks to delineate the conflictual, ambiguous aspects of this world of signs, those very things from which formalistic techniques and operations would most like to escape, and from which they believe themselves actually to have escaped. The seeming paradox of this search for traces of fascinating tensions in logic consists of the fact that it is precisely such tensions and ambivalences that logic *eliminates* (or at least is supposed to eliminate). Fascination analysis can do only two things in this domain: (a) pick up traces of what has been eliminated, that is, investigate how the absence of ambiguities in formalisms *reveals itself* with them; and (b) draw background assumptions into the foreground, that is, clarify which contingent, historical, intellectual *situations* have led precisely to this logical "anti-fascination strategy." Thus, on the one hand, moments of fascination will be analyzed with reference to their disappearance, or—as I would like to say—their disappearing presence; on the other hand, they will be considered in terms of a dynamic that arises with the logical abolition of another captivating, ominous fascination and the embarkation in a new direction, supposed to both break captivation and provide liberation. This movement that breaks captivation is one of *analysis*—that is, the systematic disconnection and separation of various intermixed components. Analysis is precisely a liberating and a purifying movement: a secular, rationalizing, *ritual purification*.[15] Our fascination analysis thus asks, on the one hand, what it is exactly from which one will be liberated by means of the new techniques that serve to differentiate, decouple, and at the same time establish new relations. On the other hand, it asks about what new kind of fascination one may thereby end up in. What is thus investigated are the instruments and techniques developed precisely as a refusal of fascination, as means of eliminating tension, as themselves latently, silently exerting their own power of fascination.

15. The early Carnap spoke emphatically of the "purification of the theory of knowledge from false problems" (Rudolf Carnap, *Scheinprobleme in der Philosophie* [Hamburg: Felix Meiner, 1961]). Wittgenstein, in the *Philosophical Investigations,* offers his well known (self)-critical thoughts on the conception that "the proposition and the word that logic deals with are supposed to be something clear-cut" (sec. 105) and proposes to give up "the *preconceived idea* of crystalline purity" (sec. 108) (*Philosophical Investigations,* ed. G. E. M. Anscombe [New York: Macmillan, 1958]). Arthur Danto observes, from the perspective of the 1980s, that in the early phase of analytic philosophy, logical construction and reduction went hand in hand with a "purgative enthusiasm" ("Analytical Philosophy," *Social Research* 47 [1980]: 612–34, 622).

This analytic distillation allows us to read, for example, in the perfect figure of the Aristotelian syllogism, which of course is not a formal construction in the modern sense, but which is nevertheless paradigmatic for the establishment of the thought of the formal,[16] the following essential operations: first of all, the operation of establishing a linguistic unit, a first proposition taken to be true, a premise that is the basis of all further propositions. This act, which constitutes a purely linguistic point of beginning, signifies a denial of all of the basic conceptions valid for the ancients, and at the same time an elimination of the concern with genealogical derivation, a cultural liberation from the demonical and fateful ancient Greek interpretation of the order of nature and of generation, of the eternal becoming and passing away. The analysis of fascination sees the obliteration of origins through the operative establishment of a point of beginning as the liberatory kernel of the establishment of premises.

The second operation that dismisses the power of fascination but that thus itself becomes an object of fascination is the establishment of the variable. The variable makes possible a detachment or disengagement from the particular, from the given exemplar, from the word and the thing to which the word refers with all of its specific properties. As a clearly visible but empty space, it functions as a silent operator—it only shows itself, without expressing anything. As a logically interpreted sign, which formally registers that in its place the introduction of variables is possible, the variable is exempted from a permanent interpretation. It shows not only that a name must be entered in its place, or that a concept or a predicate can be introduced, but also that a wealth of such introductions is possible. The variable is thus an economical instrument. The variable is only restricted by means of quantification (which Aristotle had not, of course, formalized) and the use of other variables. The invention of the Aristotelian term-variable is the invention of the term *par excellence*. As such a limit concept, it is only meaningful to the extent that it is unequivocally distinguished from other terms. The formal distinction of the sign is thus not only restrictive, but at the same time it opens up the possibility of the combination of signs; that is, restriction qua delimitation is compensated for with a combinatoric. Signs become symbols only when they are connected to other signs. What thus

---

16. "If A is asserted of all B and B is asserted of all C, then A is necessarily asserted of all C" (Aristotle, *Analytica Priora, Aristotle's Prior Analytics: A Revised Text With an Introduction and Commentary by W. D. Ross* [Oxford: Clarendon, 1949], 37–39).

arises is a logical symbol system, the inner symbolic relations of which are mute and can be grasped in a single glance. *AB, BC: AC.*

Another feature that is interesting from the point of view of fascination analysis becomes clear when one asks about the source of the power of inference of the syllogism. What makes a syllogistic deduction from two premises into a compulsory consequence? Above all, it is the analysis of the structure of the scope of the terms. If one predicate with the conceptual scope *A* (being mortal) can be attributed to all of the objects that have another conceptual scope *B* (living thing), and if *B* understood predicatively (being a living thing) can be attributed to all things with the conceptual scope *C* (human being), then the conceptual scope of *C* (human being) is also subsumable under that of *A* (being mortal). Inferability is thus the effect of an implicative and correlative scheme of classification of terms or a conceptual part-whole relation. To this is added the application of the well-known principles of logic (identity: $A = A$; the law of noncontradiction: what is true cannot be false at the same time, and vice versa; *tertium non datur*: what is neither true nor false is logically uninteresting), that is, principles of distinction and exclusion. The exclusion of all ambivalences and the introduction of a regulated binary structure, which presents itself as logical evidence, as a consistent way from *alpha* through *beta* to *gamma*, silences its own compulsory character and reconstitutes itself as the logical mode of necessity. In deduction as well, we can see at work "the passion for derivation" (Heinrich), the urge to liberate oneself from fascination as a captivating force, to liberate oneself, namely, from the mythological-genealogical chain, the cult of origins and descent, which at the same time excludes the origin and has to set up again and again an identity that derives from the origin.

The introduction of the vocabulary of fascination into a cultural field that is precisely characterized by the lack of all ambiguity makes explicit how the project of formalization is a *technique of disambiguation* and therefore a strategy of resistance and liberation from fascination, and thus from discordant states of affairs. At the same time, it shows that this formal technique of "breaking the spell" can generate a new fascination, the fascination with form.

How helpful are these fascination analytical suspicions for a feminist critique of logic? What is revealed and what is concealed in logical formalism? I will discuss these questions by considering some aspects of Frege's idea of a conceptual notation.

Frege's Conceptual Notation

The *prima facie* most interesting monument to logical evidence, and thus to the retrospective consideration of what logic *shows*, is the two-dimensional notation used by Gottlob Frege for the construction of his system of logic. This conceptual notation,[17] in which the dash symbols are extended into a web-like geometric model, has an intuitive or even aesthetic quality to it. This was also Frege's reason for introducing such a formalization, since he felt that the sign should be the "intuitive representative" of a thing that is "in itself" not intuitable, "the concept."[18] Above all, it was a matter for him of making up for a deficiency of the mathematical logic of his time, namely, the fact that it was stuck "expressing in words," a properly "logical progression." "The arithmetical language of formulas," says Frege, "lacks expressions for logical connections."[19] Concepts are not supposed to be given to apprehension but are rather to be produced with efficient, logical means.[20] The production of concepts out of "logical connections" can nevertheless be brought to intuitive realization in a two-dimensional linear symbolism—and this seems to me to be relevant to an analysis of fascination—only when we abstract from our intuition and let ourselves go through a certain *training of the gaze*.

Intuition consists of our "following" out the consequences in a direct way, our beginning from the antecedent sentences and being led to a conclusion. Frege's method of notation requires us perhaps, if we are to be true to this intuition, to follow a different direction of consequences. If we attempt to read the signs in the usual way from top to bottom, we will not success-

---

17. Conceived in 1879 by Frege as "Conceptual Notation: A Formula Language of Pure Thought Modelled on the Formula Language of Arithmetic" (*Conceptual Notation and Related Articles,* trans. and ed. Terrell Ward Bynum [Oxford: Clarendon Press, 1972]) and transfigured in 1893 in *Basic Laws of Arithmetic* as the foundation of mathematics in logic (trans. and ed. Montgomery Furth [Berkeley and Los Angeles: University of California Press, 1964]).

18. In Frege, *Conceptual Notation and Related Articles,* 88.

19. Frege, "On the Scientific Justification of a Conceptual Notation," in ibid., 88.

20. In his polemic against Boole, Frege emphasizes the difference between his own procedure and that of Boole, insofar as Frege rejects Aristotle: "For in Aristotle, as in Boole, the logically primitive activity is the formation of concepts by abstraction, and judgment and inference enter in through an immediate or indirect comparison of concepts via their extensions. . . . As opposed to this [method of Boole's], I start out from judgments and their contents, not from concepts. . . . I only allow the formation of concepts to proceed from judgments" ("Boole's Logical Calculus and the Concept-script," in *Posthumous Writings,* ed. Hans Hermes, Friedrich Kambartel, and Friedrich Kaulbach, trans. Peter Long and Roger White [Oxford: Basil Blackwell, 1979], 15–16).

fully get to the conclusion or to the judgment, because the judgment, with the "judgment stroke" used to its left, is to be found at the very top, at the beginning of the whole set of operations. If we want to follow the splits and subdivisions of the lines through to the end in order finally to get to the main path of the judgment, we have to alter the direction of our reading and begin from the bottom.[21] Frege, however—and this is the point—does not want to change our psychological habits of perception as such. Rather, he asks us to grasp the fact that we have proceeded from the judgment, only by means of the "assertoric force" of the supplied consequent. In his posthumous essay "Introduction to Logic" (1906), he complains that this was evidently difficult to understand:

> The sentence expressing the first thought is the consequent, the sentence expressing the second the antecedent. It is now almost 28 years since I gave this definition. I believed at the time that I had only to mention it and everyone else would immediately know more about it than I did. And now after more than a quarter of a century has elapsed, the great majority of mathematicians have no inkling of the matter, and the same goes for the logicians. What pigheadedness![22]

Seeing logically, logical evidence, presupposes a training, a disciplining not only of the gaze, but also a *logical re-vision* of the "natural" order of the syllogism. This revision *shows* itself; it becomes *evident in formalism*. My thesis is, however, that logic shows and *silences* it. But what does it mean to say that logic *silences*?

A correlation between demonstration and silence is immediately apparent in the fact that every formalism consists of written, stable signs, which in a certain sense just stand there mutely. As distinct interpreted signs, they do not require (in the ideal case) any interpreting speech. These mute, written signs can also be silently manipulated.[23] Frege's conceptual notation

---

21. See also Sybille Krämer, *Symbolische Maschinen: Die Idee der Formalisierung in geschichtlichem Abriß* (Darmstadt: Wissenschaftliche Buchgesellschaft, 1988), 177f.

22. Frege, *Posthumous Writings*, 186.

23. Rudolf Carnap, who attended Frege's 1910 lecture course, "Conceptual Notation," noted in his autobiography: "He [Frege] seldom looked at the audience. Ordinarily we saw only his back, while he drew strange diagrams of his symbolism on the blackboard and explained them. Never did a student ask a question or make a remark, whether during the lecture or afterwards. The possibility of a discussion seemed to be out of the question" ("Intellectual Autobiography," in *The Philosophy of Rudolf Carnap*, ed. Paul Arthur Schilpp [La Salle, Ill.: Open Court, 1963], 5).

sharpens this general correlation insofar as it takes its departure from the judgment, that is, from the logically true and necessary consequent. This measure has the effect both of marking out the logically relevant territory ahead of time and of rendering discussion of subjectively negotiable "outlooks on truth" superfluous.

"Literary" thoughts as well come forth in the dress of assertoric sentences. According to Frege, these are a misleading peculiarity of "spoken language" from which judgmental assertions must be disentangled in order to yield the thoughts themselves and represent them each with their own sign. This is especially clear in the way in which Frege connects negation and the judgmental assertion, while equally distinguishing them. Take the following question as something to be judged: "Is three greater than five?" If we had two different kinds of judgments, affirmative and negative ones, as for example, with Kant, the answer would be: "It is false that three is greater than five." Frege, in contrast, says: "The negation of the thought that three is greater than five is true."[24] The operator for negation is not related to the judgment itself but rather to that which is judged. The expression "the negation of A is asserted as true," which is symbolized in the conceptual notation as ⊢─── ─A, leaves open the component of the sentence in natural language to which the negation, expressed as "not" or with a negative prefix, is coupled. Take, for example, the sentences: "The pope is not a popular man among feminists," or "Feminists do not like the pope." According to Frege we would have to say: "The negation of the thought that feminists like the pope, or that the pope is popular among feminists, is true." We thus always have "affirmative" judgments. The Fregean conception of the judgment thus "silences" or eliminates negation, but in such a way that this silencing shows up.

The judgment stroke that cannot be overlooked and that stands at the very beginning is a normative truth-sign. The banishment of the negation from the judgment does not at all mean that it "vanishes" altogether. Transformed into a logical concept that is of use for the univocal metamorphosis of the truth value of the "content," negation, once "liberated" from the psychology of judgment, can consequently be introduced as an operator in the calculus. What is achieved here is an interesting decoupling, but one in which the separated components in a "cleaned-up form," so to speak, as a calculus, can once again be related in a calculable fashion. The classical

---

24. Gottlob Frege, "Negation," in *Logical Investigations*, ed. P. T. Geach, trans. P. T. Geach and R. H. Stoothoff (New Haven: Yale University Press, 1986), 69.

logical principle *duplex negatio affirmat* (a double negation is an affirmation) is henceforth compatible in a trouble-free way with the situation where every judgment has been purged of negation.

Two further interesting aspects of this project from the perspective of our fascination analysis are: (1) Frege's struggle against everyday language, and (2) his establishment of time invariance. Considering the first: when it comes to "protecting thought from error," language proves to be "deficient." Says Frege, "It does not even meet the first requirement which we must place upon it in this respect; namely, being unambiguous." Language—colloquial and scientific language—is not only an inadequate medium, it seems to Frege, but also it is, at least partially, plainly insidious: "The most dangerous cases [of ambiguity] are those in which the meanings of a word are only slightly different, the subtle and yet not unimportant variations."[25] The "softness and instability of language" must have something opposed to it, Frege warns, in the context of a discussion of inference, of presuppositions that "can easily slip in unnoticed." "We need," he says, "a system of symbols from which every ambiguity is banned, which has a strict logical form from which the content cannot escape."

Only a perfect chain of symbols from which nothing can "escape," to which nothing can illicitly "slip in," guarantees the scientifically required univocity. At the same time—and this brings me to the second point—it succeeds, by means of such a symbolic chain, in mastering time and the changes in content that appear as effects of time. Truth values must not be dependent on the vagaries of time, lest logic decay into a "psychological wash-basin." As many of Frege's remarks make clear, his proposed foundation of mathematics in logic—and this at a time when mathematical definitions such as those of the function and the number threatened to lose their sharpness as a result of the influence of psychology on the other sciences—was an attempt to construct an unassailable basis for a theory of mathematics currently influenced by empiricism and the philosophy of consciousness. Mathematics in the Platonic sense had to be reestablished more securely, and in such a way that it could overcome armed modern "challenges." The greatest modern challenge, however, was *time in the form of the process*—in other words, *temporal relativity*. Hence Frege's complaints should be interpreted as vehement protests *against contingency*. As a result, it is only fitting that he considers the "judgment stroke"

---

25. Frege, *Conceptual Notation and Related Articles*, 84.

as a kind of "time-blockade" (K. Heinrich), as a marked symbol that stands at the beginning and at the same time indicates the end of the logical operation.

The metatheoretical experience of the fascination analysis of some key moments of Frege's conceptual notation has thus brought to light in broad outline and clarified the threats from which a logic that both aligns itself with the ideal of mathematics and claims to provide a foundation for it would liberate us and has shown the new and promising results of this protective revision. The first threat is the Babylonian confusion of natural language(s), even if its colors and nuances constitute all of what we love so much about poetic language. It is deceptive to construe grammatical structure as logical structure. If we thus substitute for the ordinary "word language" a semantically well-thought-out and formally powerful artificial language, we will possess a "formal language of pure thoughts," *purified* from all intentions and psychological dispositions, from uncertainties about judgment, and from the multiplicity of meanings of logical connection. *Purification* goes hand in hand with a *training of the gaze* in such a way that what is not logically relevant can be ignored. What results from this, however, is a new form that once again captivates the gaze.

What of this is susceptible to a "feminist" treatment? It should by now be clear that fascination analysis is not an attempt to sell an old hat as a new one; it neither claims that what is silenced by logic is "the feminine," nor does it claim that logical signs and rules are simply forms of representation of "the masculine." Frege's concept of the function does not, perhaps, have anything at all to do with gender attributes; likewise the hallowed principle of bivalence is gender neutral, even if gender as a rule is described in terms of oppositional concepts that are to some extent two-valued. One can examine all logical concepts, principles, and rules, only to become convinced that logic is not in the least colored by gender.

What fascination analysis can nevertheless show is that this formidable disinterestedness in gender and in all media that represent the thoughts of genus and class, just like its disengagement from natural or mythological genealogy, is not established entirely without effort. The production of univocity and (gender) neutrality can be shown explicitly in the formal languages of logic. Fascination analysis can, above all—and this, in my view, is its point—uncover a peculiarity inherent in the process of the establishment of logic, namely, that *this process of construction silences itself*. Logical constructs, such as the "law" of noncontradiction or the operator for negation, take on an almost naturalized form; that is, they attain—as in

Frege's "judgeable content" or "thoughts"—their own ontic status ("the realm of thought"). What appears, as a result, is an artifact that no one has in fact made, a construct without construction, an epistemic technique without technician and epistemic actor.

"But this," one might say in opposition to the practitioner of fascination analysis, "is precisely what is peculiar to logic—that it has no personal, institutional, social, and certainly no gender-specific authority, but only has a purely formal authority accessible to all." This potential objection is, however, no objection at all. The practitioner of fascination analysis has never doubted that it is precisely this effect that was intended: a liberatory effect that is all the greater, the more "natural" logic appears to us, the more it succeeds in winning over the title of self-evidence. Insofar as fascination analysis at the very least attempts to reconstruct a silenced process and to reveal the "naturalizing effect" of logical constructions, it does not challenge their liberating, *exculpatory* function, but rather accentuates it.

The critical accent is to be placed more on the question of how it can be thought that disambiguation, purification, de-psychologizing, and the laying aside of contingency—in a word, analytic distillation and formalizing detemporalization—have presented (and continue to present) what remains a fascinating project and—the feminist accent—whether this *form fascination* itself does not in some way have androcentric (and in an inverse way also gynocentric) markings. I thus return to the heuristic sketched at the beginning of this essay, the examination of apparently neutral concepts and conceptions in terms of their perhaps tacit gender ascriptions. That is, has it been necessary to eliminate to the same degree "masculine" and "feminine" gender ascriptions in order to attain a liberating, logical gender-indifference? Is it not still possible to locate unanalyzed traces in logical concepts, especially traces that refer to the amalgam of "masculine-neutrality"? Is there also, in this case, a corresponding "feminine-neutrality?" And if so, should the project of neutralization then be carried out in a sharper and at the same time feminist-analytic way; or on the contrary, should explicit gender parameters be openly introduced into logic?

It must be noted, first of all, that fascination analysis poses more questions than it is capable of answering on its own terms. Perhaps it is the case that this metatheoretic experience is restricted to the function of generating questions, while the answers to these questions can be won only through other methods. Nevertheless, we can give an answer to the first question that is in keeping with fascination analysis. We can say, that is, whether logical formalization tacitly has androcentric or gynocentric markings. The answer is that there are in fact no such markings if we leave behind all background assumptions and the situational context of these constructions. But, on the other hand, if we include boundary conditions, traces of the "masculine" and the "feminine" are immediately evident. Thus the concept of "form" as well as the project of "formalization," considered historically, have had, since Aristotle, a "masculine" connotation; and the bearing of persons with regard to epistemic techniques established along these lines can perhaps be seen as marked by gender. More precisely, we can distinguish four moments here: (1) the de-demonization of language as a "masculine" project of formalization; (2) the return of fascination as an unspoken form-fascination; (3) the "feminine" perception of this "form fetishism" along with a gradual development of resistance to it; and (4) a feminist reconstruction and destruction of gender-specific connotations in the fascination history of logic.

What is peculiar about this is that the excess fascination of the formal science of logic hides within itself an alluring "masculine"-oriented perception that is revealed for the first time to a "feminine"-oriented gaze, one that resists its captivating power. As Leibniz very appropriately remarked, the symbolic cognition that we practice in arithmetic and algebra (we could also include here a mathematically oriented logic), is a "blind" mode of cognition,[26] but nevertheless one to which, from an historical perspective, empirical men have been more willing to entrust themselves than empirical women have.[27] The "feminist reconstruction and destruction" of gender-specific connotations mentioned above under (4) indicate the point at which we have taken leave of fascination analysis and thus also from a metatheory, that point at which we must venture something like a first-order theory. The general question with which I will introduce the last section of this paper is thus:

26. Gottfried Wilhelm Leibniz, *Betrachtungen über die Erkenntnis, die Wahrheit und die Ideen (Meditationes de Cognitione, Veritate, et Ideis)*, in *Philosophische Schriften und Briefe 1683–1687* (Berlin: Akademie Verlag, 1992), 30f.

27. This is not, of course, to assert that there are either "gender characteristics" or their positive or negative correlations with symbolic cognition. Women were simply excluded from this discourse on almost all levels of social institutions. That the latter, if socio-institutional restrictions were done away with, could explicitly be interested in the innovative symbolic sciences—and with this also in the Leibnizian project for a *characteristica universalis*, a *calculus ratiocinator*, or even an *ars inveniendi et iudicandi*—is shown in the scientific exchange between Leibniz and Countess Sophie, as well as her daughter Sophie Charlotte, who would later become the Queen of Prussia.

Have There Been Feminist Innovations in Logic?

This question can only be answered provisionally because we are still, even after twenty years of feminist philosophy, [28] in the following situation: philosophers whose work focuses on feminist philosophy pay little or no heed to logic and formalization; and philosophers who concern themselves with logic and formalization pay little or no heed to feminism. Why this is so cannot be gone into here. However plausible this pointed description of the situation may be, the following remarks, or rather desiderata and suggestions for possible projects, are intended as a sketch of alternatives.

Neutrality, Context, and Situational Semantics

In her 1977 essay *The Myth of the Neutral "Man,"*[29] which has since achieved a legendary status, Janice Moulton problematizes the ambiguity of gender-neutral terminology in English linguistic usage. As a demonstration she considers the well-known textbook example of the syllogism, the first premise of which is:

> All men are mortal.

Most people, says Moulton, would like to take the term *men* as neutral and understand the proposition as a "statement about the whole human species." But if a neutral usage was indeed intended, then "this paradigm of valid syllogisms" would be invalid, since the second premise usually runs

> Socrates is a man.

The term *man* is not used neutrally here. Proof: if it were used neutrally, then one could replace the name "Socrates" with the name of a female human being or that of a child without sacrificing the validity of the syllogism. The attempt at substitution

---

28. See the discussion report of the APA panel "Feminist Philosophy After Twenty Years," reprinted in *Hypatia* 9, no. 3 (1994): 183–224.
29. I refer to the revised edition, Janice Moulton, "The Myth of the Neutral 'Man,' " in *Women, Knowledge, and Reality*, ed. Ann Garry and Marilyn Pearsall (Boston: Unwinn Hyman, 1989), 219–32.

Sophia is a man

either makes the syllogism false or turns Sophia into a man.[30]

Another example of "obvious failures of gender neutrality" is the following inference:

Man has two sexes.
Some men are female.

Janice Moulton shows by means of these, as well as a whole series of other examples, that there are many contexts in which attempts to use such terms as *he* and *man* in a gender-neutral way lead to "false, comical or offensive sentences," even when they are intended as gender-neutral. What can be learned from this?

Mouton pleads neither for a modification of the syllogism or other form of inference, nor for granting the terms she investigates a gender-specific validity. Rather, she makes manifest a general linguistic phenomenon, which she calls "parasitic reference": "A gender-specific term, one that refers to a high-status subset of the whole class, is used *in place of* a neutral generic term."[31] Semantic theories should thus take account of such parasitical reference, namely, of the fact that the reference of an expression in one context can be codetermined by its use in other contexts in which it is not explicitly present.

I would like to make two brief additions to this analysis. First of all, it must be pointed out that this consequence has only a limited validity, since it is won from data of a specific domain, everyday English language. If we were transported into everyday German language, we would not have problems of a similar sort: *Alle Menschen sind sterblich. Sokrates / Sophia ist ein Mensch.* Or: *Menschen haben zwei Geschlechter. Einige Menschen sind weiblich.* I do not by any means intend to exclude the fact that in certain contexts and language situations, not only in other languages, there can be ambiguities regarding the gender specificity and neutrality of concepts. The

---

30. Ibid., 227. She explains further: "Although some people might argue that in this context the syllogism 'Sophia is a man' can be read as 'Sophia is a human being,' they will recognize that many other people will not take it this way."

31. Ibid., 231. A structurally similar phenomenon is apparent in brand-specific usage referring to consumer goods: if I were to say in spoken-English usage, "Have you got a Kleenex?" I would also be satisfied with any other brand of facial tissue. If I say "I have to go buy another pair of Levi's," it may in fact happen that I come home with a completely different label.

most well-known example of this in the German language, which was "discovered" in the 1970s by means of feminist sensitivity to language, is the lower case *man*, with which a (pseudo?) neutral, anonymous subject is indicated. The substitution of this with the lower case word *frau*,[32] which at first had a persistent irritant effect on linguistic convention, has in the meantime been dropped even by feminists. And this, in my opinion, with justification, since the terms *Mann* and *Frau* have become ever more in need of clarification following the transformation of women's studies into gender studies.

My second remark is concerned with the relationship between sensitivity to language and logic. Moulton's analysis incorporates what is indeed a traditional logical deduction, the syllogism, in her examination, but her efforts are not motivated by a critique of logic but by linguistic issues. She orients herself in grammar and in the usage of a natural language, not attempting to express her results in such a way that they can be presentable in another formalism. How, I ask myself, does the "parasitic reference" of gender-specific terms (i.e., their status conditions, the parasitic neutralization consequent upon their generalized usage) lend itself to symbolic notation? In other words, why do I find no feminist attempts in the research programs of "situational semantics" and "natural language quantification," in which at the intersection of linguistics and logic the attempt is made to analyze semantically the differential natural language expressions for singular and general quantification and thereby also to further refine logic? Thus, for example, Jon Barwise, in the construction of his language L(ss), which is designed to represent a situational semantics with model theoretic means, has defined the pronouns *he* and *she* as well as the word *other* as "dependent elements." Dependent on what? On "other factors," which remain to be specified. This renders interpretable sentences like "Every student has her favorite teacher and every teacher has his favorite student."[33] Barwise takes his departure from the situationally conditioned character of the understanding of expressions in the English language, just as Janice Moulton does. But while Moulton restricts herself to a discussion of classical argument models like the syllogism in which problems occur, Barwise seeks to

---

32. This first appeared in Verena Stefan, *Häutungen: Autobiographische Aufzeichnungen, Gedichte, Träume, Analysen* (Munich: Frauenoffensive, 1975).

33. Jon Barwise, "Noun Phrases, Generalized Quantifiers, and Anaphora," in *Generalized Quantifiers: Linguistic and Logical Approaches,* ed. Peter Gärdenfors (Dordrecht: D. Reidel, 1987), 1–29. See also Jon Barwise and John Perry, *Situations and Attitudes* (Cambridge, Mass.: MIT Press, 1983), and the other contributions in Gärdenfors, *Generalized Quantifiers.*

construct a new formalism capable of solving such or similar problems. Is this another case of form-fascination? Perhaps, but it would nevertheless be interesting to see how a feminist sensibility would appear in the garb of an artificial language.

Epistemic Logic

Lorraine Code, in her book *What Can She Know? Feminist Theory and the Construction of Knowledge*,[34] formulates the thesis "The sex of the knower is epistemologically significant" and thus attempts to take the well-known formula

$$S \text{ knows that } p$$

and remove its generality, insofar as the epistemic subject is inevitably marked by gender. What is intended is a feminist critique of the universalistic and perhaps androcentric construction of an anonymous cognitive subject. We can thus present the epistemic predicate (knows) as a two-place relation, but in such a way that the relatum S is to be gender-indexed:

$$K(S_f, p)$$
$$K(S_m, p)$$

To be sure, a whole string of questions immediately arises: (1) How do we know whether S_f and S_m know different things, similar things, or identical things when they "know, that p?" (2) How can it be established whether the epistemic predicate does or does not have a different content following the differentiation of the epistemic subject? (3) How is "feminine" knowledge to be distinguished from "masculine" knowledge? From Lorraine Code's thesis it follows only *that* the two are distinct and this on the ground of the gender of the one who claims to know something, but not *how* these differences are constituted. Let us take an example:

> Anna knows that the ball is round.
> Paul knows that the ball is round.

---

34. Lorraine Code, *What Can She Know? Feminist Theory and the Construction of Knowledge* (Ithaca, N.Y.: Cornell University Press, 1991).

(Some possible background assumptions: Anna thinks of a handball, since at present she plays handball often, even though she was at one point a forward on the local women's soccer team; Paul is thinking about a soccer ball, since he had previously played soccer often, even though at the moment he has just finished playing table tennis and thus could also be thinking of a ping pong ball. Neither Paul nor Anna have ever played ball, but both know simply that balls are round.)

Lorraine Code would like to object that this sort of knowledge, namely knowledge of propositions about "simples," about "medium-sized, stable objects" like balls, apples, chairs, tables, and books, to which one ascribes the correct predicate represents only a small but not really interesting part of that which one can know. In particular, her criticism is that such examples are always presented as paradigmatic illustrations of knowledge. To the contrary, complex personal knowledge, a knowledge "about people" and not "about objects" is more interesting. This knowledge is knowledge that is first generated through interaction with others.

This is not to be contradicted, but we may ask: What does it mean more precisely? How might this complex, socially created knowledge that is tied essentially to people be modeled? One general answer given by Lorraine Code is "to take subjectivity into account."[35] With this, in my view, not exactly new, peculiarly prefeminist-sounding suggestion, Code would like not only to criticize the "positivist-empiricist orientation" of the theory of knowledge, but would also like at least to relativize the unquestioned privileging of "scientific knowledge" inherent in "S-knows-that-p epistemologies." "Taking subjectivity into account" thus means, above all, the formulation of an "epistemology of everyday lives."[36]

Lorraine Code makes no proposal about how to render her critique of the classical S-knows-that-p epistemology more precise in a formal-constructive way. The possibility, however, of taking the vague postulate of the "epistemological significance of gender" and of the "personal relevance of knowledge" and sharpening it up and verifying it with a model of a *nonclassical, epistemic logic,* suggests itself immediately. Unfortunately, to the best of my knowledge there are no such feminist attempts at present. Elsewhere I have made a first attempt at a self-ascriptive epistemic language game about gender concepts, at an analysis in a semi-formal manner of sentences of the

---

35. See Lorraine Code, "Taking Subjectivity into Account," in *Feminist Epistemologies,* ed. Linda Alcoff and Elizabeth Potter (New York: Routledge, 1993), 15–48.

36. Ibid., 16.

form "I know that x is an F,"[37] but it is possible to take this further. An epistemic logic is, in contrast with classical logic, parameterized; that is, its truth values are rendered situational, temporal, and interactively limited. And—so one could provisionally claim—they are thus relativized in a gender-specific and personally relevant way. How then can, for example, the symbolization of the "acceptation logic" of Werner Stelzner[38] be modified, so that the postulates of Lorraine Code can be formulated as parameters, assuming that they can at all be formulated in this way?

Stelzner distinguishes between predicates of "inner acceptation" (A^i) and predicates of the availability to an external acceptation (A^e and A_n). While A^i is only temporally or situationally limited, for A^e and A_n "the further parameters of the epistemic auditor or the communication partner must be introduced."[39]

$A^i(x,p,t)$—in words, this reads "x adheres to the explicit inner acceptation of p in interval t"—allows for a system x, for example "I, K.T." in a determinate, time-specific situation, accepted and held to be true by me, "that I can be anything, but not a woman." I could bring into play with the predicate A^i a surprising number of subjectivities, perhaps even more than Lorraine Code would like. Thus more parameters are at once required. The communication variant of acceptation is, in contrast, the more complex and more difficult. In this case, it would be necessary to prove the "epistemological significance" of the introduction of the gender parameter.

$A^e(x,p,t,y)$—or in words something like "x fulfills in the interval t the act of explicit external acceptance vis-à-vis y"—brings the "epistemic auditor" y into play. Were I to express the above-mentioned innerly accepted opinion in a temporally specific situation, namely "not being a woman," vis-à-vis another person, a field of auditors, a community, or even vis-à-vis a computer system, I would certainly have to reckon with widely divergent reactions. One who, on the one hand, without denying the conventional indications of the feminine (e.g., name, typical behavior, clothing), refuses to conform to these conventions in certain situations, at least innerly, may find either complete understanding or complete resistance. Is y as a symbol

---

37. See Käthe Trettin, "Braucht die feministische Wissenschaft eine 'Kategorie'?" in *Denkachsen: Zur theoretischen und institutionellen Rede vom Geschlecht*, ed. Theresa Wobbe and Gesa Lindemann (Frankfurt am Main: Suhrkamp, 1994), chap. 3.

38. Werner Stelzner, *Epistemische Logik: Zur logischen Analyse von Akzeptationsformen* (Berlin: Akademie Verlag, 1984).

39. Ibid., 38. The form $A_n(x,p,t,y)$ says that the acceptations of the act of assertion fulfilled in A^e are attainable in n steps.

for the epistemic communication partner thus construed too nonspecifically? How does it allow for specification? And what type of specification could produce gender differentiation, which usually operates with the opposed concepts of "woman" and "man" and their grammatical derivatives "feminine" and "masculine"? Must it not—and this is my main question—already be clear a priori what is meant with the concept of gender, no matter whether such a concept is supposed to be introduced as a vague postulate (as with Lorraine Code), or as an epistemic parameter (i.e., as a relevant measure for expressions of knowledge, belief, and opinion) as in the latter attempt?

In general, the concept of gender has been understood in feminist studies since the end of the 1980s to be a socially and culturally bound variable. Gender is all of that which we contingently attribute, generally following a taxonomy of living things, and specifically in the differential classification of the human species, and which is thus equally contingently attributed to us, whereby precisely this contingency steps forth as "naturalized." Thus the term *gender* appears to carry an externally stabilized and unchangeable content. This naturalizing effect has been criticized from the perspectives of discourse theory and psychoanalysis,[40] *but not logically.* It is true that Sandra Harding speaks in the final chapter of her book *Whose Knowledge? Whose Science?* of both "the transformed logic of science" and "a transformed logic of feminism,"[41] but one searches in vain for a "logical" transformation in the narrower sense of the term. It is possible that it is senseless to formalize gender attributions, especially when these furthermore, as Harding points out, can be correlated with other parameters like "class, race, and sexual preference," which thus prevent there from being any independent, privileged "category" of gender for feminist research. But can we philosophically uncover the possibly problematic privileging of gender if we do not first establish an analytic instrument more precise than ordinary language?

This very brief flight into epistemic logic has, I hope, made it clear that (a) the attempt at a parametrization of gender can clarify and render more precise the purported epistemological significance of the cognitive subject. How then can we introduce such a parameter? As a marking of x, and this

---

40. Butler, *Gender Trouble*, as well as the subsequent debate, at times itself critical, generated by this critique, finally represented in *Feministische Studien* 2/93 and in Wobbe and Lindemann, *Denkachsen*.

41. Sandra Harding, *Whose Science? Whose Knowledge? Thinking from Women's Lives* (Ithaca: Cornell University Press, 1991), 307-12.

perhaps only when an addressee y, an epistemic auditor, comes into play? Also for y? Or could we allow the actors to remain neutral, requiring that epistemic predicates, that is, Stelzner's "acceptation forms" (to accept, assert, understand, believe, have an opinion about, know, etc. something) be marked with gender? How would something like this look? It has been made clear through a logical analysis that (b) we need a much clearer concept of gender in order to be able to maintain the postulate of epistemological significance. But do we have such a concept? Is the concept of gender to be so construed that it can have the same status as, say, the concept of time? So that we can then take the sets g (genus) and t (tempus) as equivalently ranging functions? But here the question of whether this makes any sense at all from a feminist perspective is not yet broached. It could be established that (c) epistemic actors be construed directly from a feminist perspective as *logically gender-indifferent* interpretation actors.[42]

Concluding Remarks

Formal analyses for the sake of clarifying philosophical problems from a feminist perspective have until now only rarely been attempted. Even more seldom has been constructive work in logic. I consider this situation to require change. Those for whom classical logic is too rigid for the investigation of specific problems must not abandon logical analysis. This is not to mention the fact that in the last thirty years a whole number of nonclassical logics (process and action logic, nonmonotonic deduction, relevant logic, many-valued logics, epistemic and deontic logics) have appeared, which can—perhaps with suitable modifications—be workable; it is also possible to construct new artificial tools. Such constructions need not be "feminine" logics, just as none of the logics named above are "masculine." Rather they would be additional logics capable of better comprehending the complex semantic problems of the practice of gender attribution.

Is a feminist critique of logic thus possible? Yes, but only when this implies a logical critique of gender concepts and their usage.

---

42. See Trettin, "Braucht die feministische Wissenschaft eine 'Kategorie'?"

GEORG SIMMEL
Modernism and the Philosophy of the Sexes

8

Ursula Menzer

Translated by Melanie Richter-Bernburg

Georg Simmel is looked on as the founder of formal sociology and is also regarded as one of the foremost representatives of *Lebensphilosophie*. Social theory and philosophy thus crossed paths in his work from the beginning. His analyses of his own period at the turn of the century, which were

This essay originally appeared under the titles "Georg Simmel, die Weiblichkeit, das Geld und die Moderne" and "Einleitung" and "Philosophie der Kultur und Philosophie der Geschlechter: Sexistische Zwietracht allenthalben," in *Subjektive und objektive Kultur: Georg Simmels Philosophie der Geschlechter vor dem Hintergrund seines Kultur-Begriffs,* Feministische Theorie und Praxis, published by Barbara Schaeffer-Hegel, Centaurus-Verlagsgesellschaft Pfaffenweiler, 1992.

grounded in cultural philosophy, were soon forgotten and have been ignored in the reception of his work.

During the last few years, Simmel's essays on cultural philosophy and aesthetics have been reappearing.[1] Among these essays are such varied and unusual studies as those on the handle of a jug, fashion, flirtation, adventure, the tensions of life in the big city, and the sociology of mealtime, as well as essays on the feminine and the relations of the sexes. This has given rise to a steadily increasing familiarity with his work and to something of a Simmel renaissance. His critique of culture is once again being discussed, and the far-reaching elements of a theory of modernism in his work, which anticipate the central motifs of the twentieth century, is now recognized. Walter Benjamin picked up his concept of modernism and his sociology of the big city in the 1930s, and the Chicago School followed suit in the 1950s. In fact, many traces of Simmel's philosophy are to be found in the writings of various authors, for example, in the early work of Georg Lukács—who was Simmel's pupil—and in that of Ortega y Gasset, Bloch, Adorno, and the recently deceased Günther Anders.

One of the keys to an understanding of Simmel's philosophy is the broadly defined concept of culture that is central to a number of the essays in his multifaceted work. As the concept is elaborated, it becomes increasingly metaphysical in nature, moving decidedly beyond a narrow definition of culture that is limited to art and its reception.

Simmel defines as cultural all created expressions and differentiations of life—for example, the organization of labor and social life, law, social norms and moral values, science, technology, art, and so on. The cultural products of human intelligence and creativity come to being and continue to exist in the tension between life as it expresses itself directly and its articulation through form. Cultural processes, with their interaction of life and form, inner and outer, subject and object, creation and destruction, are conceived by Simmel paradigmatically as processes of the soul which, in the

---

1. Georg Simmel, *Philosophische Kultur: Über das Abenteuer, die Geschlechter und die Krise der Moderne: Gesammelte Essais: Mit einem Nachwort von Jürgen Habermas* [Philosophical culture: On adventure, the sexes, and the crisis of modernism: Collected essays: With an afterword by Jürgen Habermas] (Berlin, 1983). The publisher's bibliographical note indicating that the first edition appeared in Potsdam in 1923 is incorrect. It appeared in Leipzig in 1919. Early versions of the essays on the questions of the sexes appeared in part in newspapers and in a first book publication in 1911; they were revised for the next and for following editions. See also Georg Simmel, *Das Individuum und die Freiheit: Essais* [The individual and freedom: Essays] (Berlin, 1984).

course of its self-realization, develops and formulates its potential. In other words, culture is the "path of the soul to itself."[2]

This parabolic formula, inspired by the Spencerian theory of evolutionary differentiation, describes the structure of cultural development as process; it applies both to culture in general and to cultures in particular. Its inherent dynamics determine the reciprocal relationship between the individual and society, as well as the internal relationships of individuals themselves. Thus, all collective and individual intellectual processes of development typically undergo complex, dynamic differentiation. Proceeding from a unified state of uniform indifferentiation, through stages of differentiating analysis, to an integrating synthesis, "Culture is the path from closed unity through an explicated variety to an explicated unity."[3]

In the process of differentiation, the objective, though not necessarily the subjective, cultural level of individual subjects rises. The overall complexity of the processes increases and therefore also the complexity of the contradictions. The tension in the relationship between life and form is fundamentally conflicted in nature; it is marked by an immanent antagonism that can intensify to become a tragedy of culture.

Remarkably enough, Simmel does not draw on a traditional object of cultural philosophy in developing his concept of culture but bases his investigation on one of the most influential principles of organization in civilized social life—money. The major results of Simmel's thinking appeared in 1900 in his magnum opus, *The Philosophy of Money*.[4] At the end of this work, strands of a general definition of culture are combined with a concrete diagnosis of the times to issue in an analysis and critique of the contemporary condition of culture.

The linking of philosophy and money may at first seem astonishing. But since philosophy, in contrast to the sciences, has no genuine object on which it is fixed as a discipline, it can, in principle, declare anything to be its object and treat it according to its own strictures. *The Philosophy of Money* is not, of course, a book on economics. Simmel's study is an attempt to define the entirety of all forms of economic traffic as a special case of cultural expression. The idea of the economy is subsumed under the all-encompassing concept of culture. In a later phase of his work, during which there was an increase in Nietzschean motifs and during which he came under the influ-

2. Simmel, *Philosophische Kultur*, 183.
3. Ibid., 185.
4. See now Georg Simmel, *Philosophie des Geldes*, ed. David P. Frisby and Klaus Christian Köhnke (Frankfurt am Main, 1989).

ence of the French proponent of *Lebensphilosophie,* Henri Bergson, Simmel subordinated his concept of culture to the more comprehensive metaphysical paradigm of "life."

Beginning with a general survey of his own philosophical position, Simmel argues his value-theory approach to a "philosophy of money": "If there is to be a philosophy of money, then it can only lie on either side of the economic science of money. On the one hand, it can present the pre-conditions that, situated in mental states, in social relations and in the logical structure of reality and values, give money its meaning and its practical position."[5]

The analytical discussion of the prerequisites for the creation of money in the first part of Simmel's study is followed by a second, synthetic part that is concerned with the effects of money on the individual and collective emotional disposition and on the social shaping of life in general. It is concerned, that is, with culture as influenced by monetary processes.

Simmel's discussion is based on a variant of the nominalist conception of money—already formulated in Aristotle—that remains a subject of controversy between schools of thought to this day: money is understood by the economic subject as an eminently practical invention. As such it is at the service of rationalized processes of exchange, not the least of whose promises is that of greater justice. Simmel was optimistic that highly developed monetary conditions could mitigate social competition.

Dealing with money is incredibly familiar to us. We learn to handle it as children: given to us in the form of an allowance, it serves more as a tool of pedagogical socialization than as a field for practical exercise in daily life or as a concession to unbridled wishes. Money has to be apportioned; its disbursement is projected into the future; and unfortunately, it has to be earned. It is earned, or acquired, at different rates. It is increased or decreased. It is liquid or it is tied up. A person sells himself or herself, completely or partially, for money, in order to buy different things. And money works for you.

But who really understands what processes are in operation behind this seemingly natural and self-evident given? Inexorably, it draws one area of life after another into the all-powerful categories of buying and selling, feasibility and egotistical executability. Everything has a "price." Everybody has a price—provided it is high enough to parry a sense of cheap betrayal

---

5. Georg Simmel, *The Philosophy of Money,* trans. Tom Bottomore and David Frisby (London, 1978), 54 (*Philosophie des Geldes,* 61ff.).

with a propped-up sense of one's own high value. This creates social structures that, from the perspective of circulation, appear to be transparent because they are shot through with an abstract, uniform network of prices and costs. It also creates structures that are corruptible at all levels, even the most mundane, but especially those of power and the intellect.

In 1844, Karl Marx described money as follows in his early essay, "National Economy and Philosophy":

> Since money, as the existing and active concept of value, confounds and confuses all things, it is the general *confounding* and *confusing* of all things—the world upside-down—the confounding and confusing of all natural and human qualities.
>
> Whoever can buy bravery is brave, though he be a coward. As money is not exchanged for any one specific quality, for any one specific thing, or for any particular human essential power, but for the entire objective world of man and nature, from the standpoint of its possessor it therefore serves to exchange every quality for every other, even contradictory, quality and object: it is the fraternisation of impossibilities. It makes contradictions embrace.[6]

Marx's inverted world, described in correspondingly paradoxical phrasing, is the European world of the developed monetary economy. In that economy, money—as the mediating agent and common measure of all things—determines social and personal processes that go far beyond economic transactions. This threatens to destroy the private refuge. Money as the means of exchange par excellence reduces the multiplicity of particular qualities to quantitative units of value. It therefore delivers up to comparability that which is incomparable.

Simmel could not have known of Marx's early writings, which were published only in 1932—fifty years after the appearance of Marx's major work, *Das Kapital*, and fourteen years after Simmel's death. Nevertheless, similar formulations are to be found in Simmel's *Philosophy of Money*—though his assessment of the nature of the peculiar matter is entirely different. And both Simmel and Marx make use of an erotic metaphor (which they probably found in the same source, Shakespeare's *Timon of Athens*): the kiss as

---

6. Karl Marx, "National Economy and Philosophy," in *Karl Marx and Frederick Engels, Collected Works*, vol. 3, *Marx and Engels: 1843–1844* (New York, 1975), 326 (Karl Marx, *Frühschriften*, ed. Siegfried Landshut [Stuttgart, 1953]).

the symbol of exchange,[7] as the "embodiment of social interaction" and the relativity of all things.

Simmel saw his *Philosophy of Money* as a contrast to Marx's theory of money. Simmel's express purpose was therefore to "construct a deeper level" beneath historical materialism, which defined itself as the highest state of consciousness and which laid claim to having sufficiently examined the constitutive conditions of intellectual and social phenomena. For while Marx explains man's being and actions as the result of economic conditions, Simmel subsumes economic processes under the cephalopod culture of *Lebensphilosophie*.

In the universal cultural cosmos, money develops its antagonistic effects as one of the most important creations of practical reasoning. It owes its creation and increasing importance in the modern age to the immanent dynamics of culture and the tendency toward depersonalization and objectification of all life processes. As an especially progressive construct, it possesses—in addition to affirmative characteristics that promote freedom—negative, alienating powers. They are responsible for what Simmel diagnosed as the dichotomy between the inwardness of the soul and an outwardly oriented objectivity, something that is prototypically modern. All cultural progress is therefore accompanied by profound manifestations of alienation.

Unlike Marx, Simmel did not envision the distant strategic goal of an allround developed individual in a free society of free individuals. His philosophical and sociological approach does not wave a revolutionary flag; it is more likely to take recourse to metaphysical argument than to visions; it is more distanced; and it is phenomenologically descriptive. In this sense it does not participate at all in the faddish fin-de-siècle pessimism of a cultural critique based on civilizational ennui and irrational argument, a critique whose anti-intellectualism was later placed in the service of a fascist regime. Yet Simmel did take into account the shortcomings of modern society, lamenting the fragmentation and loss of the whole personality, which he thought of as the true purpose of all culture. In that sense he deplored the inexorably growing dominance of external privilege under the dictates of money.

In the interactive processes of social change, money plays a supportive role. The general aim of replacing subjective, personal relationships with neutral, objective ones is provided with an equivalent that is characterized

---

7. See Simmel, *Philosophy of Money*, 54; *Philosophie des Geldes*, 61.

by absolute indifference to content and application. Faced with the diverse negative and ambivalent characteristics of money, Simmel also reflects on the welcome consequences of ongoing processes of objectification. He sees in them, for instance, an opportunity for new freedom, since certain dependencies become obsolete—those resulting from coercion in the family, for example, or the arbitrary labor relationship of serfdom. The dissolution of old dependencies does away with the fundamental, traditional assurances that are usually set up to protect those who are not free or capable of protecting and taking responsibility for themselves. Here we may think of the various political and legal restrictions on women denied responsibility; the image of woman that is an orientation for behavior as well as a limitation obligating her to compliance; the related feminine values of honor and morality that continue to exercise their repressive effects to this day but no longer go unquestioned. The more radical wing of the women's movement—which was only beginning to form during Simmel's lifetime—subjected to question all of the measures designed for the guidance of wives according to the standardization. As a consequence, it destroyed the framework of dependence on home and husband that was experienced as quite pleasant by women.

Nevertheless, the possibility of achieving a higher level of free development is conditional upon overcoming the old need for security and the familiar pattern of delegation of responsibility. Periods of change, with their irritating lack of orientation, are painful to all—for different reasons. Yet as long as they are perceived and turned to productive use, these critical phases are precisely the ones that form the basis for social learning processes.

According to Simmel, the fundamental experience of the modern age,[8] with its characteristics of presentness, tempo, rhythm, distance, and subject-object dichotomy, is based on a permanent circulation of goods and money, on sale, purchase, and consumption. (Art alone remains a sphere of authentic production, and Simmel later turns to art with increasing interest.) In Simmel's view, socially distributed production and consumption are thus subject to the laws of exchange. This means that the socialization of the human being is based primarily on relations of exchange, not on labor or the production sector as maintained in Marx's theory. Exchange is a "sociological construct sui generis" and finds in money its symbolic correlation:

---

8. See D. P. Frisby, "Georg Simmels Theorie der Moderne," in *Georg Simmel und die Moderne*, ed. H.-J. Dahme and O. Rammstedt (Frankfurt am Main, 1984), 35ff.

"Money is totally indifferent to the objects because it is separated from them by the fact of exchange. What money mediates is not the possession of an object but the exchange of objects."[9]

From the perspective of the subject, the modern personality is being increasingly dissolved in monetary relations: it appears either as a deliverer of labor or of goods, as purchaser, consumer, or money giver, and in this way becomes caught up in a network of external connections. However, to the degree that the modern personality disappears, as it were, behind its functions, its powerlessness in the face of subjective conditions also disappears. For Simmel, therefore, money is not centrally important simply as a representative of value but as a category of replacement of personal dependencies by externally and technically determined ones. This function of money mediates a historically new dimension of freedom. Purely monetary relationships bind the individual only anonymously to the group as an abstract whole; they therefore echo the relationships an individual has, through money, with things.

On the other hand, Simmel's praise of money, which is based on what he sees as an ultimate gain in individual autonomy, confronts historic and modern phenomena that consist in the subjection of the entire personality to the measure of money and payment. Among these phenomena are prostitution, purchase of brides and marriage for money, slavery, monetary fines and wergild, and bribery.

The most important point in Simmel's investigation is the question of the meaning of the money economy for individual freedom. He comes to the conclusion that it establishes the conditions for a more significant absence of constraints and thus for new possibilities of freedom. The point at which old constraints and the new freedom intersect is also the place where the difference in the sexes is to be situated.

Simmel mentions the women's movement in his *Philosophy of Money* in a discussion of the overall development of freedom. In his later philosophical writings on questions of gender and femininity—the subject of our discussion—the existential component of freedom disappears, as will be shown, in favor of an ontologizing, and to a considerable degree sexist, polarizing conception.[10]

Simmel does not use the concept of freedom to reformulate traditional

---

9. Simmel, *Philosophy of Money*, 211; *Philosophie des Geldes*, 264.
10. See my lecture on this subject, "Weiblichkeit und Kultur," in *Was Philosophinnen denken: Eine Dokumentation*, ed. Halina Bendkowski and Brigitte Weisshaupt (Zurich, 1983).

ideas of gender under the conditions of modernism. His dualist gender model defines cultural differentiation and development essentially on the side of the masculine, while the feminine continues to be linked with the principle of wholeness and being and therefore remains conceptually heteronomous. Simmel thus explicitly relinquishes the chance to provide an anchor for the idea of the autonomy of women. Precisely because modernism is characterized by the bourgeois individual's having been able to free the self increasingly from externally determined structures, the gender-based restrictions on women in Simmel's concept of the sexes are particularly grave.

Simmel hoped that the development of a money culture would lead to a decrease in social competition, but this evidently did not lead him to consider a model of potential freedom applicable to both sexes equally or the dismantling of a society based on gender status. Men are therefore the true beings of modernism and of culture, while women represent timeless premodernism.

Against the theoretical background of Simmel's dynamic concept of freedom in a modern money economy—as developed in his *Philosophy of Money*—Simmel's philosophy of the sexes seems remarkably inconsistent, or at the very least one-sided. This raises the overall question of how we are to evaluate the rupture in his work. The contradiction, for example, between his philosophy of culture or his sociology and his philosophy of the sexes cannot readily be regarded as the result of an open, fragmentary theory of modernism. Rather, it makes clear that philosophical thinking is only partly free of the normative power of the fact and the constellations of interests. Philosophy itself is also always part of the system.

Simmel's Essays on the Philosophy of the Sexes

It may seem trivial to note that human beings appeared in two variants, male and female. It is less trivial to ask how the two variants react to each other, how they imagine they will react to each other in the future, and how they understand themselves and each other in light of the fact that each of them lays claim to human completeness. Behind these theoretical questions lies another, quite concrete question about the nature of practical life together. It is a question about new possibilities for love between the sexes, for love that is not governed by a kind of pre-formed order—even if the opinion persists that the relationship between the sexes is adequately determined by the connection of nature. As we know and probably agree on from other contexts, we can speak of the nature of the human being only in very considered fashion. When we talk about nature, we are talking about the *concept* of nature, that is, about a construct. This insight must also be applied to a discussion of the nature of the sexes and their relationship to one another. If it is not, we rapidly find ourselves subject to the usual clichés and unable to go beyond the point where the question originally arose in response to insufficient answers.

Georg Simmel's achievement is that he subjected the feminine and the relationship of the sexes in the modern age to renewed thought. His metaphysics of the sexes is a thematic complex made up of various studies. At the center is his 1911 essay on "Das Relative und das Absolute im Geschlechter-Problem" (The relative and the absolute in the problem of the sexes).[11] This essay attempts to define the relationship of the sexes to one another and the essence of each of the sexes as an independent form of existence. It expands the framework of the general cultural approach by including the explosive subject of power.

By constructing principles that are polar opposites, Simmel escapes the systematic difficulty arising from the fact that men and women are—first or finally?—also always human but that humans are always gendered; that is, they appear as men or women. Thus, he does not mark the point at which the two diverge, but instead contrasts the difference that makes up the "male principle" with the difference that makes up the "female principle." However, the differences stand in relation to one another as the One and the Other, as norm and deviation. The "male principle" is accorded a higher degree of generality, for it also represents the generally human. Thus, the tradition of identifying the male with the human is not abandoned by Simmel, although he explicitly lays claim to doing so. The double structure of the male-human provides the backdrop for Simmel's definition of the feminine.

Simmel's "Weibliche Kultur" (Female culture),[12] the first version of which appeared in 1902, is to be understood as a direct reaction to the

---

11. Georg Simmel, "Das Relative und das Absolute im Geschlechter-Problem" (1911), in *Philosophische Kultur*.

12. Georg Simmel, "Weibliche Kultur" (1902/1911), in *Philosophische Kultur* (see the translation by Guy Oakes, "Female Culture," in *Georg Simmel: On Women, Sexuality, and Love* [New Haven, 1984]). See also Cornelia Klinger, "Georg Simmels 'Weibliche Kultur' wiedergelesen—aus Anlaß des Nachdenkens über feministische Wissenschaftskritik," *Studia Philosophica* 47 (1988).

women's movement. In it he deals with the possibility of realizing the desires and demands of women. Nevertheless, he weighs not the political and social chances of the movement's success, but the chances that objective culture can gain substance through the women's movement. He is concerned with the "relationships in principle of the female being to objective culture." Positing a female "being a priori" leads Simmel to consider the cultural productivity of women and a possible increase in the qualitative stores of the objective intellect should the demands of the women's movement for active participation be met. "Female Culture" thus deals with the relationship between specifically feminine consciousness and the formal conditions for cultural creation. Simmel's concept of culture becomes relevant in this context.

One phenomenon that Simmel stresses and considers to be specifically feminine—flirtation—should be mentioned here because it is based on structures that were laid down in "Female Culture" and expounded in his later major work on the metaphysics of gender. The "playful vacillation between Yes and No," the "simultaneity of accommodation and denial"[13] turns out to be a variant of a function of the universal passivity of the feminine, something Simmel regards as a structural characteristic.

Whereas Simmel's first essay on the problem of gender, "On the Psychology of Women,"[14] adopts the empirical method and remains within the framework of sociology, his later texts place heavier emphasis on metaphysics.

Simmel's essays on the philosophy of the sexes and the philosophy of culture are marked by a peculiarly vibrant vagueness that constantly defies categorization. They owe their character to a "metaphysical mobility of the intellect" that attempts to dissolve the material contents and products of thought in the unity of thinking itself, in what could be thought of as a constantly flowing state. In the ambiguity of this "dissolving"—in which the goal is always part of the path and the result part of the current process—the result of thought is linked to the subjective experience of thought. The stance that shines through the texts conveys an intense impression of a search for deliverance that pushes its efforts to the edge of calculated disso-

---

13. See Georg Simmel, "Flirtation," in *Georg Simmel*, trans. Oakes, 134; "Die Koketterie" (1909), in *Philosophische Kultur*, 83, 93.

14. "Zur Psychologie der Frauen," *Zeitschrift für Völkerkunde und Sprachwissenschaft* 20 (1890). See also Georg Simmel, *Schriften zur Philosophie und Soziologie der Geschlechter*, ed. H.-J. Dahme and Klaus Christian Köhnke (Frankfurt am Main, 1986). This volume includes versions published in newspapers and the early, unrevised versions of Simmel's main essays on the question of the sexes.

lution. Yet Simmel's studies do not exhaust themselves in attaining stylistic-formal proportion; they also produce concrete statements and conclusions. To borrow a metaphor from chemistry, their supersaturated solutions set free "crystallizations" (as Simmel frequently calls the products and forms of the intellect)—for example, the concept of the feminine.

Simmel's essays are masterpieces of differentiation that take apart their object in order to reveal a network of relationships and associations, analyses and analogies, polarizations and metaphors, of examples, comparisons, and typologies. An intellectual topography appears before the inner eye, and its cross-connections, points of reference, parallels, correlations, and ramifications give the texts—in spite of their intended openness and lack of finality—an aura of extreme hermeticism. This leaves them in considerable need of explication and therefore open to varying interpretations. The approach taken in this study attempts to do justice to the complex structure of the texts as well as to their varying levels of difficulty.

My examination of Simmel's philosophy of the sexes—against the background of his concept of culture[15]—combines thematic systematization with a critique of ideology. Systematization of the various issues Simmel addresses is designed, on the one hand, to disentangle his many overlapping themes, and, on the other hand, to bring together scattered statements into coherent thematic complexes. Parallel to these descriptive and interpretive approaches, the study will subject Simmel's definable statements to critical reflection because of fundamental doubts about the tenability of his thesis of the "a priori feminine."

In general, Simmel's metaphysics of gender are under suspicion of being ideological. His understanding of the feminine can be explained on the basis of our historical consciousness and the knowledge of conventional nineteenth-century values. His claim to general validity beyond that period and for all time, as well as his transhistorical definition of substantial and transcendental structures of the feminine, is strictly rejected here. His claim springs from a conservative stance and is paired with a restorative intent that omits the progressive moment. Moreover, it is anchored largely in common prejudices and reaffirms stereotypes.

No one would expect Simmel to adopt feminist positions or to represent the high point of feminist consciousness. But in light of his noble philosophical maxims (and his interpretation of the world and the human), it is not

---

15. Ursula Menzer, *Subjektive und objektive Kultur: Georg Simmels Philosophie der Geschlechter vor dem Hintergrund seines Kultur-Begriffs* (Pfaffenweiler, 1992).

too much to expect that, as a philosopher, he stand up for and defend the principle of the freedom and dignity of the individual, whether male or female. This is the standard against which he must allow himself to be measured.

Simmel diagnoses *our* culture as thoroughly male—and we can only agree with that. In the course of our study of his philosophy of the sexes, it will become clear that his philosophy of culture and all that it involves takes as its main subject the structure of a culturally conceived masculinity. Woman is excluded de facto from the realm of objective culture. She is also excluded theoretically, and may participate at most in those areas where she is not a threat to man. The definition of woman does not merely run along lines of exclusion but also of inclusion in a sector that is designated as hers.

This study consciously avoids confronting Simmel's image of the feminine with any kind of new, "progressive" image of woman. Various, more recent feminist approaches are usually just attempts at revaluation that are theoretically still bound to traditional ideas. Even older philosophical women's studies appear to provide no satisfactorily workable concept. Nor can this be the goal. For the task is primarily one of deconstruction, that is, of breaking down traditional patterns and clichés and investigating the patterns of prejudice that are behind almost all variations on the definition of the feminine; it is not to fix hastily upon positive definitions. The traditional concept of the feminine is, moreover, to be understood as derivative and merely complementary to a self-declared "gender neutral" concept of the generally human (that is, masculine). Marianne Weber speaks with keen insight in this context of the "male being in need of a complement"[16] that forms an essential part of this concept.

The point of departure for philosophical women's studies would at first appear to be a criticism: The "feminine" as an object of philosophical reflection is only justifiable if its position in historical and current philosophical production is subject to a critical review based on a critique of ideology. The purpose of this review would be to reject the "eternal" claims to supremacy of a male principle based on power and to secure equal rights and chances for women in society and for women philosophers in philosophy. What is necessary is to conquer an intellectual territory that lies beyond the tension between conformity and dissidence. A further aim is to win back women's history and to work toward a philosophical identity that is not

---

16. Marianne Weber, "Die Frau und die objektive Kultur," in *Frauenfragen und Frauengedanken* (Tübingen, 1919), 102.

subjected per se to the norms of male self-awareness. Philosophical women's studies therefore unites an interest in critical insight with an interest in political emancipation. To regard the "feminine" as a genuinely philosophical object within the context of a transcendental philosophy that seeks justification for the difference between the sexes in general categories of reason would make a mockery of every tradition of Enlightenment to which philosophy still feels bound. Only the gradual retreat of the "feminine" from philosophy through the deliberate destruction of prejudices that have the force of truth in the heads of men and women will be likely to guarantee the self-evident entry of women philosophers into philosophy. Men and women are without doubt beings of gender, but there is no serious reason to assume that gender makes a difference in their ability to think or their ability to reason. Nevertheless, their experiences and perspectives—that is, the contents of reason—are readily distinguishable and define the cultural difference between the masculine and the feminine. At the same time, that content provides the basis for a new category of analysis—gender[17]—and for a methodological expansion of philosophical women's studies into philosophical gender studies.

Feminist philosophy has adopted a very basic concept of gender and derives from it a demand that we rethink the conditions under which traditional philosophy came into being and the context in which it is exploited. This critical reception is one of the main supports of the highly ambitious project of feminist philosophy, that is, of philosophical research on gender. Its goal can be described briefly as follows: to analyze patriarchal ways of thinking and their potential for creating prejudicial structures, and to expose androcentric perspectives in speech among a generality that considers itself to be gender neutral.

From this point of view, a positive philosophy of the feminine would be misguided, counterproductive, and politically dangerous. For the time being at least, or so it seems to me, the power of utopian thinking can come only from negation.

Such considerations, more or less programmatic in nature, form the background for my choice of an approach to the discussion of Simmel's philosophy, one that combines hermeneutics and a critique of ideology. To

17. See *Die Philosophin, Forum für feministische Theorie und Philosophie*, Tübingen 1 (1990), devoted to feminist theory, philosophy, and the university; see also ibid., vol. 2 (1990), devoted to gender. See also *Denken der Geschlechterdifferenz: Neue Fragen und Perspektiven der feministischen Theorie*, ed. Herta Nagl-Docekal and Herlinde Pauer-Studer (Vienna, 1990).

provide for interpretive balance for his philosophy of the sexes and the resulting construction of the feminine—as reinforcement, so to speak—it is useful to draw on the philosophy of culture of Simmel's later phase, especially since it has been assumed from the beginning that structural parallels can be demonstrated. Moreover, Simmel himself establishes a connection between the philosophy of the sexes and the philosophy of culture by basing his concept of culture on an examination of the possibility of feminine production of culture. The textual basis for a study of Simmel's concept of culture is provided by his tightly focused essay, "The Concept and Tragedy of Culture,"[18] as well as by his essays "On the Nature of Culture"[19] and "The Conflict in Modern Culture."[20]

Gender and Culture

The core of Simmel's concept of culture is a conflict-laden and potentially tragic dichotomy between subject and object. In analyses that are to be understood as Simmel's diagnosis of the times, this dichotomy takes on particular significance because the condition of modern culture is lamented as profoundly disparate and lacking in syntheses. There is a gap between the interactive and mutually necessary elements of subjective and objective culture; and this leads to rigidity despite bustling activity, or to chronic loss of form despite stylization.

Increasing differentiation in labor processes, the automatism of technology at all levels of production, the dominance of instrumental reason, and the functionalization and abstraction of social and personal relationships through the "omnivalence" of organization by money are alienating people from each other and from themselves. Practical constraints take the place of human-centered, meaningful ends and turn means into goals, thus making necessary an ever sharper division between public and private life and activ-

18. "Der Begriff und die Tragödie der Kultur," in *Philosophische Kultur*. For an English translation, see *Georg Simmel: The Conflict in Modern Culture and Other Essays*, trans. and with an introduction by K. Peter Etzkorn (New York, 1968).
19. "Vom Wesen der Kultur," in *Brücke und Tür: Essays des Philosophen zur Geschichte, Religion, Kunst und Gesellschaft*, ed. Michael Landmann with Margarete Susman (Stuttgart, 1957).
20. Georg Simmel, *Der Konflikt in der modernen Kultur* (Munich, 1918) (see *Georg Simmel*, trans. Etzkorn).

ity. Production and exchange, creative activity and reception proceed increasingly according to their own immanent rules, come in contact or permeate each other less and less, and therefore fail to fulfill their actual cultural purpose, which is the fully developed, integrated personality.

Under the conditions of this culture, the modern individual is in a hopeless uproar at the demands placed on him or her, or is paralyzed by the lack of orientation. The "path of the soul" borders on the abyss or ends in a blockade.

The schism between subjective and objective culture also opens up in Simmel's philosophy of the sexes; there it reaches its culmination, as it were, because the subject-object dichotomy embodies a gender-specific variant of doubling. The female principle is assigned to the subjective side with its reproductive and receptive components; the male principle functions as the representative of objective culture. At the same time, the male principle encompasses the entire dichotomy. The dualistic, conflicted being with cultural consciousness is a member of the male sex. "The path of the soul to itself" describes the paradigmatic existence and development of the man. The woman is already at one with herself. But never more than that.

In Simmel's model of gender, the two opposite ways of being and thinking that make up the female and the male principle are structurally determined by unity and wholeness on the one hand, differentiation and duality on the other. Grouped around these fundamental ontological and cognitive determining factors are a number of characterizations of the male and female absolute that are defined primarily through their relationship to sexuality. Simmel thus shifts the female absolute to gender itself, the male absolute to the idea, which transcends sexuality. Male sexuality articulates itself in relational terms and is directed toward woman in general, toward the feminine absolute; the orientation of woman is toward the man as individual. A man seeks in a woman a single example of the generic type, while a woman seeks in a man a special example of the human being.

The specific, polarizing differentiations of the male and female principle in Simmel's model of the sexes can be summarized as follows:

Male Principle	*Female Principle*
Intellect/Idea	Nature/Instinct
Concept	Substance
Differentiation	Wholeness
Superdualistic harmony	Predualistic harmony

Dichotomy/dualism	Unity
Development	Completeness
Becoming	Being
Individual	Genre
Tragic fate	Sad existence
Objective	Subjective
Historical	Unhistorical
Active/acting	Passive/suffering
Productivity	Reproduction
Inspired elemental creativity	Semiproductivity
Centrifugal dynamic	Centripetal dynamic
Expansive	Gravitative
Relational sexuality	Essential sexuality
(Sexuality = Doing)	(Sexuality = Being)
Transcends sexuality	Subtends sexuality (mother)
Transcendence	Immanence
More-than-life	Life

Study of Simmel's model leads to the following conclusions: Simmel's polarizing conception of the sexes and the philosophical gynecology it encompasses presents humanity as fragmented, both in the male and in the female. However, the feminine, as he defines it, is far more restricted anthropologically and is more thoroughly circumscribed in conception than is the masculine antithesis. The female type is oriented toward immediate gender specifications, whereas the male sexual type arises precisely through its release from this liability. Simmel ignores the lack of evolutionary simultaneity and the ontogenetic chances for the development of men and women—discussing complex, historic relativity only superficially—and draws on different sources for the definition of the male and the female principle. Thus, the concept of woman is derived primarily from the biological category of her sex, while the concept of man is derived from the culturally mediated category of the genus. The choice and extent of the definitional framework predetermines the results—the desired results. Woman is a generic being; man represents culture with all its achievements (including, of course, civilization's destructive potential). Given this starting point, Simmel's concept of the man is inevitably more richly and more dynamically formulated than that of the female. Therefore, characteristics that are by tendency neutral and non-gender-specific accumulate in the man, and this provides a basis for identifying the man with the universally human.

When Simmel rejects the male as a general principle on historic grounds—only to revive it structurally afterward—he places metabrackets around the masculine-feminine polarity, guaranteeing the so-called male intellect a monopoly on definition. The male principle turns into a super-principle, and everything that does not have to be linked to the givens of female biology can be subsumed under the heading "male." In principle, every characteristic that seems relevant to social dominance and power can be monopolized as "male." Characteristics with no potential for power devolve to woman.

We cannot fail to recognize that at the theoretical level, Simmel's definitional logic parallels a function of the logic of power as actually practiced: the limitation of the feminine to biological, gender-specific parameters, and its exclusion from culture. Simmel thus extends into the abstract a historically proven pattern at the service of male hegemony. But this in no way justifies its claim to transhistorical validity.

The situation is similar with regard to the systematic polarity of manifest structures of the masculine and feminine as posited by Simmel. It is possible to accept as description something that is not acceptable—and certainly not desirable—as "immutability." In concrete terms, alienated sexuality on the one hand stands in opposition to externalized sexuality on the other—frigid, solipsistic sexuality versus sexual activism and the will to power. Though these two forms of sexual existence are complementary to each other, both are isolated and incomplete in relation to an integrated humanity—by exclusion from what is human in the broadest sense in the case of the female principle, and by marginalization in the case of the male principle. Female sexuality is desexualized through ontologization; male sexuality is made abstract through functionalization. That the masculine and the feminine arrive at harmony in this condition, as a sentimentalized Enlightenment would have it, may give rise to amazement. For the idea of an encounter between feminine-centripetal gravitation and the male-centrifugal dynamic evokes an image of cosmic catastrophe rather than of harmonious union. The romantic sensibility logically formulated the answer of its age to this fateful demand: Long live yearning! Death lies in fulfillment (or as Kleist puts it, death is fulfillment).

The ideological, patriarchal pathos of division defines as its high point the polarization of structures of reason. Men and women are each assigned different forms of thought and knowledge. As with the entire concept of the sexes, the deficiencies of one side are defined here—quite precariously—by way of the deficiencies of the other. That is, by assigning structures of reason to the sexes, Simmel constructs a one-sidedness and insufficiency that "come together again" in a completeness that embraces both sexes. As we know, Kant was clear-sighted enough to recognize that without intuition concepts are empty, and without concepts intuition is blind. His view is a warning that is thrown to the winds by a zeal for polarization that lacks compelling justification. Though it can be assumed that male and female conditions of life correspond to a different type of consciousness, the formal structures of reason are the undivided and equal property of human beings.

In his metaphysical construction of the male-female relationship, Simmel retraces, at the philosophical level, the social exclusion of woman from the centers of power and turns it into the rule. This shows that philosophy itself can make only conditional headway against the normative power of the factual. Powerful interests in the form of ideologies set loose by a duped consciousness stand in the way of the freedom of the intellect and of honesty. The exaltations of the intellect know no bounds when the dichotomy of Western thinking is superimposed on the problem of the sexes. Ideas of submission and domination form the point of connection and transition that makes one particular tradition of thought well-suited to this purpose, for it subjects the world to dichotomy and hierarchy and hypostatizes the relations of the sexes as endless discord. If doubts are noted, there are immediate expressions of concern, particularly among men, about jeopardizing the erotic tension between the sexes. And the language used is notably energetic, seeming to draw its potency directly from the existing gradient. Simmel decrees that the Other must not necessarily be the Subordinate, that it can occupy an equal and equivalent position. But his concept of the feminine, which lacks all the determinants of autonomous humanity, refutes his stated intentions.

Simmel prescribes for the feminine an independent canon of norms in order to protect it from codified and institutionalized masculinity. However, in doing so, he merely formulates what he professes to replace: a correlative standard. When he goes beyond the immediate biological invariables, what Simmel understands as the feminine orients itself, *ex negativo,* toward the image of the human-masculine in order to function as its foil. This lack of independence is particularly clear in connection with the cultural presence of the feminine. It is situated primarily in the "gaps" that male culture either leaves or is unable to fill. The ideal of the feminine outlined by Simmel is obviously dictated by male needs for supremacy and complementarity. In addition to its professed pragmatic function for the self-awareness of woman, this ideal has a useful side effect: it guarantees that woman is kept out of male-occupied territories and that fear of female competition is banned.

Marianne Weber calls the results of Simmel's thought the "subjective ideal of the thinker." In her opinion, Simmel has not laid claims to universal validity. But skepticism is in order with regard to Weber's well-meaning assessment. The fact that Simmel claims transhistorical truth for his concept is an indication that it is more than a personal reflection or an expression of private desires; yet in spite of calling upon the highest of terminological authorities, Simmel does not go beyond mere assertions. If we take this into account, we can agree with Weber. But that does not diminish the conclusion that Simmel pulls out all the stops in order to legitimize prevailing conditions.

There can be no doubt that in Simmel's construction of the sexes, he attempts to achieve formal symmetry. But this does not conceal the nature of his assessment. The consequences he formulates point explicitly toward the exclusion of woman from objective culture (the few exceptions are allowed to take their place in the gaps) and toward confirmation of a status quo based on division of society into areas traditionally reserved for the sexes. Lines of demarcation in the distribution of tasks and of power remain unchanged; there is no provision for equal participation of the female principle in the shaping of life at all levels. The male principle emerges from Simmel's investigation with its cultural dominance and manifestations justified, knowing itself exculpated and its path toward perpetuation open.

Simmel's construction of the feminine does not liberate woman from the stamp of the deficient and inferior being. Rather, it interprets the historic product of her undoubtedly reduced social character as the essential, and instead of considering the social causes, "naturalizes" the consequences. The conclusion is that woman is incapable of development. This in turn provides the basis for seeing limits to her intellectual and creative abilities and brings the matter full circle. The constant suggestion of inferiority and the traditional ghettoization of the conditions of female life reproduce a female self-awareness of internalized barriers and low self-esteem. Woman's suppressed and destroyed talents and her ruined feelings of self-worth stand in contrast to a permanent celebration of male self-awareness and the glorified male principle of achievement. Woman's subordination and her orientation toward male desires and needs are made the order of nature and become part of the bourgeois norm. Even if external forces and institutionalized repression are dissipating, ideological postulates continue to exercise their force below the surface. Their effectiveness is constantly being reinforced.

Simmel's theory of gender in no way breaks with the tradition of the degradation of woman. In the fascist ideology of an Alfred Rosenberg, the traditional combination of denigration, mystification, and mythologization enjoys a seamless yet heightened continuation. This lends credence to Lukács's theory that *Lebensphilosophie* was a forerunner of the perversions of National Socialism as it relates to woman.

Simmel's concept of the sexes—and especially of the feminine—seems so plausible at first glance and so questionable on further examination because it is unsystematic yet catchy. It is a combination of psychological typology and scientific terminology with snippets of philosophy of the most varied provenance; and it draws on existing ideologies and structures of prejudice while paying tribute to vital interests and conventional ways of thinking. Yet philosophical concepts that are made analogous to traditional phenomena of the feminine and masculine and that suggest inevitable correspondences are nothing more than metaphors. The empirical particulars that Simmel arranges into a picture take on the character of a model; the inductive process of his analysis turns into a normative claim. Historic conditions take on the character of eternal verities when he distills from the existing gender power structure a comprehensive, a priori relationship based on the polar opposition of the male and female principles. Simmel's phenomenological starting point does not fit him into a framework of historically balanced argument. On the contrary. Simmel transforms his empirical, descriptive findings into metaphysical fundamentals.

Simmel's critique of culture for its rigidity, for the dominance of the objective intellect, and for its phenomena of alienation turns on the "subjective factor," woman, that is drawn from his philosophy of the sexes. That is nothing new, for this area was always regarded as hers. At home, at the hearth, she is allowed to create atmosphere and remove a man's armor. In this, Simmel merely confirms the polarization of objective and subjective culture. By reasserting their attribution to the male and female principles, he intensifies a dualism that goes beyond structural dichotomies to include the entire human community.

Simmel's traditional pattern of thought is firmly tied to unenlightened ideas that he cannot abandon even in light of profound changes in culture and the demands placed on the individual. As such, it provides a good example of the limits of a purely conservative critique of culture. In spite of his sensitivity to cultural trends, Simmel is not willing to distance himself from the traditional image of the human being and at least open the way for new approaches to a solution. And if he could not show an interest in the autonomy of woman because he was party to the issue, his concern about the condition of culture should have led him to more radical ideas about a theory of the sexes. We might conclude that his one-sided male thinking, deep-rooted to the point of bondage, prevented him from considering unconventional ideas. Nevertheless, shortly before his death Simmel more or less renounced his philosophy of the sexes.[21] Those who currently seek to justify or take positive recourse to Simmel must bear this in mind.

A highly gender-specific human image such as that conceived by Simmel is not suited to opening up new perspectives on the "cultural distress" Simmel laments. On the contrary. There would appear to be a connection, little studied until now, between traditional forms of culture, with their immanent tendencies toward corruption, and the polarized structures of the masculine and feminine. Precisely in highly complex conditions of life, the masculine-feminine polarity can be seen as intensifying disintegration and individual unhappiness. All the more serious, therefore, are the consequences of a concept that is *based* on these structures, one whose intent is, in fact, to restore them. What is necessary is the elimination of the dichotomy and its disastrous tendencies. A synthesis that would encompass both sexes to the greatest degree possible would therefore provide a model for

---

21. In answer to Marianne Weber's criticism, Simmel wrote in a letter to her several years before his death:

> From your discussion I do not think I must draw the conclusion that there is a deadly animosity between our views. Many of the differences are only seeming differences that arise from the fact that we observe phenomena from varying distances. It also appears to me recently that there is a convincing view that dissolves the conflict and spans the fundamental alternative of whether the essential issue for a woman lies in her being human or in her being woman. This is related to a theme that has occupied me for a long time: The elements of life, as soon as the formulation of a concept has removed them from the overall atmosphere of life and has made them independent, obey a different logic and reveal a completely different meaning than they possess within a life itself. This is also significant for the concept of the feminine; but I can talk about this only in the broadest of contexts—so broad that I do not know whether I will be able to address it in the years that remain to me.
>
> For today, with all indiscriminate male and female greetings and in unfailing respect,
> Your Simmel

(In K. Gassen and M. Landmann, *Buch des Dankes an Georg Simmel*, [Berlin, 1958], 133; trans. MR-B).

thought that points toward the future. And investigation of these issues would open up a broad field of research for philosophical women's and gender studies.

Notes on the Reception of Simmel's Philosophy of the Sexes

The reception of Arthur Schopenhauer's work had reached its high point at the time of Simmel's birth. Schopenhauer's image of the sexes in his "Metaphysics of Sexual Love" (from the second volume of his major treatise, *The World as Will and Idea*)[22] is relatively well balanced—both sexes are assumed to be equally subject to the genus within them. The definition that applies equally to both sexes in Schopenhauer is made hierarchical by Simmel. Only in Schopenhauer's later essay "Concerning Women"[23] does he give free rein to a hatred that probably had its origins in his relationship with his mother, that is, in personal conflict and not in the systematic foundations of his philosophy. Schopenhauer does attempt to objectify[24] the personal and the subjective in his treatises, but in this he is not consistently successful.

Simmel knew his Schopenhauer; and the first explicit treatment of the problem of the sexes as an object of philosophy in the nineteenth century[25]

22. Arthur Schopenhauer, "Metaphysik der Geschlechtsliebe," in *Die Welt als Wille und Vorstellung*, vol. 2 (Wiesbaden, 1949).
23. Arthur Schopenhauer, "Über die Weiber," in *Parerga und Paralipomena*, vol. 2 (Wiesbaden, 1947).
24. For example, in the following passage: "When nature split the human race into two halves, she did not make the division precisely through the middle. In spite of all polarity, the difference between the positive and negative poles is not merely qualitative but also quantitative. Thus did the ancients and oriental races regard woman; and her proper place was accordingly much more correctly recognized by them than by us with our old French gallantry and absurd veneration of women, this culminating point of Christian-Germanic stupidity. It has merely served to make women so arrogant and inconsiderate" (ibid., 658; the English translation is that of E. F. J. Payne in Arthur Schopenhauer, "On Women," in *Parerga and Paralipomena: Short Philosophical Essays* [Oxford, 1974], 2:621–22).
25. The eighteenth century discussed the question of the sexes primarily in terms of education. J.-J. Rousseau's *Emile, ou De l'éducation,* may serve as a typical example. As a rule, the polarization of the sexes led to the degradation of women, a fact made clear by Rousseau's title, which simply ignores Sophie, the female counterpart to Emile in Rousseau's pedagogic tractate. Sophie does not represent the concept of a partner with equal rights. The approach is different in T. G. von Hippel's *Über die bürgerliche Verbesserung der Weiber* (Concerning the bourgeois improvement of women). Hippel acknowledges only the immediate sexual difference between man and woman. The soul and the spirit surmount all of the gender-specific differ-

will not have been unimportant to his own philosophical reflections. Personally, however, at least as far as we can tell, he was not as excessively misogynistic as Schopenhauer, whose sensuous and passionate temperament and unhappy experiences fed his vehemence.

Simmel was apparently drawn to intellectually exceptional and educated women. His wife published her own work—which was considered important by Gertrud Bäumer and Margarete Susman[26]—under the pseudonym Marie Luise Enckendorff. Simmel's investigation of the problem of the sexes would therefore seem to have been inspired partly by motives of self-reflection and the need to clarify his understanding of himself as a male. But this understanding was not prepared to give up the position of historic superiority attributed to every man without further scrutiny; and it tried, in subtle fashion, to objectify and legitimize that position.

Nietzsche, like Schopenhauer a prominent hater of women, at least relativizes his savage statements about woman-as-such. In "Beyond Good and Evil," he writes:

> About man and woman, for example, a thinker cannot relearn but only finish learning—only discover ultimately how this is "settled" in him. . . .
>
> After this abundant civility that I have just evidenced in relation to myself I shall perhaps be permitted more readily to state a few truths about "woman as such"—assuming that it is now known

---

ences, and he therefore emphasizes equal education for boys and girls—education to becoming citizens. He sees the empirical differences between the sexes as a result of historic conditions, in particular as a result of the process of repression of women by men. Simmel reviewed Hippel's book in a newspaper article on the occasion of the hundredth anniversary of its appearance (Georg Simmel, "Ein Jubiläum der Frauenbewegung [1892]," in *Schriften zur Philosophie und Soziologie der Geschlechter*). Simmel took many thematic impulses from Hippel, but his position on the sexes is more like that of Rousseau.

26. Margarete Susman: "Gertrud Simmel, whom I revered like almost no other woman, was an important and, in her own way, great woman who dealt with all of the essential questions of life in her own independent fashion and who published four important books under the name Marie Luise Enckendorff: *Vom Sein und Haben der Seele* (1906), *Realität und Gesetzlichkeit im Geschlechtsleben* (1910), *Über das Religiöse* (1919), and *Kindschaft zur Welt* (1927)" (*Buch des Dankes,* 280; trans. MR-B).

Dahme and Köhnke are of a different opinion about the independence of Gertrud Simmel's thought; her books, they write, "offer little more than a dressed up rehash of many of her husband's ideas" (see the introduction to Simmel's *Schriften zur Philosophie und Soziologie der Geschlechter,* 12).

from the outset how very much these are after all only—*my* truths.²⁷

In this sense, Simmel's discussion introduces a new quality to the debate with its claim to objectivity and its metaphysical character. The attack on male supremacy had become, by this time, a matter of public record, had been quasi-institutionalized by the women's movement. Simple suppression from a position of power was therefore no longer enough; the "inferiority of woman" had to be scientifically proven.²⁸

The women's question was part of the spirit of the times. The women's movement frightened patriarchally minded men, and its political and social demands made them worry about their privileges. Simmel was not the only one who felt that he was being spoken to, and he made every attempt to concentrate his philosophical acumen on saving the nobly feminine—that is, the passive and submissive. Simmel's efforts to develop a philosophy of the sexes were not entirely original, though they were unique in their coherence. The ideas of the feminine in Plato and Aristotle, Spinoza and Fichte, Humboldt and Hegel, Schleiermacher and Feuerbach, Schopenhauer and Weininger,²⁹ are unmistakable, though they are not referred to explicitly. It is possible that he was not even familiar with all of them. But this would have made no difference. For most of these ideas derive from common prejudices, though they are decked out more or less elaborately in philosophical terms. We should regard them, therefore, as common expressions of the ideology of any given time, the function of which is to strengthen the status quo of male glory and supremacy.³⁰

---

27. *Jenseits von Gut und Böse*, 7. Hauptstück, 231 (trans. Walter Kaufmann, in *Basic Writings of Nietzsche* [New York, 1992], 352).

28. See, for example, P. J. Moebius, *Über den physiologischen Schwachsinn des Weibes* (Halle, 1899). In response, see O. Olberg, *Das Weib und der Intellektualismus* (Berlin, 1902). See also H. Dohm, *Die Antifeministen: Ein Buch der Verteidigung* (Berlin, 1902). In his book, Dohm also analyzed the controversial discussion of definitions of the feminine that was taking place within the women's movement.

29. On Weininger, see A. Stopczyk, "Geschlecht und Gewalt," in *Philosophinnen: Von Wegen ins 3. Jahrtausend: 1. Jahrbuch der Internationalen Assoziation von Philosophinnen e.V.*, ed. Manon Maren-Grisebach and Ursula Menzer (Mainz, 1983). For an interesting and vehement response, see H. Schröder, "Zur Neuauflage von faschistischem Antifeminismus und Antisemitismus; Oder: Vor Weininger wird gewarnt," in *Was Philosophinnen denken*, vol. 2, ed. Manon Andreas-Grisebach and Brigitte Weisshaupt (Zurich, 1986). See also Margarete Susman, *Vom Geheimnis der Freiheit* (Zurich, 1965), 115–70.

30. On this concept of ideology, see K. Lenk, introduction to *Ideologie: Ideologiekritik und Wissenssoziologie*, ed. K. Lenk, 3rd ed. (Neuwied, 1967).

With the exception of a few well-meaning but blind efforts, the ultimate search for the eternal feminine has repeatedly led—through the utilitarian harmony of its artful distinctions—to the general degradation of woman. The need for categorization, expressed in polarizing models, almost automatically produces a classificatory hierarchy; at the least, it leads to implied valuations that translate into practical discrimination.

There is, of course, a tradition of thinkers who do not set themselves up to be party or judge. One of them is Simmel's contemporary and student, Theodor Lessing. With his historic, typological distinction between female/woman/lady, he overcomes metaphysical, speculative definitions and accords the female future greater freedom. Like John Stuart Mill, to whom he refers directly, Lessing is one of those who attempts to reflect without prejudice on the question of women. Mill writes: "I consider it presumption in any one to pretend to decide what women are or are not, can or cannot be, by natural constitution."[31]

The tradition of the philosophically based isolation of woman, contained in explicitly philosophical investigations that point beyond mere anthropological glosses, does not come to an end with the nineteenth century and Simmel. This is particularly clear from the perpetuation of this line of thought in a popular philosophical, National Socialist best-seller by Alfred Rosenberg[32] and in the current apologia for Simmel's concept of the sexes by Hans Michael Baumgartner.[33]

With regard to Rosenberg, it is perhaps important to note that the aim of this discussion is not to subject Simmel's work as a whole to the suspicion of pre-National Socialist obscurantism.[34] Apart from this, however, a sexual-fascist continuity can be seen running through the entire history of our culture; Simmel is in no way unusual in this context. Identification of parallels between Simmel's work and that of Rosenberg clearly demonstrates that this continuity—in spite of the differences in detail and diction—is based on the same fundamental commonplaces.

31. John Stuart Mill, *The Subjection of Women*, "unabridged republication" of the 1869 London edition (London, 1970), 104.
32. A. Rosenberg, *Der Mythus des 20. Jahrhunderts: Eine Wertung der seelisch-geistigen Gestaltenkämpfe unserer Zeit*, 57–58th ed. (Munich, 1935), 482–513. On this work, see Ursula Menzer, "Beute des Mythos: Der Begriff der Frau in der nationalsozialistischen Philosophie und seine bedrückende Aktualität," in *Was Philosophinnen denken*, vol. 2, ed. Andreas-Grisebach and Weisshaupt, 124–33.
33. H. M. Baumgartner, "Gleichheit und Verschiedenheit von Mann und Frau in philosophischer Perspektive," *Gießener Universitätsblätter* 2 (1984): 78–95.
34. See Georg Lukács, *Die Zerstörung der Vernunft* (Neuwied/Berlin, 1972), and Hans-Joachim Lieber, *Kulturkritik und Lebensphilosophie* (Darmstadt, 1974).

Rosa Mayreder's collection of essays, *Zur Kritik der Weiblichkeit* (On the critique of femininity), was published in 1905. It can be read as a first answer to questions raised by the bourgeois and proletarian women's movement of the last third of the nineteenth century. The essays were a reaction to major changes in society and related consequences for the lives of women. Rosa Mayreder was a committed feminist who analyzed the philosophy of her times against the background of the women's movement in particular. Unfortunately, Mayreder's role in the theory of feminism is much too little noted today, though she gave precise formulation to important issues during her own times.[35]

We do not know whether Simmel knew Mayreder's work.[36] Mayreder herself does discuss Simmel's concept of culture and his philosophy of the sexes in her second volume of essays, *Geschlecht und Kultur* (Sex and culture), which appeared in 1923.[37] And in fact, from among his contemporaries, Simmel's views were countered exclusively by women theorists. In addition to Rosa Mayreder, Marianne Weber should be acknowledged in this context.[38] In her essay, "Die Frau und die objektive Kultur" (Woman and objective culture), she responds directly to Simmel's metaphysics of the sexes. She criticizes his ideas in polite and nonpolemical terms but decidedly rejects his model of polar opposites: "Polarity alone may create the happiness of union at that one 'beautiful moment,' but it does not create a lasting union rich in content. For this includes a relationship that extends to the human."[39] Apparently, Simmel did not remain untouched by Weber's criticism. Nevertheless, he could not find his way clear to an explicit revision of his views during the last years of his life.

Lewis A. Coser wrote in the essay "Georg Simmels vernachlässigter Beitrag zur Soziologie der Frau" (Georg Simmel's neglected contribution to the sociology of women) that no significant research on Simmel had taken note

---

35. Unfortunately, Rosa Mayreder's works have been only partially reissued; the recent edition does, however, include an interesting introduction; see Rosa Mayreder, *Zur Kritik der Weiblichkeit: Essays*, collected and with an introduction by H. Schnedl (Munich, 1981).

36. "My belief that Simmel still reads a lot turned out to be false. I asked him where his library was. He took me by the arm and led me into the hallway, where a very limited number of books stood on a small bookcase: 'Here,' he said; 'I don't read any longer.' The answer was given seriously but not totally without that endearing coquetry that I had already noticed before in this great person" (see K. Berger in *Buch des Dankes*, 248 [trans. MR-B]).

37. Rosa Mayreder, *Geschlecht und Kultur, Essays: Kritik der Weiblichkeit*, pt. 2 (Jena, 1923).

38. Weber, "Die Frau und die objektive Kultur."

39. See ibid., 133.

thus far of his contribution in this area.⁴⁰ It was left to women theoreticians and the women's movement to introduce Simmel's investigation of the question of the sexes and of the feminine into the current discussion. Coser does note that Simmel makes statements that would "make present-day feminists uneasy." Coser is particularly appreciative of the fact that Simmel broaches the subject of the dilemma of modern woman in a male culture; as to the means Simmel suggests for overcoming the dilemma, however, Coser remarks that the "wealth of Simmel's sociological ideas fails him." Coser writes: "Poor Simmel. When it was a question of a prescription for curing the suffering of modern woman, he took recourse to traditional remedies. On closer examination, the female culture of the future reveals a strong similarity with the world of the educated woman in the Berlin of his times. Simmel's diagnosis was extremely modern, his treatment quite Wilheminian."⁴¹

Marielouise Janssen-Jurreit analyzed Simmel's ideas a number of years ago in her comprehensive study, *Über die Abtreibung der Frauenfrage* (On the abortion of the women's question).⁴² Janssen-Jurreit's discussion presents Simmel as a representative of a philosophy of history that regards history as the fulfillment of the conflict between the sexes⁴³ (see, e.g., Hegel and Spengler). And in fact, in his ambitious essay on flirtation, Simmel defines the man-woman relationship as the primary social form:

> Here as elsewhere, the relationship between the sexes provides the prototype for countless relationships between the individual and the interindividual life.
>
> ... Then in the final analysis the ubiquitous experience that a large number of generally human forms of conduct would have their normative paradigm in the relations of the sexes proves this.⁴⁴

---

40. L. A. Coser, "Georg Simmels vernachlässigter Beitrag zur Soziologie der Frau," in *Georg Simmel und die Moderne*, ed. Dahme and Rammstedt.

41. Ibid., 89. Marianne Ulmi shares this view; see *Frauenfragen—Männergedanken: Zu Georg Simmels Philosophie und Soziologie der Geschlechter* (Zurich, 1989). In her study, Ulmi criticizes me for discussing only the "Wilhelminian" part of Simmel's concept of the sexes (see Menzer 1983, n. 10 above) and ignoring what Coser calls the "main strands" of his argument.

42. M. Janssen-Jurreit, *Sexismus: Über die Abtreibung der Frauenfrage* (Frankfurt am Main, 1979).

43. Ibid., 67ff.

44. Simmel, "Flirtation," in *Georg Simmel*, trans. Oakes, 149, 150 ("Die Koketterie," in *Philosophische Kultur*, 95, 97).

Janssen-Jurreit responds that it would be superfluous to write essays and learned articles and assert in ideological terms that the differences between the sexes are differences in the form of being if it were a question of unalterable natural facts that assert themselves in spite of all historic norms. She comes to the following conclusion: "Since all previous literature and philosophy is a contribution toward securing and stabilizing the male ego, the possibility of an independent female will—and of resistance—must be eliminated in every conceivable way using every possible dialectical trick."[45]

Jürgen Habermas conjectures in an afterword to the new edition of Simmel's *Philosophische Kultur* that Simmel's essays on female culture and the problem of the sexes will meet today with a positive response "in those areas of the women's movement that base their hopes and claims on specifically female, specifically motherly qualities."[46] But it should be noted that the conservative trend in the feminist movement remains tied to traditional designations of woman's being and role, especially since it does not do away with ideas of polarity but attempts a mere reorientation in its evaluation of the feminine.[47]

Hans Michael Baumgartner has undertaken a study of Simmel's concept of the sexes and its present-day validity. He compares P. Lersch's *Vom Wesen der Geschlechter* (On the nature of the sexes)[48] with Simmel's metaphysics of the sexes and gives preference to Simmel's approach since he believes he can show that Simmel's fundamental model of polarity is fruitful. Baumgartner argues that this model can be justified in transcendental terms and that it prevents ideologization.[49] But he devotes not a thought to the fact that the model itself could be ideological in structure or that it is situated in an ideological context.

A recent volume containing Simmel's *Schriften zur Philosophie und Soziologie der Geschlechter* (Writings on the philosophy and sociology of the sexes) makes available Simmel's scattered newspaper articles and essays. His two major essays on the subject of the sexes and female culture, known to us from the collection *Philosophische Kultur,* are con-

---

45. See Janssen-Jurreit, *Sexismus,* 72.
46. See Jürgen Habermas, "Simmel als Zeitdiagnostiker," in Simmel, *Philosophische Kultur,* 252.
47. See Manon Maren-Grisebach, "Frau und Natur," in *Was Philosophinnen denken: Eine Dokumentation,* ed. Bendkowski and Weisshaupt.
48. P. Lersch, *Vom Wesen der Geschlechter,* 4th ed. (1950) (Munich, 1968).
49. See Baumgartner, "Gleichheit und Verschiedenheit," 93.

tained in this volume in earlier versions. The two editors of the volume regard Simmel's discussions as historic documents that are, on many points, no longer tenable. However, they also regard his writings on the question of women as exemplifying "in miniature" the development of his thought.[50]

---

50. See the introduction to Simmel, *Schriften zur Philosophie und Soziologie der Geschlechter,* ed. Dahme and Köhnke, 14. The position of the two editors in the study of Simmel's ideas is characterized by a remarkable magnanimity, just as the mega-project of an edition of Simmel's complete works (projected to take twelve years) and the parallel historic series edited by Ottheim Rammstedt are notable for a conception that keeps them almost entirely free from criticism of Simmel. It would appear that critical voices are jealously excluded by the small circle of those who are making a living from Simmel studies—the object they have taken possession of and exploited must not be damaged. In the meantime, however, the *Simmel Newsletter* has been founded (the first number appeared in the summer of 1991, ed. O. Rammstedt et al.). We can hope that it will become a forum for all those engaged in research on Simmel and that it will promote a free exchange of information instead of attempting to manipulate the debate from the heart of an academic industry with its own concrete interests.

9 | EXPLICATING THE IMAGE OF WOMAN IN PSYCHOANALYTIC DISCOURSE
Sigmund Freud's Theory of Femininity

Christa Rohde-Dachser

Translated by Stephanie Morgenstern

To undertake a systematic deconstruction of psychoanalytic discourse that would aim to expose its latent gender ideology, a close examination of Freud's formulations of "femininity" (1923, 1925, 1931, 1933) is crucial in many respects:

1. These works present the core explications of the *psychoanalytic image of the feminine*. This image serves as the starting point for a systematic

This essay is a slightly abbreviated translation of "Explizierte Weiblichkeitsentwürfe im Diskurs der Psychoanalyse: Die 'Theorie der Weiblichkeit' bei Sigmund Freud," chapter 4 in *Expedition in den dunklen Kontinent: Weiblichkeit im Diskurs der Psychoanalyse*, ed. Christa Rohde-Dachser (Berlin and Heidelberg: Springer, 1991), 55–75.

critique of the allegedly gender-neutral concerns of psychoanalytic discourse.
2. The Freudian portrait of femininity illustrates with rare clarity *the role played by unconscious fantasies in generating the myths intrinsic to the construction of psychoanalytic theory*— in particular, the construction of its ostensibly "objective" formulations of gender difference (see also Schlesier 1981; Rohde-Dachser 1989).
3. This portrait also allows inferences as to the *content and structure* of the unconscious fantasies involved in this cycle of explanation and remythologizing.
4. Its broad resonance suggests that we are dealing with fantasies of the *collective unconscious*.
5. Although Freud does not present it as such, his theory of femininity can also be read as a *theory of patriarchal socialization* (Mitchell 1974); it reveals the unconscious processes that are effective in the socialization of the sexes in patriarchal society and that contribute to the perpetuation of its typical gender relations.

I share Renate Schlesier's view that only a systematic investigation of Freud's constructions of femininity and of their role in the history of psychoanalysis can provide the theoretical means to move beyond these positions once and for all. I do not believe we can do this simply by toning them down to harmlessness, or by having them incrementally replaced. "Freud's theory of femininity [is] not a detachable element of psychoanalysis . . . with basic tenets that can be altered or discarded without repercussions to the whole. *Rather, it proves to be the touchstone by which the claims to explanatory power, the logical consistency, and the constitutive methodological and epistemological interests of psychoanalysis can be gauged*" (Schlesier 1981, 11; my emphasis).

In what follows, I will begin by summarizing the central theses of Freud's theory of femininity in point form in order to perform a hermeneutical investigation into the unconscious meaning of the resulting text. In so doing, I will treat Freud's views of female development and psychology as though they were expressions of *unconscious fantasies translated into theoretical terms*. I presuppose that by using standard psychoanalytic techniques, unconscious fantasy can be extrapolated from theory, exposing the fantasy's underlying structure in concepts as close as possible to real experience (Bion 1965) and then reformulating it in terms of the end in view. Strictly speaking, the point of departure for such an operation ought to be the original

Freudian text; however, a comprehensive textual analysis of this kind is beyond the scope of the present investigation. Such pragmatic considerations aside, I hold that presenting an abstract of Freud's thought in propositional form and using this as the basis for hermeneutic interpretation is justified by our interest in fantasies of the collective unconscious (cf. Lorenzer 1986). As these are psychic structures with a certain degree of generality, they can probably be discerned—at least at their levels closest to consciousness—even within the relatively crude framework of the text expressed in point form.

Freud's Theses on Femininity

Boys *and* girls are both born "male" (i.e., active). Boys remain so. For the girl, the difficult road to "femininity" (i.e., passivity) begins with the discovery of gender difference.

The discovery that she has no penis is a great disappointment for the girl. From then on, she feels worthless, incomplete, "castrated." She blames her lack on the mother. In her disappointment, she turns her attention from the mother to the father.

From this point on she desires her father's penis, not as an object of lust, but for the sake of her own narcissistic completion. Later the desire for a penis becomes the wish to have a child by the father (husband), preferably a boy (as penis-bearer). That is the only way the woman enjoys motherhood.

As a rule, penis envy lasts the woman's entire life. This is why envy is one of her dominant character traits.

Her interests are confined to the limited social network of relationships she lives in and to the fulfillment of the daily tasks these relationships entail. Because she has little ability to sublimate, she strives for nothing else. The limited radius of her activity is adequate to her needs.

Because of her deficiency in character and anatomy, she remains dependent all her life on the man as the means to her narcissistic restitution.

The woman also has the weaker sexual constitution. The libido (desire) is male. The expression "female libido" is a contradiction in terms.

The clitoris is a stunted penis.

With the development into womanhood, clitoral sexuality must be abandoned and transferred to the vagina, the "location of the man's desire."

Man acts, woman reacts.
Femininity is identical with (acquired) passivity, which is enjoyed "masochistically." (Freud 1923, 1925, 1931, 1933)

From the Theory to the Unconscious Fantasy

Our interests lie less with the familiar manifest content of these theses than with the unconscious fantasies that underlie them, and to which the manifest content indirectly alludes. In order to reach this latent level, we treat the theoretical text as if it were a "psychoanalytic text" (Werthmann 1975). It "is interpreted as if it contained a second text, and in such a way as to bring this second text to light. . . . The classic designations for this second text are 'the unconscious,' or the 'unconscious fantasy' " (Werthmann 1975, 123). Its reconstruction is considered complete if *all* elements of the original text are integrated and locked into a meaningful structure (Sandner 1988; Rohde-Dachser 1989).

This reconstructed text exposes the unconscious fantasy hidden in Freud's theory of femininity. It could be translated into the language of the secondary process as follows:

> "I am all that matters to my mother (later: my wife). As she is dependent upon me, she will never leave my side. I need not share her with anyone. She needs me; I do not need her. My penis guarantees my ownership of her. She herself has nothing for which I could envy her. On the contrary, she envies me. I am the one who loves and desires her, and not the other way around. She herself is without desire. That is also why she will never long for someone else. Without me she knows no pleasure. She lives only through me, and not I through her. Whatever suffering this may bring her, I am not to blame. This is what she wants.
>
> Because this is the case, I need never fear
>
> > that I will become the passive object of her love or of her desire (I was not even this as an infant)
> > that I will have to share her love with another (as a girl she was already exclusively committed to her father)

> that I could be overpowered by her desire or that I will fail before it (her libido is weaker than mine)
> that she could have sexual pleasure without me (she does not have the appropriate sexual organs for it)
> that I could be envious of her (she has nothing to arouse my envy)
> that she could be dissatisfied with her situation (her family is her world)
> that she will actively direct her interests elsewhere than towards me (she is not interested in cultural activity)
> that I could become guilty towards her (e.g., by making her pregnant)
>
> These convictions grant me security. I am happy and proud to be a man."

Structure and Function of the Unconscious Fantasies in Freud's Theory of Femininity

Thus the hermeneutic reconstruction of Freud's theory of femininity leads to a somewhat surprising conclusion. The woman, as depicted by Freud, is a creature of second-class gender, marked by penis envy, condemned because of her bodily defect to a life-long search for narcissistic restitution via a penis-bearer. Yet she reemerges here as a central figure in the (man's!) fantasy, around whom revolve not only a great many of his wishes, but, more importantly, many of his fears as well. The unconscious fantasy scenario taking shape here warrants further explanation. This must be done at two levels: the level of content and the level of form. I will begin with the latter.

Unconscious fantasies betray their origin, among other ways, by their cognitive structures. Now the point of departure for the fantasy at hand is the image of the penisless, "castrated" woman—the person without a gender of her own, the negative version of the man, the creature of lack. What such a construction presupposes is the idea of a *single* kind of genital organ—the penis—which one either has or does not have. In the worldview of *phallic monism* (Chasseguet-Smirgel 1964, 1976), nothing heteronomous exists: there is no second sex.

Following Freud (1923), it is with this fantasy that the boy responds upon his discovery of gender difference. It is a deeply *narcissistic* one: he, who understandably believed that all people had the same gender, *his* gender, finds his expectation was mistaken. He explains this by supposing that the other (female) gender must be missing something, or have lost something, or have had something taken away. Thus he interprets the world according to his own image with no awareness of alternative points of view, taking himself as the measure of all things. The fantasy of the woman's castration is the product of this childlike logic. It obviously generates further fantasy images (cf. Sandler and Sandler 1988, 153), which we encounter in the reconstruction of the Freudian text.

These inferred fantasies can probably also be traced back to that stage of a child's development at which scientists of various disciplines locate the discovery of gender difference and the construction of gender identity.[1] There is considerable evidence that the fantasizing explored here represents an attempt of the (male) child to make sense of the experience of gender difference in a way that favors the consolidation of a secure (male) gender identity. The *thought structures* within which the castration theory takes shape can also be linked to this period. For instance, the theory latches onto a single, conspicuous feature of the body—the penis—to the exclusion of other, equally possible criteria of difference; this structure is typical of the preoperational thought of the three- to six-year-old described by Piaget (cf. Piaget and Inhelder 1966). The egocentric orientation of the above fantasy (i.e., its exclusive orientation to the [male] child, and to his perspective as the only one possible), as well as the child's inability to change perspectives even in the face of contradictory experiences, are also characteristic of this stage of development (cf. Oerter and Montada 1987, 420ff.).

Investigating the defense mechanisms manifested in these unconscious fantasies yields a similar result. We are mainly dealing with the mechanisms of *splitting, projection, denial, idealization, and devaluation*. Psychoanalytic object relations theory associates them with the early phase of human development, where they are gradually—although never completely—replaced

1. Psychoanalysts date the discovery of gender difference at the child's second or third year (Mahler et al. 1975; Roiphe and Galenson 1981). According to Kohlberg's extensive empirical research, the construction of gender identity occurs mainly in the period from the child's second to fifth year (cf. Kohlberg 1966, 1969). Yet toward the end of the second year, the child has already developed an irreversible core gender identity (cf. Stoller 1968). In addition to more recent research results, Ethel Person (1983) offers a good overview of the partially contradictory psychoanalytic theories of the pre-Oedipal formation of female and male gender identity.

by *repression* at the end of the child's third year (cf. Kernberg 1975). But there may also be powerful repressions that become effective *in conjunction with* these more primitive defense mechanisms: there is some evidence that the fantasy images analyzed here are so-called screen fantasies—fantasies mobilized and sustained in order to conceal another, more frightening fantasy (cf. Greenson 1958; Rohde-Dachser 1979). In fact, the recurring fantasy of the castrated woman is very likely to fulfill such a screening function. This means that the boy can call upon it any time new information (for instance, the sight of the vagina) threatens to evoke another, more frightening fantasy. Screen fantasies operate as a kind of inner refuge: when summoned to the rescue, they help deny the unsettling information and pacify the awakened fear ("she does not even have genitals of her own, as she is castrated").

These fantasies divide living creatures into those with and those without a penis, which, furthermore, lays the basis for a *construction of reality* in which woman and man each occupy a predetermined place. The creator of this view of reality is a boy who, in doing so, positions himself securely in the realm of the father, with the conviction that he is indispensable to the mother. She therefore cannot turn from him, from the "beatus possidens" (Abraham 1921, 74), as he can from her. In this narcissistic universe, the castrated woman, deprived of her difference, appears banished to a satellite existence as a mirror to boy/man's penis-warranted grandeur. Because he is her center and she his mirror, he is also the one who can distance himself, while she must remain in place—a place which is also his, as she has no place of her own. Her autonomous existence is as unthinkable as her autonomous gender.[2]

Thus, with the image of the castrated woman the boy creates both his narcissistic mirror and the foundation of his male gender identity. From then on the boy—and later the man—will seek out experiences that confirm his worldview, and will attempt to bring the external world into harmony with it. Against this background, Freud's theory of femininity can also be

---

2. The mother depicted here is also the "mother of the *rapprochement*" as described by Mahler (cf. Mahler et al. 1975). The time of the discovery and working out of gender difference in the second half of the child's second year coincides with the "crisis of *rapprochement*" with which children respond, according to Mahler, upon the discovery of their separation from the mother. In this phase of development, the child would seek an optimal distance from the mother, while he or she feels torn between fear of separation and fear of becoming one with her again. In this situation it is important that the mother remain stationary so that the child can be sure she will still be there when he or she returns. Clearly, this immobile "mother of the *rapprochement*" is stably integrated into the worldview of phallic monism.

interpreted as the unconscious search for an identity of thought and an identity of perception for the fantasy of the castrated woman and all further fantasies derived from it.

This is not the first expression of this conjecture. In 1926 Karen Horney was already drawing attention to the striking similarities between a boy's fantasies and the psychoanalytic theory of femininity. In doing this, she also contemplated the possibility that the myth might return as a theoretical construct: "The present analytical picture of feminine development (whether that picture be correct or not) differs in no case by a hair's breadth from the typical ideas that the boy has of the girl" (Horney 1926, 29). She illustrates the postulated parallel as follows:

Responses of the boy	[Psychoanalytical] images of female development
He naively assumes that the girl also has a penis	For both genders, only the male genitals have a role to play
He observes the absence of a penis	She sadly discovers the absence of a penis
He believes that the girl is a castrated, mutilated boy	She believes that she once had a penis and was castrated
He believes that the girl was subjected to a punishment that could also threaten him	She conceives of castration as a form of punishment
He believes the girl to be inferior	She believes herself to be inferior; envies the penis
He cannot imagine how she could ever overcome this loss, or this envy	She never overcomes the feeling of lack and inferiority, and must constantly overcome her wish for masculinity
He fears her envy	She constantly wishes to avenge herself against the man for his greater possession.

The parallels do more than simply demonstrate the striking correspondence between the levels of infantile (male) fantasy and psychoanalytical theorization of femininity and gender difference. They are also a compelling sign that these psychoanalytical constructions of femininity are products of the *male unconscious* and that their original function probably was to help the boy make sense of the discovery of gender difference, to ground his masculine gender identity, and thus to secure himself a place in patriarchal society. In this society, according to Mitchell, both sexes hope theirs will not be the feminine place (Mitchell 1974, 517).

This is also where the elementary *projection mechanism* first becomes visible. This mechanism will be of increasing concern to us because it is central to the determination of the woman's place in patriarchy. By means of projection, the woman is assigned a fate that actually applies to the man (or, at least, applies to them both) yet that the man brackets out of his self-definition and relegates entirely to her. The parts of the self excluded this way are deemed feminine from then on. The man no longer discerns them in himself, but only in the opposite sex; he no longer needs to feel like the party concerned. This projection mechanism begins to take shape with the discovery of gender difference: the young boy looks at the girl and sees that she has no penis. Freud describes the way this sight arouses massive fears of castration, which apply to his own genitals. His conclusion, "*she* is castrated, not I," consistently shows the same projective direction. These elaborations upon his fears—

"*she* has insufficient genitals, not I;
she must feel inferior, not I;
she has grounds for grief and envy, not I;
she is punished, not I;
she must break away from Mother (i.e., fulfill the "change of object"), not I"

—lead to the generalization:

"*she* is the one to whom bad things happen, not me!"

All of these fantasies serve to reassure the male child in his sense of self and security. The castration model derived from them turns out to be the *fundamental defense fantasy against the boy's fears, which stem from the (male) past unconscious.* Now this fantasy does not seem to be burdened by the repressive quality that Sandler and Sandler (1983) generally postulate for the contents of the past unconscious. What we find, rather, are highly elaborate constructions, formed as secondary processes, that explain why something is—or more importantly, why something is *not* (why, for instance, a woman has no genitals, is penisless, castrated).

This suggests that so far our hermeneutic exploration has reached an area of unconscious fantasizing whose contents could probably have passed the consciousness threshold with relatively little conflict because they were directed into the *present unconscious* and made socially acceptable. They are cloaked in metaphors (e.g., the Image of the castrated woman) that are quite likely to belong to the *past unconscious* and seem to have no present explosive power. (On the rhetoric of the metaphors of the past unconscious, see also Sandler and Sandler 1984.) One could even wonder whether one is dealing, rather, with words emptied of their affective content (Lorenzer 1970), which would indicate that a process of desymbolization has taken place in which the discarded symbolic representation no longer contains its referent.

Still, something remains notably unclear. Does Freud's theory of phallic monism—as is often maintained—describe a boy's fantasy that will allow room for other views of the female as soon as it has fulfilled its functions—above all, the consolidation of the male gender identity and the overcoming of the narcissistic shock linked to the discovery of gender heteronomy? Or, on the contrary, does the theory of phallic monism lay the groundwork for a *fundamental defense constellation*—for instance, against the common human experience (which in fact lasts beyond childhood) of dependency upon the "omnipotence" of the early mother? Might it in fact constitute a secret worldview, ascribed to psychoanalysis, which can be presented as nothing more than a boy's fantasy (or as a neurotic fantasy) if its ideology is threatened by critique? The openness of these questions strengthens the impression that something crucial is *not* being discussed. The defensive aspect of the constellation must not be overlooked.

The Unfinished Process of Explanation

Along similar lines, Renate Schlesier argues that the process of explanation in Freud's theory of femininity is left unfinished. In doing this, she draws attention to the many *negations* it contains, which our work up to this point has also been attempting to reconstruct. Femininity, according to Schlesier, appears in Freud's theory as thoroughly negative—that is, as defined by a lack: "Thus, it would seem to follow logically that Freud does not claim that his construction has resolved the 'puzzle of femininity' " (Schlesier 1981, 166). And yet the castration model of the female, borne of the boy's fantasy, was not made the object of further analysis. Freud suggested that underlying the mythological symbol of horror, the Medusa head, is the "horror of woman" as such (Freud 1923, 144), which is also triggered by the sight of the penisless female genitals. This seemed so "natural" to him, so self-evidently grounded in anatomy, that he never took into consideration its potentially defensive nature (Schlesier 1981).

To resume the process of explanation here, where it was left off, we will undertake a further transformation of Freud's theory of femininity—this time with the explicit assumption that we are dealing with a defense fantasy whose negations refer indirectly to what is being defended. We proceed from the premise that what is being defended can be made accessible if the empty spaces left by the negations are filled—in fact, filled by what is explicitly negated in them. For this reason, we return to the text we transformed earlier in order this time to investigate its negations. In doing this, we concentrate on the images presented both of the woman herself, and of that which she is denied. In order to proceed straight to the result, we will do without the reconstruction of the individual steps of this text analysis, which the reader herself or himself could do at any time.

If we gather the negations from the original thesis text, the image we find of the woman is very familiar:

she has *no* wishes or interests independent from the man;
she has *no* drives independent from the man;
she has *no* autonomous sexual desire;
she has *no* genitals of her own;
she has *no* other possession of any value;
she has *no* superiority and *no* power over the man;
she has *no* allies (i.e., the boy/man has no rivals);
and, last but not least, she makes *no* complaint.

Were we to create a reverse image of these negations, we would end up with a complex of images that we may suspect will contain all that is defended and taboo in the Freudian view of women. This complex of images, the mirror image of the castrated woman, centers on a woman *independent from the man, with genitals of her own and an autonomous sexual desire.* What the patriarchal image of femininity excludes—and Freud's is a prime example—is what the patriarchal man does not want to consider: *the idea of the woman which is identical to the idea of his broken mirror.* It involves:

her independence
her power (superiority)
her sexual organs
her desire
her possessions (*her* breasts, *her* children, *her* ability to give birth)
her allies (his rivals)
her lack of *envy* (which negates his fetish)
her reproach—his guilt.

I will call this the image of the Other Woman in order to highlight her nature as a subject. What is it that makes the image of the autonomous woman so dangerous that she must be imprisoned behind a defensive fortress of this kind? What would happen if the woman of this fantasy succeeded in breaking out of her dungeon? One thing is clear: she would at least be *visible,* and clearly not suffering from the lack that the male gaze imputes to her (and that the castrated woman adopts). She would appear in her entirety: an autonomous, desiring, and desirable woman—*the embodiment of his wish*. However, in this decisive moment the position of the male subject is overturned. From the glorious center of the mother/woman's attention, he becomes a desiring subject confronted with another (female) subject who ceases, at that very moment, to be his mirror.

Having established this, we have come closer to discovering what it is that evidently not only arouses the desire for this Other Woman but also justifies the fear of her. My thesis is that this fear is bound up in many respects with the break in the man's narcissistic universe described above, in which the *present unconscious* recognizes a danger. Other interpretations—for example, the commonly cited fear of incest associated with this wish, or the fear of the power of the "early" mother—are related to the *past unconscious* and, in my view, could therefore not convincingly explain what triggers and sustains the fear in the here and now. According to Sandler and Sandler (1983), the censorship effective in the *present unconscious* would be directed at the desires surging from the *past unconscious* because they present a danger *now,* to the adult man. For example, the desires may be deemed grossly inappropriate, unsuitable to the (male) self-image, or associated with the anticipation of shame, injury, and defeat. This male wish, directed to the figure of the Other Woman emerging from the haze of his defense fantasies, must therefore be threatening because it disrupts a *present equilibrium.*

Now such a threat can be conceived in many ways. The male wish stimulated by the confrontation with the Other Woman could be one that tempts the man to become a son again, to bring himself into a dependent position, whereas his male identity up to that point had been formulated on the basis of superiority and dominance over the castrated woman. In addition, the fulfillment of the wish can be denied him. This would cause a situation of potential powerlessness and thus of shame and injury in relation to a powerful object, which will then become the trigger of both disappointed aggression and narcissistic anger. And finally, the man himself can also fail before his wish.

I would like to consider these different sources of fear a little more closely. The wish awakened by the Other Woman, according to our conjecture, threatens a man who not only wants to penetrate the genitals of the promised woman, but also wants to sink himself into them. This is reminiscent of the small child snuggling up to the mother's body, experiencing there his first moments of bliss, back at a time when he had only a vague sense of his masculinity. Thus the wish for the Other Woman could lead the man back behind the threshold of his masculinity. The woman who throws off patriarchal devaluation and is aware of her own resources would be in a position to deny him his wish, making her the *embodiment of refusal*. She is the possessor of the desirable body that promises the wish's fulfillment, just as the body of the mother had promised *everything* before the male gaze declared it castrated. But this body is at her own autonomous disposal. By Other Woman's very existence, she contradicts the illusion of her body's perpetual accessibility, which the boy/man's unconscious fantasy had seemed to guarantee, and reveals the absurdity of the narcissistic demand for this accessibility. In doing this, she *provokes his shame and anger*.

The Other Woman, who may deny the boy/man his wish, or may ignore it altogether because she pursues goals of her own according to rules of her own, inevitably arouses the man's *narcissistic anger*. At a primitive level, her potential refusal and the presumptuousness it implies are grounds enough to provoke violence, real or fantasized. This is how she becomes the personification of evil, which only appears in the secondary process as *male* evil: since her very existence suffices to arouse evil, this is reason enough to lay the blame for it on her. The fantasy of her castration and the devaluation it entails seem to avert this danger, and, along with it, the danger of another fantasy that may be even more frightening: the no-longer-negated image of the vulva and vagina, associated with the idea of the desiring woman, reminds the man—as they once did the boy—of the possibility of his own failure, his inability to satisfy the woman with his own genital endowments.

This recurring castration metaphor (within and outside psychoanalysis) also serves to turn this male experience of fear into a threat inflicted on him from the outside. Instead of "I am afraid of failing" or "I have failed," it becomes: "*She* (seldom *he*) could castrate me (has castrated me)." Shame is thus converted into aggression, which is easier to bear only because it has an external target: the woman becomes the culprit.

Apparently, it is the Other Woman who can set all this in motion: she can rob the man of this masculinity, infantilize him, brand him a beast—indeed, this is what she is said to want. This means she uses her "power" sadistically against the man; and even if she does not, the fact remains that she could. Because she is arbitrarily merciful or merciless, the man could easily feel himself the prey of her impulses. In a word: *she is guilty of the effect she may or may not have.* Sooner or later, in this narcissistic structure of thought, she is inevitably transformed from the *embodiment of the wish* to the *embodiment of evil.*

The Other Woman, the female subject, who briefly emerged from behind the image of the castrated woman and confronted the man as *you* instead of as his mirror, is therefore banished to a new construct. As counterpoint to the devalued, castrated woman, we find the "frightening woman"—the other side of the coin. Both sides serve to neutralize the threat of the autonomous female subject in that they either devalue or demonize her.

Thus, a *double image of womanhood in psychoanalytic discourse* begins to take shape: the appearance of the Other Woman (the female subject) in the narcissistic universe of the man represents for him both the *loss of the mirror* and the *manifestation of the wish*. The loss of the mirror is accompanied by anger and the fear of fragmentation; the manifestation of the wish arouses the kind of fantasies and fears discussed above. All of these responses appear in what is projected onto the female subject, according to this pattern:

Response of the man	*What is attributed to the female subject*
Narcissistic anger	She is angry
She should be castrated!	She wants to castrate me
I am greedy for her	She wants to devour me
She should return to her dependent existence	She wants to make me her son again
I would like to destroy her	She wants to destroy me
I would like to return to her	She wants to monopolize me

This is the network of attributions into which the image of the Other Woman disappears, in order to make room for yet another masculine construct: the "frightening woman." No longer the embodiment of his devalued self, this is instead his negative, terrifying, evil self: the *Medusa,* the personification of horror in female form, who turns a man to stone ("petrifies" him) if he looks her in the face.

It is well known that for Freud the severed head of the Medusa signaled the possibility of castration, just as the sight of penisless female genitals did. In becoming petrified (the equivalent in the unconscious of becoming erect), the man simultaneously expresses and negates his fear (Freud 1940, 273). Instead, we have sought to determine the meaning of the castration metaphor at the level of the *present unconscious.* It was natural for us to read the construct of the "frightening woman" (the Gorgon, the Medusa, etc.) as a negative mirror that warns: "Look away, or you could recognize yourself and be unable to bear what you see." The fact that this frightening construct may have its origin in the *past unconscious* is just as immaterial as the recurring related question of whether she was the mother of the "Oedipal disappointment" or the "early almighty" mother (on this matter, see also Sandler and Sandler 1984). Our question instead is: What is the present, immediate cause of the demonization of the female, and what would be seen in the Medusa's countenance if she were to be looked in the eye *now?* The message directed at the man—"Do not look; it could mean your death!"—suggests that the aspects of evil depicted above bear with them a message of mortality, which is projected into the face of the demonized woman. Thus she is also the source of a death threat, and avoiding her gaze becomes a strategy for survival.

The fantasy systems discussed here, it seems, are constantly translated into theories of psychoanalytic discourse, which grants them a certain legitimacy. As a result other fantasies—for instance, fantasies of an autonomous, *non*castrated woman—cannot make themselves likewise known. How has this come to be? The question must be given at least a preliminary investigation.

From the Analyzed to the Analytical Mythos—the Shaping of an Identity of Perception and an Identity of Thought

Unconscious fantasies can only persist over time if they are confirmed by perceptions of the outside world—that is, if one's sense impressions convey a correspondence between the internal fantasy scenario and the external world. How do the unconscious fantasies about gender difference described here add up to such an *identity of perception* (Freud 1900)? Even more importantly, how are they validated by seemingly logical (i.e., secondary-process) deductions within the framework of a scientific theoretical model? In other words, how does an *identity of thought* take shape? For the sake of clarity, we will address these issues separately at first, although it will become clear that both levels of validation—the levels of sense perception and of thought—are tightly woven together in practice. This is especially true in the process of *staging* (*Inszenierung*), in which unconscious fantasy, intellectual theory, and interpersonally generated "reality" are effectively integrated.

Establishing an Identity of Perception

Unconscious fantasies about one's own sex, the opposite sex, or gender relations are validated fundamentally by sense impressions—or rather, by the biased selection of sense impressions. When this happens, what is fantasized is discovered to exist in reality and—where necessary—is interpreted into compatibility with the meaning of the unconscious fantasy. The prime example for an identity of perception formed this way is the (male) sight of female genitals: after carefully tuning out or discarding all other perceptions that are possible in this situation, the boy registers a single negative sense impression, "no penis!" which entails the conclusion "therefore castrated!" The image of the castrated woman, thus construed and internalized, can be invoked whenever necessary and can always be revalidated by the same process of selective perception.

A similar principle is at work in the part of unconscious fantasizing that deals with male and female personality constructs—that is, fantasy constructions whose derivatives accessible to consciousness correspond most readily to the structure of gender stereotypes. It goes without saying that there *are* women dependent upon men, that there *are* mothers who wish only for a boy and never want a girl, women who have little interest in sex or whose super-ego is corrupt, women who seem to suffer unnecessarily or who passively wait to be "rescued," and so forth. One comes across them often in one's own experience, and even more frequently in the mass media. These perceptions serve as "proof" that the unconscious fantasy is in fact real. Conflicting observations, or simply the experience of the living diversity of male-female relationships, can do nothing to shake this conviction.

Insofar as these discrepant observations are given any significance at all, they will figure as the famous "exceptions that prove the rule"—as is familiar enough from stereotype research (see, for example, H. Tajfel 1981).

Freud himself was known to reason this way. By his own admission, in order to explain any phenomenon that did not cohere with his image of woman and of gender relations, he would invoke his thesis of human "bisexuality":

> In conformity with its peculiar nature, psychoanalysis does not try to describe what a woman is—that would be a task it could scarcely perform—but sets about enquiring how she comes into being, how a woman develops out of a child with a bisexual disposition. In recent times we have begun to learn a little about this, thanks to the circumstance that several of our excellent women colleagues in analysis have begun to work at the question. The discussion of this has gained special attractiveness from the distinction between the sexes. For the ladies, whenever some comparison seemed to turn out unfavourable to their sex, were able to utter a suspicion that we, the male analysts, had been unable to overcome certain deeply-rooted prejudices against what was feminine, and that this was being paid for in the partiality of our researches. We, on the other hand, standing on the ground of bisexuality, had no difficulty in avoiding impoliteness. We had only to say: "This doesn't apply to *you*. You're the exception; on this point you're more masculine than feminine." (Freud 1933, 116–17)

One comes across this kind of argumentation again and again—though rarely so barefaced—in psychoanalytic statements about gender difference. It follows a characteristic pattern: a priori assumptions about the "male" and "female" are invoked, which in "reality"—in individual men and women—can materialize in many different combinations and therefore ought not to prejudice a norm. What it means, in fact, is that the a priori assumptions can never be refuted by reality: the men and women one meets in everyday life simply become further examples of the many possible combinations of "essentially" male and female character traits within a single person.

This reveals Freud's theory of femininity as a closed system of thought; given that it supplies both a norm and interpretations of deviations from the norm, the deviations themselves become immanent to the system, and the norm is no longer falsifiable. A case in point is the imputation of penis envy that has burdened (and still does burden) women in psychoanalysis who resist the traditional confinements of their gender roles and rebel against the imposition of male will. And this occurs even within psychoanalytic institutions themselves. The more vehement this rebellion, according to this logic, the greater the alleged penis envy, and vice versa. In a circular argument such as this, identities of perception and thought work in very close fraternity. The androcentric metaphor of "brotherhood" is particularly apposite here: what is validated this way is *male* fantasy thought, just as the Freudian theory of femininity is a manifestation of the *male* unconscious.

Establishing an Identity of Thought

In the operations of the formation of an *identity of perception* for unconscious fantasies described so far, secondary-process, logical, or even pseudological "proof" played only a subordinate role. This changes if we now explicitly inquire into the formation of an *identity of thought* for these fantasies, whose derivatives assemble into what clearly declares itself to be a theory (as in the case of the Freudian theory of femininity). Relatively high demands are then made on the theory's logical consistency, compared to corresponding constructs in everyday psychology. Yet we are dealing with the perplexing phenomenon that a theory apparently devised to bring unconscious fantasies to light, and thereby under the control of the Ego, is clearly also being used to legitimate these fantasies and to validate them as a theory in themselves. This way the original theory's logical consistency can suffer no apparent loss; it already *is* what lends credibility to (what may amount to) a process of rationalization. What makes this rationalization possible? What must happen so that fantasy and "truth" can coexist within the same theoretical construct, without this being noticed?

First, the *prevailing institutional conditions* certainly play a role. Once a theory is advanced, the more respected the professional group of its adherents, and the more undisputed the scientific standing of its founder within these experts, the less the theory will be questioned. This is especially the case when the profession has come to agree that the theory is valid and has granted it paradigm status (cf. Kuhn 1962). A critic of the dominant paradigm is then easily branded a dissident and is more often eliminated from the group than granted an opportunity to provide counterevidence. Still, this does not relieve the adherents of the established theory from having to explain the most patent contradictions in the dominant paradigm or to take a stand in some other way when these contradictions appear.

It is my impression that, in the case of Freud's theory of femininity, this paradigm maintenance occurs mainly by a *process of ongoing disavowal*. Few analysts today still speak unselfconsciously about "penis envy" or "female masochism"; still, these complexes of images persist in the literature (for reasons that are, at first, hard to grasp) as a *negation* that must constantly be reexplained. For decades there has been no psychoanalytic book, no journal article on the theme of femininity without the requisite specialist discussion of the classic Freudian images. The unconscious, which knows no negation, says to itself: "What is constantly repeated must be true!"

In addition to these factors specific to the field, there are certain thought operations drawn from the theory itself that seem well suited to reinforce unconscious fantasies by being expressed as scientific theories. Freud's theory of femininity has already been competently investigated in this regard (see, for instance, Schafer 1974; Irigaray 1974; Schlesier 1981). This is why I will only refer to a few thought operations that appear destined to be inadvertently mythologized by the use of scientific language (see further references in Barthes 1957). These are, most significantly, *misattributions, omissions, the overextension of theoretical concepts, associations, dissociations, arguments by analogy, metaphorical turns of phrase,* and the unnoticed *concretization of metaphors*—a process that Mentzos (1971) has also described as "regressing desymbolization."

One finds in Freud and his orthodox followers a characteristic drift between *metaphor and factual claim*, between *fantasy and reality*. The shift of level occurs unnoticed, such that attention is not drawn to the contradictions this generates in the discourse, or to their need for clarification. Thus Freud repeatedly states that the little girl responds to the discovery that she has no penis with the *fantasy* that she is castrated—yet he almost simultaneously speaks of the "*discovery*" of her castration," of the refusal "to accept *the fact* of her castration," and of the woman's need to conceal her *sexual inferiority*" (Chodorow 1978, 189; my emphasis). The clitoris is spoken of as a "stunted" penis, or as an organ that "in *reality* is only an insufficient substitute for the penis" (Chodorow 1978, 190; my emphasis). On the significance of the penis, one reads in Abraham: "To begin with, the girl has no sense of inferiority regarding her body and therefore cannot succeed *at first* in acknowledging that, compared with the boy's, it shows *a defect*" (Abraham 1921, 70; my emphasis). And: "Let us keep in mind that sexual activity is linked to the male organ, that the woman is therefore in a position only to stimulate or to stifle the libido of the man, but is otherwise compelled to an attitude of passive expectancy!" (96; emphasis in original).

We are dealing here with a covert *concretization of metaphors*—the loss of their "as-if character," just as one finds in the mental disturbances of borderline patients (cf. Mentzos 1971; Rohde-Dachser 1979). Along similar lines, Schafer draws attention to the *overextension of theoretical concepts* and to the *misattributions* it entails, both of which generate the same mystifying effect: "To mention just one more problem: Freud was too quick to favour the designation penis envy for the complex array of feelings, wishes, and fantasies of which penis envy is, after all, only a part, though often a most intense and consequential part. Here the influence of phallocentrism can hardly be overlooked" (Schafer 1974, 348).

Omissions arise, above all, from a lack of interest in the subjective experience of women and mothers, except when it comes to negative feelings about their womanhood and the worth of their gender. Schafer writes about such "gaps" in Freud's work: "It seems that he knew the father and the castrate in himself and other men but not the mother and the woman" (Schafer 1974, 357). All of these inclusions and omissions are woven into a theory text and integrated, in turn, into a network of *associations and dissociations*. This network, quite independently from its original logical context, takes on the form of a fantasy.

Finally, in *arguments by analogy*, a conjecture gains legitimacy by means of a comparison: in the process, the object selected for comparison takes on a normative function. We see this, for instance, in Freud's claim, which he relativized more cautiously elsewhere: "The male sex-cell, is actively mobile and searches out the female one, and the latter, the ovum, is immobile and waits passively. This behaviour of the elementary sexual organisms is indeed a model for the conduct of sexual individuals during intercourse" (Freud 1933, 114).

Confirmation of the Unconscious Fantasy by Means of Staging

In addition to these operations, which validate unconscious fantasies by shaping identities of thought and perception, there is the operation of *staging (Inszenierung)*. Through staging, unconscious fantasies of gender difference strive to become realized so as to supply, in the psychically external world, the correspondence required for their preservation. Staging works by *role allocation* and by *role adoption* (cf. Sandler 1976).

What the Freudian theory of femininity actually seeks is to describe how the woman *comes to be,* and not what she *is* (cf. Freud 1933, 114). To this end, it has at its disposal a whole array of explicit and latent *role allocations* for the opposite sex. They concern the "development of a little girl into a normal woman" in which, according to Freud, it can be expected that "constitution will not adapt itself to its function without a struggle" (1933, 117). This claim suggests that we cannot count on the woman willingly adopting the limitations ascribed to her by virtue of her sex—a sex into which "nature" has obviously woven a distinct contradiction between "constitution" and "function." If, in spite of this obstacle, she resolves to take on this difficult journey and the renunciations it entails, she will then become a "proper" woman according to the latent normative requirements of this theory. (For example, these requirements include replacing the clitoris with the vagina as the leading erogenous zone at the appropriate developmental stage; cf. Freud 1905, 221) This "proper" woman is sent a latent message, construed according to the pattern of *narcissistic collusion* (Willi 1975): "You are defective, whereas I am complete. If you are ready to accept your castration and to idealize my genitals instead, then you can take part in my completeness. Follow me, be subordinate to me, be a part of me; this is the way to heal your defect!" The negative version of the same message would say: "You should not notice that you are also fully adequate—and could exist—without me."

Drawing upon our earlier hermeneutic explanation of the Freudian image of femininity, this message can become even more diverse. It could go, for example, as follows:

"Be my mirror!
You are nothing without me, but with me you are everything!
Remain castrated!
Do not do what compels me to demonize you!
Spare me from the vision of the Gorgon's head!
Prevent that I should come to know myself!
Never let me know that you are doing all this for me!"

Sandler (1976) holds that the addressee of latent messages such as these understands the sense of the staging unconsciously and takes on the role that has been, just as unconsciously, assigned to him. If this is true, then he accepts, by the same token, the promises, rewards, deceptions, and disappointments covertly associated with the role. This may well also be the case for the latent messages contained in Freud's theory of femininity, which women have been hearing and absorbing for some time. A critique of psychoanalytic theory of femininity undertaken within the field of psychoanalysis would therefore have to question, fundamentally, what it could mean for women if they were to take leave of the expectations associated with these roles. I believe we could best describe such a leave-taking as a "farewell to daughterly existence" (Rohde-Dachser 1990), with all the consequences of guilt feelings and desolateness that pave the way to an independent being.

REFERENCES

Abraham, K. [1921] 1971. "Äusserungsformen des weiblichen Kastrationskomplexes." In *Psychoanalytische Studien,* vol. 2, ed. J. Cremerius, 69–99. Frankfurt am Main: Fischer.

Barthes, R. [1957] 1964. *Mythen des Alltags.* Frankfurt am Main: Suhrkamp.

Bion, W. R. [1965] 1977. "Transformations." In *Seven Servants: Four Works by Wilfred R. Bion.* New York: Jason Aronson.

Chasseguet-Smirgel, J., ed. [1964] 1970. *Female Sexuality: New Psychoanalytic Views.* Ann Arbor: University of Michigan Press.

———. [1976] 1986. "Freud and Female Sexuality: Some Considerations of the Blind Spots in the Exploration of the 'Dark Continent.'" In *The Role of the Father and the Mother in the Psyche.* New York: University Press.

Chodorow, N. [1978] 1985. *The Reproduction of Mothering: Psychoanalysis and the Sociology of Gender.* Berkeley: The Regents of the University of California.

Freud, S. [1900] 1953. "Interpretation of Dreams." In *Standard Edition,* vols. 4 and 5. London: Hogarth Press.

———. [1905] 1953. "Three Essays on the Theory of Sexuality." In *Standard Edition,* 7:125–243. London: Hogarth Press.

———. [1923] 1953. "The Infantile Genital Organization: An Interpolation into the Theory of Sexuality." In *Standard Edition,* 19:140–53. London: Hogarth Press.

———. [1925] 1953. "Some Physical Consequences of the Anatomical Distinction Between the Sexes." In *Standard Edition,* 19:243–58. London: Hogarth Press.

———. [1931] 1953. "Female Sexuality." In *Standard Edition*, 21:223–43. London: Hogarth Press.

———. [1933] 1953. "Femininity." In *Standard Edition*, 22:112–135. London: Hogarth Press.

———. 1940. "Medusa's Head." In *Standard Edition*, 18:273. London: Hogarth Press.

Greenson, R. G. [1958] 1982. "Characters in Search of a Screen." *Journal of the American Psychoanalytic Association* 6: 242–62.

Horney, K. [1926] 1984. "The Flight from Womanhood." *International Journal of Psycho-Analysis* 12, 360–74.

Irigaray, L. [1974] 1985. *The Speculum of the Other Woman*. Ithaca: Cornell University Press.

Kernberg, O. F. [1975] 1978. *Borderline Conditions and Pathological Narcissism*. New York: Jason Aronson.

Kohlberg, L. 1966. "A Cognitive Developmental Analysis of Children's Sex Role Concepts and Attitudes." In *The Development of Sex Differences*, ed. E. E. Maccoby. Stanford: Stanford University Press.

———. 1969. "Stages and Sequence: The Cognitive-Developmental Approach to Socialization." In *Handbook of Socialization Theory and Research*, ed. D. A. Goslin. Chicago: Rand McNally.

Kuhn, T. S. [1962] 1976. *The Structure of the Scientific Revolution*. Chicago: University of Chicago Press.

Lorenzer, A. 1970. *Kritik des psychoanalytischen Symbolbegriffs*. Frankfurt am Main: Surhkamp.

———. 1986. "Tiefenhermeneutische Kulturanalyse." In *Kultur-Analysen*, ed. H. D. König, A. Lorenzer, et al. Frankfurt am Main: Fischer.

Mahler, M. S., F. Pine, and A. Bergman. [1975] 1978. *The Psychological Birth of the Human Infant*. New York: Basic Books.

Mentzos, S. 1971. "Die Veränderung der Selbstrepräsentanz in der Hysterie: Eine spezifische Form der regressiven De-Symbolisierung." *Psyche* 25:669–84.

Mitchell, J. [1974] 1976. *Psychoanalysis and Feminism: Freud, Reich, Laing, and Women*. New York: Pantheon Books.

Oerter, R., and L. Montada. 1987. *Entwicklungspsychologie: Ein Lehrbuch*. Vol. 2. Rev. and enl. ed. Munich: Psychologie Verlags Union.

Person, E. S. 1983. "Woman in Therapy: Therapists' Gender as a Variable." *International Review of Psycho-Analysis* 10:193–204.

Piaget, J., and B. Inhelder. [1966] 1972. *The Psychology of the Child*. New York: Basic Books.

Rohde-Dachser, C. [1979] 1995. *Das Borderline-Syndrom*. 5th enl. ed. Bern, Stuttgart, and Vienna: Huber.

———. 1989. "Unbewußte Phantasie und Mythenbildung in psychoanalytischen Theorien über die Differenz der Geschlechter." *Psyche* 43:193–218.

———. 1990. "Über töchterliche Existenz: Offene Fragen zum weiblichen Ödipuskomplex." *Zeitschrift für Psychosomatische Medizin und Psychoanalyse* 36:303–15.

Roiphe, H., and E. Galenson. 1981. *Infantile Origins of Sexual Identity*. New York: International Universities Press.

Sandler, J. 1976. "Gegenübertragung und Bereitschaft zur Rollenübernahme." *Psyche* 30:297–305.

Sandler, J., and A.-M. Sandler. 1983. "The 'Second Censorship,' the 'Three-Box Model,' and Some Technical Implications." *International Journal of Psycho-Analysis* 64:413–25.

———. [1984] 1985. "Vergangenheits-Unbewußtes, Gegenwarts-Unbewußtes und die Deutung der Übertragung." *Psyche* 39:800–29.

———. 1988. "Das frühere Unbewußte, das gegenwärtige Unbewußte und die Schicksale der Schuld: Eine technische Perspektive." In *Die psychoanalytische Haltung: Auf der Suche nach dem Selbstbild der Psychoanalyse*, ed. P. Kutter, R. Paramo-Ortega, and P. Zagermann. Munich: Verlag Internationale Psychoanalyse.

Sandner, D. 1988. "Die Erfassung der unbewußten Beziehungsphantasie mit Hilfe der psychoanalytisch-empirischen Hermeneutik." *Forum der Psychoanalyse* 3:333–44.

Schafer, R. [1974] 1977. "Problems in Freud's Psychology of Women." In *Female Psychology: Contemporary Psychoanalytic Views*, ed. H. P. Blum, 331–60. New York: International Universities Press.

Schlesier, R. 1981. *Konstruktionen der Weiblichkeit bei Sigmund Freud: Zum Problem von Entmythologisierung und Remythologisierung in der psychoanalytischen Theorie*. Frankfurt am Main: Europäische Verlagsanstalt.

Stoller, R. J. 1968. *Sex and Gender: On the Development of Masculinity and Femininity*. New York: Science House.

Tajfel, H. [1981] 1982. *Gruppenkonflikt und Vorurteil: Entstehung und Funktion sozialer Stereotypen*. Bern, Stuttgart, and Vienna: Huber.

Werthmann, V. 1975. "Die zwei Dimensionen der psychoanalytischen Interpretation und der 'unbewußte Begriff.' " *Psyche* 29:118–30.

Willi, J. 1975. *Die Zweierbeziehung*. Reinbek bei Hamburg: Rowohlt.

10 | FIN-DE-SIÈCLE VIENNA: A MOVEMENT FOR OR AGAINST WOMANHOOD?
Some Thoughts on Weininger and Freud

Ingvild Birkhan

Translated by Christine Manteghi

Fin-de-siècle Vienna, with its vast sphere of influence, was a cultural microcosm, as well as a trendsetting pioneer in new developments in the confrontation of the sexes. The extensive conflict between women and men was experienced as a problem so pressing that the success or failure of the times seemed to depend on solving it. Women's protests and feminist demands could no longer be ignored. Detailed redefinitions of gender relations were carried out by the men. However, these definitions testify to a kind of scan-

This essay originally appeared under the title "Das Wien der Jahrhundertwende—eine Wende für oder gegen die Frau? Überlegungen zu Weininger und Freud," in *Denken der Geschlechterdifferenz: Neue Fragen und Perspektiven der feministischen Philosophie*, ed. Herta Nagl-Docekal and Herlinde Pauer-Studer (Vienna: Wiener Frauenverlag, 1990), 41–71.

dal or danger in woman, which were not really so new.¹ In any event, a careful distinction is made by Karl Kraus in speaking of August Strindberg: "Strindberg's truth is that the world order is threatened by the feminine. Strindberg's error is that the world order is threatened by the woman."² On the female side of the issue, the fundamental question of whether and to what extent women experience the masculine as a threat remains in the background.

In the discussion of sexual difference in Vienna in the early twentieth century, two names immediately come to mind: Sigmund Freud and Otto Weininger. Freud made the world sit up and take notice and caused an upheaval, a discussion, and continuing widespread consequences that still remain in effect today. Is Weininger in many respects his fatal antipode?³

Without a doubt, both authors pursued very different paths. Since my short essay deals with the never-ending discourse on the provocative beginnings of psychoanalysis and with the criticism of Weininger's theories, it necessarily remains within a limited framework. My investigation seeks to inquire into the cultural influences that could have shaped and supported their self-understanding as men and their theoretical concepts, albeit in different ways, with the tendency to emphasize the inherent deficiency of the "woman." In which socially recognized position with a high pretension to truth does Weininger anchor his sexual typology? Where can Freud, the great decryptor, conceivably be placed according to his objective? Such a point of departure should then direct our critical eye toward the order that has long been valid in these places and that the principled man has visibly tried to seize for himself alone again in our century in new ways. I am referring to the realm and control of art and of the religious system. Does the structuring of the sexes and the expropriation of woman in these areas follow different but nonetheless related laws?

---

1. Two especially informative investigations on this theme are Nike Wagner, *Geist und Geschlecht: Karl Kraus und die Erotik der Wiener Moderne* (Frankfurt am Main, 1982), and Jacques Le Rider, *Der Fall Otto Weininger: Wurzeln des Antifeminismus und Antisemitismus* (Vienna, 1985), which also includes the first publication of Heimito von Doderer's speech on Otto Weininger. Jacques Le Rider presents not only a critical interpretation of Weininger's works, but also clearly situates the author within a cultural context, tracing his worldview up through to fascism.

2. Quoted in the afterword by Roberto Calasso, in Otto Weininger, *Geschlecht und Charakter: Eine prinzipielle Untersuchung* (Munich, 1980), 666–67.

3. Joshua Sobol, *Weiningers Nacht*, ed. Paulus Manker (Vienna, 1988). This work contains an essay by Jacques Le Rider, who poses this question, 135–39.

The Heterosexual Matrix in *Geschlecht und Charakter*

I will begin with Otto Weininger's *Geschlecht und Charakter*,[4] published in 1903. Is whatever is set in motion there simply a delusional system? If this is really true, then it was a general delusion of the entire period, and it would be revealing in this sense. For *Geschlecht und Charakter* had a fascination previously unheard of, and also the unspoken approval of a secret readership. The work was not only read by well-known intellectuals to be skeptically dissected and rejected,[5] but it was even recommended and defended by them.[6] The philosopher Jodl had accepted it—admittedly in an abbreviated version[7]—as a dissertation. Kraus, Strindberg, Wittgenstein,

---

4. *Geschlecht und Charakter* (Munich, 1980) includes Weininger's diary and letters from August Strindberg, as well as essays written from a present-day perspective by Annegret Stopczyk, Gisela Dischner, and Roberto Calasso. All subsequent references to Weininger's *Geschlecht und Charakter* will refer to the English edition, *Sex and Character*, trans. unknown (London: William Heineman and New York: Putnam's Sons, 1906[?]) and will appear as parenthetical references within the text.

5. It is always surprising that so few people publicly distanced themselves in writing from this work. Freud's brief remarks are quite restrained when, for example, he says: "Weininger (the young philosopher who, highly gifted but sexually deranged, committed suicide after producing his remarkable book, *Geschlecht und Charakter* [1903]), in a chapter that attracted much attention, treated Jews and women with equal hostility and overwhelmed them with the same insults." Freud then draws a connection to the Oedipus complex ("A Phobia in a Five-year-old Boy," in *The Standard Edition of the Complete Psychological Works of Sigmund Freud*, trans. Strachey, 5:36, n. 1). In a short statement with special reference to the concept of bisexuality and the psychophysiological perspective of the first part of *Geschlecht und Charakter* as quintessence, Rosa Mayreder sees in the book a phallocracy in the narrow sense of the word: "By denying that even the most masculine woman—that is, the woman with the highest content of arrhenoplasma—has a soul, while acknowledging its presence in the most feminine man, Weininger ties the soul to the most primary indicator of gender and unintentionally elevates the phallus to the carrier of the soul" ("Zur Kritik der Weiblichkeit," in *Essays*, ed. Hanna Schnedl [Munich, 1981], 45).

6. August Strindberg's enthusiasm for Weininger was so unconditional that he acknowledged that he had completely solved the problem of women. Why should a man live at all and devote himself to a woman? "[B]ecause I believed to find that our bond with the earthly spirit of woman was a sacrifice, a duty, a test. We may not live as gods here below; we must walk through the mire" (from a letter of Strindberg's to Artur Gerber, quoted in Sobol, *Weiningers Nacht*, 132).

7. In particular, the disreputed sections entitled "Das Wesen des Weibes und sein Sinn im Universum" and "Das Judentum" did not exist then; these were first included in the book version of *Geschlecht und Charakter* as chapters 12 and 13 respectively. Here I would also like to mention the various drafts of his dissertation. Some manuscripts of Weininger's that were first discovered a few years ago in the archives of the Österreichische Akademie der Wissenschaften date from before the final approval of the dissertation in 1902. The manuscripts are entitled *Eros und Psyche: Biologisch-psychologische Studie und Zur Theorie des Lebens*. Hannelore Rodlauer, who has also thoroughly reexamined the course of Weininger's educa-

and Gütersloh, to name just a few, largely approved of it. Doderer even celebrated Weininger in 1963 as a hero and "monument to the reality of spirit."[8]

The book not only shows the suffering of a confused individual, but because it makes such sweeping generalizations, it is also radically offensive to others—above all to women, about whom dreadful things are said that can all too easily be inflammatory. Outrageous things are also said about Jews, as Hannelore Schröder has pointed out.[9] For Weininger, the definitions given for the female Other were also applicable to Jews.[10]

The very young, extremely well-read Weininger draws from philosophical texts of ancient times through the twentieth century.[11] Wherever he is concerned with defining the true essence of man and his exalted ethical responsibility, Weininger points impassionedly to Kant. He maintains his reference to the intelligible ego as a central theme throughout his occasionally contradictory, but by and large consistent, theses against women.

To what extent the constructs of the gender duality in human existence show many faces when seen through the lens of anthropology, to what extent they are historically determined phenomena—neither question seems to be significant in Weininger's eyes. A philosophy of nature and historical investigation beyond the transcendental difference remains unexplored. This lack of philosophical reasoning bears consequences for his concept of the gender dichotomy in which he goes beyond other philosophical gender differentiations in his unmistakable rejection of the feminine.[12]

---

tion, is overseeing the publication of these texts. A prepublication of selected texts can be found in Sobol, *Weiningers Nacht*, 195–98.

8. Heimito von Doderer, "Rede auf Otto Weininger," in *Der Fall Otto Weininger*, by Jaques Le Rider (Vienna, 1985), 247.

9. Hannelore Schröder, "Zur Neuauflage von faschistischem Antifeminismus und Antisemitismus; Oder: Vor Weininger wird gewarnt," in *Was Philosophinnen denken II*, ed. Manon Andrea-Grisebach and Brigitte Weisshaupt (Zurich, 1986), 134–56.

10. According to Theodor Lessing in his work *Der jüdische Selbsthaß*, "Woman and Jew, to him [Weininger] those were two different names for the aspect of nature that he feared and avoided" (quoted in Otto Weininger, *Über die letzten Dinge* [Munich 1980], appendix, 206). It is meant as only a small indication of Lessing's longtime attempt to see antifeminism and anti-Semitism as a single entity—a problem that is still discussed today.

11. "Weininger comes to a definition of what was seldom said but was nevertheless decisive in forming the basis of the philosophical tradition through ancient times, the middle ages and the modern." Such is the interpretation of Cornelia Klinger in her sound and critical essay, "Das Bild der Frau in der Philosophie und die Reflexion von Frauen auf die Philosophie," in *Wie männlich ist die Wissenschaft?* ed. Karin Hausen and Helga Nowotny (Frankfurt am Main, 1986), 62–84.

12. Significant is the fact that, and the manner in which, women since have dealt with and further developed the conceptions of sexual difference in philosophy. Important aspects are

When the "female" is the theme of discussion, the ideal form of the abstractly feminine is meant to be characterized. As the author expressly formulates, the feminine is also present in man.[13] But this femininity is de facto precariously related to real women and only for the purpose of degrading them.[14] How is the man defined from Weininger's point of view? A few quotes may serve to reflect his ideas: "The pure man exists in the image of God" (398). The man lives "in a conscious connection to the entire world" (222). And "aggrandized, fully developed masculinity" is equated with "genius" (242). In any case, he consistently maintains that the man is ego, monad, personality, sense of duty.

How is the woman characterized in relation to this man? The answer is insulting. A key to deciphering all the problems regarding sexual difference seems appropriate: the woman is none of that, she is not a person. Here, probably more decisively than ever before, woman is stripped of her humanity through the words of a man, while man is made analogous with *Mensch*.[15] In the context of the relationship of nothing to something, woman consistently represents the negative pole: "The female was not made according to the divine image" (389). "F is not a monad and, therefore, is not a reflection of the universe" (243). "The absolute female has no ego" (240). "Logical axioms form the basis of all concepts, and these are absent in women" (243). "Personality and individuality, the (intelligible) ego and the soul, desire and (intelligible) character—all of this describes one and the same and which within the sphere of mankind is only attributable to M and

---

dealt with by women philosophers in Herta Nagl-Docekal, ed., *Feministische Philosophie*, Wiener Reihe: Themen der Philosophie, vol. 4 (Vienna, 1990).

13. The concept of bisexuality that was so important to Freud and Weininger (and that brought crisis to the friendship between Fließ and Freud with the delicate plagiarism affair) is referred to here. In my opinion, it is a questionable model in many respects; not only in that the female pole is/was judgmentally deemed to be the lesser, but the concrete historical examples of women's oppression are thereby also easily forgotten.

14. What he first introduces as an abstract term, namely "F" or "female," is repeatedly changed, in his choice of words, to "woman" or "women." The same is also true for "M." Were this not so, it might seem only natural to see these categorizations in a different light—perhaps they would not appear to be the dreadful result of a long development that tends toward driving the separation of spirit and matter to its utmost. Yet on the other hand, hadn't this separation already been fundamentally linked to gender polarity for a long time? [Trans. note: The original German text uses *Weib* or *W* to refer to what is indicated here as "female" or "F."]

15. The presumptuous generalization of the man as *Mensch* (i.e., human being) is the focus of the book *Diotima: Philosophinnengruppe aus Verona: Der Mensch ist zwei: Das Denken der Geschlechterdifferenz*, trans. Veronika Mariaux (Vienna, 1989). In the preface to this book, I attempt to address the crisis of the mother image within the context of the development of philosophy.

is absent in F" (241). The female is not nameless without reason. Her waiting for the man is "only a waiting for the moment, in which she can be completely passive" (354). His concentration on human/male spiritual existence prevents the author from ascribing an existence to the female. He reduces his conceptions to a simple formula: "Consequently, woman does not exist" (384). "Women have no essence and no existence; they are not, they are nothing" (383).

This radicalization produces some fatal elements in the differentiation between female and male. First, the female void can be endlessly filled with characteristics—in the case of Weininger these are, as expected, contemptible characteristics. He does not cede the woman even *one* good quality: not pity, goodness, or fairness, and neither shame nor loyalty, all of which require continuity and thus an intelligible ego. Arbitrary examples are drawn from the past and present that are supposed to prove women's nonhumanity as well as their lack of logic and morality. In places where the woman shows herself to actually be something, she appears as a profound fabrication, in that she imitates the language of man and in that she—a shapeless being, receptive, impressionable, hypnotizable—is determined by man. Weininger also mentions hysteria in the same breath.[16]

On the other hand, how can woman as such not represent the continual fear that man himself, being so close to nothingness, may be consumed, may lose himself in the nothingness of the female, may merge with her and possibly himself degenerate into a female? In my opinion, the idea that this being is supposed to be only a void, and as such is only his diametrical opposite in an ontological differentiation, and that she herself does not distinguish herself separately from him, must inevitably represent a frightening state of affairs for him. In one way then, the female is indistinguishable from him. And this female draws her essence and existence from him. Numerous traditional delimitations, which have usually defined woman in relation to man as less active, less intelligent, and less social, become obsolete when seen from this perspective.

But the problem extends even further. Because the long process of the male search for identity culminates in the complete equation of the man with *Mensch,* even the woman in her role as mother does not appear as fundamentally "human." But with this turn to the mother, Weininger as-

---

16. Christine von Braun undertakes to thoroughly interpret the hysteria that Weininger characterizes as the "organic mendacity" of the female as *the* phenomenon of female defiance (*Nichtich: Logik, Lüge, Libido* [Frankfurt am Main, 1985]).

signs to her a certain ability, a personal, not wholly reprehensible female will, which is separate from the male will. She aspires to have a child; she aspires to motherhood in the spirit of preserving the human race.[17] The way Weininger assigns the desire to procreate primarily to woman, not to man/father is conspicuous. The previously outlined negative depictions of the female suddenly seem to exist alongside her recognized maternal side. In this context of the mother figure, we encounter a sentence that comparatively addresses the male-female planes, by means of which a new dimension of the dynamic of the gender separation appears: "In her [that is, woman/mother], everything attains life. . . . In this respect, she is comparable in her lowly physical sphere to the genius" (308).

Wherein specifically does the foundation of Weininger's virile self-consciousness lie? In my opinion, the question must be associated with a key aspect of his theory: the focus is on creativity, production, the genius that produces. What is strongly maintained and focussed upon is the genius of the man—the genius that looks at the woman and imagines that he, in his existence as genius, surpasses the female genius mentioned above. This is not the man who thinks of himself primarily in terms of his sense of responsibility, his legal jurisdiction, or his public exercise of power. This man compares himself with his mother—and Weininger says this. He sees the origin of life, the children, as being inextricably connected to her. What is significant for her is an ability that he also has. When she gives birth, so does he—in a more noble sphere, of course, under more noble conditions, namely, in the realm of "spiritual production" (331). She produces only a lowly life form, while he breathes a higher form of life into all living things.[18]

The author zealously ensures that this *true* concept of genius is attributed solely to the man. "Whoever . . . may wish to change and expand the concept of genius so that women under him also have a small place within the definition, would thereby already have destroyed the concept" (242). "The genial *Mensch* already has the woman, like everything else, completely

---

17. Weininger makes frequent references to Plato. The idea that the "spiritual child," the product, has a higher value than the "bodily child" appears already in Plato's *Symposium*. But production is also decisively associated with the male desire to procreate, which Weininger apparently finds so difficult to accept that he puts the female desire to have the child in the forefront and thereby basically recognizes the woman as the "mother of life," whom he then also bestows (referring to the prostitute) with the face of death. He deals with this in detail in the tenth chapter.

18. In this respect, Weininger opposes man with his art not only to woman, but also to the universe as a whole.

within himself" (242)—a male mimesis of the female birth experience. So nothing is foreign to the genius ego. It is the dream and claim of the man that he gives birth and that he carries the woman within himself. As the true genius (and therefore, according to Weininger, expressly in opposition to her despicable reality), he can give her a countenance full of beauty and morality. He gives her a soul.[19]

The domain sanctioned in our culture where genius can find its specific freedom and where the re-creation of woman can find its highest expression is art.[20] Unlike, for instance, the social sphere of communication, which is defined by actions, woman may appear here in the realm of the great male genius as bearer of values. Weininger focused on the artist as the most basic form of the man and genius, whereby, as was already said, the endowment of the female with a soul is an essential determining factor. He very hesitantly recognized the genius of scientists.[21] In the course of these considerations, it should not be forgotten that a certain stage in the development of art is reflected here.[22]

But why does man direct his art, his Eros—which in *Geschlecht und Charakter* is sharply distinguished from the sexual physical confrontation—so much toward woman? The author provides an astonishing answer to his own mystery: "Perhaps in the process of his anthropogenesis, the man retained the divine, the soul for himself alone through a metaphysical act that is not fixed in time. . . . He compensates for this injustice of his in the tribulations of love, in and with which he attempts to give the woman back the soul he once robbed from her" (341). Are private eroticism and public art/eroticism then an attempt to correct a fundamental injustice toward the woman? If such experiences in fact exist, then a "feeling of guilt" must also be present—a precarious subject that is not further explored.

But an alarming fact remains as part of this astonishing answer: this fe-

---

19. The eleventh chapter, "Eroticism and Aesthetics," revolves around his idea "that what one believes to be the morality of the female" is actually "the 'interjection' of the soul of the man into the female" (236).

20. Weininger understands the relationship between art and nature as such: "Art therefore creates nature, and not nature art" (32b).

21. "The scientist is the one who, stands . . . *beneath* the philosopher and *beneath* the artist. The latter two earn the title of genius, the mere scientist never" (219). Waltraud Heindl directs her attention to the character of the male cult figure in her article "Geschlecht ohne Charakter, Otto Weiningers Kultfiguren," in *Österreich und der Große Krieg 1914–1918: Die andere Seite der Geschichte*, ed. Klaus Amann and Hubert Lengauer (Vienna, 1989). I am indebted to Theres Kühn for this reference.

22. One should bear in mind the extent to which Richard Wagner was the epitome of an artistic genius to both the Weininger father and son.

male being, who is declared not to have a soul, can herself never be a lover. So whom does the man love, then, when he falls under the spell of Eros? A lucid explanation points us in the direction of what is probably the only possibility: "In all love, the man loves only himself" (332). In all love, the eroticist seeks his own (higher) self, that which he is supposed to be, and makes woman simply "a vessel for the idea of his own perfection" (353). But it is not only that Eros and artistic genius are so obviously bound to the subjective male existence; if at all possible, nothing that is remembered or is worth remembering should come to the erotic man from woman: "[E]ven the highest eroticism uses woman not as an end in itself, but instead consistently as a means to an end, namely, purely to represent the ego of the lover" (331). In a confusing lack of differentiation, the ideal woman represents nothing more than the male ego.[23] Such explanations stand in gross conflict with the lives of real women and are highly questionable forms of the feminine.

Are not these two poles—the man's impassioned privilege of artistic creation that is so absolutely asserted and that was developed over the course of centuries, and the model of femininity that is presented in *Geschlecht und Charakter*, the radically asserted lack of self in the woman—closely related? Do they not mutually require each other's existence? Exactly because this woman in and of herself has neither an end nor a worth, she becomes a boundless medium for male projections.[24] On the other hand, when she is looked at only as a male creation, this image dissolves; this empty woman, the transfigured mother/Madonna and pure lover, collapses all too easily in her illusiveness. The loss of unity with the imagined lover is imminent.

When man does not encounter woman in the realm of art/eroticism as described above, but they instead desire each other as sexual beings in a genital coitus, the fear of the most extreme danger—failing to achieve the true self—prevails. The epitome of this failure is woman; however, accord-

---

23. Fundamental aspects of this problem are comprehensively addressed in Janine Chasseguet-Smirgel, "Das *Ichideal:* Psychoanalytischer Essay über die 'Krankheit' der Idealität," in *Literatur der Psychoanalyse*, ed. Alexander Mitscherlich (Frankfurt am Main, 1981).

24. A work that addresses the importance of the projection phenomenon in literature is Silvia Bovenschen, *Die imaginierte Weiblichkeit: Exemplarische Untersuchungen zu kulturgeschichtlichen und literarischen Präsentationsformen des Weiblichen* (Frankfurt am Main, 1979). In her article entitled "Inszenierung der inszenierten Weiblichkeit: Wedekinds *Lulu*—paradigmatisch" (43–60), she examines Wedekind's dramas *Erdgeist* and *Die Büchse der Pandora*, which caused quite a commotion in the period shortly before and after the turn of the nineteenth century.

ing to Weininger, man also bears a diabolical stigma for his eventual failure of self-realization—namely, the expression of his desire to come in contact with the woman. The fate of the phallus/penis is represented in the image of hell present in the *Divina Commedia:* "[T]he center of Dante's hell is Lucifer's genitals" (400). But the woman represents the man's potential to sin. She who can never know the longing for a soul wants nothing other than the unification of herself with another, copulation, and insatiable, universal sexuality—as a consequence of her lack of a soul. She wants to be violated, always wants to be an object so that she can at least be something. Copulation is the function of the woman in the universe.

I do not want to go into the relationship between these "insights" and statements that the author considers to be previously unheard and undiscovered with patterns of argumentation that have recurred over the centuries, like the many extreme examples to be found in the *Hexenhammer*. I would only like to mention that the turn-of-the-century woman who is so prototypically condemned to passivity yet at the same time possesses an insatiable sexuality is not here accused, as in the period of the witch persecutions, of decidedly aggressive, destructive activity. And the responsibility for the traumatizing sexuality then does not fall upon her, for the man alone strives toward higher ends. He must practice abstinence. Accordingly, Weininger says: "[T]he woman is only sin, and this only by way of the man's sin" (402). "When the man became sexual, then he created the woman" (401). She is thus once again produced by him, but now as his own undoing.

However, the woman/mother, who is not to be interpreted only as a nonman and a "void," who is not to be simply placed in a series of the man's creations, who can not be only a fabrication and an imitation of the masculine, remains as a reality. Weininger's solution (or the *primum movens* of his series of theories?) lies in the offensive gesture of associating motherhood with animal existence and rejecting it as a possible "human" spiritual phenomenon. "Motherly love is an instinctive urge: even the animals are not less familiar with it than human beings. This in itself proves that this kind of love can not be true love, that this altruism is not true morality" (297). The son makes the mute mother aware of this, and he also decides that he is a *Mensch* precisely by distinguishing himself from her. I do not want to question his necessary distinction from the maternal world, but a problematic point still remains. This distinction in Weininger's context is not so much to be understood as a reflection of independence and being different, but rather as a male transgression in a deeply critical respect. Deeming man superior is fundamental to the male progression. Does the man, throughout his whole life, see the physical sexual act as the reprehensible obligation to devote himself to an animalistic existence that he then wanted to transcend by breaking with and differentiating himself from his mother?

Sin is actually already present in the very will to be born, according to Weininger. A *circulus vitiosus* follows, which includes a degradation of the generating man/father and of parenthood in general, as the following statements indicate: "[E]arthy fatherhood ... is ... insignificant" and "ensuring the continuance of the race can not be a moral responsibility" (458). Parenthood in general is immoral.[25] The problem of genealogy, of generations, of extending men's existence by having children, is placed on the back burner.

With this abasement of the mother in the struggle for autonomy (or rather autarchy) on the part of Weininger's man, it should at the same time not be forgotten to what a great extent the man defined himself in terms of being a genius, in which case he closely links himself to the maternal productive ability and thus to an idealized female object. Horror stricken, he rejected only *that* woman who does not correspond to this pure love object.

But from his philosophical perspective, which helped influence his idea of the striving toward autonomy, the "other" Weininger proposes women's emancipation. A certain way out exists for the real woman. She is never completely a woman, but rather, according to the controversial concept of bisexuality, she is also partly a man. The basic claim is essentially that she may become a man insofar as it is possible. In this manner, Weininger approves of the women's emancipation movement as long as women ultimately submit to ethical principles. Whether or not the possibility exists, in the course of women's emancipation, for "the categorical imperative [to] come to life in the woman" is Weininger's actual concern. Does the woman, the sexual difference as it were aside, then join the brothers as a sister? If this is conceded to her, it appears as if suddenly the crucial problems—of the disunity of the sexes, of the borderline figure of the ambivalent mother and prostitute, of the genius existence that due to "natural" circumstances is granted only to man, and of the scandalous fall into sexual complications—are or could be resolved. Then what is the status of the "law of the family"?[26]

---

25. "[I]t is immoral to procreate a human being for any secondary reason, to bring a being into the limitations of humanity, the conditions made for him by his parentage" (*Sex and Character*, 346).

26. George Wilhelm Friedrich Hegel, *Hegel's Phenomenology of Spirit*, trans. Miller (Oxford: Clarendon Press, 1977), 274: "Consequently, the feminine, in the form of the sister, has

An indispensable precondition for any emancipation, according to Weininger, is suddenly presented at the end of the book: the responsibility for "the upbringing of all of mankind [must be] taken away from the mother" (460).

The Father System in *Totem and Taboo*

The second issue that I would like to address, as I mentioned at the start of this essay, is the question of Sigmund Freud. Freud, too, notices the woman's status as an object at many levels. However, this diagnosis does not cause him the same anxiety that is evident in Weininger, and his statements are far less vehement and degrading. He conjures up images of female inferiority on the basis of the gender situation and the division of functions according to sex. But the woman is not entirely deprived of the status of being a human being.[27]

Since Freud, unlike Weininger, does not base his theories on the idea of a "finished" individual, but rather (to summarize the most important points) directs his examination toward the process of human development, he vividly calls to mind the sometimes very significant influence of the female Other in each individual's development—the role of the so-called phallic mother and the mother as an early love object. The male will is to decisively intervene with his own intentions in the emotional drama of the developing person. The intervention referred to here is the Oedipal conflict. It is the father who intervenes and sets the new course. From this point on, the male child clearly provides the standard for psychoanalysis; and the patriarchal social law and its language are responsible for further development, espe-

---

the highest intuitive awareness of what is ethical." But woman is not destined to further advance in this direction. Hegel further argues that the "law of the family" allows woman neither to become conscious of nor to attain the moral essence. This alone shows how little Weininger, who makes an appeal for emancipation, takes into account the basic obstacle preventing the independent status of woman, although a clear philosophical understanding of the problem presented by this "law of the family" had existed for a long time. This does not mean, however, that Hegel sees or seeks a way to overcome this law. Luce Irigaray traces Hegel's investigation of the sister in "The Eternal Irony of the Community," in *Speculum of the Other Woman*, trans. Gillian Gill (Ithaca: Cornell University Press, 1985).

27. The concepts I am outlining here occur primarily in the following essays of Sigmund Freud's: "Femininity," "The Infantile Genital Organization," "Some Psychical Consequences of the Anatomical Distinction Between the Sexes," and "Female Sexuality."

cially for shaping sexual differences, whose irreversible development occurs, according to Freud, in this early stage of childhood.

From where does this primary authority of the father that Freud claims in his system originate? Here I repeat the question posed at the beginning: To which cultural influences are the male self-consciousness and the consistent basis from whence the woman is interpreted, bound? I will answer this question first with reference to *Totem and Taboo*.[28] In my opinion, Freud's writings on cultural theory reveal that the structure of the traditional religious order remains decisive as a kind of higher authority in supporting gender polarity. My view opposes Freud's own position as it appears, for instance, in the 1930 preface to *Totem and Taboo,* that science is unconditional and that he himself was "completely estranged from the religion of [his] fathers as from all others" (293). It is a pronouncement whose assuredness is surprising in view of his work *Moses and Monotheism*, which Freud began a few years after this declaration.[29] My view is not that his religious position as such is preserved, but rather that essential elements of the religious order that has been in effect for centuries are redefined in terms of a male hegemony as opposed to attributing them to a transformation due to science.

Turning now to *Totem and Taboo*—which was written in 1912/1913—with its study "Die infantile Wiederkehr des Totemismus," the discussion of which must necessarily remain very brief, I would like to characterize how the femininity that was shattered by the prism of psychoanalytical interpretation fades and becomes voiceless when the theme of the active participation of women in the cultural process arises.

Freud undertakes to record, from his perspective, early stages of religion in the totemist phenomena and to extend the interpretation to the development of the concept of God on into the present.[30] He summarizes what he sees as the results of his study: "So, I would like . . . to declare the finding that the beginnings of religion, morality, society, and art all intersect in the Oedipal complex. . . . It comes as a great surprise to me that even these

---

28. Freud, *Totem und Tabu: Einige Übereinstimmungen im Seelenleben der Wilden und der Neurotiker*, in *Studienausgabe*, 9:287–387. Parenthetical references in the text are to the English edition: *Totem and Taboo, Standard Edition*, 13:ix–99.

29. Freud, *Moses and Monotheism, Standard Edition*, 23:7–137. He had produced an outline for this work already in 1934.

30. Freud repeatedly had to defend his views against condemnations from the field of ethnology. Edith Seifert, who makes frequent reference to *Totem und Tabu*, addresses this problem in the first chapter of her study, "Was will das Weib?" in *Zu Begehren und Lust bei Freud und Lacan* (Weinheim, 1987).

problems of the inner life of the masses should be resolved from a single concrete point, namely, the status of the relationship with the father" (156–57). That all things moral and religious can be explained—and how—by the relationship to the father was advanced by Freud in his later combination of a certain model of the ur-horde of Darwinian origin with totemism. The shift that Freud brings to the complex considerations of numerous scholars on the rich spectrum of exogamy and in the totemist phenomena is this very return to a forceful, strong individual within a horde. Darwin himself also mentions other models of a possible social ur-condition of humankind. The existence of a single man who is the strongest, and who retains all the women for himself, is the most important element for Freud. This strong one then becomes the *father* of the ur-horde, while the dispossessed are the sons.[31]

The truly relevant thing about the position of the father is his access to the sexual object, the freedom to which only he is entitled, in short, to "sexually use" (a Freudian formulation) all women.

In this manner, the first sexual encounter takes on meaning. It does not fade behind the image of the ur-father, and it is not only fixated on Lucifer as with Weininger. But it is influenced by the elementary power of a violent, property-seizing father. And the subject of birth and giving birth, the subject of the ambiguous origin of humankind, or a conception that is incommensurate with the confiscatory ur-encounter are all very obviously bypassed in Freud's cultural theory. The mother remains in the shadows unless she appears in the context of the feared incestuous libido of the male child.

With this dominance of the father that was first introduced as a natural supremacy, Freud paves the way to the exclusive father-god. But still no reason is offered that would justify giving this figure, and the power and force incarnate in him, the name of "father" along with respect and affection—especially on the part of the oppressed sons. No pressing reason seems to exist for Freud for including the specific fate of the dependent daughters in his cultural theory.

---

31. The following statements from *Moses and Monotheism*, in which Freud still offers his construction from *Totem and Taboo* a quarter-century later as a valid theory, shows that he essentially upholds his father model: "The strong male was lord and father of the entire horde and unrestricted in his power, which he exercised with violence. All the females were his property—wives and daughters of his own horde and some, perhaps, robbed from other hordes. The lot of his sons was a hard one: if they roused their father's jealousy they were killed or castrated or driven out" (81).

Returning to the subject of the father-son axis, a necessary break without which the process leading to the father would not have even been initiated—a kind of fall from grace—lies between this tyrannical master, who supposedly can be seen in the animal kingdom, and all the socioreligious organizations that develop thereafter one by one. This break is the revolt of the sons.[32] "In the beginning was the act." Freud cites Goethe in explaining the murder of the horde's ur-father. *This* action toward *this* father turns out, furthermore, to be the origin of culture. Yet beyond their thirst for power, another motivating factor for this violent act, which was carried out *collectively* by the sons, was their sexual demands, their envy of the ur-father's possession of all women. The aggressive rebellion of these sons, who are at the mercy of this omnipotent one, seems to Freud to be an obvious and irrefutable theory. It is the decisive conflict. It is the deed of Oedipus.

What hardly presents any problem whatsoever is the prospect of a female will. Was there no sovereignty at all on the part of women? Was the male individual's power of possession so universally accepted? Shouldn't the goals and desires of women have had a different basis? Would the mothers really have agreed to the exclusion and oppression of the sons?[33] And should this father's incestuous conquest of the daughters be looked at as being so insignificant, when the son's redemption is given a much greater importance in psychoanalysis?[34]

Whether and to what extent the (eliminated) male tyranny is already based on an offense against the woman, making this property-seizing individual out to be a natural phenomenon is probably supposed to raise him above all critical judgement. It is a transgression that according to Freud is basically carried on by the sons and that remains unaddressed. After the act against the father, the woman still remains under the control of the male

32. Freud does not even consider the participation of the women and daughters. Edith Seifert undertakes in *Zu Begehren und Lust bei Freud und Lacan* to in part include the daughters in the transgression against the father and to trace their eventual further development.

33. Freud still at times counts on mothers who incite their sons to action or provide them with special protection, but this fact does not change the serious consequences of his initial position, since he on the whole retains the structure of culture/religion according to his Oedipal model.

34. That the father's (or other male relative's) incestuous violation of the daughters is not taken seriously even today, despite its frequent occurrence, but is in many ways concealed and excused as if it were simply an inalienable right of the father's, is clearly shown and rightly so in Josephine Rijnaarts, *Lots Töchter: Über den Vater-Tochter-Inzest,* trans. Barbara Heller (Düsseldorf, 1988).

will in Freud's model.[35] After the slaying, the brothers recall the dead, absent father. From this moment on, they draw up contracts; and they share the father's absolute power, an important consequence of which is their renunciation of the sexual objects of their own clan. They provide incest taboos and ensure exogamy in the interest of the male order and male solidarity. Freud traces these taboos with respect to avoiding incest back to the childhood Oedipal conflict of each individual. But returning to the topic of the brothers, they perceive the loss. Driven by a burning feeling of guilt, they revert to a "posthumous submission" to the father. "The dead father became stronger than the living one had been" (143).

The reversal, the turn toward the "dead father," is fulfilled now, according to Freud, in the worship of a certain animal in the totemist system. This animal acts as a surrogate father. The repudiation of his killing represents an abrogation of the act. The ceremonial slaying of the animal is ritual repetition, a constant and also jubilant reminder of the brotherly alliance and the venture of having violated the paternal order. The totem feast is a consumption of the fatherly essence, the appropriation of the father's qualities; it signifies a strengthening of the clan's unity. A totem animal becomes their progenitor. "Features were thus brought into existence which continued thenceforward to have a determining influence on the nature of religion" (145).

That psychoanalysis could shed more light only upon *certain* religious principles, as he sometimes maintains, is contradicted by Freud's attempt to base the act that initiates culture in this very confrontation of the father and sons.

The subject of the woman and culture is pushed aside. The sex difference and sexual urges are indeed the focus of attention in psychoanalytical perception, but the woman still has no active role in religion/culture. Here, the conflict-laden dialogue between father and son prevails. The emergence of culture, especially the genesis of religion, is presented in such a way that the

---

35. Even if Freud, as already mentioned, was subject with *Totem and Taboo* to ethnological criticism, how much the theories of cultural anthropology were, conversely, influenced by the production of a patriarchal psychoanalytical theory must also be considered. Is not this question important, for instance, to the understanding of the preconditions necessary for the theories of Claude Lévi-Strauss on the exchange of women? See Lévi-Strauss, *Elementary Structures of Kinship,* trans. Bell and Sturmer (Boston: Beacon Press, 1969). Georges Bataille, too, seems to assume that men give away women: "Marriage is a matter less for the partners than for the man who gives the woman away, the man whether father or brother who might have freely enjoyed the woman, daughter or sister, yet who bestows her on someone else" (*Eroticism,* trans. Dalwood [San Francisco: City Lights Books, 1986], 218).

woman is expropriated or excluded from the very start, as if the woman had always been silent and passive in the course of cultural development.[36]

How he can do this is virtually incomprehensible, but Freud must close his eyes to the existence of the female totem (and the need to explain it) and the totemist ancestral mothers in order to comply with his unmistakable objective; they apparently offer a too flagrant contradiction to his one-sided approach. Freud's "overlooking" of female religious/cultural positions is not any less astonishing when the transition from totemism to religious systems that possess certain conceptions of God in a narrower sense is established.

The focus of discussion is the "clan deity, in whose supposed presence the sacrifice is performed" and who is newly embraced in the totem feast or sacrifice (147):

> How does the god come to be in a situation to which he was originally a stranger? The answer might be that in the meantime the concept of God had emerged—from some unknown source—and had taken control of the whole of religious life; and that, like everything else that was to survive, the totem meal had been obliged to find a point of contact with the new system. The psychoanalysis of individual human beings, however, teaches us with quite special insistence that the god of each of them is formed in the likeness of his father, that his personal relation to God depends on his relation to his father in the flesh and oscillates and changes along with that relation, and that at bottom God is nothing other than an exalted father. As is the case of totemism, psychoanalysis recommends us to have faith in the believers who call God their father, just as the totem was called the tribal ancestor. (147)

Freud continues:

> We know that there are a multiplicity of relations between the god and the sacred animal (the totem or the sacrificial victim). (1) Each

---

36. In *Moses and Monotheism*, Freud somewhat more specifically addresses the idea that the absolute power that was set free in the elimination of the father was in part bequeathed to women. Since Freud holds to the premise that divinities arose out of the humanization of totem animals who represent the father, the specified problem with regard to female divinities, as well as the problem regarding the structure of the matriarchy, which Freud in essence accepts, remains. That a revolution occurred—namely, the "return of a single father-god of unlimited dominion" (84)—is discussed, but not what this meant as a moment of cultural "expatriation" of women.

god usually has an animal (and quite often several animals) sacred to him. (2) In the case of certain specially sacred sacrifices—"mystic" sacrifices—the victim was precisely the animal sacred to the god. (3) The god was often worshipped in the shape of an animal (or, to look at it another way, animals were worshipped as gods) long after the age of totemism. . . . We are relieved from the necessity of further discussion by the consideration that the totem is nothing other than a surrogate of the father. (147–48)

God, then, is a new creation deriving from the very source of all religious education, namely, the longing for a father. Over the course of time, the intensification of this longing is supposed to have produced transformations, changes in the various religious systems.

Is it necessary to emphasize the obvious facts that refute the Freudian paradigms? Female divinities also existed; animals were holy to the female gods, as well; there were also sacrifices made to them, and they, too, could take on the form of an animal in myths—to name only a few. All of this could not have escaped an authority and a reader of Frazer like Freud. Even the inevitably necessary exclusion of facts as demanded by the handling of a specific theme would be insufficient to explain *this* obvious omission. The intention of offering a "theory of origin" for religion/culture is, in any case, too broad. The effects are too influential and serious, as is their significance for the present. As mentioned above, it is all too transparent that without this exclusion, the concept of totemism would already have lost its credence.

The subjugation of the woman—who appears unquestionably as quasi-natural object of regression, desire, and exchange—must be exposed and rejected in general, but especially so in the field of psychoanalysis. I am aware that *Totem and Taboo* has long generated criticism, especially from the camp of ethnology, and that the results of new investigations have overturned the validity of much of this work. The question I am interested in, however, is what the author noticed and nevertheless "had to" conceal for the purpose of advancing his concept of the Oedipal cultural father.

It is obvious that femininity and divinity, that femininity and culture were not and are not to be separated in the history of humanity as it occurs in *Totem and Taboo* in the context of psychoanalysis. Not only for the sake of historical accuracy, but also from the present social and individual perspective, which is influenced by psychoanalysis, it is necessary to persist in asking the question: What insight could the "other" facts in the cultural domain of the past have revealed—insight perhaps into the impossibility of Freud's or any analogous theory of origin? Which multifaceted female-male cultural confrontations, which complex mother-daughter or sister-sister clashes that are observable in culture, which cultural metamorphoses of female origin would have become manifest? Why should important forms of incestual barriers not also have been inaugurated by women/mothers? It should not be thereby assumed from the outset, however, that female parallels exist for the male ur-father situation sketched by Freud.

The brief allusion to female divinities first appears in Freud's treatise after the paradigm of the ur-father, his murder and his "return" as totem/God are established and presented to us as a solid edifice. In one sentence, "the institutions of maternal rights recognized by Bachofen (1861)" are mentioned, questionably presented, and then immediately dismissed again from the historical context of religion (428). The failure to characterize the existence and longtime paramount significance and multitude of goddesses, who are not even all exclusively mother goddesses, and to shape, classify, and interpret them in the light of psychoanalysis, in no way upsets Freud's line of argumentation: "I cannot suggest at what point in this process of development a place is to be found for the great mother-goddesses, who may perhaps in general have preceded the father gods." And without further reflection, he continues, "It seems certain, however, that the change in the attitude to the father was not restricted to the sphere of religion but that it extended in a consistent manner to that other side of human life which had been affected by the father's removal—to social organization" (149).

When, thereafter, the female divinities (who remain anonymous in this context) once again become the focus of attention along with their (name-bearing) heroes, they appear neither as bearers of culture nor as life-giving or life-taking divine women in a cosmic dimension. How frequently the goddesses are representatives of power, justice, and wisdom is not acknowledged. Here they are only thought of reproachfully in relation to the sons who "conduct incestual relations with the mother in defiance of the father" and then must pay for it with their lives. Thus, the sacrificial death of heroes by or for a female divinity is to be interpreted as a consciousness of wrongdoing done to the father. Their return, their rebirth is called resurrection.

Freud's cultural theory and his Oedipus theory mutually illuminate, influence, and support each other. The condition leading to the origin of religion is supposed to be the Oedipal transformation of the male individual. The content, structure, and goal of the Oedipal conflict are supposed to be the core of religion/culture. The period preceding the Oedipal change and the corresponding time before religion/culture are thus denoted as an era of nature.

The period of the special relationship with the mother, the time when the maternal other is at the center of attention, is not to be called "culture." The cultural birth is supposed to first arise with the father. That implies that in the history of humanity, substantial active female participation in religion/culture is not supposed to have existed. The existence of female divinities, as far as their genealogy is discussed at all, is supposed to be due primarily to the forbidden incestual desires. The relationship between religion and the social order that is otherwise so relevant in Freud's eyes seems less interesting when a goddess is the point of discussion. Nothing of that which was said of male gods, their function of effecting collective action, for instance, is even remotely considered for the female divinities. Cultural dialogues or conflicts between mother and daughters, and consequently the important and manifold interactions of female children with the mother, are not essential to the discussion. Exalted mother figures, their possible relation to the exalted father, and their deprivation of cultural power and replacement by this father are clearly subject to condemnation.

The issue of the Oedipal break and of the pre-Oedipal phase has of course subsequently been further examined,[37] and the issue of female divinities has also been explored from various angles. Whether thereby the division that equates the feminine with a nature that must be controlled and the masculine with culture and a strong nature is carried out *ad absurdum* remains open to question.

Thus, Freud allows the widespread involvement of female divinities in cultural orders to become lost in his journey into the past and even more so in his discussion of the unconscious basis of religion/culture. This very fact that he wants to find only a male god and the longing for a father does not allow me to say that he is literally bound to this system like a true believer. But he is strongly influenced by his own objectives that themselves largely derive from our religious tradition. It is clear from the way the question of the origin of the father religion is posed in *Totem and Taboo* that the generally accepted religious foundation is abandoned as an illusion. But that Freud primarily wants or is able to find and illustrate only the emergence and significance of patriarchal religion shows that with his psychoanalytical

---

37. The role of the relationship between pre-Oedipal and Oedipal in the process of establishing cultural meaning is explored thoroughly and subversively (with a special emphasis on art) in Julia Kristeva, *Revolution in Poetic Language*, trans. Margaret Walker (New York: Columbia University Press, 1984).

perspective he wants to extend the scope of power of the traditional father system and to prevent the permeation and upsetting of the sociocultural sphere by women. If it was Freud's hope that "scientific spirit, reason" would gradually achieve "dictatorship in human emotional life,"[38] should we then think he would have desired the participation of women in this "dictatorship"—apart from considering the desirability of this dictatorship?

Without a valid religious reference to the patriarchal system, the dominant role of the father as a powerful ruling authority could appear to be relative. Was it not necessary to reestablish the father's status?

In order to have some kind of irrefutable certainty for the social preeminence of the man, it now seems necessary to also scientifically anchor it in an inherent male predominance. Freud's argumentation is not free from this biological determinism. However, I do not want to dwell on this idea, but rather I want to again address the development of the Oedipal relationship, which alone inaugurates religion/culture.

The sons' aggressive action and the (also sexual) omnipotence of the father—both elements are requisite and converge in the guilt complex and the reacknowledgment of the father to create a male-dominated process. The woman, as matter and as the property of the father, is a necessary precondition for *this* initiation of religion/culture, which is reflected in the sons'/brothers' claim to possession that follows the "act."

Even if this important decisive point in the ontogenetic and so-called phylogenetic development does/did exist, and even if this view of "the female" and this power over "the female" exists/existed, then in my opinion, the problem is the tendency toward the *absolutization* and the *perpetuation* of this (also historico-cultural) Oedipal revolution. Why not reevaluate this caesura that is part of our culture and exceed and transform it?

Crossover of Father Positions and Mother/Son Status

After stressing the alienation and asymmetry of the sexes under male domination at the turn of the century, in a brief third section, I would like to emphasize certain interrelations between the described positions and texts of both authors. Looking back now to Weininger's *Geschlecht und Charakter,* this catastrophic text should, on the one hand, be clearly distinguished

---

38. Quoted in Chasseguet-Smirgel, *Ichideal,* 210f.

from the approach in *Totem and Taboo*. Yet on the other hand, some common factors between them need to be outlined.

In his evaluation of the situation at the turn of the nineteenth century, and in his rapid movement through the ages and cultures—including, indirectly, non-European ones—Weininger is unable to perceive any cultural traces of women. In a homogeneity that is barely conceivable, men are the actors. Freud, who investigates in a different way, and more extensively, finds female influences on culture but without really allowing them to come to the forefront in his discussion.

How should this phenomenon, this absence of women, be interpreted? Is it that woman naturally could not satisfy the criteria of being a person? Or is it that this culture, which is so radically dominated by men, must be seen as being *"inhumane"* as a result of this very domination? The latter explanation is offered by neither Freud nor Weininger. When *Geschlecht und Charakter* is looked at in the context of Freud, it can now be said that even without emphasizing the significance of a powerful father figure who possesses women, and the necessity of his existence for the sons' usurpation of power, woman is directly and radically confronted with man made in the image of God, and with the standards of male socialization, autonomy, and creativity that have developed over the course of time. In comparison to this (developing) man, she inevitably appears to be a void, to be a subhuman being—so much so for Weininger that he does not even begin to deal with the real woman and with genital sexuality.

Psychoanalysis insists on the important difference and the important interaction between the father and the developing male. The central figure is *the* father, who is at first master over the women. He is visibly elevated and gives the systematic circumstance of cultural theory definition. That the emotions and theorems of Weininger were not bound to the law and authority of an exalted father is by no means what I wish to say. But in his definition of the man, Weininger did not include the father as causal and essential; he neither recognized nor discussed nor explained his existence. His theoretical structure in many respects conceals the foundation upon which his theories are built. Since the role that the father plays in this nonexistence and nonessence of the woman is dependent on this structure, it remains indistinguishable. Which characteristics are significant for the father and whether he fulfills the characteristics of the Freudian father are not openly demonstrated either.

But wherever *the* female is presented for discussion, the mother becomes a key issue. The key to Weininger's differentiation between woman and man can be found, in my opinion, in the relationship and the boundary drawn between mother and son. Recalling the most important thing: it is said that the historical woman/mother from whom the son liberated himself became a life-giving animal to him, and all *fécondité* became revolting to him. The woman that remains is soulless and fatefully sexual. Whether a particular father image had an influence on making the woman/mother this way is not seriously considered. The man/son at least wants to create the woman as she is supposed to be[39]—as his exalted artwork. In becoming one with her, the idealized object, he also becomes significant to an exalted father. Would an actual relationship with a woman have destroyed this association? Another way leading to the approval of the woman is obstructed for Weininger. With his expansive definitions of genius and ego, Weininger sacrificed clearly drawn boundaries of the male individual. He therefore oscillates between the threatening necrophile fantasy of omnipotence and the despair of the ego that has sunken into profound loneliness.[40]

In view of such a fanatic rejection, daring separation, and at the same time narcissistically idealized control of the mother in the aesthetic sphere, as posited in Weininger's *Geschlecht und Charakter,* Freud's conscious return to religious tradition and his multifaceted demonstration, analysis, and postulation of the father role and of the generational question take on considerable meaning. Through psychoanalytical awareness, the father event and the fatherly will are substantially incorporated into male existence and development, and the progression of the sons/brothers can be traced back to it in the totem animal and the figure of the father-God.

When an exalted father (what is referred to here is, for instance, the unquestioned correlation of the man with the image of God) is adopted as a hidden fundamental aspect of *Geschlecht und Charakter,* the question arises: In view of the total inferiority of the female Other that is established here, is it not a reasonable assumption that this exalted father is unacceptable as a sexual being who is seeking a sexual relationship with the woman?

From this perspective, the Freudian conception of the ur-father once again becomes very telling: the ur-father was a sexual being. In the end, it is acknowledged there, I think, that the father is a "divided" being; his wish

---

39. In the interpretation of Ibsen's *Peer Gynt,* woman as she should be in order to contribute to the redemption of the man is once again the focus of attention.

40. Weininger quite frequently and very insistently refers to the loneliness of "the significant person" who is sustained by the belief in "his possession of an 'I' or soul, which is solitary in the universe, which faces the universe and comprehends it" (167).

for, and relationship with, the female Other, which is essential to him, is not disputed and is also not entirely dismissed for the sons.

For Weininger, the father figure was decisive for the trend toward a self-birth of the ego and for his rejection of, and attack against, the sexual procreative act—of course, necessary deprivation, postponement, or limits within the range of sexual possibilities and desires are not included here. Thus, this father figure can only have denied the significance of the relationship to the female Other. Quite obviously, viewing the exalted father as incomplete, as a "divided" being in this way, is unacceptable.

In principle, Weininger would have to explicitly view every father who has sexual contact with the mother in a dismal light. Such a father would have to be damned along with Lucifer. Had the young author (apart from only a few comments) not wholly ignored the man as father and excluded him from his discourse on sexual difference, his outcry against sexuality would also have openly condemned the fathers, the cultural authorities. Would the relinquishment of a "pure" father figure have been the most basic injury and therefore impossible for Weininger? Did paternal purity have to be preserved at all cost while disgrace was simply allowed to fall upon the mother? The power of Weininger's God was obviously rooted in the radical rejection of sensuality. Freud, on the other hand, ultimately allows his ur-father to be regarded as a sexual being.

But what motivates Freud to underestimate and to rule out the participation of exalted mother figures in culture, to force women, as harbingers of culture, into the shadows, and not even to allow them to appear at the horizon?[41] Is the equation of the origin of culture with the Oedipal situation so unalterable? Is his father system so completely devised according to the principle of the father's absolute power over the female sexual being that any admission of female cultural activity and autonomy casts doubt on it? Would a more explicit reminder of a cultural mother system have upset his system? The impression that male supremacy is absolutely necessary for the existence of culture in general would have thus been undermined.[42] The

---

41. I would like to present evidence for how deeply, on the other hand, the "cultural incompetence" of woman raised doubts about her ability to be a human or lovable being. In the words of August Strindberg, "Not the opinion but the fact that woman is a rudimentary man . . . , that the man created culture in its entirety . . . shows his superior position . . . strange that this simple truth first had to be discovered, as if the possibility of an erotic relationship were grounded upon keeping this a secret" (quoted in Le Rider, *Der Fall Otto Weininger*, 51).

42. Shortly after completing this article, the essay "Das Kästchenproblem: Zum Psyche-Mythos bei Freud" by Gerburg Treusch-Dieter came to my attention. It is worth mentioning since *related references* appear and the author furthermore poses the question of whether it

strictly philosophical ethical question, whether or not the woman is the "means to an end," and whether the cultural code in which her existence is interpreted as an existence solely for the man and child can be perforated, may not be addressed for such obvious reasons.

Taken in its totality, the theory of the ur-father horde, too, is symptomatic in character and is intended to keep the contempt for women alive. But in comparison to Weininger's catastrophic imagination of the heterosexual matrix, the gender model as conceived by Freud in certain aspects offers a potential point of departure.

---

can be assumed "that in his 'Motiv der *Kästchenwahl*,' Freud touches upon the very flip-side of his system of cultural theory" (92); here, woman appears in the form of the Moira, before whom "every cultural effort becomes ineffectual" (93). Treusch-Dieter's article appeared in *Mythen der Rationalität*, ed. René Weiland and Wolfgang Pircher (Vienna, 1990).

11

WOMAN: THE MOST PRECIOUS LOOT IN THE "TRIUMPH OF ALLEGORY"
Gender Relations in Walter Benjamin's *Passagen-Werk*

Astrid Deuber-Mankowsky
Translated by Dana Hollander

"The historical projection of the experiences which underlie the *Fleurs du mal* is what this study should offer"[1]

Walter Benjamin worked on the project entitled *Passagen-Werk*, the "Arcades Project," for over thirteen years. He left behind one thousand pages

---

This essay originally appeared under the title "Die Frau: Das kostbarste Beutestück im 'Triumph der Allegorie,' " in *Concordia: Internationale Zeitschrift für Philosophie* 21 (1992): 2–20.

1. Walter Benjamin, "Zentralpark," *Gesammelte Schriften*, vol. 1.2, ed. Rolf Tiedemann and Hermann Schweppenhäuser (Frankfurt/Main: Suhrkamp, 1974), 673. This edition of Benjamin's writings is henceforth cited as *GS*. "Central Park," trans. Lloyd Spencer with Mark

of quotations, interwoven with his own brief aphoristic comments. The *Passagen-Werk* also includes independent texts that grew out of his work on the project. The longest of these are "The Work of Art in the Age of Mechanical Reproduction"; "The Paris of the Second Empire in Baudelaire" (intended as the middle part of a book Benjamin planned on Baudelaire, which was written for the *Zeitschrift für Sozialforschung* but was later rejected by Horkheimer and Adorno); and the revised version of the "flaneur" chapter of the Baudelaire book, "On Some Motifs in Baudelaire" (which did eventually get published in Horkheimer and Adorno's journal). The *Passagen-Werk* also includes the collection of aphorisms entitled "Central Park"—which gathers particularly those motifs that would have been decisive for the third part of the Baudelaire book—and, of course, the well-known "Theses on the Philosophy of History."

During the 1930s, in the Bibliothèque Nationale in Paris, the German émigré Walter Benjamin, virtually obsessed, buried himself in texts from the nineteenth century in order to record from them passages, in his tiny handwriting, as if they were treasures. If some critics today cite "writer's block" or the tendency that overcame Benjamin to be a "copyist"[2] in order to explain what prevented him, despite years of work, from actually writing the *Passagen-Werk*, then this indicates a misconception of the task Benjamin set for himself. For it was an infinite task in several respects. In the "convolute" entitled "Theory of Knowledge, Theory of Progress," Benjamin formulated the following approach as a "modest methodological proposal for the cultural-historical dialectic":

> It is very easy to establish oppositions, according to determinate points of view, within the various "fields" of any epoch, such that on one side lies the "productive," "forward-looking," "lively," "positive" part of the epoch, and on the other side the fruitless, retrograde, and obsolescent. It is even the case that the contours of this positive part will only emerge clearly when profiled against the negative. On the other hand, every negation has its value solely as background for the delineation of the lively, the positive. So it is of decisive importance to apply a new partition to this initially excluded, negative part so that, by a displacement of the angle of vi-

---

Harrington, in *New German Critique* 34 (winter 1985), 43. All translations modified where necessary.

2. Cf. Pierre Missac, *Walter Benjamin's Passages*, trans. Shierry Weber Nicholsen (Cambridge: MIT Press, 1995), 66ff., esp. 75–76.

sion (but not of the criteria!), a positive element emerges anew in it too—something different from that previously signified. And so on, ad infinitum, until the entire past is brought into the present in a historical apocatastasis.[3]

This statement expresses an attitude that reproaches any kind of scientific deduction—be it the most differentiated dialectical development of a historical state of affairs—with what it sacrifices to the idea of progress on which it is based.[4] Thus, though the commentaries in the *Passagen-Werk* include exclamation marks and repetitions in the form of self-quotations, there are no last words, no firm judgments that would allow a matter to be laid to rest in order to proceed to the next step. There is always an "on the other hand," a "yes, but"; behind every ambivalence that is determined, another one opens up.

This process extends progressively deeper—for it is oriented toward what is dead, toward what has been rejected, marginalized, or forgotten. It makes the historian into a "herald who invites the dead to the table."[5] With this, the process subverts the boundaries of philosophy and nonphilosophy, the feelings of shame that have been carefully put in place by traditional philosophy. In contrast to an empathetic (*einfühlend*) reconstruction of a historical state of affairs, Benjamin's construction of history presupposes the destruction of the harmonious illusion of history and of the present. It becomes a procedure of deconstruction that always also refers to the present.

The "modest methodological proposal" stipulates that no experience be excluded from the philosophical concept of experience, not even those experiences that would normally be excluded as private. And this consideration was probably what led Benjamin, in his last writings, to call into question the taboo of the gender neutrality of thinking and of philosophy. It is what led him to use the disappearance of woman in the nineteenth century as a

---

3. Benjamin, *Das Passagen-Werk*, GS 5.1 (Frankfurt: Suhrkamp, 1982), ed. Rolf Tiedemann, 573. *The Arcades Project*, trans. Howard Eiland and Kevin McLaughlin (Cambridge and London: Harvard/Belknap, 1999), 459.

4. It is just this work of memory, which is directed against the repression and forgetting of what is barbaric about "civilization," of what has been and is continually sacrificed to civilization, that prompts the literary scholar Sigrid Weigel to take Walter Benjamin as a starting point for her reflections on the "topography of the sexes" and on the specificity of feminine writing. Cf. Sigrid Weigel, *Die Stimme der Medusa: Schreibweisen in der Gegenwartsliteratur von Frauen* (Reinbek bei Hamburg: Rohwolt, 1989), 267ff. and *Topographien der Geschlechter: Kulturgeschichtliche Studien zur Literatur* (Reinbek bei Hamburg: Rohwolt, 1990), esp. 15ff., 180ff., 204ff.

5. *Passagen-Werk*, GS 5.1, 603. *Arcades Project*, 481.

paradigm for the absence of experience that in his view characterized the self-alienated modern man.

Now, Benjamin writes, the past in its entirety, ad infinitum, must be brought into the present. But this is not as regressive as it sounds and as is often suggested in the secondary literature. Rather, it is connected to the project of reclaiming or remembering an experience that had been overtaken by the modern age. Thus, in the end it is the present for whose sake the past, as Benjamin writes, must be redeemed or remembered. This experience presupposes the experience of difference. It is not available to a monological process of reflection on the part of the subject. Benjamin thinks of it as a constructed experience, as an experience to be constructed in confrontation with the past. What is at stake here is the present, from political relations to social and technical "revolutions" to the most private impressions.

The fact that the present is thus also at stake is another reason why Benjamin's task is an infinite one. An indication for what is problematic about this undertaking may be found in the continually changing process to which the *Passagen-Werk* was exposed over the years. For in spite of the theses about the "poverty of experience" during his time and their radicalization in the thesis that in modernity "experience," *Erfahrung,* had been replaced by "lived experience," *Erlebnis,*[6] the point of departure for Benjamin's philosophy nevertheless remained a struggle concerning experience in a highly personal sense.

Benjamin's manner of proceeding presupposes a reflective look at one's own personal development that doesn't idealize, that doesn't confuse the personal with the private, and that doesn't lose itself in reflection. For this attitude, Benjamin coined the term *Geistesgegenwart,* which can be translated as 'presence of mind' or 'presence of spirit.' This slightly ominous-sounding term is one of the supports of Benjaminian "historical materialism." Presence of mind denotes an anticipatory understanding of those moments of the present that justify an interruption in time. Such moments

---

6. The term *Erlebnis,* which can be translated roughly as 'lived experience,' along with the term *Einfühlung,* which appears frequently in this essay and is translated as 'empathy,' is a technical term. Both of these concepts belong to Wilhelm Dilthey's (1833–1911) epistemology of the human sciences of which Benjamin was critical. According to Dilthey, the task of the historian consists of *einfühlendes Verstehen,* an "empathetic understanding," and of *Nacherleben,* the attempt to identify with lived experiences of past epochs. Benjamin's "minor methodological recommendation" is directed against this "empathy" of historicism, while his concept of "experience" is directed against the notion of lived experience (*Erlebnis*) that was a central term of Diltheyan philosophies of life.

allow one to pose questions to history that are constitutive of the present situation or that make possible the examination of those questions' basis in experience.

Presence of mind is thus absolutely necessary if one wants to approach the concept of experience that Benjamin has in mind. His undertaking is not unlike "an 'ascesis,' *askèsis*, an exercise of oneself, in the activity of thought," as Foucault formulated it.[7] The expression "presence of mind" makes reference to the kind of historical work Benjamin has in mind in the above-cited redemptive figure of the "herald who invites the dead to the table." That this has a great deal to do with an attempt to reclaim the possibility of experience, and thus with an attempt to reclaim oneself, is evidenced, for example, by the fact that the figure of Baudelaire became ever more central to Benjamin's work on the *Passagen-Werk*—not only Baudelaire as a poet, but Baudelaire as a "heroic subject of modernity."[8] This man, who belonged to the world of asocial and marginalized figures, who was a brooder and an allegorist, a provocateur who lived in protest and repudiation, whose "only sexual communion was realized with a whore,"[9] for whom the lesbian woman, the mannish woman, became a heroic ideal, who transmitted hysteria to men, and who compared the poet to a prostitute, in the end became for Benjamin " 'the place where he would stage all [his] ideas and all [the] battles' he had fought during his life, battles with himself and with the world."[10] In his examination of Baudelaire, he sought to gain clarity about the "totality" of his "generation's experiences,"[11] to situate these experiences historically and to anchor them in their societal framework. What interested him about the *Fleurs du mal*, then, was not "any ingenious ordering of the individual poems, let alone . . . any secret key," but rather "the ruthless exclusion of every lyrical theme which did not bear the imprint of Baudelaire's own sorrowful experience."[12]

    7. Michel Foucault, *The Use of Pleasure*, vol. 2 of *The History of Sexuality*, trans. Robert Hurley (New York: Pantheon, 1985), 8.
    8. "The hero is the true subject of *modernité*." "Das Paris des Second Empire bei Baudelaire," GS 1.2, 577. "The Paris of the Second Empire in Baudelaire," in *Charles Baudelaire: A Lyric Poet in the Era of High Capitalism*, trans. Harry Zohn (London: New Left Books, 1973), 74.
    9. Benjamin, "Paris, die Hauptstadt des XIX. Jahrhunderts," in *Passagen-Werk*, GS 5.1, 54. "Paris, Capital of the Nineteenth Century," trans. Edmund Jephcott, in *Reflections: Essays, Aphorisms, Autobiographical Writings*, ed. Peter Demetz (New York: Schocken, 1986), 157.
    10. Cited in Momme Brodersen, *Spinne im eigenen Netz: Walter Benjamin: Leben und Werk* (Bühl-Moos: Elster Verlag, 1990), 1990, 249. *Walter Benjamin: A Biography*, trans. Malcolm R. Green and Ingrida Ligers, ed. Martina Dervis (London: Verso, 1996), 234.
    11. Ibid., 261/248.
    12. "Zentralpark," 658. "Central Park," 32.

In the course of Benjamin's study of these experiences, the changes that came over the relations between the sexes in the nineteenth century became more and more important for him. In Baudelaire, Benjamin came to see less and less the solitary individual; instead, he came to see in him the solitary, disintegrating *man*.[13] According to Benjamin's interpretation of industrial modernity, it is in the disappearance of sexual difference—which is the flip side of the submission and functionalization of woman—that the originary experience of the (male) individual, his self-alienation, culminates. This occurs not primarily in the loss of traditional ties, but in the loss of the experience of difference. For Benjamin, however, the recognition of difference is the condition of the possibility of love; the elimination of difference is the entrance into hell.

Thus the strength of Benjamin's method turns out to lie not in the fact that he realizes the task he has set for himself but in his insight into certain questions, which has not lost any of its relevance to the present day.

"Baudelaire's readers are men."[14]

Presence of mind, we noted earlier, led Benjamin to concentrate more and more on the figure of Baudelaire, to construct in Baudelaire the "hero of modernity," and to represent in Baudelaire the decline of masculinity. Benjamin demonstrates his own presence of mind quite concretely not only by theoretically criticizing the division of "private life" from "public life" (*Geschäftsleben*), but also by subverting this opposition to the point of in-

---

13. Here one might object that personal experiences make their way into every philosophy and that this is by now well known. But the method presented here is directed precisely against this idea of personal experience as a more or less unconscious influence. First, it proceeds from the assumption that—in view of a development in which language is degraded ever further into a strategic discourse deployed for the purpose of achieving control over all living things—the possibility of experience as societal experience has been exhausted within this society. The discussions that have taken place within feminist philosophy, discussions that concern the question of a "female subject" or of "female experience," eloquently testify to this aporia: How are we to take recourse to an unadulterated female experience if nothing has been as much the object of definitions, ascriptions, and disfigurations as "woman"? And how would we be able to do without such a recourse, as long as collective memory (even if it is present only in the rarest moments), or the longing for it, has not yet completely disappeared?

14. "Zentralpark," 673. "Central Park," 43.

corporating his own "private life" and private experiences into his philosophical reflections.

Part of a man's private life is his relationship to the other sex. In the avant-garde circles of the 1920s, in the wake of the crisis that befell bourgeois masculinity, along with all its values, after World War I, this was an area of much experimentation and discussion.[15] Benjamin was familiar with these discussions and experienced the crisis of masculinity in a very personal way. Not only did he not manage to support his family, but he remained, even after he himself became a father, financially dependent on his parents; and in the end, he didn't even manage to have his *Habilitation* thesis officially recognized.

Thanks to Hans Puttnies's and Gary Smith's 1991 volume entitled *Benjaminiana*,[16] we now have direct access to the so-called *privata* and even into the *privatissima*. In this book, we learn about Benjamin's "open" marriage with his wife Dora Kellner-Benjamin—a strong and highly independent woman, who for several years supported the family with her work as a translator and writer—as well as about their rather ugly divorce in 1930. We also know about his love affair with the sculptor Jula Cohn and about the affair with Asja Lacis. However, both the voyeuristic interest in Benjamin's private life and the designation of a separate category of *privatissima* are subverted by the fact that Benjamin dedicated his most important books to the women who helped shape the course of his life: To Dora Kellner he dedicated the *Origin of German Tragic Drama;* to Jula Cohn he dedicated the "Elective Affinities" essay, in which the social institution of marriage is an important theme; and to Asja Lacis, about whose influence on Benjamin with respect to his Marxist turn enough has been written, he dedicated *One Way Street*. That these dedications say something about his relationships to these women and are not merely concessions to convention, that Benjamin actually did not separate his "privata" from himself in the manner that

---

15. The literary scholar Ulrike Baureithel convincingly shows how the "dissolution of patriarchal values that resulted from war and inflation" influenced, as a "prime theme," the "dominant discourse" of literati during the Weimar period, especially that of the "Neue Sachlichkeit" movement. The contexts of these discussions were well known to Benjamin. To what extent they entered into his late writings would have to be examined case by case. Ulrike Baureithel, "Kollektivneurose moderner Männer. Die Neue Sachlichkeit als Symptom des männlichen Identitätsverlustes—sozialpsychologische Aspekte einer literarischen Strömung," *Germanica* 9 (1991): 123–43.

16. Hans Puttnies and Gary Smith, eds., *Benjaminiana: Eine biografische Recherche* (Giessen: Anabas Verlag, 1991).

might be suggested by the *Benjaminiana* volume, is evidenced by an excerpt from his 1931 diary:

> On the whole, however, the three great loves I have experienced shaped my life not only with respect to its course and its periodization but also with respect to the subject of this experience. I have gotten to know three different women during my life, and three different men within me. To write the story of my life would mean to portray the rise and fall of these three men, and the compromise among them.[17]

To make this life, with its many breaks, into something that could be experienced was one of the aims of the *Passagen-Werk*.

The love relationships with all three of these emancipated women failed. Benjamin would spend the following years alone and in exile. As a loner—a somewhat neglected, single man—as an intellectual, on the margin of society, he is not independent of women. He is offered help from his divorced wife, who runs a guest house in southern France during the war, and is also supported financially by the publisher Sylvia Beach and the poet Winifred Bryher, among others. Gisèle Freund—whose book on the history of photography Benjamin reviewed—was among his closest friends, as were the fashion critic Helen Grund and the librarian and author Adrienne Monnier. What tied Benjamin to these women was not only the support he received from them but also a lively intellectual exchange. In other words, he listened to them. The *Passagen-Werk* itself testifies to the fact that he took these women more seriously on an intellectual level than is typical of the conventional habits of the "genius." In the "convolute" he wrote under the heading "Fashion," we find several long excerpts from Helen Grund's essays about the essence of fashion; Adrienne Monnier, for whom Benjamin had translated a text into German, is also cited on several occasions. She is the source, too, of the noteworthy sentence, "Baudelaire's readers are men." Benjamin included it in the collection of aphorisms entitled "Central Park," along with the following sentences:

> Women are not fond of him. To the men he represents the depiction and transcendence of the lewd side [*côté ordurier*] of their libidinal

---

17. Cited in Rolf Tiedemann, Christoph Gödde, and Henri Lonitz, "Walter Benjamin 1892–1940," *Marbacher Magazin* 55 (1990): 145.

life [*Triebleben*]. If one goes further, Baudelaire's Passion reveals itself in this light as being for many of his readers a *rachat* [repurchasing, redemption, e.g., of annuity, atonement] of certain elements of their libidinal life.[18]

"Male impotence—the key figure of solitude"[19]

Under the heading "Central Park," in which Adrienne Monnier's remark appears, Benjamin collected the most important theoretical reflections that were to go into his Baudelaire book, "A Lyric Poet in the Era of High Capitalism," which was never finished. Some of these motifs recur in "The Paris of the Second Empire in Baudelaire," which was originally planned as the second part of the book. Of the first and third parts only the titles are known: "Baudelaire as Allegorist" and "The Commodity as Poetic Object." In "Central Park," there is strikingly frequent mention of "male impotence," of the "lesbian woman," of the whore, of the male drives, of images of women, of infertility, of the feeling that pregnancy is unfair competition, and of the "sacrifice of masculine sexuality."[20] Far from wanting to draw a personal psychogram of Baudelaire, Benjamin seeks to grasp the "historical index" and the "social grounds"[21] for this impotence.

The texts in which these theoretical fragments would have been developed more fully never materialized. Thus, concerning the question of how sexual difference plays into Benjamin's critique of modernity, we remain dependent on the interpretation and detailed reading of the fragments, commentaries, and quotations.

Let us begin with Baudelaire, whose "unique importance," as Benjamin writes in a letter, "consists in having been the first one, and the most unswerving, to have apprehended, in both senses of the word, the productive energy of the individual alienated from himself—agnosticized and heightened through concretization."[22] This he did in his person (and) as a poet. In

---

18. "Zentralpark," 673. "Central Park," 43–44. The parenthetical note after the word *rachat* is by the translator of "Central Park."
19. Ibid., 679/47.
20. Ibid., 670/40.
21. Ibid., 663–64/36–37.
22. Letter to Horkheimer dated April 16, 1938, cited in *GS* 1.3, 1074. English translation in *The Correspondence of Walter Benjamin, 1910–1940*, ed. Gershom Scholem and Theodor W. Adorno, trans. Manfred R. Jacobson and Evelyn M. Jacobson (Chicago and London: University of Chicago Press, 1994), 557.

his depiction, Benjamin suspends the distinction between Baudelaire the poet and Baudelaire the person. For the experience that Baudelaire, who after all turned poetry into a form of introspection, expresses in his poems is for Benjamin a "hollowing-out of the inner life."[23] What he demonstrates through Baudelaire is the "demontage" that modernity implements through the very "individual" that it had brought into being.

But of course Baudelaire is not a bourgeois individual in the usual sense: He has no family and no public life or life of commerce (*Geschäftsleben*). For him there is no essential division between private and public life. While "the bourgeoisie endeavored to compensate itself for the inconsequential nature of private life" by retreating "within its four walls,"[24] Baudelaire has no such place of refuge. While the private man "has no intention of extending his commercial (*geschäftlich*) considerations into social ones,"[25] since his private space, in which he represses both types of considerations, represents for him his universe, Baudelaire strives, in a movement that is at once modern and highly unmodern, to make the city into his "interior." In the space where people meet each other as businesspeople and where all those who are not businesspeople, who are without a private life in the true sense, become asocial, Baudelaire is on a futile search for refuge. He experiences solitude in the crowd. The very fact that he exposed himself to this and that he did not allow himself to be calmed by his wife in the sequestered *Gemütlichkeit* of home makes him for Benjamin the quintessential "modern hero." It makes him capable, through his person and in his poems, of "giving form to modernity." As a hero without an inner life, unneeded and solitary, Baudelaire plays the role of the portrayer of heroes and thereby produces nothing more than protest. And it is at this point that sexual difference, or rather its disappearance, comes into play as a paradigm for Benjamin's critique of modernity.

For Benjamin describes the "erosion of inner life" that is performed by Baudelaire as the gender-specific erosion of masculine inner life. The modern hero is no construct of thought; he is a gendered being, endowed with a modern libidinal life, a being with a perverse libidinal life, with the libidinal life of a fetishist. His needs correspond to, and give rise to, the modern "order of the sexes."[26] According to Benjamin, it is in fetishism that the

---

23. *Passagen-Werk, GS* 5.1, 440. *Arcades Project,* 348.
24. "Das Paris des Second Empire," 548. "The Paris of the Second Empire," 46.
25. "Paris, die Hauptstadt," *GS* 5.1, 52. "Paris, Capital," 154.
26. Cf. the title of the book by Claudia Honegger: *Die Ordnung der Geschlechter: Die Wissenschaften vom Menschen und das Weib* (Frankfurt/New York: Campus, 1991), 44.

socially prescribed (mis)relation between the sexes finds its adequate expression.

Woman appears in Benjamin's notes as a prostitute or as a masculinized woman; as a lesbian, a heroine of modernity, or a factory worker, who also has taken on masculine traits. Three things are especially conspicuous here: (1) that the housewife, wife, and mother, who was the subject of so many literary efforts in the eighteenth and early nineteenth centuries does not come up at all; (2) that throughout, Benjamin talks about the appearance or image of woman, but never of "woman" or "the feminine in and for itself"; and (3) that Benjamin makes practically no attempts, in his notes on Baudelaire, to make essential determinations about women—a practice that was particularly prevalent among his contemporaries.

Benjamin's disinterest in the primary role of women in bourgeois society—the role of housewife and mother—is probably tied to various factors. His disinterest in the real situation of the majority of women is certainly a decisive factor. Another reason lies in the fact that it is only recent feminist research—beginning in the 1970s and, more recently, that of Lieselotte Steinbrügge in particular—that pointed to the system-stabilizing function that was and is occupied by women as the "moral sex" (as Steinbrügge calls it).[27] A further important reason, however, is that it was Benjamin's approach to concentrate not on "normal" scenarios, but on prominent, extraordinary lives, in order to distill from them the scandal of the "normal."

The women encountered by Baudelaire in the public sphere of the city were the prostitute and the "masculinized" woman of letters. Of course, both prostitution and the assimilation to masculine norms, which was required of women of letters and female intellectuals as much as it was of female factory workers, were also the only means of escape that bourgeois industrial society held out to women outside of the family. There was neither a place nor a language for women to engage in self-reflection. As Claudia Honegger writes in her 1991 book *Die Ordnung der Geschlechter* (The order of the sexes), "The modern discourse of female self-reflection" no longer existed in the nineteenth century, or it existed only as a "murmuring which was naturally sequestered in a gender-segregated public sphere."[28] In careful textual analyses, Honegger shows how in 1800 medical anthropology put an abrupt end to this discourse of female self-reflection by simply

---

27. Cf. Lieselotte Steinbrügge, *Das moralische Geschlecht: Theorien und literarische Entwürfe über die Natur der Frau in der französischen Aufklärung* (Weinheim/Basel: Beltz, 1987).

28. Honegger, *Die Ordnung der Geschlechter*, 44.

deriving the supposedly gender-based deficiency of woman, her designation as mother and housewife, from physiology and thus objectively and scientifically legitimizing it: "From this point onward," Honegger concludes,

> all female self-reflection would be confronted with, and would have to contend with, these "laws of nature." These become a great epistemological barrier behind which many themes disappear for a long period, themes that in the great transitional phase before 1800 were still being discussed in a framework that was also one of social theory: couple-based individuation, cultural autonomy and intellectual self-realization, rational love, and the systematization of feminine morality.[29]

The nineteenth century thus becomes a time of a "disorder of the sexes" in which sexual difference is determined as a relation of complementarity, but in which difference as an experience is systematically excluded. In other words, in the construction of woman, the possible difference of woman is stifled by the determinations of a phallocratic discourse. As soon as she wants to raise her voice, woman is forced to speak in the language of man.

The leveling of sexual difference that takes place as part of this process becomes for Benjamin the paradigm of the loss of an experience of difference as such. Far from morally condemning, in a hypocritical manner, Baudelaire's predilection for prostitutes—according to Benjamin, it was only with a prostitute that Baudelaire was able to realize sexual communion—he declares it to be a key figure for the isolation of the modern human male, for the hollowing-out of modern man in the midst of his technologized world. The modern man is the fetishist man. He replaces woman with a dead object. According to Benjamin's reading, this is precisely what woman is for Baudelaire:

> Woman in Baudelaire: the most precious loot in the "Triumph of Allegory"—the life that means death. This quality belongs most unqualifiedly to the whore. It is the only thing which one may not bargain with her for, and for Baudelaire, this is all that counts.[30]

Baudelaire does not allow for difference; he kills woman by denying her otherness, by inundating her with meanings in order to "empathetically"

---

29. Ibid., 43.
30. "Zentralpark," 667; "Central Park," 39.

identify himself with (*sich einzufühlen*) that which alone remains as an other: death.

"What's the point of speaking of progress to a world sinking into rigor mortis."[31]

Baudelaire's fetishism is neither a purely private nor a purely sexual phenomenon. According to Benjamin's reading, it simply serves to express the figure of the banishment of difference that is characteristic of modernity as a whole. For in Baudelaire's fetishism, in the fetishism that Baudelaire as a poet introduced into lyric poetry, we find that the schema of the commodity fetish that Benjamin borrows from the Marxist analysis of capital and the linguistic schema of allegory are superimposed on one another. Thus the whore represents at once the "becoming-human of the commodity"[32] and allegory as such—that is, for the "life that means death."

Both the Marxist and the psychoanalytic concepts of fetishism refer to so-called "archaic fetishism":[33] the investment of an object with magical powers; by suspending the fact that this significance has been ascribed to the objects by humans, the object itself is treated as divine. Like the archaic fetish, the sexual fetish and the commodity fetish owe their existence to a concealment of how they came to be, or how they came to be produced. Accordingly, in sexual fetishism an object is sexually cathected; it then stands for that which woman does not have, the phallus. Real sexual desire, however, is only possible after one has abstracted from the fact that sexual cathexis has been produced by the fetishist himself. That is, for the fetishist the object itself has become the phallus and is no longer what it once was, a use object. For the shoe fetishist, the shoe no longer has anything to do with the object that a woman puts on in order not to get cold feet.

This is the very same mechanism that Marx has in mind when he speaks of the commodity fetish. The "commodity" is the product of the commodity-producing society. It is not just some random thing, that is, a use object,

---

31. "Was soll das, einer Welt, die in Totenstarre versinkt, von Fortschritt reden" (ibid., 682/50).
32. Ibid., 671/42.
33. On this point, and on what follows, see the helpful account given by Ulrich Erckenbrecht, *Das Geheimnis des Fetischismus: Grundmotive der Marxschen Erkenntniskritik* (Frankfurt and Cologne: Europäische Verlagsanstalt, 1976), esp. 69ff.

but it is a thing that has both use value and exchange value. That is, it is a thing with a certain price. The price, however, is the product of an abstraction. It presupposes that things that have nothing to do with each other—for example, a glass of beer and a pack of cigarettes—have been compared to, and made equivalent with, each other. Now the essential characteristic of capitalist, commodity-producing society is that it produces commodities not primarily because of their immediate use or use value but because of their exchange value. That is, commodities are produced for the market. It is more or less irrelevant what is produced. All that matters is that they be sold. A further essential quality of capitalism, one that is decisive for the commodity fetish in Marx's sense, is that the exchange value become independent of the use value. The price of the commodity is independent of the origin of the exchange value, that is, of the human labor that imbues a thing with value; it seems to belong to the commodity as a supersensible quality. And thus, as if touched by a magical power, products appear to us on the market, in the words of an advertising executive recently heard on Austrian television, as "personalities with their own character traits," in order to whisper to us: "Buy me."

All three forms of fetish owe their existence to the investment of a thing with a meaning; second, they are products of an abstraction in which the concrete thing itself, in its specific determination, is forgotten, is submerged, and disappears; and third, they function as true fetishes only when their origin, their becoming—that is, the process of abstraction to which they owe their existence—itself becomes obscured, when it too is subject to abstraction.

It is just this description—to return now to the *Passagen-Werk*—that applies also to the schema of allegory that Benjamin had already developed in his *Habilitation* thesis, *The Origin of German Tragic Drama*. Like the concept of fetishism for Marx, allegory for Benjamin serves as an epistemocritical category. An ambivalence inheres in both economic fetishism and allegory. Each presupposes a constant process of abstraction in order to exist and to function. Like Marx, Benjamin presupposes both the organization of society and the psychological and physical activity of individual subjects whose survival in organized capitalist society depends on their engaging in this self-destructive activity of abstraction. Unlike Marx, however, Benjamin does not count on progress and on the dynamic inherent in the social process.

Benjamin is concerned not only with the critique of capitalism but also with the critique of the idealistic self-image and self-understanding of humanity on which the Marxist critique of capitalism is based. This is connected with his deep skepticism about the revolutionary power that supposedly resides in the experience of labor, in the experience of the production process, and also with his critique of Marxism's understanding of nature. Both are expressed, for example, in a passage from a letter to Adorno dating from the year of Benjamin's death, in which he writes:

> But even if, in fact, what is at issue in the aura is a "forgotten human something," the issue is not necessarily what is actually present in work. The tree and the shrub, vouchsafed to people, are not made by them. Thus there must be something human about objects that is *not* bestowed by work. I would, however, like to leave it at that.[34]

Benjamin's skepticism about faith in technical progress is illustrated by a citation from a manuscript in which Benjamin noted the most detailed version of his plan for the Baudelaire book. It brings us back to allegory. The lyric poetry of Baudelaire, he writes, "stands at the place where the nature of things is overwhelmed and becomes transformed by human nature. Since then, history has shown that he was right not to rely on technological progress for this [transformation]."[35]

The overwhelming of nature of which Benjamin is speaking here presupposes a specific devaluation of the world of things that does not come into being with commodity-producing capitalism but that is its condition of possibility. Thus, while the Marxist theory of the commodity fetish makes it possible for Benjamin to situate the experience of the allegorist Baudelaire historically and socially, it does not go far enough for him as an epistemo-critical category, because it does not conceive of the sphere of experience broadly enough and does not even touch on the sphere of thought and language. But it is the latter that concerns Benjamin. And because the commodity fetish, like the sexual fetish, can only come about through the ascription of meanings and the process of abstraction, his critique, which he bases on allegorical intention, goes much deeper and is directed also at these. This critique reaches its highest point in the determination of what Benjamin calls the "de-souling" (*Entseelung*) of woman; in this it demonstrates the phallocraticism of modernity. For this is precisely what de-souling, or deper-

---

34. Letter to Adorno dated May 7, 1940, cited in *GS* 1.3, 1134. *The Correspondence of Walter Benjamin*, 629.
35. Manuscript cited in *GS* 1.3, 1152.

sonalization, is: the degradation of woman into a prostitute, who under capitalism represents at once the embodiment of the commodity and the becoming-human of allegory: "In the body that has been robbed of its soul [*im entseelten Leib*], which is nevertheless still available to desire, allegory and commodity are united."[36] The real woman, however, disappears by virtue of being transformed into a prostitute. Having been made into an object, she serves, just like a thing, as the bearer of abstract meanings that have been projected into her.[37]

It is not the case, however, that the destruction of woman passes men by without taking its toll. From a philosophical perspective, the only possible remaining experience in modernity is an empathy with meanings projected, in the abstract, onto a soulless (*entseelt*) world; or, as Benjamin writes in the Baudelaire book, "a kind of mimesis of death," such as "manifests itself a hundredfold in Baudelaire's writings."[38] It is a world without love and is, as Benjamin expresses so well, that "same historical night at the onset of which the owl of Minerva (with Hegel) begins its flight and Eros (with Baudelaire) lingers before the empty pallet, torch extinguished, dreaming of bygone embraces."[39]

"The world of the commodity resists its deceptive transformation through its distortion into allegory."[40]

But what of the "positive part" of Baudelaire's undertaking, which Benjamin, as he writes in his "modest methodological proposal," claims to have discerned in each negative, "obsolescent" branch? Benjamin distills this positive part from the ambivalence that inheres in allegory, and he illustrates it with reference to Baudelaire himself, to the person Baudelaire. The positive aspect of allegory is its destructive side. The latter prevents empathy with dead abstraction, which is something promoted by the commodity fetish as well as by sexual fetishism. Allegory is hostile to such empathy, for allegory

36. Ibid., 1151.
37. Christina von Braun speaks of the "disappearance of woman" in a similar sense in *Nichtich: Logik, Lüge, Libido* (Frankfurt/Main: Verlag Neue Kritik, 1985).
38. "Das Paris des Second Empire," *GS* 1.2, 587. "The Paris of the Second Empire," 83.
39. *Passagen-Werk, GS* 5.1, 439. *Arcades Project,* 347.
40. "Zentralpark," *GS* 1.2, 671. "Central Park," 42.

belongs to thinking—to bottomless and unrestrained thought. And in the end, allegory continually leads the allegorist into a situation of failure. The further the allegorist thinks—and the compulsive fixing of meanings compels him to do continually extend the reach of his thought—the closer he comes to an insight into the compulsiveness of what he does. The meanings that have been fixed become ever more arbitrary and devoid of content until they finally come to mean nothing at all. In allegorical thought, thinking is transformed into pensiveness; allegorical thought makes the allegorist into a melancholic.

In the schema of allegory, thought is never suspended, nor does an illusion of a harmonized whole invite one to empathetic enjoyment. The allegorist can never be comforted by any illusory certainty. Destruction is something he experiences on his own person. This is why it is not given to Baudelaire to give himself over to the *Gemütlichkeit* in which the "private man" of the nineteenth century has installed himself. But this also means that it is not given to him, as it is to the private man, to "[enjoy] his alienation from himself and the others."[41]

Baudelaire experiences modernity in his own person. But this also means that he cannot continue playing a man in a seemingly uninterrupted manner. For where there is no longer woman, man can no longer exist either. Where woman is forced into masculinization, there begins the "feminization" of man; in a certain sense, he begins to share her fate. This is evident in the case of Baudelaire on several levels. As a poet in the modern age, dependent on the market and forced to "claim the dignity of a poet in a society that no longer had any dignity to confer,"[42] Baudelaire experiences his affinity with the prostitute. He must sell himself. He protests against this, in that he adopts the feminine form of refusal, that is, with hysteria.[43] It is in the impotence, finally, of which Benjamin so often speaks, that Baudelaire performs this emasculation on his own body.

Baudelaire's heroism lies in his refusal or inability to participate in dreaming the dream of progress and to enjoy his own self-alienation, in his inability to pretend that nothing was going on. And it is even in this heroism that he comes to resemble the masculinized woman, as the "spiritualized"

---

41. "Paris, die Hauptstadt," *GS* 5.1, 50. "Paris, Capital," 152.
42. "Zentralpark," *GS* 1.2, 665. "Central Park," 38.
43. Christina von Braun interprets male hysteria as a form of "refusal to let the sexual being be destroyed." In this connection, she also interprets impotence as a symptom of male hysteria. von Braun, *Nichtich: Logik, Lüge, Libido*, 324ff.

(*vergeistigt*) woman who he makes into a lesbian and singles out as one of his "heroic ideals."[44]

Nevertheless, Benjamin himself pointed out that Baudelaire had no real interest in the real lesbian woman—indeed, that it would never have occurred to him to "to champion the lesbian woman publicly in his writings."[45] That he nevertheless chose her to be a "heroic ideal" is connected with what remains of sexual difference despite its leveling: the capacity of woman to bear children. Pregnancy, however, had to be experienced by Baudelaire, as Benjamin notices astutely and notes on several occasions, as "unfair competition." It is just this competition that Baudelaire eliminates with his conception of the lesbian heroine, thereby eliminating woman's final, corporeal difference.

The Voice of the Modern Woman

In the course of his studies of the nineteenth century, Benjamin came upon an unusual text that seems to have at once fascinated and troubled him. This text was written by a woman, the Saint-Simonian Claire Démar, and is entitled "Ma loi d'avenir" ("My Law of the Future").[46] It appeared in 1834, one year after Claire Démar's suicide, in the independent women's journal *Tribune des femmes*. In it, the author proposes a program of radical feminist social critique and a conception of a new female subjectivity to emerge in the framework of modernity.[47] Indeed, the "question of woman" was one of the central themes of Saint-Simonianism, and in a certain sense the discourse of "feminine self-reflection" experienced a further short renaissance in the 1830s. But none of the texts written by women can be

---

44. Cf. "Das Paris des Second Empire," *GS* 1.2, 594. "The Paris of the Second Empire," 90.

45. Ibid., 597/93.

46. Claire Démar, "Ma loi d'avenir," in *Claire Démar: Textes sur l'affranchissement des femmes (1832–33), suivi de Symbolique groupale et idéologie féministe saint-simoniennes*, ed. Valentin Pelosse (Paris: Payot, 1976); "My Law of the Future," in *Feminism, Socialism, and French Romanticism*, ed. Claire Goldberg Moses and Leslie Wahl Rabine (Bloomington: Indiana University Press, 1993), 178–203.

47. Cf. Astrid Deuber-Mankowsky, "Weibliches Interesse an Moral und Erkenntnis. Am Beispiel der Feministin und St.-Simonistin Claire Démar (circa 1800–1833)," in *Denken der Geschlechterdifferenz*, ed. Herta Nagl-Docekal and Herlinde Pauer-Studer (Vienna: Wiener Frauenverlag, 1990).

compared with the one by Claire Démar in terms of its radicalism. "In the widely ramified literature of the time which deals with the future of woman," it is, as Benjamin rightly remarks, "unique in its power and passion."[48]

In this text, Démar not only settles accounts, without any illusions, with the male law of bourgeois society, but also exposes the slave-like character that women have taken on in the course of their oppression. She demands not only the abolition of marriage, which she understands as a publicly sanctioned form of prostitution, but also demands the elimination of paternal law and the abolition of property. She passionately criticizes Christian morality and its hierarchization of spiritual and sensuous love. For what she envisions is the "free union of the sexes" in a love in which body and spirit come into their own, a love that is free and passionate and that is not subject to any legal regulation. "And it is for this reason," she writes, "that today we feel and demand the rehabilitation of stigmatized flesh, tortured for so many centuries under the Christian law that consecrated the unjust predominance of one principle over the other."[49]

Claire Démar is, however, sufficiently realistic to postulate, in addition to the mystery that she demands for the union of the sexes, the abolition of gender-specific division of labor. The mystery of love presupposes, she writes, that both partners be materially independent of one another. And thus she, who had after all so adamantly defended the rights of woman, arrives, logically and in near-despair, at the conclusion that equal rights in the modern age are only attainable if all difference is eliminated, and provided that the individuals subject themselves to a public functionalization and streamlining:

> And so:
> No more paternity, always doubtful and impossible to prove.
> No more property, no more inheritance.
> Classification according to ability, compensation according to work.
> Consequently:
> No more maternity, no more law of blood.
> I say no more maternity:
> Indeed, once woman is delivered and emancipated from the yoke

---

48. "Das Paris des Second Empire," *GS* 1.2, 594. "The Paris of the Second Empire," 91.
49. Démar, "Ma loi d'avenir," 74; "My Law of the Future," 188.

of tutelage and protection of man, . . . once man no longer pays her the price of her body, then woman's existence and social position will derive only from her own ability and her own works.

For that to happen, the woman must create a work and fulfill a function.—And how could she, if she is always condemned to spend a more or less long period of her life attending to the upbringing of one or more children? Either the work will be neglected and poorly done or the child will be badly brought up and deprived of the care his weakness and lengthy period of development demand.

You want to liberate *woman!* Well then, bring the newborn from the bosom of the *blood mother* to the arms of the *social mother,* the *professional nurse,* and the child will be better raised. . . .

Then and only then will man, woman, and child all be liberated from the law of blood and from exploitation of humanity by humanity![50]

Claire Démar's vision of the future shows in sharp contours what the emancipatory potential of modern women, men, and children holds in store: a fully rationalized society in which the value of the individual is determined exclusively by his or her function in the whole—where the contours of this "whole" themselves become ever more blurred and the individuals become ever more empty.

Benjamin cites the conclusion of Démar's manifesto in "The Paris of the Second Empire in Baudelaire." "Here," he comments, "the image of the heroic woman which Baudelaire absorbed may be seen in its original version."[51] The heroism of Claire Démar consists in her engagement for mystical love and her tragic failure in relation to reality. Her "free woman" is a construct; she is the counterpart of the modern man embodied in Baudelaire, and her fate is comparable to his. The experience of love, which is what Démar was emphatically concerned with, is not given to either of them. For what underlies Baudelaire's ideal of androgyny is the figure of empathy. Thus, the heroine, like the hero, turns out to be an available role in the tragedy and masquerade of modernity. "The virtuoso of empathy," writes Benjamin at one point, "really does not go out of himself. His highest

---

50. Ibid., 93–94/202.
51. "Das Paris des Second Empire," *GS* 1.2, 595. "The Paris of the Second Empire," 91.

achievement consists in having made his own I so empty, so free of all the ballast of personhood, that he feels at home in every mask."[52]

The virtuoso of empathy thus reproduces on the level of the relation between the sexes the empathy for the commodity, which whispers its "Buy me" to the consumer, as well as the empathy of the prostitute for her client, whose every wish she promises to fulfill. In the same way, modern man empathizes with the feminine ideal that he has brought into being. Empathy is the exact opposite of the experience of love. Love presupposes the experience, the recognition, and the bearing of difference and the experience of the other in his or her own being. It is fulfilled in the lovers' drawing nearer to each other by becoming similar to one another, but never in their empathy for one another.[53]

The "Teaching" of Claire Démar

In the *Passagen-Werk*, under the heading "Anthropological Materialism," Benjamin copied several passages from Claire Démar's manifesto. He terms her expositions a "teaching," evidence for his regard for her. He defends her against the "reaction of the established bourgeoisie," against its contempt,[54] and he remarks in at least three places in his notes that anthropological materialism must be incorporated into dialectical materialism.

What probably fascinated Benjamin about Claire Démar is her plea for the rehabilitation of sensuousness, her critique of the hypostasis of spirit by Christianity, and her radical defense of the mystery of love in the free meeting of the sexes. And although it was defeated by modernity, Démar's true "teaching" consists in its having shown the necessity of writing against the limits of modernity and in having thereby demonstrated the necessity of feminine self-reflection.

Benjamin refrained from fixing a feminine essence. He was certainly no

---

52. Manuscript cited in *GS* 1.3, 1179.
53. In this connection it is necessary to consider the concept of "mimesis" (though to do so here would exceed the scope of this paper). See, for example, the following from a diary entry by Benjamin: "It became clear to me that I changed radically every time a great love gained power over me. This is because of the fact that a true love affair makes me similar to the woman I love." Cited in Brodersen, *Spinne im eigenen Netz*, 188; *Walter Benjamin: A Biography*, 172.
54. Cf. *Passagen-Werk*, *GS* 5.2, 973ff. *Arcades Project*, 809ff.

feminist, nor did he work toward equal rights for women. But in his late writings, in his notes and commentaries, he demonstrated that a thought that allies itself with experience cannot get around thematizing sexual difference. And such a thematization must reflect upon the sexuality of the one who philosophizes in a form that—when it is read somewhat against the grain—reveals the beginnings of a thought that makes room in itself for an openness to the sameness and otherness of the other sex.

This seems to me to be a good argument in favor of Benjamin's "modest methodological proposal," which perhaps also includes a few points of departure for a feminist-oriented philosophy.

A LEGACY OF THE ENLIGHTENMENT
Imagination and the Reality of the "Maternal" in Max Horkheimer's Writings

Mechthild Rumpf

Translated by Melanie Richter-Bernburg

> A child always has a right to absolute happiness with respect to its mother.
> —Max Horkheimer (1939)

The image of the good mother is an archaic fantasy that, although it was not first dreamed up during the Enlightenment, was given well-defined form during that period. A mother's love was accorded great importance for the development of the child even if the various norms and expectations did not produce a uniform image. The two poles in the discussion of the maternal ideal are reasoned, measured love on the one hand, and immediate feeling on the other.

This essay originally appeared under the title "Ein Erbe der Aufklärung: Imaginationen des 'Mütterlichen' in Max Horkheimers Schriften," in *Feministische Studien: "Zwischen Tugend und Affären"* (Weinheim: Deutscher Studien Verlag Weinheim, 1989), 55–68.

The definition of the role of the mother and its ideological elevation was linked to the nonrecognition of the female subject, the binding of woman to her being as mother. Through her domestic agency, she was to represent that moral, loving power that was, to be sure, regarded as the "other" in relation to reason but that could be subsumed and controlled in the name of a "reasoned community" and in the interest of "humane" male individuality.

We still know little about the real mothers of the Enlightenment. But there are, for instance, reports of the gleam in Kant's eye when he spoke of his mother.[1] And he is reported to have said that he owed his morality and his striving for knowledge to her: "I will never forget my mother, for she planted and nourished the first seed of the Good in me, she opened my heart to the impressions of nature; she awakened and expanded my concepts, and her teachings have had a lasting, healthy influence on my life."[2]

The critical theory of Adorno and Horkheimer resorts to the history of the Enlightenment in two ways. It formulates the critique of subjective, theoretical, and practical reason as well as the critique of social conditions and relationships. The analyses themselves are based on an idea of reason that Horkheimer calls the *concept of reason*.[3] Marxist theory represents a point of reference for the anticipation of a reasoned society from which the ideological veil of all previous systems of "objective reason" has vanished. Marxist ideas fade in Horkheimer's critical theory, but they can still be identified in their frequently encoded form.

Specific concepts of reason are fundamental to our search for the conscious and unconscious motives of Enlightenment philosophers assigning a specific place to the "feminine." What was expected of a woman was love and attention to the concrete subjectivity of others, qualities that no state—no matter how perfect—and no society could guarantee. I believe that this has always been known but that it has seldom been understood as an aspect of "male identity." The nonrecognition of such subjective potential and such orientations for action has determined the history of male self-understanding.

This is where my particular interest in the critical theory of Adorno and

---

1. Hartmut Böhme and Gernot Böhme, *Das Andere der Vernunft: Zur Entwicklung von Rationalitätsstrukturen am Beispiel Kants* (Frankfurt am Main, 1983), 485.
2. Ibid.
3. Max Horkheimer, "Zum Begriff der Vernunft" (The concept of reason) (1952), in *Gesammelte Schriften* (Frankfurt am Main, 1985), 7:34.

Horkheimer begins.[4] In what follows I examine the significance of the difference between the sexes in the context of an "Enlightenment that has begun to reflect on itself." I concentrate on a few of Horkheimer's writings because they cling to a specific legacy of the Enlightenment, that is, to the maternal as the sole task of women. I demonstrate the importance of the "maternal"—its psychological representation in the subject—for Horkheimer, the imagination and the idea of reality expressed in his thought. I pursue the question of whether Horkheimer's critique of reason in the interest of a liberated humankind remains bound to a strictly male perspective and thus reproduces, or even exceeds, the gender metaphysics of the Enlightenment or whether, in his radical critique of reason, the indispensability of "undamaged" maternal love is given a new basis in the division of labor between the sexes.

The first task is to clarify the perspective that is tied to the memory of a possible objective content of reason (which is what is meant by "the concept of reason"). Horkheimer does not formulate a starting point for reestablishing a concept of objective reason; rather, he formulates a critique of reason and of social reality. "Social theory . . . was the heir to the older systems of thought," he writes in his *Eclipse of Reason* (1947), and the task of philosophy is self-critique. What must be analyzed is the chasm between subjective and objective reason, how it is "perpetuated . . . by all the doctrines that tend to triumph ideologically over philosophical antinomy in an antinomic world."[5] Philosophy cannot eliminate or reconcile this "chasm"; it can only illuminate the source. For Horkheimer, it is decisive to think in terms of practices that change society, even if he can no longer identify an identical,

---

4. The following discussion is part of a broader examination that I can only outline here; see Mechthild Rumpf, *Spuren des Mütterlichen: Die widersprüchliche Bedeutung der "Mutterrolle" für die männliche Identitätsbildung in Kritischer Theorie und feministischer Wissenschaft* (Traces of the maternal: The contradictory meaning of the "mother's role" for the constitution of male identity in critical theory and feminist scholarship) (Frankfurt am Main, 1989), chap. 1, "Mystische Aura." See also idem, "Das 'moralische Gefühl': Zur Frage der Aktualität von Max Horkheimers Moralkritik" (The "moral sentiment": On the question of the actuality of Max Horkheimer's critique of morals), in *Zwielicht der Vernunft: Die Dialektik der Aufklärung aus der Sicht von Frauen* (The ambiguity of reason: The dialectic of the Enlightenment from the point of view of women), ed. Christine Kulke and Elvira Scheich (Pfaffenweiler, 1992), and idem, " 'Mystical Aura': Imagination and the Reality of the 'Maternal' in Horkheimer's Writings," in *On Max Horkheimer: New Perspectives*, ed. Seyla Benhabib, Wolfgang Bonß, and John McCole (Cambridge, Mass., 1993).

5. Max Horkheimer, *Eclipse of Reason* (New York, 1947), 146, 175, and 182. (Translated into German and cited in the original version of this essay from *Zur Kritik der instrumentellen Vernunft* [Frankfurt am Main, 1985], 139, 163–64, 170.)

emancipatory subject, a class subject, since fascism: "The conscious or unconscious motive that inspired the formulation of the systems of objective reason was the realization of the impotence of subjective reason with regard to its own goal of self-preservation. These metaphysical systems express in partly mythological form the insight that self-preservation can be achieved only in a supra-individual order, that is to say, through social solidarity."[6]

Horkheimer reflects systematically on only *one* central condition of "metaphysical systems": the powerlessness of the subjective reason of the male, the economic subject within bourgeois society. But that is only one side of self-preservation. In his critique, Horkheimer excludes the fact that in history to this point, the male subject has been just as dependent on the "private" side of self-preservation, on the satisfaction of his psychological and physical needs, on the creation and renewal of his potential for work. When Horkheimer formulates "respect for individual life"[7] as one goal of society, he assumes a life that has always been guaranteed by the care and love of the woman.

The motherliness of women and the devotion of a wife remain the unspoken basis of bourgeois society as well as of its possible transformation into "social solidarity" of male subjects. From a feminist perspective, this concept of reason is open to criticism because it is conceived only from the perspective of the male subject.[8] An asymmetrical relationship between the sexes is tacitly assumed; with regard to a "reasoned society," the family as women's sphere of action appears to be indispensable.

On another, *subject-related level,* the significance of the maternal love of the woman becomes a more subtle but also a more open topic of discussion. This is the level on which Horkheimer discusses the dimensions of experience on which the possibility of objective reason can still be based in order to pave the way for an end to the destructive power of merely subjective reason. Maternal love takes on great importance for Horkheimer in this context. In his essay "The Concept of Man" (1957), for example, he develops the following idea:

> Maternal love does not consist simply in feeling or even in attitude; it must also express itself properly. The well-being of the little child

---

6. Ibid., 175 (164).
7. Ibid.
8. See, for example, Horkheimer's critique of Hegel in "Autorität und Familie" (1936), in *Traditionelle und kritische Theorie* (Traditional and critical theory) (Frankfurt am Main, 1970) ("Authority and the Family," trans. Matthew J. O'Connell in *Critical Theory* [New York, 1972]); and see note 5 above.

and the trust he has in people and objects around him depend very largely on the peaceful but dynamic friendliness, warmth, and smile of the mother or her substitute. Coldness and indifference, abrupt gestures, restlessness and displeasure in the one who attends the child can *introduce a permanent distortion into his relationship to objects, men, and the world, and produce a cold character that is lacking in spontaneous impulses.* This was recognized, of course, as far back as Rousseau's *Emile* and John Locke, and even earlier. Only today, however, are people beginning to grasp the factors involved in the connection of which we are speaking. It does not take a sociologist to recognize that a mother who is pressed by other cares and occupations has a different effect than the one she wants.[9] (my emphasis)

The interaction between mother and child is understood by Horkheimer as a practice that creates meaning prior to all language, as the constitution of a potential for experience and for a libidinous relationship to the self and to the world. Memories of mimetic relations to people and to things that precede a conscious subject-object division and the delimitation of ego structures are associated with the maternal. It is not identity, distance, and domination that mark the source of the human in these positions but nearness and solidarity, love and play.

The "maternal" does not become the absolute "other" of reason but stands in contrast to the *instrumental half of reason.* It appears as the metaphoric expression of a philosophical thought that contains the utopia of intact intersubjectivity. This thought recalls a concept of reason based on the idea of noninstrumental relations, recognition of the other, morality, the right to happiness, and enlarged freedom—reconciled with the concept of a "self-sustaining" individual.

The thesis of the importance of maternal love is contradicted by the figures of thought in *Dialectic of Enlightenment* (1947). There the self-destruction of reason through forms of internal and external domination of nature, and the elimination of "meaning" in the legacy of magic and myth, leave behind not a trace of the uniquely maternal in the subject. The male ego is

---

9. Max Horkheimer, "Zum Begriff des Menschen" (1957), in *Gesammelte Schriften,* 7:60 ("The Concept of Man," trans. Matthew J. O'Connell in *Critique of Instrumental Reason* [New York, 1974], 8). See also idem, "Der Mensch in der Wandlung seit der Jahrhundertwende" (The change in mankind since the turn of the century) (1960), and idem, "Bedrohungen der Freiheit" (Threats to freedom) (1965), both in *Gesammelte Schriften,* vol. 8.

identical only with itself, and society demands the denial of "tender family ties." Insofar as Horkheimer does not reflect this "result" in the context of a foiled, mutual recognition in the relation of the sexes, he holds, in paradoxical fashion, to the utopia of the maternal as "prehistoric"—as a principle of "social criticism" ("Authority and the Family," 1936)—and remains bound to the division of labor between the sexes.

The Image of the Mother Loses Its "Mystical Aura"

This raises the question of how the "maternal" in Horkheimer can take on special meaning when, through the historical-philosophical perspective, only the destruction of the memory of one's own origins is confirmed.[10] The sociopsychological view of the biographical development of male subjects marks the point of departure in Horkheimer's thought from which he hopes to break through the historical-philosophical isolation of *Dialectic of the Enlightenment,* drawing perhaps on the following statement in the text:

> Men had to do fearful things to themselves before the self, the identical, purposive, and virile nature of man, was formed, and something of that recurs in every childhood.... Man's domination over himself, which grounds his selfhood, is almost always the destruction of the subject in whose service it is undertaken; for the substance which is dominated, suppressed, and dissolved by virtue of self-preservation is none other than that very life as functions of

---

10. "Indeed, it was necessary that reason free itself and become independent from objective moments in order to escape the blind force of nature and in order to dominate nature to the degree that, today, admittedly gives us a feeling of horror. Reason did not become aware of this liberation as a necessary yet at the same time seeming liberation. It threw together mythology and superstition along with everything that cannot be reduced to the limited subjective spirit. It was not in what reason can accomplish but in its *self-enthronement* that misfortune lay, that brought with it self-destruction. Subjective reason once refused, with the hybris that is inherent in all blindness, to admit that it does not owe its independent existence to itself but to a large degree to the division of labor, to the process of the conflict between man and nature. The more deliberately it denies this, the more emphatically it must present itself to itself and others as an absolute being, finally to ban itself ... as a qualitas occulta to the realm of spectres" (Horkheimer, "Zum Begriff der Vernunft," 33ff.).

which the achievements of self-preservation find their sole definition and determination: it is, in fact, what is to be preserved.[11]

It is this "something" that leaves open the possibility of redefining the relationship between phylogenesis and ontogenesis. Within the process of the constitution of the male subject, Horkheimer sees a chance that the legacy of the Enlightenment, the "identical, purposive character" and self-limitation of reason, will not repeat themselves blindly. This constitutive process is absorbed into Horkheimer's concept of culture.

Corresponding to the concept of reason is a *concept of culture*[12] that is not "something for special occasions" or merely "edifying." For Horkheimer, culture maintains its claim to truth as long as it is able to articulate itself as a thorn in the side of false generality. In 1952 this diagnosis sounded gloomy—it was directed against the existing culture industry and against conservative attempts to turn culture into a "corrective" against economic-technical reason. Adorno in particular was unyielding in the face of regressive tendencies in which Goethe and classical music, for example, were regarded by the fascists as a neutralized cultural asset. The memory of this incomprehensible time must be taken into consideration in order to understand the following analysis: "The splitting off and neutralization of culture is no help against the destructive work of subjective reason. What is important is not to overcome the contrast between subjective and objective reason by deciding in favor of an alternative, or from the outside by ameliorating the contrasts or hypostatizing ideas but by immersion in the contradictory matter itself."[13]

It is not immediately clear from this formulation that culture includes the family. Since "Authority and the Family" (1936), Horkheimer had seen family structures and processes as part of the cultural sphere, with a "definite, even if relative life of their own."[14] With regard to the classical era of the bourgeoisie, the result was a moment of resistance to the mere rationality of means and ends.

After fascism, Horkheimer had to redefine the origins and place of the powers that could oppose the functionalization of reason and the coldness

---

11. Max Horkheimer and Theodor W. Adorno, *Dialektik der Aufklärung* (1947) (Frankfurt am Main, 1971), 33, 51 (*Dialectic of Enlightenment,* trans. John Cumming [New York, 1982], 33, 54–55).
12. See Horkheimer, "Zum Begriff der Vernunft," 32.
13. Ibid., 33.
14. "Authority and the Family," 59 (172).

of individual life and of society as a whole. The collective and subjective experience is not absorbed in the merely identical ego of reason:

> Subterraneously, without one's own knowledge, something of that power still exists. Otherwise all happiness would succumb to the dividing powers of subjectivity. What makes life worth living at all in this late, present day draws on the warmth that is inherent in any desire, any love of a thing: happiness itself has archaic features, and the *logical consistency with which they are eliminated* brings with it unhappiness and the emptiness of the soul. In pleasure at a garden, there still trembles that cultic element that gardens had when they belonged to the gods and were cultivated for them. If those ties are once severed, there may remain an after-image of that pleasure and that happiness, but its inner life will be extinguished.... The aesthetic receptivity of the human being has its prehistory in idolatry: belief in the goodness or sanctity of a thing necessarily precedes, historically, the pleasure in its beauty. The case is similar for such a decisive category as that of human dignity.... The subterranean relationship to a not quite forgotten experience, to a deeply ingrained insight, which does not satisfy the statistical criterion yet retains its claim to truth, still gives such ideas, which define our civilization, life and legitimacy.[15] (my emphasis)

Horkheimer speaks of the "logical consistency" with which the "archaic features" of happiness are eliminated. Here he names no subject that brings this about, but a hint is already contained in the image of maternal love sketched in "The Concept of Man" (1956).[16] For Horkheimer, where the "principle of equality" penetrates the family, the contrast between cultural and social spheres vanishes.[17] Through the pursuit of a career and the turning of "mother's love" into a science, a woman would become equal to a man only in a negative sense; her thoughts would be reified, and her maternal abilities would disappear. The argument concerning the loss of maternal love, which Horkheimer had formulated in "Authority and the Family" in 1936, is actualized in a particularly impressive way in "Authoritarianism and the Family" (1949):

---

15. "Zum Begriff der Vernunft," 32.
16. See quotation above on page 307.
17. See the discussion in the section that follows.

Her whole attitude toward the child becomes rational; even love is administered as an ingredient of pedagogical hygiene. . . . The spontaneity of the mother and her natural, unlimited protectiveness and warmth tend to be dissolved. Therefore, the image of the mother in the minds of children sheds its *mystical aura*. . . . Women have paid for their limited admission into the economic world of the male by taking over the behavior patterns of a thoroughly reified society. The consequences reach into the most tender relations between mother and child. She ceases to be a mitigating intermediary between him and cold reality and becomes just another mouthpiece for the latter. Formerly she endowed the child with a feeling of security which allowed him to develop a certain *independence*. He felt his love for his mother reciprocated and somehow lived on this emotional fund throughout his life. The mother, cut off from the community of the males and despite an unjustified idealization being herself forced into a dependent situation, *represented a principle other than reality;* she could sincerely dream the dreams of utopia with the child, and she was his natural ally whether she wished it or not. Thus there was a force in his life which allowed him to develop his own *individuality* concomitantly with his adjustment to the external world. Together with the fact that decisive authority in the house was represented by the father and therefore asserted itself, at least to a minimum, through an intellectual interaction, the role of the mother prevented the adjustment from happening too suddenly and totally and at the expense of individuation. Today, since the child does not experience the mother's unrestricted love, his own capacity for love remains undeveloped.[18] (my emphasis)

The destructive power of subjective, formalized, and instrumental reason now includes the last residue of experience on which Horkheimer's concept of reason could draw for support. With this interpretation, the "maternal" would lose its importance as a resistant force; now it would be the mothers who brought to an end the dialectic of the Enlightenment in the ontogenetic

---

18. Max Horkheimer, "Authoritarianism and the Family," in *The Family: Its Function and Destiny*, ed. Ruth Nanda Anshen (New York, 1949), 389. (Translated into German as "Autorität und Familie in der Gegenwart" and cited in the original version of this essay from *Zur Kritik der instrumentellen Vernunft*, 277ff.).

process and who irrevocably fixed the most sinister of results—hopelessness of any change.

But this view, which would come close to being a prognosis for the neutralization of culture, is contradicted by Horkheimer himself. I will turn to this in the following discussion, in which I reconstruct Horkheimer's argumentation in the context of "Authority and the Family."

The "Maternal" as the Social Principle in Prehistory

With the studies for "Authority and the Family," a sociopsychological perspective was opened up in 1936 that was to encompass the intrapsychic dynamics of the dominated. The main starting point for the analysis of the relationship between culture and society and the mediating functions of the family is that the coercion exercised by material conditions on the single individual has been partly "internalized" in the historical process and that the dominated are thus fixed in their roles. Horkheimer understands the historical process of internalization of external force not only under the aspect of affirmation but also as a dialectic of accommodation and possible resistance. Using the example of morality and romantic love, he shows that social development was, at the same time, the condition for breaking with society. The institutions of culture thus acquired—here he was interested above all in marriage and family—a "definite even if relative life of their own."[19] In the diagnosis of the present in 1936, this "life of their own" appears to be at a standstill:

> Bourgeois thought begins as a struggle against the authority of tradition and replaces it with reason as the legitimate source of right and truth. It ends with the deification of naked authority as such (a conception no less empty of determinate content than the concept of reason), since justice, happiness, and freedom for mankind have been eliminated as historically possible solutions. . . . The fullest possible adaptation of the subject to the reified authority of the economy is the form which reason really takes in bourgeois society. ("Authority and the Family," 72, 83 [184])

19. Horkheimer, "Authoritarianism and the Family," 59 (Autorität und Familie," 172).

Horkheimer already sees a change in the origins of the bourgeois struggle against traditional authority: the particularity of reason finds expression in the postulates of duty and obedience in Protestantism and in the abstract philosophical concept of the individual, even as it dissolves in reality in light of the class structure of developing bourgeois society and the seemingly rational authority of the "free contract." It is decisive for Horkheimer that the structural change in authority in the family and society leads to a strengthening of domination and subjection, while it is robbed of its possibly intersubjective dynamic, the possibility of dissolution: "In the consciousness of the present age, authority is not even a relationship but an inalienable property of the superior being, a qualitative difference" (103 [210]).

Blind obedience in the face of the anonymity of social structures and reified authority is no longer an act that is forced upon one from the outside but is now the unconscious reaction of the single individual: "The family, as one of the most important formative agencies, sees to it that the kind of human character emerges which social life requires, and gives this human being in great measure the indispensable adaptability for a specific authority-oriented conduct on which the existence of the bourgeois order largely depends" (98 [206]).

Horkheimer sees in the function of the father in constituting the (male) child the same contradiction of the bourgeois idea of emancipation that led to the perpetuation of the "naked authority as such." The bourgeois idea of education rejected blind obedience and instead called for the use of reason, which was understood as insight into the reality and necessity of subjection. At the same time, however, in the authority of the father, it perpetuated an order willed by God. The psychological, legal, moral, and economic strength of the father appears to the child to be a position granted by nature. Thus, the "structure of authority as it exist[s] outside the family" is "anticipated in large measure.... To recognize facts means to accept them" (100–101 [208]).

For the present, Horkheimer formulates the exclusively negative side of this principle: people are no longer taught "to look for the reasons of things"; they tend, in masochistic fashion, to "surrender [their] will to any leader whatsoever" (110 [215]). Since paternal authority in its irrational features now comes to the fore against a background of impenetrable social conditions, the *virtual behavior of the father (coercion/mildness)* no longer has any importance, for the "drive to submission" is created more essentially by the structure of the family itself than by the "conscious intentions and methods of the father" (111 [216]). That the family stands in an "antagonistic" relationship to society is explained by Horkheimer here through "sexual love and especially . . . maternal care" (114 [219]), while all humane features are eradicated in the figure of the father.

If, in the history of bourgeois thought, the metaphysics of gender legitimized the exclusion of the woman from certain cultural and social spheres of action, in Horkheimer the exclusion becomes the basis for a difference between the sexes that can be formulated as a critique of society. Even though he recognizes the reification of the woman as a "sex object" and "domestic servant," he assumes that she *not only* "acts" [*wirke*] in this function, but that she acts as a person (as does a man!) in the family (114ff. [219ff.]):

> [C]ivic life . . . always had an essentially negative character. . . . But common concerns took a positive form in sexual love and especially in maternal care. The growth and happiness of the other are willed in such unions. A felt opposition therefore arises between them and hostile reality outside. To this extent, the family not only educates for authority in bourgeois society; it also cultivates the dream of a better condition for mankind. In the yearning of many adults for the paradise of their childhood, *in the way a mother can speak of her son* even though he has come into conflict with the world, *in the protective love of a wife for her husband,* there are ideas and forces at work which admittedly are not dependent on the existence of the family in its present form and, in fact, are even in danger of shriveling up in such a milieu, but which, nevertheless, in the bourgeois system of life rarely have any place but the family where they can survive at all. (114 [219], emphasis mine)

Yet there is still the question of the source of the "ideas and forces" that are alive in maternal care and love for a husband, in spite of all reification. Horkheimer draws closer to a new explanatory context that does not point to the nature of woman or the being of the female: "To the extent that any principle besides that of subordination prevails in the modern family, the woman's maternal and sisterly love is keeping alive a social principle dating from before historical antiquity, a principle which Hegel conceives 'as the law of the ancient gods, the gods of the underworld,' that is, of prehistory."[20]

20. Ibid., 118 (222). I have discussed this idea in greater detail in *Spuren des Mütterlichen*, chap. 3.

The social principle preserved in maternal love is phylogenetically older than all conscious human laws: it is a mythic legacy—embodied for Hegel in the figure of Antigone—but one that cannot maintain itself by its own strength. The authority of the husband and the subordination of the wife and children is, to be sure, an objective law; but in the love of the wife and mother, it is, as it were, transcended: the wife is an object, but by breaking through this status and giving more love than she can expect in return, and thus by implicitly criticizing bourgeois society's abstract principle of exchange, she places her actions in a relationship antagonistic to the existing order. She thinks of her son, through whom the intimation of a better society is to be preserved—or will he only be reminded of this idea later on in the protective love of his wife?

Horkheimer's thesis that in her love a mother represents a social principle of prehistory touches on the question of the "sublation" of the myth. Horkheimer writes later, in 1945, that "in the true enlightenment, that which is identical with philosophy, mythology will not be shouted down. Its power will be appeased."[21] We can add here, in relation to this idea, that in the process of constituting male subjectivity, this "female," prehistoric power is rather "shouted down" than "appeased."

In his discussion of Antigone in "Authority and the Family," Horkheimer attempts to clarify two issues—the source of the "moment of *individual selfhood*, recognizing and being recognized" as a social principle, and its fading into history, phylogenetically and ontogenetically. Antigone's suicide and her last words in Sophocles' tragedy—"If this seems good to the gods, / Suffering, we may be made to know our error"[22]—are interpreted by Horkheimer as depriving myth of its power. He writes: "When she thus renounces all opposition, she simultaneously accepts the principle of male-dominated bourgeois society: bad luck is your own fault."[23]

The antagonistic moment, which is supposed to be contained in the love of woman as a prehistoric social principle, can be conceived of only as conscious resistance. This is the point of Horkheimer's conclusion, which he tries to link with the fading of this resistance in modern history in the last part of "Authority and the Family" and in later texts.[24]

---

21. Max Horkheimer, "Verstreute Aufzeichnungen, 1940–1949" (Scattered notes, 1940–1949), in *Gesammelte Schriften*, 12:301.
22. Cited in Horkheimer, "Authoritarianism and the Family," 117 (225).
23. Ibid., 121 (220).
24. Ibid. See also *Dialectic of Enlightenment*, "Juliette" discussion and "Mensch und Tier."

However, instead of asking in what way the "prehistoric social principle" can fall, intrapsychically, under the authority of patriarchal law, Horkheimer seeks the conditions under which the problematic male character comes into being through the change in "maternal practice," in which—as a result of the "dependency" of woman—there is immediate expression of the "influence of a mind dedicated to the prevailing order of things."[25] Nevertheless, the thesis of the "accommodation" or "subordination" of woman does not provide a basis for statements about the *concrete* expression of maternal behavior. Horkheimer's construction of an immediate connection between the "dominant spirit" and damaged maternal love leads logically for him to a fading of the utopian dimension and the resistant moment in the male subject.

Horkheimer develops a second type of argumentation in an analysis of the Oedipus conflict, through the "dissolution" of which the "devaluation of purely sensuous pleasure" is defeated. Above all, "every sensuous element must be strictly banned from the son's tenderness for his mother":

> Under the pressure of such a family situation the individual does not learn to understand and respect his mother in her concrete existence, that is, as this particular social and sexual being. Consequently he is not only educated to repress his socially harmful impulses . . . but, because this education takes the problematic form of camouflaging reality, the individual also loses for good the disposition of part of his psychic energies. ("Authority and the Family," 121 [224])

Here, Horkheimer formulates a clear connection between the suppression of drives and the nonrecognition of the woman in the process of constituting the male subject. Precisely because he does not only understand the mother as the object of the son's drives, he nears the reproduction of male identity in one aspect. That identity must develop by setting itself off from the mother and from previous experience because the father imago becomes increasingly abstract and because it is the irrational male authority that represents socially dominant principles. Such an interpretation would not problematize the Oedipal conflict as such, but only its asymmetrical structure and repressive form, the culturally specific different valuation of masculinity and femininity, of maternal and patriarchal practice. The Oedipal problem-

---

25. "Authoritarianism and the Family," 120 (224).

atic does not lead to a prejudgment of the asymmetrical relationship of the sexes; but as a product of previous history and culture, this is what gives the Oedipal event its specific symbolic import and the ego its reduced functions: "The forced separation, expressly represented by the woman and especially by the father, of idealistic dedication and sexual desire, tender mindfulness and simple self-interest, heavenly interiority and earthly passion forms one psychic root of an existence rent by contradictions."[26]

The outcome of the Oedipal phase as sketched here reproduces the separation of reason and sensuousness and the damaging of both areas: "Reason and joy in its exercise are restricted; the suppressed inclination towards the mother reappears as a fanciful and sentimental susceptibility to all symbols of the dark, maternal, and protective powers. Because the woman bows to the law of the patriarchal family, she becomes an instrument for maintaining authority in this society."[27] Horkheimer does not explain how the mother controls the Oedipus conflict by making a taboo of sexuality, or how she bows to the law of the patriarchal family.[28] But in this way he negates the explosiveness of his thesis that with the male, repressive form of the Oedipus conflict, suppression of drives, nonrecognition of the woman, and becoming unconscious of the legacy of the mother are related. This unpleasant, almost unconscious insight must not—at least so it seems—become a critical thought that could undermine the ideology of maternal love.

The maternal, antagonist principle is not recognized in the process of the constitution of the male; it is negated or becomes unconscious—but this is an indication for Horkheimer that maternal love itself is no longer existent. Yet this view neglects the fact that psychic reality and external reality do not act as mirror images of one another. Maternal practice cannot be deduced effortlessly from theoretical structural categories, and its existence does not fade because it is not represented in culture and in the male subject.

---

26. Ibid., 121 (224). This motif is developed further in the "Juliette" discussion in *Dialectic of Enlightenment*.

27. "Authoritarianism and the Family," 121 (225).

28. An attempt at an answer is made only in the *Dialectic of Enlightenment*: "Like her [Circe, M.R.], women under the pressure of civilization are above all inclined to adopt the civilized judgment on woman and to defame the sex" (Gleich ihr [Kirke, M.R.] sind unterm Druck der Zivilisation Frauen vorab geneigt, das zivilisatorische Urteil über die Frau sich zu eigen zu machen und den Sexus zu diffamieren [66]). With an eye to the contemporary situation, Horkheimer's later formulation reads: "The equation of women and sex is disappearing" (!) ("Concept of Man," 17) (Die Identität von Frau und Sexus geht verloren[!] ["Zum Begriff des Menschen," 67]).

Still, the latest formulation of the premonition that loss of the "mystical aura" could be tied to the relationship between the sexes is formulated in "Authoritarianism and the Family" (1949). There it is not the structure of authority or instrumental reason as such that is to be deciphered in sociopsychological terms, but its barbaric form, the fascist character: "It is this configuration of submissiveness and coldness which more than anything else defines the potential fascist of our time."[29]

Both of these aspects are seen by Horkheimer as being the result of a nearly complete lack of concrete relations to parents. Holding fast to familial, patriarchal authority became abstract "once the inner substance of the family had dissolved." In *The Authoritarian Personality* (1950) Theodor W. Adorno and his colleagues had shown that submissiveness is the result of suppressed rebellion against the father. On the other hand, coldness is shown in a "rejection of pity—of that very same quality which used to reflect more than anything else the mother's love for her child."[30] This statement loses its aspect of truth in the following paradoxical structure of argumentation: the thesis of the "conscious *rejection* of love for the mother" by the male child is *negated* insofar as Horkheimer attributes to the maternal self *no substance* because the relationship between mother and child has in fact withered.[31] Horkheimer makes that which cannot be dissolved vanish—the difference between the psychic "remaking" of the "maternal" and true "maternal" behavior; between the mother imago and the real mother and wife; between the "mystical aura" and social nonrecognition, yes, true contempt for the dimensions of its significance.

This is a key passage in Horkheimer, one that answers the question of where, in the future, the reason for a failed individuality and mere instrumental reason is to be sought: in the presumed empiricism of the mother-child relationship, where there is a seamless realization of the tendencies toward totalization of social processes of rationalization.

Outlook

The aporia in Horkheimer's discussion of the importance of the maternal for the constituting of the male subject and its fading in history points the

29. Horkheimer, "Authoritarianism and the Family," 391 (280).
30. Ibid., 393 (281).
31. Ibid., 393 (282). See also "Familie" (1956), in *Soziologische Exkurse*, ed. Institut für Sozialforschung, and note 19 above.

way to a fundamental problem that I can formulate here merely as a thesis: with the introduction of the maternal, Horkheimer potentially formulated an intersubjective approach toward existing subject-philosophical premises; however, in the end he remains bound to the philosophy of the subject. That is why he causes that which cannot be eliminated—the conscious and unconscious traces of childhood—to vanish. The nonidentical represents a hope, and that hope he simultaneously destroys.

The objection that Horkheimer does not systematically consider the *difference between internal and external reality* is of central importance. He constructs a reflexive relationship between the real behaviors of mothers and the "mystical aura" of the maternal. But the "mystical aura" expresses at the same time the nearness and the distance from what is actually experienced; it is at one and the same time a creation and an involuntary memory.

The male idea of happiness, which for Horkheimer is the source of utopian thinking, has its roots, not in the experience of the lost perfect happiness of childhood, but in the togetherness of sensuousness and denial. Horkheimer asserts the "right" of the child to "absolute happiness with respect to its mother." Adorno's answer to this was: "That is very closely related to the question of the single child. It is all a question of the reconstruction of childhood. . . . The great force with which we extend beyond regression depends on the depth with which we penetrate this level."[32]

It is not by chance that Horkheimer does not speak of "wish" or "claim"—but of the right of the child to absolute happiness. But this view presupposes a relationship free of conflict and an identity of mother and wife that is free of conflict. If there were such a thing as absolute happiness, there would no longer be any happiness.

---

32. See note 1 above.

13 REASON, GENDER, AND THE PARADOX OF RATIONALIZATION

Elisabeth List

The idea of reason is not just one philosophical idea among many others. It is the core idea of modernity, the idea separating the new era of the scientific revolution and the early Enlightenment from the dark Middle Ages. In the last decades of the twentieth century, this image of reason has become the target of several critiques, one of them the feminist critique. This chapter tries to pinpoint the arguments specific for a feminist critique of reason and to illustrate some of the results of this critique by discussing what has been called the "paradox of rationalization" and the solution provided by a feminist approach to understanding reason.

Dialectics or Paradox? Accounts for the Crisis of Reason from Marx to Habermas

The feminist critique of modernity and its underlying idea of reason draws, at least in some of its arguments, upon the program of Critical Theory. It is therefore necessary to look at both the commonalities and the differences between a feminist critical social theory and Critical Theory from Adorno/Horkheimer to Habermas.[1] The differences will become evident with respect to the issue of rationality, especially of the role of instrumental reason for the process of modernization and its consequences for an adequate understanding of reason. Albrecht Wellmer, in a recent paper on "Reason, Utopia, and Enlightenment,"[2] proposes to read Habermas's theory of communicative action as a solution for the problem posed by what has been called the "paradox of rationalization."[3] Implicit as it seems in Weber's description of the process of modernization and rationalization, this problem is also inherent in the *Dialectic of Enlightenment* and the account of the fate of reason in the course of modernity as it is given by Horkheimer and Adorno.[4] If Critical Theory claims both to inherit and to transform the traditional idea of reason, it should be able to cope with this issue. I will argue that this is not possible without addressing and criticizing the implicit genderization of received ideas of reason or rationality. In this respect it seems that Critical Theory is in need of further elaboration.

Critical Theories

Critical Theory has its roots in Marx's critique of Hegelian philosophical idealism, which he saw as a form of false consciousness and as the ideology

---

1. For a survey of related issues, see Herta Nagl-Docekal, *Kritische und feministische Theorie Ein Bericht*. In *Theologie zwischen Zeiten und Kontinenten: Festschrift für Elisabeth Gössmann*, ed. T. H. Schneider and H. Schüngel-Straumann (Fribourg, Basel, Vienna: Herder, 1993), 1:224–38.

2. Albrecht Wellmer, "Reason, Utopia, and the Dialectic of Enlightenment," in *Habermas and Modernity*, ed. Richard J. Bernstein (Cambridge, 1985), 35–66.

3. For an account of the Weberian version of this paradox, see Wolfgang Schluchter, "Die Paradoxie der Rationaliserung in Zum Verhältnis von 'Ethik' und 'Welt' bei Max Weber," in *Zeitschrift für Soziologie* 5, 3 (1976): 256–84.

4. Max Horkheimer and Theodor W. Adorno, *Dialektik der Aufklärung: Philosophische Fragmente* (Frankfurt am Main, 1969).

of the ruling class. As Wellmer points out, already in Marx we find the configuration of three theoretical interests as characteristic for Critical Theory: (1) a critique of the ruling form of reason, (2) a utopian perspective for an ideal form of social life, and (3) the intellectual beliefs and hopes of the Enlightenment. This last motive, argues Wellmer, has been in danger of being lost in a dialectical move from hope to despair. What has gone wrong with Critical Theory and its relation to rationality?

Let us begin with the founding father of Critical Theory, Karl Marx. As far as the issue of rationality is concerned, it can be said that Marx took an optimistic attitude toward science and technology and their emancipatory potential. This attitude, and his neglect of the rational potential of social and political interaction, made Marx prone to a scientistic or instrumental concept of rationality. Such an unconditioned commitment to the beliefs of the Enlightenment tradition is no longer present in the more recent version of a critical theory of society in the tradition of historical materialism. The historical evidence of fascism and the ways it succeeded in making use of science and technology for its political aims led Adorno and Horkheimer to replace the progressive dialectic of productive forces, including technology and the sciences, by a negative dialectic of progress and enlightenment, written in terms of Weber's theory of modernization. In both Weber and Adorno/Horkheimer, as in Marx, purposive and formal rationality, or "instrumental reason," as they call it, are taken as analytical categories adequately describing the structure of modern societies. Both Weber and the authors of the *Dialectic of Enlightenment* present a pessimistic diagnosis of the process of increasing rationalization of social structures and its consequences. Nevertheless, Wellmer maintains, they implicitly appeal to a more comprehensive, emphatic idea of reason, which they did not and could not fully spell out.

A similar perspective on the history of Critical Theory has been elaborated by Seyla Benhabib in her book *Critique, Norm, and Utopia*, especially with respect to the question of whether the utopian potential inherent in the early articulations of Critical Theory in the thirties and forties of the twentieth century could be brought to bear on the project of a communicative ethics as Habermas proposes.[5] More recently, she has made explicit that the concept of moral agents as implicit in moral theories in the tradition of Kant, especially J. Rawls's *Theory of Justice* and Habermas's ethics of dis-

---

5. See Seyla Benhabib, *Critique, Norm, and Utopia: A Study on the Foundations of Critical Theory* (New York, 1986).

course, is in need of revision to do justice to feminist critiques of these moral theories.⁶ In the following pages, these issues concerning the state of ethical theory will not be addressed in detail. Instead, rationality will be treated in a more descriptive manner as a paradigm for action, much as it has been conceived of by Max Weber and later also by Adorno and Horkheimer. In such a theoretical framework, the term *rational is used* to characterize not only human action but also social processes. A short comment is thus in order on the term *rationalization,* which for the present purpose should not be given a psychoanalytic meaning. *Rationalization* here means a cultural process of the "articulation of functionally rational norms"⁷ for specialized and differentiated spheres of public social life. Rationalization as a cultural process of this type, however, had very ambivalent, if not contradictory consequences. So in Weber, rationalization connotes both emancipation (from traditional social powers, the dark and enchanting forces of older times) *and* objectification. In other words, it means gains *and* losses with respect to the autonomy and spontaneity of the individual. Weber gives impressive descriptive accounts of the tension between these two tendencies without, however, suggesting possible solutions. On the contrary, his pessimistic outlook on the process of modernization presents objectification, the loss of freedom and meaning of individual life, as a historical if not logical result of rationalization. Given that rationality is an unconditioned human good, this view indeed seems to imply something like a "paradox of rationalization."

Horkheimer and Adorno take a similar attitude toward rationality. For them, as a consequence, it is the sphere of art that comes to be the locus of realization for the ideas of happiness and harmony—a locus beyond the sphere of discursive rationality. This indeed cannot be regarded as a solution for the paradox of rationalization. For as Wellmer states, the work of art as a mode of reconciliation between humans and nature "can state only a transhuman state of affairs, but not a life form of speaking and interacting individuals."⁸ And, he concludes, "From the vantage point of an idea of reason which can be explicated only in terms of a transdiscursive aesthetic rationality, the functional, systemic and cognitive differentiation process of European society can be conceived only as being geared in the process of

---

6. See Seyla Benhabib, "The Generalized and the Concrete Other: Visions of the Autonomous Self," *Praxis International* 5 (1986): 402–24.
7. Thomas Luckmann, "On the Rationality of Institutions of Modern Life," *European Journal of Sociology* 1 (1975): 3–15.
8. Wellmer, "Reason, Utopia, and the Dialectic of Enlightenment," 49.

instrumental rationalization. This is the ironical agreement of Critical Theory and Max Weber."[9]

According to Wellmer, the only way out of the impasse and the paradox of rationalization would be a conceptual change, a change of the framework for the discourse on rationality itself—the development of a philosophical framework replacing purposive and formal rationality with a more comprehensive concept of rationality. This is what Habermas tries to do in his *Theory of Communicative Action,* especially in his critique of Weber's concept of rationality. According to Habermas, it is the concept of communicative rationality that can avoid the one-dimensional view of rationality inherent in Weber's theory of modernity.

Contexts and Limits

It should not be denied that such a conceptual move is in order. But it is questionable to think that it was primarily the move from epistemology to aesthetics—as recommended by Adorno and Horkheimer—that led to the failure of the Dialectic of Enlightenment, seen as a story of reason, of Critical Theory itself. What makes for the peculiarity of the emphatic concept of reason guiding traditions of critical thinking like Critical Theory is, as Wellmer himself clearly states, its *inherent relation to ideas about the human individual and human social life*. Thus, it seems more promising to look at these ideas in order to understand the paradoxical consequences of modern notions of rationality than to look at its cognitive or discursive features.

A satisfactory solution posed by the paradox of rationalization would consist of a twofold task: first, to show that the unreflected use of a concept of a self-sufficient reason and a strategy of rational action, isolated from its context, necessarily leads to paradoxes; and second, to acknowledge and to be aware of the limiting conditions, the constraints of rational action. *Thus, such a solution depends on whether we can adequately describe these contexts and limits in terms of a history and theory of modern societies.*

Taking these considerations as a framework for understanding reason, Habermas's version of a critical theory of modern societies, although of considerable interest as a point of departure for feminist theory, is in need of complementation and critique because it is to a certain degree gender

9. Ibid.

blind, both in its way of conceptualizing the dual structure of society and in its underlying idea of rationality.[10]

To begin with the second point mentioned, Habermas, in his theory of rational discourse, to a certain degree avoids the dramatic staging of the role of reason and its place in history that is inherent in Enlightenment stories of the progress of reason. In these accounts of the drama of universal rationalization, the self-images of sciences and philosophy are the self-images of a "Race of Heroes and Supermen," which Bacon hoped would come about. Whatever else it will be, a feminist critique of such images of reason will amount to a demasculinization of the image of reason. It will take sides with those who are ready to replace a totalizing rhetoric or, to use a phrase borrowed from Richard Bernstein, a "rage" for or against reason by a more modest and moderate discourse about its limits and merits.[11] However, Habermas, while critically aware of the social context of the development of ideas of reason, seems to deny the relevance of certain types of contextuality in his own account of communicative rationality. In his response to Carol Gilligan's proposal to view "contextual relativism" as a mode of moral judgment, he makes it clear that he is not ready to regard questions of situational limits or constraints as systematically relevant for an adequate philosophical account of practical reason.[12]

Not surprisingly, feminist critiques of male/mainstream ideas of reason all raise the issues of the denied and repressed contextuality and situatedness of rational practices.

Situated Knowledges: The Feminist Contribution to Epistemology

That there *are* such limits of rationality as a feature of human agency is quite evident. There are, for instance, limits set by the various media and

---

10. For an excellent critical examination of the explicit and implicit role of gender in Habermas's social theory, see Nancy Fraser, "What's Critical about Critical Theory? The Case of Habermas and Gender," in *Unruly Practices: Power, Discourse, and Gender in Contemporary Social Theory* (Oxford, 1989), 113–43.
11. Richard J. Bernstein, "The Rage Against Reason," in *Philosophy and Literature* (1985/2): 186–200.
12. Jürgen Habermas, *Moralbewußtsein und kommunikatives Handeln* (Frankfurt am Main: Suhrkamp, 1983), 169–200.

forms of symbolic articulation, by the capacities of human mind, by the conditions of embodiment of knowledge, and especially by the social and cultural context of human experience. To consider these limits means to accept that they render all claims of full reflexivity, all claims of self-sufficiency for the thinking and reflecting subject as source of knowledge, as untenable. Moreover, it means to change fundamental ideas about what it means to do philosophy that is both *real* and *good*.

A theory of knowledge elaborating the limiting conditions of experience and discourse is being developed from different angles—phenomenology, semiotics, psychoanalysis—and has recently been put forward, especially by feminists.[13] Summarizing the insights brought about by these new attempts to understand human reasoning would involve the following points: (1) the openness of the process of reflection; (2) the essential mediation of all notions of epistemology and ontology, especially the notion of object and subject through symbols that are socially constructed and discursively produced; (3) the unavoidable impact of the unconscious in all efforts to transform embodied, implicit experience into explicit contents of concepts, statements, theories; and (4) the notorious presence of the desire for closure in the construction of knowledge systems as revealing the working of the unconscious masculine self in philosophical and scientific discourse.

To take account of these features does not imply per se that claims for validity or truth are, as poststructuralists seem to believe, in principle illegitimate. Neither does it, as defenders of traditional epistemology seem to hold, lead to relativism, because the conditions in question are not arbitrary, but are empirical givens. Nevertheless, a critical awareness of the unavoidable situatedness and contextuality of cognitive and discursive practices will change the idea of reason as guiding our philosophical endeavors.

Having to cope with age-old definitions of femininity as "the other" of reason, feminists have good reason to insist on the issue of the limits of reason. As a consequence, they have proposed as a leading idea for a feminist theory of knowledge the concept of *positionality*. This concept, as it has been proposed by Linda Alcoff and others,[14] could also be useful to explain

---

13. See, for example, Dorothy Smith, "A Sociology for Women," in *The Prism of Sex: Essays in the Sociology of Knowledge*, ed. J. E. Sherman and E. T. Beck (Madison: University of Wisconsin Press, 1979), 135–87; and *The Everyday World as Problematic: A Feminist Sociology*, (Boston 1987); Jane Flax, "Postmodernism and Gender Relations in Feminist Theory," in *Signs: A Journal of Women in Culture and Society* 12/4 (1987): 621–43; Linda Alcoff, "Cultural Feminism versus Poststructuralism: The Identity Crisis in Feminist Theory," in *Signs* 13/3 (1988): 405–36.

14. See Alcoff, "Cultural Feminism versus Poststructuralism."

why traditional epistemology and the history of ideas of reason and rationality are marked by a continuous denial of the issue of limits and contingency, and what could account for this special form of cognitive repression. It has already been mentioned that in the symbolic order of traditional philosophical discourse, the image of women or the feminine has its place as the image of the other. As such, it served and still serves as the very foil onto which the thinker, the philosopher, could project the uneasy but suppressed suspicion and awareness of the fragility of his own system of knowledge. In other words, it is the unreflected positionality of the philosopher as a male subject that both led him and, in the context of a patriarchal society, that gave him the possibility of denying his own experience of lack, incompleteness, limit, and difference by projecting them, as female, onto the "other" of his cultural self.[15]

This line of thought gives us a first hint of a feminist account of the paradox of rationalization: The unintended destructive consequences of rationalization and modernization, which appear as paradoxes against the background of the ideals of the Enlightenment, might result from the repression of anxieties and experiences of lack, of weakness and dependence, that were eliminated from the philosophical image of the self in the name of reason and that became part of a devalued image of femininity. Seen in this way, it is the patriarchal unconscious of an androcentric cultural tradition that brings about the paradox of rationalization. There are remarks in Adorno and Horkheimer suggesting that they hold a similar view;[16] however, it seems that this insight of early Critical Theory has been lost in its later reformulations.

Dual Societies

To regain what Critical Theory seems to miss in its story of the "dialectics of reason," a systematic account of the sociohistorical context would be necessary in order to understand *how the repression of incompleteness*

---

15. See Michele Le Doeuff, "Women and Philosophy," in *French Feminist Thought: A Reader*, ed. Toril Moi, 181–201 (Oxford, 1987).
16. Horkheimer and Adorno, *Dialektik der Aufklärung*, 68–69.

could develop as a stable and culturally accepted attitude and pattern of thinking.[17]

On the first pages of his three volumes on the sociology of religion, Max Weber mentions what he holds to be one of the fundamental principles for the organization of capitalist economy: the principle of the separation of household and enterprise. In his comprehensive studies of the emergence of institutions and forms of action in modern society, however, he did not systematically include the analysis of family and private life. Weber seems to regard the separation of the private sphere of social reproduction from the domains of a rationally organized economy and politics as indispensable, not because he sees the first as a necessary requirement for the second, but because he locates in the sphere of privacy all those elements of meaning and action that are essential for the human condition but that resist integration into the prevailing patterns of purposive and formal rationality. Thus, the elements of the aesthetic, the personal, and the erotic appear in Weber's account of modernity as fundamentally irrational residuals in the context of a thoroughly rationalized world.[18] In other words, the whole realm of gender and the problems of gender relations are excluded from the dynamics of rationalization.

It should be kept in mind that it is in the context of his sociology of religion that Weber at least touches on the issues of erotic life. Although Weber is aware of the importance of these issues for religious intellectuals and the ascetism they favored,[19] they remain marginal for his account of the process of rationalization. For Weber it is the tension between the two intellectual spheres of religion, on the one hand, and of science, on the other—the tension between religious enchantment and scientific enlightenment—that is experienced as paradox in the context of a culture that accepts both religion and science as value systems. According to Weber, the ideas of religion and enlightenment are irreconcilable—and the tension between them must be sustained as long as one is not ready to give up one of the two value systems and its respective worldview.[20]

Does Habermas's dual conception of modern society take into account

---

17. See Vigdis Songe-Möller, "Sexual Metaphors in Early Greek Philosophy," in *Gender—an Issue for Philosophy? Proceedings of the Nordic Symposium for Women in Philosophy*, no. 2 (Oslo, 1994), 101–20; for the culture of modernity, see Alice A. Jaardine, *Gynesis: Configurations of Women and Modernity* (Ithaca: Cornell University Press), 1985.

18. Max Weber, *Gesammelte Aufsätze zur Religionssoziologie* I (Tübingen, 1920), 10.

19. Ibid., 556–64.

20. See Schluchter, "Die Paradoxie der Rationalisierung," 277.

the reality of gender and gendered life-world? Habermas, following Weber's account of the process of modernization, reformulates the paradox of rationalization in terms of an increasing tension between what he calls "system" and the life-world, where "system" means the complex, differentiated, and formalized structures and organizations of economy, administration, and political institutions. The tensions or conflicts between system and life-world, according to Habermas, should and could be overcome by an emancipatory politics. The goal or telos of emancipation would be a rationally led life of individuals no longer subjected to the imperatives of system maintenance.

What would a "fully rationalized life-world" thus understood amount to? The answer to this question should be found in Habermas's idea of communicative rationality. If Wellmer's interpretation of Habermas's account is correct, the view or ideal of individual life that it presupposed indeed has to be called "gender blind." Evidently, such an interpretation of the idea of a rationalized life-world as the reconstruction of Marx's ideal of a free association of producers takes for granted something like a "natural division of labor between the sexes"—once more drawing a picture of a life-world where it is men who make rational decisions concerning life, while it is women who take care of it and reproduce it.[21]

In short, Habermas, in his view of the dual organization of modern society, accounts for the *essentially gendered nature of the organization of modern society according to the principle of separate private/public spheres* no more than does Weber. If this is the case, it is the task of a feminist critique to close this gap in received theories of modernity. This would require an answer for the following three questions: (1) When and how has a pattern of gender relations developed in such a way as to organize male dominance? (2) How has the same process of social transformation contributed to the emergence of separate spheres of the domestic and private? (3) How have the ideas of reason and knowledge, and the image of the knowing subject, become incorporated into this type of a dual and asymmetric organization of gender relations as power relations?

Origins

These are questions of interest not only for a feminist critique of sexism and male dominance but also for social theory and for a theory of rationality.

---

21. For a more detailed account of Habermas's interpretation of the role of the worker and the citizen and its gendered subtext, see Fraser, *Unruly Practices*, 124.

Classical theories of modernity from Marx to Habermas have ascribed to the family and the private sphere a marginal role in the process of modernization, although this is the social realm where children are raised and socialized and thereby undergo those fundamental psychogenetic and symbolic processes that make of them members of society as a thoroughly gendered universe. These processes have been studied primarily by psychoanalysis and cultural anthropology. Although in many cases explicitly sexist, these theoretical disciplines provide the conceptual and theoretical tools to answer the questions concerning the relationship between social evolution, gender roles, and images of reason.[22]

Because our main issue here is the image of rationality in modern societies, it is not possible to give a satisfactory account of the history of the private/public split and the history of gender roles and gender images.[23] With respect to the first question, it should at least be mentioned that recent feminist research critically rereading Engels's explanation for the oppression of women in his book on the family, private ownership, and the state has shown that it was not the emergence of the state, but an earlier type of kinship corporate society that led to the establishment of patriarchy as the prevalent form of social organization.[24] The reason for that was the advantage of patrilocal residence for both the accumulation and control of economic wealth, which meant, first of all, advantages for the exploitation of female labor. As Coontz and Henderson assume, the change from egalitarian matrilineal residence to patrilocal societies with hierarchical patriarchal structures has been preceded by violent conflict between different lineages and conflicts between different groups of men within one lineage competing for the products of female labor, resulting in forms of social stratification stemming from social relations between men, especially in warfare and trade.[25] These are topics open to debate and further research, but they give an idea of how the worldwide historical victory of patriarchy might be explained. Patriarchy, in this context, means female domestic work and the control of the fruits of this work by men—that is, the form of "natural division of labor between the sexes" as taken for granted by classical Marxism and social theory. To give a very short summary of a long story: The

---

22. See Gale Rubin, "Traffic in Women: Notes on the 'Political Economy' of Sex," in *Toward an Anthropology of Women*, ed. Rayna Reiter (New York, 1975), 171–84.

23. For a more comprehensive account, see Gerda Lerner, *The Creation of Patriarchy* (Oxford: Oxford University Press, 1986).

24. See Stephanie Coontz and Peta Henderson, "Property Forms, Political Power, and Female Labour in the Origin of Class and State Societies," in *Women's Work, Men's Property: The Origin of Gender and Class* (London, 1986), 111.

25. Ibid., 141.

rise of a thoroughly androcentric culture, of monotheism, cults excluding women, and similarly patriarchal traditions of knowledge, was preceded by outbursts of violence against women.

With respect to the third question, concerning the relation between gender roles and images of reason, it can be said that the ideas of reason still prevalent today took shape in early Greek science and philosophy and therefore in a social and cultural context that was clearly patriarchal. The separation of the *oikos* as the realm of subsistence, of economic production, and of social reproduction on the one hand, and of a public sphere that was the place for the cultivation of rational discourse on the other, was one of the important features of Greek society.[26] I use the term *dual society* for such an arrangement of social life, an arrangement that is intimately related to the division of labor between women and men and that was, of course, the social basis for the philosophical constitution of both reason and gender that took place in this period.[27]

Modernization for Whom?

After the Middle Ages, with the rise of capitalism, a new type of a dual society emerged. Just as the modern civil state has not abolished existing forms of the division of power and gender but only indicates that kinship relations have lost their significance as principles of political order, so the expansion of industrial production for a free market did not render superfluous the traditional forms of private subsistence production.[28] On the contrary, as feminist historians have shown, it is this type of private subsistence production that provided the material basis for the process of modernization and rationalization. It was the work of women, including child rearing, caring labor, education, and socialization, but to a great extent also the production of use-values, of goods satisfying the immediate material needs

26. See Sara Pomeroy, *Goddesses, Whores, Wives, and Slaves: Women in Classical Antiquity*, 2d. ed. (New York, 1984); and Hanna Arendt, *The Human Condition* (Chicago, 1958).

27. A more detailed account of this crucial step in the formation of philosophical thinking can be found in Vigdis Songe-Möller, "Sexual Metaphors in Early Greek Philosophy."

28. For the transformation of the political function of patriarchy in the political philosophy of John Locke, see Linda Nicholson, "Gender and History," and Lorenne M. G. Clark, "Women and Locke: Who Owns the Apples in the Garden of Eden?" in *The Sexism of Social and Political Theory*, ed. Lorenne M. G. Clark and Lynda Lange (Toronto/Buffalo/London, 1979), 16–40.

for food, clothing, and so forth. All these were requirements for the efficient organization of a public economy and of industrial production, and this is what is implied by the Weberian principle of "separation of household and enterprise," although Weber does not elaborate on it in this way.

In the face of a culminating crisis of the traditional forms of family life and reproduction, theorists of modernity recently have begun to acknowledge the importance of the dual structure of society for the process of modernization. Now they have come to realize that the allegedly *universal* process of rationalization, the modernization of industry, administration, and public life has, in fact, been a "halfway modernization."[29] Until very recently it has systematically excluded the private realm, which has been regarded as the realm of women's life and work. According to Dubiel, the deeply contradictory character of capitalist modernity results from the very fact that its realization depends on the possibility of exploiting or making use of premodern forms of labor and symbolic orientation, such as religion or traditional values of solidarity.[30] But of course the most important of such "premodern" resources are the modern ideologies and ideas of femininity, of women's housework and caring work in the private sphere.

We are living in a historical period with a more general awareness of the dual structure of modern society. Why, one could ask, has the polarity and complementarity of "private femininity" and "public masculinity," praised by the writers and philosophers of the last century as functional and eternal, become not only visible, but at the same time problematic, in the recent decades? Is it because, under the conditions of late capitalism, privacy and family are being gradually subverted and deprived of their role as elementary units of subsistence and as a place of stable primary relations by the dynamics of a progressively modernized market economy? In other words, the process of modernization has begun to undermine its dual social ecology, which turns out to have been a necessary requirement for its very existence.

We are now in a position to give an interpretation of what has been called the paradox of rationalization. If it is the case that modern society can exist only in dependence on forms of life that are, according to its own understanding, "premodern," then the imperative of progressive and comprehen-

---

29. Ulrich Beck, *Risikogesellschaft: Auf dem Weg in eine andere Moderne* (Frankfurt, 1986).
30. Werner Dubiel, "Autonomie oder Anomie: Zum Streit über den nachliberalen Sozialcharakter," in *Die Moderne—Kontinuitäten und Zäsuren*, ed. Johannes Berger (Göttingen, 1986), 270.

sive modernization or rationalization as a universal social norm must be, in the long run, self-destructive for modern society. At the same time, the very imperatives of modernization were massively related to the androcentric premises in its understanding of reason, and its dependence on the resources of life as provided by the work and the activity of women remained implicit or repressed.

Even if we see plenty of evidence that this is the case, it does not mean that the destructive effects of modernization must be conceptualized as paradoxical effects of rationalization. Taking into account the reality of dual society and its organization by dividing genders, the problem of how the maximization of rationality, be it formal or purposive rationality in Weberian terms, can have such damaging and irrational results appears much more as the logical outcome of the constellation described than as a paradox.

If this is the case, of course, it leads us to question the concept of rationality guiding the process of modernization. This is what both Wellmer and Habermas propose to do. But efforts to replace problematic concepts of rationality to save the life-worlds of individuals remain abstract as long as they fail to address the material grounds for their persistence. These material grounds, seen from a feminist perspective, are the forms of patriarchal organization of social life. *Consequently, the crisis of modernity as well as the "paradox of rationalization" could be explained as unintended effects of the tacit genderization both of rationality and social agency.*

The Gendered Social Context of Rationalities

The effects of genderization on notions of rationality and social agency could be shown by locating the evolution of prevalent concepts of rationality in the history of dual/patriarchal societies. The dual organization of social life and complementary cognitive and emotional patterns defining the practice and meaning of gender is usually regarded in terms of a theory of social evolution, and from this perspective it appears as a functional requirement for the process of social differentiation and evolution, a development that evidently came along with the political subordination of women and their restriction to private sphere and with the rule of men in the public sphere. But theories of evolution of this type are not, as scientific theories claim to be, "true accounts of what really happened," but are narratives, stories of origin, most often stories of the male heroes of reason, of pioneers fighting against a wild nature, servants of the good of mankind. I say mankind, because they are stories written by men and for men, denying and justifying their violent and repressive episodes and effects for women. In short, the ideas of reason and ruling emerged from a subtext of the history of male dominance as a universal historical necessity; and the idea of reason, both in the history of philosophy and in modern science, remained embedded in images of masculinity and ruling.

This holds also for the "grand narration" of the rise and progress of modernity and its core ideas of rationality and of philosophical reason, an idea, which despite its universal claim, is thoroughly masculinized. Thus, the image of the "man of reason"[31] in the writings of Kant and Fichte consists at least of the following three characteristics: (1) The capacity to reason and to calculate rationally; (2) autonomy and the capacity for self-maintenance, both economically and as citizen and subject of political rights; and (3) the ability to control affect and emotions.[32] In his essay on "Protestant Ethics and the Spirit of Capitalism," Max Weber shows how such an ideal type or rational action could develop from a religious background,[33] and feminist research on the personality structure of scientists reveals its relationship to the image of gender.[34] Not surprisingly, it is the same paradigm of the rational actor that forms the conceptual core of individualist social theories since Max Weber.

Seen in the context of the genderized social ecology of modernity, it is clear that the ideal of the "man of reason" or of "abstract masculinity," as Nancy Hartsock calls it, is neither self-sufficient nor universal—as is claimed by the philosophers defending it. It could only develop as a correlate to its counterpart of "concrete femininity," which makes for the traditional bourgeois image of the ideal woman, housewife, and mother. Her respective paradigmatic qualities are (1) prudence and skill in managing the domestic concerns, "concrete practicality";[35] (2) caring and concrete responsibility for the lives and needs of her husband, relatives, and children;

---

31. This term was coined by Genevieve Lloyd in her book *The Man of Reason: 'Male' and 'Female' in Western Philosophy* (London, 1984).

32. Kant's *Ethics and Philosophy of Law* can count as a paradigm case for this image of reason and also for the tradition of intellectual asceticism in the history of western philosophy. See Robin May Schott, *Cognition and Eros: A Critique of the Kantian Paradigm* (Boston: Beacon Press, 1988).

33. Max Weber, *Gesammelte Aufsätze zur Religionssoziologie*, 17–206.

34. Evelyn Fox Keller, *Reflections on Gender and Science* (Boston, 1985).

35. For Rousseau in this respect, see Le Doeuff, "Women and Philosophy," 189.

and (3) empathy, sensibility, the ability to create an atmosphere of intimacy and emotional security.

In other words, traditional ideas of femininity reflect a clear awareness of the role of women for the maintenance of the everyday lives of individuals. Therefore, even writers like Rousseau must ascribe to women *some* rational capacities. But at the same time, they are eager to insist that these are not capacities with the dignity of *pure and universal reason.*[36]

Thus, we conclude that the philosophical concern with the question *"Which reason?"* should shift to the question *"Whose reason?"*[37] It may turn out that the idea of reason underlying the discussed theories of modernity tend to mythologize and reify certain aspects and traits of rational agency due to an image of reason that serves to satisfy unconscious desires for power and to provide at the same time a rationale for exploiting "other rationalities" by denying them the name of reason. *Doctrines of a self-sufficient, universal reason are then the epistemological justification for, and ideology of, a dual society, justifying the exploitation of women as reproducers of immediate and concrete life.*

Furthermore, they are mistaken theories of rationality, of society, and of the subject insofar as they (1) deny the contingencies and situatedness of all human practices; (2) celebrate the ideal of an isolated, solitary, and self-sufficient individual; and (3) claim an unlimited sovereignty over the emotional dynamics of conscious, embodied human life.

The traditional image of pure reason has been criticized in all of these three aspects—by phenomenology with respect to the first, by Habermas in his theory of communicative action with respect to the second, and by psychoanalysis with respect to the third. But it is only feminist criticism that shows how these three traits are related in the image of gender. By revealing the unconscious of an androcentric and patriarchal culture, the feminist critique of modernity accounts for the contradiction between the explicit norms of the Enlightenment and the destructive consequences of the process of rationalization operating according to the code of abstract masculinity. Seen from a feminist perspective, the self-destructiveness of rationalization is no longer a paradox. It is the logical outcome of the suppression of those aspects of humanity that have been relegated to the female and excluded from the concern of a masculinized idea of reason.

---

36. Ibid.
37. Compare here Sandra Harding, *Whose Science? Whose Knowledge? Thinking from Women's Lives* (New York, 1991).

In the forgoing considerations about the so-called paradox of rationalization, I have tried to reconstruct theories of rationalization in the context of theories of modernity from Max Weber to Jürgen Habermas. I have argued that they all fail because they fail to give a satisfactory account of the social division of labor between women and men as their organizing principle of society.[38] Closing this gap has been the main effort of feminist research in social theory and history. Critical Theory claimed to be both a theory of society *and* of reason. Consequently, a profound criticism of its claims must question the concept of rationality operating in its theoretical context.

This issue has become the central focus of feminist criticism of traditional epistemology and philosophy of science, especially in the debates around psychoanalytic and poststructuralist theories of discourse.[39] From such a perspective it seems clear that Critical Theory does not question the claims of a rationalist account of human reason and its claim that intellectual capacities are sufficient to understand the human condition. This is because it does not overcome the androcentric view of the human as reason. Therefore, the elaboration of the feminist critique drew from other philosophical traditions that are critical toward the rationalist heritage: the tradition leading from Nietzsche to Foucault, Derrida, and Lacan.

One issue that has become a special concern for feminist theories about reason and gender is the issue of body and embodiment.[40] Only a philosophical framework not neglecting the phenomena of the embodiment of human existence can account for the central role of gender in philosophical discourses about human understanding and reason.[41] Both gender and reason are essentially embodied, as much as is human life in general. And only such a philosophical framework will be able to make sense of sexuality, procreation, and birth—not as part of "woman's nature," but as essential features of the human condition.

The realm of embodied experience that has been excluded from the concerns of philosophical discourse about concepts of reason *is* the realm of

---

38. For a detailed criticism of Habermas in this respect, see Nancy Fraser, *Unruly Practices*, 113–43 (first published in *New German Critique* 35 [spring/summer 1985]: 97–131).

39. For a representative collection of issues in this field, see Linda J. Nicholson, ed., *Feminism/Poststructuralism* (New York/London: Routledge, 1990).

40. See Alison M. Jaggar and Susan R. Bordo, eds., *Gender/Body/Knowledge: Feminist Reconstructions of Being* (New Brunswick: Rutgers University Press, 1986); Judith Butler, *Gender Troubles: Feminism and the Subversion of Identity* (New York/London: Routledge, 1990); and *Bodies that Matter: On the Discursive Limits of "Sex,"* (New York/London: Routledge, 1993).

41. Mark Johnson, *The Body in the Mind* (Chicago: University of Chicago Press, 1987).

gender experience; and, in the last resort, it is the repression of this domain of experience that gives rise to the destructive effects of the historical process of societal rationalization, guided by a concept of abstract, disembodied reason. Because the impulses coming from this vital sphere of embodied experience are repressed and transformed by, and in the context of, a violent patriarchal organization, they are targets of violent forms of control. This makes for the alliance between some forms of rationalization and violence.

If this is the case, taking a position beyond the *Dialectics of Enlightenment* would mean changing its underlying notions of reason, but at the same time it would mean a transformation of the prevailing images of gender. Above all, it would require the subversion of the androcentric gender bias of received concepts of reason and rationality—not by denying gender, but by explicitly taking account of its discursive construction as one of the most important features of what we experience as social reality. This will be the point of departure for feminist attempts to rewrite the project of theorizing—a project that despite critical revisions will, after all, remain indebted to the heritage of Critical Theory, at least as long as feminist thinking will be committed to its genuine political orientation.

CONTRIBUTORS

Heidemarie Bennent-Vahle teaches philosophy at the Catholic Professional School (Fachhochschule) in Aachen, Germany, and at the Euregio-College in Wuerselen, Germany. Her recent publications include *Philosophinnen-Lexikon*, co-edited with U. I. Meyer (Leipzig: Reclam, 1996), *Grundriss einer Weltweisheit für das Frauenzimmer*, co-edited with Johanna Charlotte Unzer (Aachen: Ein-Fach-Verlag, 1995), and " 'O mein Herz springt in Tausend Stück'—zum Briefwechsel zwischen Kant und Maria von Herbert," in *Die Philosophin: Forum für feministische Theorie und Philosophie* 14 (1996).

Ingvild Birkhan is a lecturer in the Department of Philosophy and the chairperson of the Coordination Center for Women's Studies at the University of Vienna. Her recent essays on feminist theory include "Ein philosophisches Paradigma der Geschlechtersymbolik: Aristoteles und seine Zeugungstheorie," in *Körper—Geschlecht—Geschichte: Historische und aktuelle Debatten in der Medizin*, ed. Elisabeth Mixa et al. (Vienna, 1996); "Fremde sind wir uns selbst—zum Pathos von Krieg und Tod im problematischen Kontext kollektiver Identität," in *Krieg/War*, ed. Wiener Philosophinnenclub (Munich: Fink, 1997); and "Ein sprachloses Leitbild: Zur Dekonstruktion der symbolischen Verschränkung von Mutter und Tochter in Maria," in *Mutterwitz: Das Phänomen Mutter—eine Gestaltung zwischen Ohnmacht und Allmacht,* ed. Gudrun Perko (Vienna: Milena, 1998).

Astrid Deuber-Mankowski is an assistant professor in the Department of Cultural Studies at Humboldt University, Berlin, and one of the editors of the semiannual *Die Philosophin: Forum für Feministische Theorie und Philosophie.* Her numerous publications deal with feminist theory, modern philosophy, and the concept of modernity.

Christine Garbe is a professor of German language and literature and their didactic at the University of Lüneburg, Germany. Her recent works include *Literarische Sozialisation,* a book that she published together with H. Eggert (Stuttgart and Weimar: Metzler, 1995), and *Lesen im Wandel—Probleme der literarischen Sozialisation heute,* co-edited with W. Graf et al. (Lüneburg: Didaktik-Diskurse, 1998).

Ursula Pia Jauch teaches philosophy as a "Privatdozentin" at the University of Zurich, Switzerland. Her books include *Immanuel Kant zur Geschlechterdifferenz: Aufklärerische Vorurteilskritik und bürgerliche Geschlechtsvormundschaft* (Vienna: Passagen, 1989), *Damenphilosophie und Männermoral: Von Abbé de Gérard bis Marquis de Sade. Ein Versuch über die lächelnde Vernunft* (Vienna: Passagen, 1990), and *Janseits der Maschine: Philosophie, Ironie und Ästhetik bei Julien Offray de la Mettrie (1709–1751)* (Munich: Hanser, 1989).

Cornelia Klinger is a Permanent Fellow of the Institute for Human Sciences (Intitut für die Wissenschaften vom Menschen) in Vienna. She teaches philosophy as a "Privatdozentin" at the University of Tübingen, Germany. She has written a wide range of articles on feminist philosophy, German Idealism, the political and aesthetic theories of Romanticism, and related subjects. Her recent publications include *Flucht—Trost—Revolte: Die Moderne und ihre ästhetischen Gegenwelten* (Munich: Hanser, 1995); "Essentialism, Universalism, and Feminist Politics," in *Constellations: An International Journal of Critical and Democratic Theory* (New York, September 1998); "Aesthetics" in *The Blackwell Companion to Feminist Philosophy,* ed. Alison Jaggar and Iris Young (New York: Oxford, 1997); "The Concepts of the Sublime and the Beautiful in Kant and Lyotard," in *Feminist Interpretations of Immanuel Kant,* ed. Robin May Schott (University Park: The Pennsylvania State University Press, 1997).

Elisabeth List is a professor of philosophy at the University of Graz, Austria, and the chairperson of the research group "Cultural Studies" at the Faculty of the Humanities at the same university. She has been a visiting professor at Bergen, Norway, and at the universities of Klagenfurt and Innsbruck, Austria. For many years she was a board member of the International Association of Women Philosophers. Among her numerous publications, she is co-editor of *Denkverhältnisse: Feminismus und Kritik* (Frankfurt: Suhrkamp, 1989); *Die Präsenz des Anderen: Theorie und Geschlechterpolitik* (Frankfurt: Suhrkamp, 1993); and *Leib/Maschine/Bild: Körperdiskurse der Moderne und der Postmoderne* (Vienna: Turia und Kant, 1997).

Ursula Menzer is a lecturer in philosophy and a freelance author living in Hamburg, Germany. She is co-editor of *Philosophinnen: Von Wegen ins 3.Jahrtausend* (First yearbook of the International Association of Women Philosophers) (Mainz: Tamagnini, 1982) and *Subjektive und objektive Kultur: Georg Simmels Philosophie der Geschlechter vor dem Hintergrund seines Kultur-Begriffs* (Pfaffenweiler: Centaurus, 1992) and editor of *Er/Sie* (Concrete Poetry) (Paderborn: Monika Hoffmann, 1996).

Herta Nagl-Docekal is a professor of philosophy at the University of Vienna, and a corresponding member of the Austrian Academy of Sciences. She has been a visiting professor at Millersville State University, Lancaster, Pennsylvania, at the University of Utrecht in the Netherlands, and at several universities in Germany. She is one of the editors of *Deutsche Zeitschrift für Philosophie* (Berlin: Akademie Verlag). Among her recent books are *Feministische Philosophie: Ergebnisse, Probleme, Perspektiven* (Frankfurt am Main: Fischer, 1999) and two co-edited collections of essays translated from English: *Jenseits der Geschlechtermoral* (Frankfurt am Main: Fischer, 1993) and *Politische Theorie: Differenz und Lebensqualität* (Frankfurt am Main: Suhrkamp, 1996).

Christa Rohde-Dachser is a sociologist and psychoanalyst and co-editor of the journal *Psyche*. After years of clinical work and providing training and supervision at the Hannover Medical School, she accepted the professorial chair at the Frankfurt University Institute of Psychoanalysis in 1987. She is a training and control analyst in the Deutsche Psychoanalytische Gesellschaft and occupies the chair at the DPG Institute of Psychoanalysis in Frankfurt am Main. She has numerous publications on clinical issues, on the overlap between sociology and psychoanalysis, and on the psychoanalysis of female development. Her publications include *Die Sexualerziehung*

Jugendlicher in katholischen Kleinschriften: Ein Beitrag zum Problem der Moraltradierung in der komlexen Gesellschaft (Stuttgart, 1970); *Das Borderline-Syndrom*, 5th ed. (Bern, 1995); *Expedition in den dunklen Kontinent: Weiblichkeit im Diskurs der Psychoanalyse* (Heidelberg, 1991); and *Im Schatten des Kirschbaums: Psychoanalytische Dialoge* (Bern, 1994).

Mechthild Rumpf has been a professor of cultural studies at the University of Bremen, Germany, and is currently a visiting professor in the Department of Political Science at the University of Vienna. Since 1985 she has been an editor and board member of the journal *Feministische Studien*. Her numerous publications, dealing mostly with gender difference and gender relations under the conditions of modernity and with the meaning of "femininity" in Critical Theory, include *Spuren des Mütterlichen* (Frankfurt, 1989); and "Mystical Aura," in *On Max Horkheimer*, ed. S. Benhabib, W. Bonß, and J. McCole (Cambridge, Mass., and London, 1993); "Staatsgewalt, Nationalismus und Krieg: Ihre Bedeutung für das Geschlechterverhältnis," in *Feministische Standpunkte in der Politik-wissenschaft: Eine Einführung*, ed. Eva Kreisky and Birgit Sauer (New York, 1995); and "Teures Vaterland, die Wiege alles Großen und Guten": Die Befreiungskriege 1813–1815 als Altar für deutschen Volksgeist," in *Militär, Gewalt, Geschlechterverhältnis erscheint*, ed. Christine Eifler (1999).

Lieselotte Steinbrügge is Assistant Professor in the Department of Romance Languages and Literature at the Free University of Berlin. She is the author of *The Moral Sex: Woman's Nature in the French Enlightenment* (New York: Oxford University Press, 1995) and the editor, together with Hans-Erich Bödeker, of *Conceptualising Women in Enlightenment Thought* (Berlin: Nomos Verlag, 1999).

Käthe Trettin has taught at the universities of Berlin, Vienna, Freiburg, and Graz. Her main interests, apart from feminist philosophy, are philosophy of logic, epistemology, philosophy of mind and cognitive science, and, more recently, analytic ontology and metaphysics. She is the author of a book on Aristotle's and Frege's logic (*Die Logik und das Schweigen*, 1991) and several articles on feminist philosophy ("Braucht die feministische Wissenschaft eine 'Kategorie' "?, 1994; "Zwei Fragen zur feministischen Erkenntnistheorie," 1995; "Probleme des Geschlechtskonstruktivismus," 1997), on the philosophy of mind ("Kausalität und Erklärung: Zum Problem der mentalen Verursachung," 1998), and on ontology ("Tropes and Things" and "Ontology and Feminism," forthcoming).

INDEX

academia, lack of acceptance for German feminists in, 4–5
Adorno, Theodor W., 14, 29, 156–57, 202; on authoritarianism, 318; Benjamin's writing and, 282, 295; Critical Theory and, 322–24; critical theory of, 304–5; on culture, 309–12; Enlightenment discussed by, 304, 325–26
aesthetics: of art and landscape, 167–69; idealization of femininity and, 161–63
Alcoff, Linda, 327–28
alienation, Rousseau's discussion of, 79–81
allegory, Benjamin's schema of, 294–98
Allgemeine Gesellschaft für Philosophie in Deutschland, 4
amour-passion. See passionate love
analogy, identity of thought and, 250
analytic philosophy, in Anglo-American academia, 6
Anders, Günther, 202
Andreas-Salomé, Lou, 167–69
androcentrism: conceptual notation and, 191–92; German feminist discussion of, 8–10
androgyny, Baudelaire's ideal of, 300–301
anthropological materialism, Benjamin's discussion of, 301–2

Anthropology from a Practical Point of View, 106, 110–11
Antigone, Hegel's discussion of, 140–46
anti-Semitism, in fin-de-siècle Vienna, 257–58
"archaic fetishism," 293–96
Aristotle: fascination analysis and syllogisms of, 184–85; idea of feminine in, 225; nominalist conception of money and, 204; reproduction theory of, 12; syllogistics of, 26
art: historical context for, 169–74; unity of nature with, 94–99; Weininger on genius of, 262–66; women and landscape, connections in, 163–69
"assertoric force," conceptual notation and, 187–92
"Authoritarianism and the Family," 310–12
Authoritarian Personality, The, 318
"Authority and the Family," 309–10, 312–18
autonomy: of citizens, Rousseau's discussion of, 82–88; instrumentalization of women and, 141–46; justice and morality and, 89–94; money and, 208–9; Rousseau's discussion of, 81

Bachofen, J. J., 273
Bacon, Francis, 32, 326

Barth, Hans, 79 n. 2
Barwise, Jon, 195
Bataille, Georges, 135 n. 51, 270 n. 35
Baudelaire, Charles, 28, 282, 285–86; allegory schema and, 296–98; Benjamin on solitude of, 289–93; fetishism of, 293–96; as "hero of modernity," 286–89, 297–98
"Baudelaire as Allegorist," 289
Bäumer, Gertrud, 224
Baumgartner, Hans Michael, 226, 229
Baureithel, Ulrike, 287 n. 15
Beach, Sylvia, 288
beautiful: landscape and artwork, analogies with, 164–69; women and nature and idea of, 152–55
Beauvoir, Simone de: feminist discussion of, 2; instrumentalization of women and, 136–37; on sexual difference, 12–13
Benhabib, Seyla, 84, 88 n. 41, 323
Benjamin, Walter, 202, 281–302; critique of modernity and, 28; fascination with Démar's work, 298–302
Benjaminiana, 287–88
Bennent-Vahle, Heidemarie, 24–25, 85, 113–46, 149 n. 5
Berger, Renate, 67 n. 47
Bergson, Henri, 204
Bernstein, Richard, 326
Betroffenheit, German feminist discussion of, 10
"Beyond Good and Evil," 224–25
biological characteristics: culture and gender and, 217–23; Hegel's female morality and, 131–35
Birkhan, Ingvild, 26–28, 95 n. 66, 255–79
bisexuality: Freudian theory of, 247–48, 259 n. 13; Weininger's discussion of, 257 n. 5, 259 n. 13
Bloch, Jean, 150, 202
Bloch, Maurice, 131 n. 34, 150, 202
Böhme, Karen, 133–35
Boolean logic, 186 n. 20
Bossuet, 78
bourgeois society, Horkheimer's concept of "maternal" and, 312–18
Bovenschen, Silvia, 85, 263 n. 24
Braidotti, Rosi, 9, 21
Bronfen, Elisabeth, 68, 73–74
Bryher, Winifred, 288
Buck, Günter, 90
Butler, Judith, 18

Calasso, Roberto, 257 n. 4
canons of philosophy: cultural characteristics of German philosophical canon, 6–7; German feminist theory and, 22–30
capitalism, Benjamin's critique of, 294–96
Carnap, Rudolf, 183 n. 15, 187 n. 23
Cassirer, Ernst, 96
castration theory: Freud's theory of femininity and, 236–45; identity of thought and, 249–50
"Central Park" aphorisms (Benjamin), 288–93
Chicago School, 202
citizenship, autonomy of, Rousseau's concept of, 82–88
civilization, Rousseau on misery of, 82–88
Cixous, Hélène, English translations of, 1–2
Clément, Catherine, English translations of, 2
Code, Lorraine, 26, 196–200
Cohn, Jula, 287
collective unconscious, Freud's theory of femininity and, 232, 234–55
"Commodity as Poetic Object," 289
commodity fetishism, of Baudelaire, 293–96
complementarity theory of sexes, Rousseau's *Julie* and, 58–61
Complete History of England, 77
"Concept and Tragedy of Culture, The," 215
concept of culture, Horkheimer's discussion of, 309–12
"Concept of Man, The," 306–7, 310
concept of reason, Horkheimer's critical theory regarding, 304–19
concept-script, Frege's discussion of, 26
conceptual notation: feminist critique of logic and, 180; Frege's development of, 186–92
"Concerning Woman," 223
concretization of metaphor, identity of thought and, 250
Condorcet, Jean Antoine de, 22–23, 34–38, 43
"Conflict in Modern Culture," 215
conscience, Rousseau's discussion of, 80–81
consciousness, Hegel's discussion of, 121–23
constructionism: conceptual notation and, 190–92; feminist theory and, 15
context, feminist innovations in logic and, 193–96
"contextual relativism," 326
Coole, Diana, 85–86, 162 n. 27

Coontz, Stephanie, 331
correct argumentation, principles of, 177–80
Coser, Lewis A., 227–28
Critical Theory: German feminist discussion of, 29–30; modernization and, 337–38; reason in context of, 322–24
Critique, Norm, and Utopia, 323
Critique of Pure Reason, gender difference in, 107–8
culture: father system in Freud's *Totem and Taboo,* 267–75; feminist theory and, 17–20; gender and, 215–23; in German feminist theory, 6; Horkheimer's concept of, 309–12; money and, Simmel's discussion of, 205–9; Simmel's critique of, 202–3; Simmel's philosophy of the sexes and, 212–15, 226–30

Danto, Arthur C., 183 n. 15
Das Kapital, 205
Davidoff, Leonore, 162
death, femininity and, in Rousseau's *Julie,* 67–74
deconstruction, French feminist theory and, 2
defense mechanisms, Freud's theory of femininity and, 236–40
Démar, Claire, 298–302
Derrida, Jacques, 337
Descartes, René: equality of sexes discussed by, 34–35; feminist critique of, 33–34, 43
"de-souling," Benjamin's concept of, 295–96
Deuber-Mankowsky, Astrid, 28
dialectic, Hegel's concept of, 120–23
Dialectic of Enlightenment, 29, 307–9, 317–18, 322–23, 338
dichotomy systems, feminist theory and, 21
"Die Frau und die objektive Kultur," 226
Die Ordnung der Geschlechter, 291–93
Die Philosophin: Forum für feministische Theorie und Philosophie, 4
difference feminism: principles of, 13–14; utopian strain of, 16
differentiation: Simmel's philosophy of the sexes and, 212–15; Weininger's concept of, 260–66, 276–79
Dilthey, Wilhelm, 284 n. 6
Diotima: Philosophinnengruppe aus Verona, 259
Dirscherl, Klaus, 95 n. 69

disambiguation technique, fascination analysis and, 185
Dischner, Gisela, 257 n. 4
Discours de la méthode, 34
Discourse on the Origin of Inequality, 40–41, 80 n. 7, 91–92
Discours sur l'histoire universelle, 78
discursive constellation, feminist theory and, 15
distinction principle, fascination analysis and, 185
Divina Commedia, 264
divinity, in Freud's *Totem and Taboo,* 272–75
division of labor: gender and culture in, 215–23; idealization of femininity and, 159–63; Rousseau on gender-specific division, 88
Doderer, Heimito von, 256 n. 1, 258
dominance, feminist discussion of, 10
dualism of gender, German feminist discussion of, 10–11
dual societies: origins of modernization and, 333–34; paradox of rationalization and, 328–30
duplex negatio affirmat, conceptual notation and, 189–92

Eastern European feminist studies, translations of, 2–3
Eberle, Matthias, 164 n. 35, 169 n. 49
Eclipse of Reason, 305
economics: Rousseau's discussion of, 87 n. 37; Simmel's *Philosophy of Money* and, 203–9
education: Hegel's female morality and, 132 n. 38; Rousseau on limitations of, for women, 83–88, 223 n. 25; Rousseau's philosophy of history and, 90–94
egoism: Hegel's female morality and, 133–35; reason and, 310; Rousseau and origins of, 40–41
einfühlendes Verstehen, 284 n. 6
Einfühlung, 284 n. 6
"Elective Affinities," 287
Emile and Sophie, or The Solitary, 87–88
Emile ou de l'éducation, 39–43; autonomy discussed in, 83; paradox of passionate love in, 52; women's powers discussed in, 64 n. 42

emotional development, Hegel's female morality and, 132–35
empathy: Baudelaire as virtuoso of, 300–301; German concept of, 284 n. 6
Enckendorff, Marie Luise (pseud.), 224
Engels, Friedrich, 141, 331
English usage, feminist innovations in logic and, 194–95
Enlightenment: French Enlightenment, feminist critique of, 31–44; German feminist theory and, 6–7, 22–26, 33–44, 86–88; Horkheimer's discussion of, 303–19; Marx's Critical Theory and, 323; philosophy of history and, 78–99; sexual equality during, 86–88
Entseelung, Benjamin's concept of, 295–96
epistemic logic, feminist theory and, 196–200
equality of sexes: Condorcet's view of, 34–39; Enlightenment discussion of, 34–44; Kant and Schopenhauer's discussion of, 103–12
Erfahrung, in Benjamin's work, 284
Erlebnis, in Benjamin's work, 284
Eros und Psyche: Biologisch-psychologische Studie und Zur Theorie des Lebens, 257 n. 7
Esquisse, 37–38
ethics: Critical Theory and, 323–24; family as keeper of, in state, 127–30; female as resource for, 113–46; Hegel's different ethical worlds, 123–27; instrumentalization of women and, 138–46; of sexual difference, Kant and Schopenhauer on, 108–12
Ethik Menzer, 110
evolutionary differentiation, Simmel's philosophy of culture and, 203
exclusion principle, fascination analysis and, 185
experience, in Benjamin's work, 284
explanation, role of, in Freudian femininity, 240–45

family: ethical function of, within state (Hegel), 127–30; ethical worlds of Hegel and, 123–27; female morality and, 130–35; Fichte's concept of, 113–14; Hegel's law of, 113–20, 265; Horkheimer's concept of "maternal" and, 306–7, 312–18; idealization of femininity and nature of, 158–63; instrumentalization of women and, 136–46; Protestant ethic regarding, 168–69; role of, in modernization, 330–32; Rousseau's view of, 86–88
fantasy, Freud's theory of femininity and, 27, 232–55; confirmation by staging of, 250–52; identity of perception and, 246–48; identity of thought and, 249–50
fascination analysis: conceptual notation and, 190–92; feminist critique of logic and, 179–80; method of, 180–85
fascism, Horkheimer on, 309–10
"Fashion," 288
fatherly law. *See* patriarchy
female morality, familiy and, 130–35
"female principle" of Simmel, 210–15; gender and culture shaped by, 216–23
feminine antithesis, German feminist discussion of, 10–11
feminine self-reflection, 298–99
femininity: artwork and landscape connected with, 163–74; and death, in Rousseau's *Julie*, 67–74; fin de siècle rejection of, 259; Freud's theory of, 231–55; in Freud's *Totem and Taboo*, 267–75; gender and culture and, 219–23; Horkheimer's concept of reason and, 304–19; instrumentalization of women through, 136–46; money and, 208–9; nature and, 149–73; as otherness, 11–13; as scientific unknown, 32–33; Simmel's philosophy of the sexes and, 212–15; subject and thesis concerning nature and, 151–55; Weininger's discussion of, 260–66
feminist epistemology: critique of Kant and Schopenhauer, 102, 104–8; situated knowledges and, 326–28
feminist theory: assessment of, 11–12; Benjamin's work interpreted by, 291–93; conceptual notation and, 187–92; critical theories and, 322–24; critique of reason by, 31–44, 322–38; English translations of non-English works, 1–2; epistemic logic and, 196–200; in fin-de-siècle Vienna, 255–79; formalism and, 175–80; innovations in logic and, 193–200; logic critiqued in, 175–200; nature as discussed by, 149–73; Simmel's philosophy in context of, 201–30, 213–15, 223–30
Ferry, Jean-Marc, 173 n. 55
fetishism: of Baudelaire, 293–96; Benjamin's discussion of, 290–93; of modern hero, 28

Fetscher, Iring, 79
Feuerbach, Ludwig, 225
Fichte, Johann G., 335; on gender differences, 86; idea of feminine in, 225; on marriage, 113–14, 117
Fictions of Feminine Desire: Disclosures of Héloïse, 46 n. 1
Fin-de-siècle Vienna, feminist theory, 255–79
Fleurs du mal, 282, 285–86
Fliess, Wilhelm, Freud and, 259 n. 13
flirtation, Simmel's "Weibliche Kultur" and, 211–15, 228–29
formalism: conceptual notation and, 187–94; feminist theory and, 175–80
Foucault, Michel, 17, 144 n. 65, 285, 337
Frankfurt Congress on the Future of the Enlightenment, 33
Frankfurt School, Critical Theory of, 9
freedom, money and, Simmel's discussion of, 207–9
Frege, Gottlob, 25–26, 180; conceptual notation of, 186–92
French Enlightenment, feminist critique of, 31–44
French feminist theory, English translations of, 1–2
Freud, Sigmund: father system in *Totem and Taboo,* 266–75; feminist theory and, 17; fin-de-siècle movement and, 255–79; Fliess and, 259 n. 13; German feminist discussion of, 26–28; identity of perception, 245–48; identity of thought, 245–46, 248–50; radical tradition and, 9; theory of femininity of, 231–55; Weininger and, 257 n. 5
Freund, Gisèle, 288
fusis, Schopenhauer's concept of, 108–12

Garbe, Christine, 23, 34 n. 8, 45–74, 85 n. 28, 98–99
garden metaphor: art in context of, 169–74; in Rousseau's *Julie,* 61–67, 97–99
Gatens, Moira, 21
gaze theory, conceptual notation and, 189–92
gender contract, feminist of concept of, 19 n. 42
gender difference: in Benjamin's *Passagen-Werk,* 281–302; child's discovery of, 236 n. 1; conceptual notation and, 191–92; culture and, 215–23; epistemic logic and, 199–200; ethics of, 108–12; fantasy and, 235–40; feminist theory and, 13–14, 85–88; fin de siècle discussion of, 258–66; Freud's theory of femininity and, 232–55; in Freud's *Totem and Taboo,* 270–75; German feminist discussion of, 7–12; Hegel's discussion of, 24–25, 134–35; idealization of femininity and, 158–63; identity of perception and, 246–48; instrumentalization of women and, 136–46; justice and morality concerning, 90–94; Kant's discussion of, 101–12; money and, 208–9; ontology of, 14–15; paradox of rationalization and, 321–38; philosophy of history and, 77–99; Rousseau's concept of nature and, 84–88; Schopenhauer's discussion of, 101–12, 223–24; sexuality and, 16–19; Simmel's philosophy of sexes and, 209–15; social construction and, 15–16; social context of rationality and, 334–38
Genth, Renate, 150 n. 8
Georg-Lauer, Jutta, 20
"Georg Simmels vernachlässigter Beitrag zur Soziologie der Frau," 227–28
Gerhard, Ute, 11 n. 26
German feminist theory: English translations of, 1–3; historical background to, 3–4; re-reading of canon and, 22–30
Geschäftsleben, 286–87, 290
Geschlecht und Charakter, 28, 257–66, 275–79
Geschlecht und Kulture, 227
Gilligan, Carol, 326
Goethe, W. F. von, 269
Greece, classicism and yearning for, 165–69
Grund, Helen, 288
guilt, passionate love and, 49–51
Gütersloh, Paris von, 258
gynocentrism, conceptual notation and, 191–92

Habermas, Jürgen, 29, 168 n. 46, 172 n. 53, 229; Critical Theory and, 322–25, 337; dual conception of society, 329–30, 334; rational discourse theory of, 325–26; on Weber, 172 n. 54
Habilitation thesis (Benjamin), 287, 294
Harding, Sandra, 14, 18 n. 40, 199–200
Harrison, Beverly W., 158 n. 20
Hartsock, Nancy, 335–36

Index | 347

Hassauer, Friederike, 33, 90 n. 51
Hausen, Karin, 151 n. 11
Hauser, Margit, 86 n. 32
Hegel, G. W. F.: ethical worlds of, 123–27; family as viewed by, 113–20; female as ethical resource in, 113–46, 223; on female morality in family, 130–35; on gender differences, 86, 120–23; German feminist interpretation of, 24–25; instrumentalization of women by, 136–46; on law of family, 127–30, 265; Marx's critique of, 322–24
Heindl, Waltraud, 262 n. 21
Heinrich, Klaus, 182
Henderson, Peta, 331
heteronomy, Rousseau's discussion of, 81
heuristic of suspicion, feminist critique of logic and, 178–80
Hexenhammer, 264–66
Hippel, T. G. von, 223 n. 25
Hirsch, Emmanuel, 82 n. 14
history: in Benjamin's *Passagen-Werk*, 283–302; fascination analysis and, 182–85; Hegel's dialectical perspective on, 120–23; Hegel's female morality and, 134–35; Horkheimer's concept of "maternal" and, 312–18; idealization of femininity and, 160–63; instrumentalization of women and, 138–46; justice and morality in, 90–94; of logic, 177–80; philosophy of, gender difference and, 77–99; Rousseau's exclusion of women from, 84–88; Simmel's philosophy of the sexes and, 219–23
Hoffmann, Paul, 160 n. 23
Holländer, Hans, 164 n. 34, 165
Honegger, Claudia, 291–93
Horkheimer, Max, 29, 130 n. 31, 136 n. 52, 282; Critical Theory and, 322–26; "maternal" motif in work of, 303–19
Horney, Karen, 238
humanity, femininity and, 14
Humboldt, Wilhelm, 225
Hume, David, philosophy of history and, 77

Ibsen, Henrik, 277
identity of perception, Freud's theory of femininity and, 245–48
identity of thought, Freud's theory of femininity and, 245, 248–50
impotence, Benjamin's discussion of, 289–93

incest, in Freud's *Totem and Taboo*, 269 n. 34
individuality: ethical function of family and, 127–30; ethics of, versus universality, 123–27
industrialization, reduction of feminine with, 158 n. 20
inequality, Rousseau on origins of, 84–88
inner life, Benjamin's discussion of, 290–93
institutional conditions, Freudian identity of thought and, 248–50
instrumentalization of women, Hegel's concept of, 136–46
Internationale Assoziation von Philosophinnen (IAPh), founding of, 3–4
"Interrelations of the Two Sexes," 105
Irigaray, Luce, 141 n. 61, 144 n. 68; English translations of, 2
Italian feminist studies, translations of, 2–3

Janssen-Jurreit, Marielouise, 238–39
Jauch, Ursula Pia, 7, 24, 101–12
Jeffrey, Kirk, 163
Jodl, Friedrich, 257–58
Journal de la Société de 1789, 35–37
judgment, conceptual notation and, 187–92
Julie, ou, La Nouvelle Héloïse, 23, 45–74; community of Clarens in, 57–61; death of Julie in, 67–74; discourse of love in, 53–57; "female place" in, 62–67; human relationships in, 91–92; paradox of *amour-passion* in, 47–53; unity of art and nature in, 94–99
justice, morality and, Rousseau's discussion of, 88–94

Kamuf, Peggy, 46 n. 1; on Rousseau's *Julie*, 59–61, 63 n. 40, 65 n. 43
Kant, Immanuel, 59 n. 27; beautiful and sublime in, 165–69; conceptual notation and, 188; Critical Theory and, 323–24; culture and gender discussed by, 219; feminist epistemological critique of, 102, 104–8; gender difference and philosophy of, 101–12; on gender differences, 86; German feminist interpretation of, 24; Hegel's discussion of, 114–15; justice and morality discussed by, 92–94; "man of reason," 335; on motherhood, 304; philosophy of history and, 81; Weininger and, 258

Keller, Evelyn Fox, 32
Kellner-Benjamin, Dora, 287
Kindlers Literaturlexikon, 84 n. 23
Klinger, Cornelia, 25, 96 n. 72, 147–73, 257 n. 11
knowledge, power and, 9
Kofman, Sarah, 93–94
Kohlberg, L., 236 n. 1
Krainer, Georg, 81 n. 10
Kraus, Karl, 256, 257
Kristeva, Julia, 19–20, 274; English translations of, 2

Lacan, Jacques, 337; feminist theory and, 12, 17; German forerunners of, 28
Lacanian psychoanalysis, French feminist theory and, 2
Lacis, Asja, 287
Landes, Joan B., 158 n. 19
landscape motif: in art, femininity and, 163–69; historical context for, 169–74; idealization of femininity and, 156–63; in Rousseau's *Julie*, 63 n. 39; women and nature and idea of, 152–55
"Landscape with Figures," 162–63
Lange, Lynda, 86
language: conceptual notation and, 188–94; logic and, 177–80
Latin American feminist studies, translations of, 2 n. 6
law, philosophy of: ethical function of family and, 127–30, 265; ethical worlds of Hegel and, 123–27; Hegel's discussion of, 114–20; Hegel's female morality and, 133–35; instrumentalization of women and, 136–46; lack of German counterpart to, 5
Lebensphilosophie, 201–2, 204, 206, 221
"Lebensphilosophie," 26–27
Lefebvre, Henri, 171 n. 53
Leibniz, G. W., 192
Le Rider, Jacques, 256 n. 1
lesbianism, in Benjamin's work, 289–93, 298
L'Esperance, Jean, 162–63
Lessing, Theodor, 26, 258 n. 10
Lévi-Strauss, Claude, 270 n. 35
liberal feminism, lack of German counterpart to, 5
List, Elisabeth, 29–30, 321–38
"lived experience," in Benjamin's work, 284

Lloyd, Geneviève, 20 n. 46, 32
logic: fascination analysis method and, 180–85; feminist critique of, 175–200; feminist innovations in, 193–200; Frege's conceptual notation of, 186–92; German feminist discussion of, 25–26
"logic of action," 177 n. 7
Lopez McAlister, Linda, 3 n. 10
love, morality and, Rousseau's discussion of, 91–92
Lukács, Georg, 121, 139 n. 59, 202, 221
"Lyric Poet in the Era of High Capitalism, A," 289

Mahler, Gustav, 237 n. 2
male hysteria, in Baudelaire's work, 297–98
"male principle" of Simmel, 210–15; gender and culture shaped by, 216–23
"Ma loi d'avenir" (My law of the future), 298–302
Man, Paul de, on Rousseau's *Julie*, 63 n. 39, 66 n. 46
Marcuse, Herbert, 115–16, 129 n. 28
Mariaux, Veronika, 259.15
marriage: Fichte's concept of, 113–14; Hegel's concept of, 116–20; Rousseau on virtue and sensibility of, 46–74, 57–61
Marx, Karl: commodity fetishism, 28; Critical Theory and, 322–24; on money, 205–8
Marxism: Baudelaire's fetishism and, 293–96; gender issues in German feminist theory categorized as, 5; radical tradition and, 9
masculinity, structure of reason by, 32–44
master-servant metaphor, Hegel's female morality and, 133–34
Mayreder, Rosa, 226, 257 n. 5
Medusa metaphor, Freud's theory of femininity and, 241, 245
memory, in Benjamin's work, 283
Mensch, Weininger's concept of, 259–66
Menzer, Ursula, 26–27, 201–30
Metaphysics of Morals, 104
"Metaphysics of Sexual Love," 24, 102, 223
Millar, John, 38
"mimesis" in Benjamin's work, 301 n. 53
misogyny: in fin-de-siècle Vienna, 257–66, 276–79; German feminist discussion of, 7
modernization: art and landscape and, 168–69, 173–74; dual society and, 330–32; gen-

der implications of, 29–30; idealization of femininity and, 158–63; impact on women of, 332–34; money and, 207–9; role of family in, 330–32; Simmel's philosophy of, 201 30
"modest methodological proposal" of Benjamin, 282–83, 296–98, 302
modesty, Rousseau's discussion of, 92–94
money, Simmel's philosophy of, 203–9
Monnier, Adrienne, 288–89
Montet-Clavié, Danielle, 67 n. 48
moral agents, Critical Theory and, 323–24
morality: characteristics of, 42 n. 18; ethical worlds of Hegel and, 123–27; female as resource for, 113–46; instrumentalization of women and, 136–46; justice and, Rousseau's discussion of, 88–94; in Rousseau's *Julie*, 63–64; unity of art and nature and, 95–99
Moses and Monotheism, 267, 268 n. 31, 271 n. 36
motherhood: Benjamin's disinterest in, 291–93, 298; female morality and family and, 130–35; Freud's theory of femininity and, 236–40; in Freud's *Totem and Taboo*, 269 n. 33; German feminist theory and, 29; instrumentalization of women and, 141–46; martyrdom of, in Rousseau's *Julie*, 69–74; as motif in Horkheimer's work, 303–19; "mystical aura," Horkheimer on loss of, 309–12, 318–19; in Rousseau's *Julie*, 58–61; as social principle in prehistory, 312–18; Weininger's discussion of, 261–66
Moulton, Janice, 193–96
myth: Horkheimer's concept of "maternal" and, 307–8; motherhood as social principle and, 315–18
Myth of the Neutral "Man," The, 193

Nacherleben, 284 n. 6
Nagl-Docekal, Herta, 23–24, 77–99
narcissism, Freud's theory of femininity and, 236–40, 251–52
"National Economy and Philosophy," 205
National Socialism, 221, 225
natural language, conceptual notation and, 190–92
nature: cultural dichotomy and, 17; female as natural moral community, 113–20; femininity and, 149–73; German feminist discussion of woman and, 25; idealization of, 156–63; landscape and artwork, connections with, 164–69; reason's domination of, 32–44; Rousseau's discussion of women and, 84–88, 162; Simmel's philosophy of sexes and, 210–15; subject and thesis concerning woman and, 151–55; unity of art with, 94–99; woman's virtue and, in Rousseau's *Julie*, 63–67
neutrality, feminist innovations in logic and, 193–96
Newby, Howard, 163
Nicholson, Linda, 84, 88 n. 41
Nietzsche, Friedrich: misogyny of, 224–25; radical tradition and, 9; rationalist heritage of, 337
nonclassical logic, feminist theory and, 177 n. 5
noncontradiction, law of, fascination analysis and, 185
Nye, Andrea, 26, 175–80

Observations on the Feeling of the Beautiful and the Sublime, 24, 101–2
Oedipal conflict: in Freud's *Totem and Taboo*, 266–75; Horkheimer's concept of maternal as social principle and, 316–18
On Certainty, 180–82
One Way Street, 287
"On the Nature of Culture," 215
"On the Psychology of Women," 211–15
ontology, feminist theory and, 14–15
"On Women," 105
ordinary language philosophy, 178–80
Origin of German Tragic Drama, The, 287, 294
Origins of the Distinction of Ranks, 38
Ortega y Gasset, 202
Ortner, Sherry, 150
"Otherness": feminist theory and, 11–13; instrumentalization of women and, 141–46
Other Woman, Freud's theory of femininity and, 242–45

paradox of rationalization: contexts and limits, 325–26; Critical Theory and, 322–25; dual societies, 328–30; feminist epistemology and, 326–28; origins of, 332–34
"Paris of the Second empire in Baudelaire, The," 282, 300

Passagen-Werk, 28, 281–302
passionate love: paradox of, 47–53; rejection of, in Rousseau's *Julie*, 53–57; Rousseau's discussion of, 46–74
passions, unity of art and nature and, 95–99
patriarchal socialization, Freud's theory of femininity as, 232, 241–45
patriarchy: culture and gender, Simmel's concept of, 218–23; female morality and family and, 130–35; femininity and, 149–73; in Freud's *Totem and Taboo*, 266–75; German feminist theory and, 22–30; Hegel's discussion of family and, 118–20; Horkheimer's concept of maternal and, 317–18; origins of, 331–32; post-World War I dissolution of, 287; in Rousseau's work, 62 n. 36, 87–88; subject and thesis of femininity and, 151–55; unity of art and nature and, 95–99; in Weininger's work, 277–79
Peer Gynt, 277
penis envy, Freud's theory of femininity and, 233–34, 235–40
perception, identity of, 245–48
personal experience, Benjamin's discussion of, 286 n. 13
phallic monism, Freud's theory of femininity and, 235–40
phallocentric representation, 12–13; Weininger's discussion of, 264–66
Phenomenology of Spirit (Phänomenologie des Geistes), 24–25, 119–20, 129–30; gender theory discussed in, 120–23; instrumentalization of women in, 138–46
Philosophie de l'histoire, 77
Philosophische Kultur: Über das Abenteuer, die Geschlechter und die Krise der Moderne, 202 n. 1, 229–30
Philosophy of Money, 203–9
Philosophy of Right, 25
"philosophy of the sexes," Simmel's discussion of, 27
pitié naturelle, Rousseau's concept of, 41–42
Plato, 225, 261 n. 17
politics: ethical function of family and, 127–30; feminist theory and, 17; instrumentalization of women and, 141–46
positionality, situated knowledges and, 327–28
Poulain de la Barre, François, 22–23, 34–35, 37–38, 86 n. 32

power, knowledge and, 9
praxis, feminist critique of logic and, 177–80
"presence of mind" in Benjamin's work, 285
private sphere: art and landscape and, 168–69; idealization of femininity and, 160–63
privatissima concept, Benjamin's life and, 287–88
projection mechanism: Freud's theory of femininity and, 238–40; Weininger's use of, 263–66
Prokop, Ulrike, 118
property, ethical function of family and, 129
prostitutes, Benjamin's depiction of women as, 289–93
Protestant ethic, family unit and, 168–69
"Protestant Ethics and the Spirit of Capitalism," 335
psychoanalytic theory: double image of women in, 244–45; feminist theory and, 17–18; fetishism, 293–96; in fin-de-siècle Vienna, 276–79; Freud's theory of femininity and, 231–55; in Freud's *Totem and Taboo*, 270–75; German feminist discussion of, 27–28
public sphere, idealization of femininity and, 160–63
Puttnies, Hans, 287

Quine, Willard Van Orman, 178

"Race of Heroes and Supermen," 326
Rammstedt, Ottheim, 230 n. 50
Rang, Brita, 150 n. 11
rationality: art and landscape and, 172 n. 53; Critical Theory and, 322–25; gendered social context of, 334–38; gender implications of, 29–30; male myth of, 149–50; origins of modernization and, 332–34; paradox of, 321–38; Rousseau on women's lack of, 39–42; situated knowledges and, 326–28
Rawls, John, 323–24
reality, Horkheimer's external-internal view of, 319
reason: contexts and limits, 325–26; critical theories of, 322–25; dual societies and, 328–30; feminist critique of, 31–44, 322; gendered context of, 334–38; Horkheimer's concept of, 304–19, 308 n. 10; mod-

ernization and, 332–34; origins of, 330–32; paradox of rationalization and, 321–38; Rousseau's critique of, 41–42; situated knowledges, 326–27
"Reason, Utopia, and Enlightenment," 322
"regressing desymbolization," Freudian identity of thought and, 249–50
relevant theory, logic and, 177 n. 7
religion, in Freud's *Totem and Taboo*, 272–75
religiosity, in Rousseau's *Julie*, 72–74
reproductive function of women: Hegel's female morality and, 131–35; Rousseau's discussion of, 85–88; Weininger's discussion of, 261–66
res cogitans, feminist critique of, 33–35
research methodology, in German feminist theory, 7
res extansa, feminist critique of, 33–35
Ritter, Joachim, 156–57, 161 n. 25
ritual purification, fascination analysis and, 183–85
Rodlauer, Hannelore, 257 n. 7
Rohbeck, Johannes, 34
Rohde-Dachser, Christa, 26–27, 231–55
role allocation and adoption, Freud's theory of femininity and, 250–52
Roman de la rose, 66 n. 46
Romantics, Hegel's rejection of, 116–20
Roos, Peter, 32
Rosenberg, Alfred, 221, 225
Rousseau, Jean-Jacques: on alienation, 79–81; German feminist interpretations of, 23–24; idealization of rural innocence in, 162; *Julie, ou, La Nouvelle Héloïse*, 45–74; justice and morality discussed by, 88–94; misery of civilization and citizen autonomy discussed by, 82–88; origins of egoism in, 40–41; paradox of *amour-passion* in Julie by, 47–53; as philosopher of history, 77–79; on sensibility of marriage, 57–61; women's abilities assessed by, 39–41, 223 n. 25, 336
Rumpf, Mechthild, 29, 303–19

Saint-Simonianism, 298
Schafer, R., 250
Schelling, F. W. J., 145–46
Schiller, Friedrich, 96, 164 n. 33, 166
Schleiermacher, F. D. E., 225

Schlsier, Renate, 232, 240–41
Schneider, Helmut J., 161 n. 25
Schopenhauer, Arthur: feminist epistemological critique of, 102, 104–8; gender difference and philosophy of, 101–12, 223–25; German feminist interpretation of, 24
Schriften zur Philosophie und Soziologie der Geschlechter, 229–30
science: Benjamin's reproach of, 283; equality of sexes and, 37–38; feminist critique of reason and, 32; in Freud's *Totem and Taboo*, 274–75; Hegel's female morality and, 132 n. 38; Simmel's philosophy of the sexes and, 221; Weininger's reticence concerning, 262
Scott, Joan, 21
Segerberg, Krister, 177 n. 7
Seifert, Edith, 267 n. 29, 268 n. 32
self-interest, Rousseau on, 41
self-preservation, Rousseau on, 41
sentiment: landscape and artwork, analogies with, 163–69; women and nature and idea of, 153–63
sexism: autonomy and, in Rousseau's work, 83–88; German feminist discussion of, 7–10
sexual fetishism, of Baudelaire, 293–96
sexuality: Benjamin's discussion of male impotence and, 289–93; culture and, 216–23; Démar's celebration of, 299–300; ethics of sexual difference and, 108–12; gender difference and, 16–19; Hegel on marriage and, 117–20; Hegel's female morality and, 132–35; Kant and Schopenhauer's discussion of, 105–8; love and, in Rousseau's *Julie*, 53–57; in Rousseau's Julie, 45–74
sexual pessimism, Kant and Schopenhauer's concept of, 108–12
"silence/silencing" concept, fascination analysis and logic, 181–85
Simmel, Georg, 156 n. 15, 161 n. 25, 166–67; assessment of philosophy of sexes, 223–30; feminist theory concerning, 201–30; gender and culture discussed by, 215–23; German feminist discussion of, 26–27; letter to Weber, 222 n. 21; philosophy of sexes, 209–15
Simmel, Gertrud, 224 n. 24
situated knowledge, feminist epistemology and, 326–28

situational semantics, feminist innovations in logic and, 193–96
Sketch for a Historical Picture of the Progress of the Human Mind, 37
Smith, Gary, 287
social agency: family and Weberian concept of, 168–69; Horkheimer's concept of reason and, 305–6
social contract: gender differences and, 19–20, 19 n. 42; justice and morality in, 89–94; legitimacy of, 82–88
Social Contract and Discourses, The, 40
socialization, money and, Simmel's discussion of, 207–9
social structure: feminist theory and, 87–88; of gender difference, 15–21; Horkheimer's concept of family and, 313–18; rationality in context of, 334–38
Society of Women in Philosophy (SWIP), 3
Spanish feminist studies, translations of, 2–3
Speculative Beginning of Human History, 81, 92–93
Spencer, Herbert, 203
Spinoza, idea of feminine in, 225
staging, Freud's theory of femininity and, 250–52
state: ethical function of family in, 127–30; Hegel on family as model of, 115–20; instrumentalization of women within, 141–46
Stegmüller, Wolfgang, 177
Steinbrügge, Lieselotte, 22–23, 31–44; Benjamin's work interpreted by, 291–93; on biologization of women, 93 n. 61; moral gender concept of, 90–91; on Rousseau's *Julie*, 59–61, 63 n. 40, 98 n. 75
Stelzner, Werner, 198–200
Stephan, Inge, 67 n. 47
Stopczyk, Annegret, 257 n. 4
Strindberg, August, 6, 256, 257 n. 4, 277 n. 41
student movement, in Germany, feminist theory and, 3, 5
subjectivity, landscape and artwork, connections with, 164–69, 171–74
subsistence production, origins of modernization and, 332–34
Susman, Margarete, 224
syllogisms: fascination analysis and, 184–85; German feminist discussion of, 25–26

Sylvan, Richard, 177 n. 7
symbolic construction, feminist theory and, 19
symbolic denominator, Kristeva's concept of, 19–20
synecdoche, discourse of, paradox of passionate love and, 49–53

Tanner, Tony, 99 n. 81
taste, Rousseau on taste in women, 39–40
technology, social development and, 37–38
teleology, philosophy of history and, 78
tertium comparationis, Simmel's concept of, 166–67
Theory of Communicative Action, 325
Theory of Justice, The, 323
"Theory of Knowledge, Theory of Progress," 282–83
"theory of origin," in Freud's *Totem and Taboo*, 272–75
"Theses on the Philosophy of History," 282
third value sphere complex, 168
thought, identity of, Freudian theory of, 248–50
"topography of the sexes" concept, 282 n. 4
Totem and Taboo, 28, 266–79
Tractatus, 180
translations of feminist theory, surveys of, 1–3, 2 n. 6
Trettin, Käthe, 25–26, 175–200
Treusch-Dieter, Gerburg, 278 n. 42
Tribune des femmes, 298

Über die Abtreibung der Frauenfrage, 228–29
Über die bürgerliche Verbesserung der Weiber, 223 n. 25
Ulmi, Marianne, 228 n. 41
unconscious: Freud's theory of femininity and, 234–35; male unconscious, femininity as constructed by, 238–40; staging as confirmation of, 250–52
universality: ethical function of family in state and, 127–30; German feminist discussion of, 8–9; individuality versus, 123–27; of reason, feminist critique of, 32

veil imagery, in Rousseau's *Julie*, 60 n. 32
Vienna, Fin-de-siècle philosophy in, 27–28
Virgin Mary, cult of, feminine idealization and, 155 n. 14

virtue, paradox of passionate love by, 50–53
Voltaire, 77
von Braun, Christine, 260 n. 16, 297 n. 43

Wagner, Richard, 262 n. 22
Walzer, Michael, 88 n. 39
Weber, Marianne, 213, 220, 222 n. 21, 226
Weber, Max, 86, 168, 172 n. 54, 323–25; on modernization, 335, 337–38; organization of capitalism and, 329–30
"Weibliche Kultur," 210–15
Weigel, Sigrid, 283 n. 4
Weininger, Otto, 26–28, 225; fin-de-siècle movement and, 255–66; misogyny of, 276–79
Wellmer, Albrecht, 322–23, 325, 330, 334
Weltbild concept, landscape and artwork, connections with, 164–69
What Can She Know? Feminist Theory and the Construction of Knowledge, 196–200
Whose Knowledge? Whose Science?, 199–200

Wittgenstein, Ludwig, 180–82, 257–58
Wittig, Monique, English translations of, 2
Woman as good as the man; or the equality of both sexes, 34
women's movement, in Germany, feminist theory and, 3
Words of Power: A Feminist Reading of the History of Logic, 175–80
"Work of Art in the Age of Mechanical Reproduction, The," 282
World as Will and Idea, The, 223
World as Will and Representation, The, 109–12
World Congress of Philosophy, German feminists' participation in, 4

Zeitgeist, gender difference in Kant and Schopenhauer and, 102, 105–12
Zeitschrift für Sozialforschung, 282
Zimmerman, Jörg, 154 n. 13
Zur Kritik der Weiblilchkeit, 226

www.ingramcontent.com/pod-product-compliance
Lightning Source LLC
Chambersburg PA
CBHW050856300426
44111CB00010B/1267